Entrepreneurship and Behavioral Strategy

A volume in
Research in Behavioral Strategy
T. K. Das, *Series Editor*

RESEARCH IN BEHAVIORAL STRATEGY

T. K. Das, *Series Editor*

Published

In Development

Entrepreneurship and Behavioral Strategy

edited by

T. K. Das
City University of New York

INFORMATION AGE PUBLISHING, INC.
Charlotte, NC • www.infoagepub.com

Library of Congress Cataloging-in-Publication Data

A CIP record for this book is available from the Library of Congress
http://www.loc.gov

ISBN: 978-1-64802-048-3 (Paperback)
       978-1-64802-049-0 (Hardcover)
       978-1-64802-050-6 (E-Book)

CONTENTS

ABOUT THE BOOK SERIES

Behavioral strategy continues to attract increasing research interest within the broader field of strategic management. Research in behavioral strategy has clear scope for development in tandem with such traditional streams of strategy research that involve economics, markets, resources, and technology. The key roles of psychology, organizational behavior, and behavioral decision making in the theory and practice of strategy have yet to be comprehensively grasped. Given that strategic thinking and strategic decision making are importantly concerned with human cognition, human decisions, and human behavior, it makes eminent sense to bring some balance in the strategy field by complementing the extant emphasis on the "objective" economics-based view with substantive attention to the "subjective" individual-oriented perspective. This calls for more focused inquiries into the role and nature of the individual strategy actors, and their cognitions and behaviors, in the strategy research enterprise. For the purposes of this book series, behavioral strategy would be broadly construed as covering all aspects of the role of the strategy maker in the entire strategy field. The scholarship relating to behavioral strategy is widely believed to be dispersed in diverse literatures. These existing contributions that relate to behavioral strategy within the overall field of strategy have been known and perhaps valued by most scholars all along, but were not adequately appreciated or brought together as a coherent sub-field or as a distinct perspective of strategy. This book series on *Research in Behavioral Strategy* will cover the essential progress made thus far in this admittedly fragmented literature and elaborate upon fruitful streams of scholarship. More importantly, the book series

Entrepreneurship and Behavioral Strategy, pages vii–viii
Copyright © 2020 by Information Age Publishing
All rights of reproduction in any form reserved.

will focus on providing a robust and comprehensive forum for the growing scholarship in behavioral strategy. In particular, the volumes in the series will cover new views of interdisciplinary theoretical frameworks and models (dealing with all behavioral aspects), significant practical problems of strategy formulation, implementation, and evaluation, and emerging areas of inquiry. The series will also include comprehensive empirical studies of selected segments of business, economic, industrial, government, and non-profit activities with potential for wider application of behavioral strategy. Through the ongoing release of focused topical titles, this book series will seek to disseminate theoretical insights and practical management information that will enable interested professionals to gain a rigorous and comprehensive understanding of the subject of behavioral strategy.

—**T. K. Das**
City University of New York
Series Editor
Research in Behavioral Strategy

CHAPTER 1

ENTREPRENEURIAL PROCESS ORIENTATION AND MULTIPLE PERSPECTIVES OF ENTREPRENEURSHIP

David F. Jorgensen
Frances Fabian

ABSTRACT

We propose the new construct of entrepreneurial process orientation (EPO) with the goal of clarifying important entrepreneurial characteristics in relation to key theoretical processes. The EPO has ramifications for improving entrepreneurial training and guiding entrepreneurs to higher success based on pursuing a person-fit alignment between their EPO and the entrepreneurial process that is pursued. We first differentiate the theoretical perspectives of discovery, creation, and effectuation in regard to their implications for different approaches to the entrepreneurial process, which in turn suggest differing optimal behaviors and skill sets. This insight suggests that entrepreneurs may vary in their suitability for pursuing particular types of entrepreneurship. To pursue an initial operationalization of the EPO construct, we propose using configurations of the subscales of the individual entrepre-

Entrepreneurship and Behavioral Strategy, pages 1–21

1

2 ■ D. F. JORGENSEN and F. FABIAN

neurial orientation (IEO; innovativeness, proactiveness, and risk-taking) as a proxy for aligning entrepreneurs to train in the dominant behaviors of their optimal theoretical perspective—discovery, creation, and effectuation. Other instruments are suggested for future study and use in building the EPO construct. We conclude with implications for theory, research, and education.

INTRODUCTION

In recent years, universities have jumped into the entrepreneurial arena (Singer, 2015; Venkataraman, 2019), in particular because of entrepreneurship's driving relationship to economic growth (Aghion, 2017). Students are often either barraged by a simplified, single, causal approach to successful startups, or exposed to a panoply of entrepreneurship frameworks. In the former case, their passions and personality may not fit well to the skills of the selected approach, and in the latter, they may find it overwhelming to attempt to master the wide set of skills associated with varied frameworks. To date, there appear to be very few examples of how to customize the entrepreneurship education experience to the bent of the student, both in regard to their interests and their skill sets.

The domain of person-environment fit research (Kristof, 1996) encompasses a wide array of perspectives, such as person-vocation and person-career fit, person-organization fit, person-group fit, and person-supervisor fit—all contained within the larger person-environment (P-E) fit theory (Hsu et al., 2019). Authors have also contended that person-entrepreneurship fit (Markman & Baron, 2003) and perceived person-entrepreneurship fit (Hsu et al., 2019) should also enter the fit sphere. While these additions add important insight to the burgeoning literature predicting entrepreneurial career success, they conceptualize entrepreneurship as a binary fit of entrepreneur/non-entrepreneur. Entrepreneurial research, on the other hand, indicates that entrepreneurship processes (and hence, skill sets) can vary widely based on theoretical perspective; in particular, we focus here on the different interests and skill sets associated with the three theoretical perspectives of discovery, creation, and effectuation.

Accordingly, we introduce the new concept of "entrepreneurial process orientation," or EPO. This orientation view proposes that there exist different kinds of entrepreneurs who will be most successful if they pursue entrepreneurial endeavors in a way consistent with their orientation, that is, have a fit between their personal characteristics and the type of entrepreneurial approach they pursue. We compose these orientations to reflect the three perspectives on venture formation of discovery, creation, and effectuation. While recent research stresses that individual-level characteristics are related to entrepreneurial intentions and success (Zhao, Seibert, & Lumpkin, 2010), the lens presented here reflects that different configurations of these characteristics are likely to exist and provide some equifinality in success if individuals pursue a corresponding emphasis in their approach to entrepreneurship.

By assessing an individual's entrepreneurial orientation, we can move beyond the dichotomous emphasis on whether an individual is fit to be an entrepreneur at all, towards better understanding and labelling of exactly what type of entrepreneur they may be: for instance, one who discovers opportunities, creates opportunities, or effectuates alongside and in the face of opportunities. Moreover, this conceptualization of an optimal fit offers specificity and direction for would-be entrepreneurs to build the appropriate set of matching competencies. Together, this combines the personality and competency approaches to entrepreneurship roles (Wagener, Gorgievski, & Rijdijk, 2010) by ensuring entrepreneurs have a key insight that will help them move forward in an already-difficult journey; that is, an understanding of how to combine, or fit, facets of their own personality to a corresponding approach to entrepreneurship processes.

Hsu et al. (2019) argue that the person-entrepreneurship fit is unknown prior to venture engagement in the entrepreneurship process. However, assessments such as the individual entrepreneurship orientation (IEO) scale developed by Bolton and Lane (2012), could provide insight into an individual's proclivities prior to engagement in the entrepreneurship process. This scale in particular produces distinguishable factors in innovativeness, proactiveness, and risk-taking, which we argue below may in turn differentially feed into the success of discovery, creation, or effectuation processes in pursuing entrepreneurship.

Below we briefly summarize the concept of fit in relation to entrepreneurship, and then follow with a review of the three perspectives of entrepreneurship, with an emphasis on their causal processes associated with success. We follow with theory development on what types of orientations should best work with the approaches associated with the three entrepreneurial perspectives. We conclude in summary that widening our understanding of the potential for entrepreneurial success of a greater variety of individuals, and in turn, designing pedagogies and programs tailored to these differences, are key initiatives for both increasing and improving outcomes in the entrepreneurship sector.

THE APPLICATION OF FIT TO ENTREPRENEURSHIP

Fit at the individual level (Brigham & Castro, 2003) has been used in many contexts, but has been largely focused on similar, albeit importantly different, phenomena: for example, person-vocation and person-career fit, person-organization fit, person-group fit, and person-supervisor fit (Kristof,

1996; Kristof-Brown, 2000; Kristof-Brown, Barrick, & Stevens, 2005a; Kristof-Brown, Zimmerman, & Johnson, 2005b; Morley, 2007). A central assumption in this approach is that the success of the studied phenomenon is contingent on a match between personal characteristics and the key environmental constraints and demands within which they work.

Fit in Entrepreneurship

Markman and Baron (2003) introduced fit to entrepreneurship by creating the "person-entrepreneurship" construct. In this perspective, the entrepreneurship choice is one in which a potential entrepreneur needs to have characteristics that match a singular depiction of the entrepreneurship process, that is, "creating new companies by transforming discoveries into marketable items" (Markman & Baron, 2003, p. 281).

Similarly, Hsu et al. (2019) delineated their perspective from person-entrepreneurship fit by introducing the construct of "perceived person-entrepreneurship fit." In their approach, true person-entrepreneurship fit can only be examined after venture engagement in the entrepreneurship process. In particular, successful entrepreneurship requires that the entrepreneur fits their personal needs with what starting a business offers, irrespective of their level of entrepreneurial self-efficacy (Hsu et al., 2019). While both of these have moved the conversation forward regarding how success in entrepreneurship is contingent on a match between the entrepreneur and a particular constellation of necessary entrepreneurial skill sets, they assume certain dominant views of the entrepreneurship process are universally applicable.

Other work has related entrepreneurial success to fit issues with more narrow features of entrepreneurship. For instance, research (Renko & Freeman, 2017) indicates value for a fit between the entrepreneur and the type of opportunity they pursue, such as social versus commercial (Riedo, Kraiczy, & Hack, 2019) or the opportunity's financial or market realities (Miller, Munoz, & Hurt, 2016; Serviere-Munoz, Hurt, & Miller, 2015). Drawing from a person-organization fit perspective, for instance, growth in small technology firms was found to be spurred by a fit between the founder's cognitive style (i.e., intuitive decision making) and the formalization of the organization (Brigham, Mitchell, & De Castro, 2010). Finally, some research suggests that oft-lauded entrepreneurial traits are likely to be successful, but contingent on a matching environment: Networking ability positively influences financial performance, but only through mediation by the new venture network size and strength of network relationships, and only for very young startups (Semrau & Sigmund, 2012). In sum, not only is there reason to believe that fit concepts are important to successful venture creation, but that such fit parameters may vary based on features of the entrepreneurial process that are necessary for particular types of startup endeavors.

Eckhardt and Shane (2003), in their advocacy for opportunities and opportunity recognition as central to entrepreneurship, argued that "the field is better served by studies of the entrepreneurial process itself than studies which focus on normative arguments for the performance of individual entrepreneurs" (2003, p. 345). We agree, with the caveat that the literature has offered very different perspectives on what is involved in the entrepreneurship process based on associated assumptions; here we concentrate on the discovery, creation, and effectuation perspectives. Each approach to the entrepreneurial process signals very different types of personal characteristics that should be successful for launching a venture.

Extending ideas from IEO (Kollmann, Christofor, & Kuckertz, 2007), we expand the idea of orientation to encompass a more comprehensive view of entrepreneurship that differs along the three theoretical perspectives, which we refer to as "entrepreneurial process orientations." With this view, entrepreneurs are not seen as "one size fits all," but rather that some individuals are likely to succeed within the analytical and strategic skills in the discovery paradigm, while others are more attuned to the creative, out-of-the-box, innovative thinking in the creation paradigm, and equally important, some individuals thrive in social networking and formulation skills necessary for success at effectuation.

Specifically, a misfit between a person's EPO and the process they actually pursue augurs a high likelihood of failure, resonant with the observations made in the entrepreneurial fit literature to date. Importantly though, by recognizing multiple process variations, many more individuals are likely to find paths to success by assuring a match between their orientation and the process they pursue. Perhaps most important of all, if universities hope to nurture the next generation of successful entrepreneurs, they need to recognize the variety of successful paths individuals can take in entrepreneurship, and teach students the requisite skills accordingly.

To begin this process, we consider how the characteristics of innovativeness, proactiveness, and risk-taking may be differentially effective for pursuing the associated entrepreneurial process approaches.

Individual Entrepreneurial Orientation

Researchers have long been interested in understanding what drives certain people to become entrepreneurs, and whether such individuals could be identified ex ante. Robinson, Stimpson, Huefner, and Hunt (1991) drew on social psychology to create the "entrepreneurial attitude orientation" that combined behavior, attitude, and emotion to differentiate entrepreneurs from non-entrepreneurs. While a successful predictor for identifying entrepreneurs, it provides very little insight on the match between the entrepreneur and the ensuing processes required for entrepreneurship.

Entrepreneurial orientation, on the other hand, is a construct that arose at the firm level and was specifically designed to be matched to patterns of strategies, in particular to new market entry (Covin & Slevin, 1991; Gupta & Gupta, 2015; Lumpkin & Dess, 1996; Wiklund & Shepherd, 2003). Kollman et al. (2007) elaborated a logic for expanding the construct to the individual level, noting that individuals, and not just firms, possess specific qualities which set them apart from others as entrepreneurial. Their original description was concerned with why levels of interest in entrepreneurship tended to vary by country, and thus they sought out cultural antecedents that would predict the five analogs in IEO paralleling the firm-level factors (Lumpkin & Dess, 1996): autonomy, innovativeness, proactiveness, risk-taking, and competitive aggressiveness.

Bolton and Lane (2012) in turn developed a popular scale for the study and measurement of IEO. Their empirics for the scale development found three of the five factors were valid and reliable: innovativeness, proactiveness, and risk-taking. Drawing from their source (Rauch, Wiklund, Lumpkin, & Frese, 2009, p. 763), the factors can be described as follows:

Innovativeness is defined as "the predisposition to engage in creativity and experimentation through the introduction of new products/services as well as technological leadership via [research and development] in new processes."

Proactiveness is defined as "an opportunity-seeking, forward-looking perspective characterized by the introduction of new products and services ahead of the competition and acting in anticipation of future demand."

Risk-taking "involves taking bold actions by venturing in to the unknown, borrowing heavily and/or committing significant resources to ventures in uncertain environments."

Conceptually, an entrepreneur should score higher than a non-entrepreneur on all of the three factors of the IEO scale. Yet, little has been expanded upon in regard to whether the three subscales may in turn have optimal configurations for different entrepreneurial processes. In the sections below, we examine the different entrepreneurial perspectives of discovery, creation, and effectuation to develop theory on how they may differ in relation to proactiveness, innovativeness, and risk-taking.

Some stipulations should be noted. Entrepreneurial process orientations represent a typology rather than a taxonomy; while there are ideal configural types for the perspectives, it is expected that EPOs can overlap across factors. For example, a discovery EPO will require some degree of innovativeness and risk-taking, though it will be argued below that it is primarily driven by proactiveness. In addition, as a typology, no one individual is likely to be a perfect type, rather they are likely instead to favor one type or another. Finally, we note that risk-taking as defined in the subscale differs from "riskiness" as presented by the discovery perspective of entrepreneurship (Alvarez & Barney, 2007) which relates to computing probabilities associated with alternative outcomes.

THREE PERSPECTIVES OF ENTREPRENEURSHIP

A question central to entrepreneurship is on the origin of new ventures; notably, whether opportunities for venture formation are discovered or created (Alvarez & Barney, 2007; Neill, Metcalf, & York, 2017). The ensuing study of opportunity exploitation on which this debate pivots has been the subject of significant attention (Alvarez, Barney, & Anderson, 2013).

Contrasts have been noted to help differentiate the discovery, creation, and effectuation perspectives. Alvarez and Barney (2007) provided a compelling comparison of the discovery and creation perspectives, distinguishing the two in depth. In response to the causal assumptions of the discovery perspective, Sarasvathy (2001) introduced the effectuation perspective as an additional exemplar of the entrepreneurial process. Key to understanding the distinction among these perspectives lies in the answer to the central quandary in entrepreneurship: "How do ventures come to exist?" This line of inquiry and its conflicting approaches are likely to generate fruitful debate for years to come (Alvarez et al., 2013). While no singular perspective can explain every process an entrepreneur may undertake to begin a venture, collectively the three perspectives of discovery, creation, and effectuation cover a broad spectrum of potential approaches.

The Discovery Perspective

Discovery research has been one of the most widely studied domains of entrepreneurship (Alvarez et al., 2013; Gaglio & Katz, 2001; Shane, 2003; Venkataraman, 1997). Discovery entrepreneurship treats an opportunity as pre-existing in the environment, waiting to be found. Accordingly, these opportunities exist independently of entrepreneurs (Alvarez & Barney, 2007) and will continue existing until they have been found, or the market moves on, leaving them undiscovered. Generally, this assumption has guided research more widely than either the creation or effectuation views, in that the existence of opportunities irrespective of entrepreneurs has been taken as given (Alvarez et al., 2013).

The discovery entrepreneurship perspective also treats entrepreneurs as a distinct group of individuals who differ from non-entrepreneurs. Moreover, these differences are salient ex ante when operating in an environment that is risky in nature (Alvarez & Barney, 2007). Importantly, as part of the process of planning that the discovery perspective follows, discovery entrepreneurs operate under expectations of attaining specific returns on their investment. Using the discovery perspective, entrepreneurs conduct various analyses that together result in a list of alternatives, all with expected returns. It is the duty of the entrepreneur following the discovery perspective to then choose among those alternatives, typically choosing the alternative with the highest possible return and/or the highest chance of attaining a competitive advantage.

Because it is so popular and effective, the causal process underlying the discovery perspective has come to occupy the bulk of educational models in venture formation. Indeed, in most traditional MBA programs (Sarasvathy, 2001) candidates are taught the causal process associated with environmental analysis: that is, discover a need that has been underserved; develop a strategy to capture all possible market share from incumbents; and protect the market from new entrants. In sum, the discovery approach, as a causal method, requires careful planning (Chandler, DeTienne, McKelviec, & Mumford, 2011) and opportunity assessment (Sarasvathy, 2001).

Because of its focus on exploiting existing opportunities, entrepreneurs following the discovery perspective must necessarily be trained in methods to perform such an environmental analysis; tools include business plan creation, business canvas maps, and opportunity assessments. Excitingly, prior experience has been shown to increase performance in discovery perspective contexts (Hmieleski, Carr, & Baron, 2015), and presumably through experiential learning methods some effect may be observable after classes at the university level. The proactiveness factor of the IEO scale, with its opportunity-seeking, forward-looking emphasis, lends itself most appropriately to said training within the discovery perspective.

The discovery process has been bolstered, though, by other views and methods over the years. In fact, Alvarez et al. (2013) noted that entrepreneurs indeed do more than "just discover" throughout the duration of their venture. For example, methods seen in the past as conflicting may be employed simultaneously (Edelman & Yli-Renko, 2010). Mainela and Puhakka (2009) found, for instance, that because in some cases an opportunity may not have any "rules" in existence for its exploitation, discovery and effectuation must work in tandem. The savvy entrepreneur in such conditions would thus need to exploit while effectuating, effectively creating the rules by which future ventures will join in exploiting the same opportunity.

The Creation Perspective

Creation entrepreneurs are thought to operate differently than discovery entrepreneurs, and are best idealized in the cultural mythos around pioneering genius. World-altering innovative inventions by the Wright brothers, Nikola Tesla, or Thomas Edison epitomize the archetypes of creation entrepreneurship. In recent eras, the disruptive innovations from such creation entrepreneurs less represent the lone engineer and more the rearrangement of long-standing industries with technological advances, such as witnessed in the strategies from companies like Netflix, Airbnb, and Uber (Sarasvathy, Dew, Velamuri, & Venkataraman, 2003). Creation entrepreneurs thus exude innovativeness through creativity and experimentation, as well as through technological leadership (Rauch et al., 2009, p. 763).

In fact, the view of an opportunity to a creation entrepreneur includes the creation of both new means as well as new ends (Sarasvathy et al., 2003). As compared to their discovery counterparts, creation entrepreneurs accordingly operate in environments of uncertainty rather than risk (Alvarez & Barney, 2007; Sarasvathy et al., 2003). When a creation entrepreneur creates an opportunity, there is seldom assurance that demand will follow supply.

The creation perspective assumes that opportunities do not exist apart from the actions of entrepreneurs (Alvarez & Barney, 2007). Without existing markets to guide investors and customers alike, the best a creation entrepreneur can do is assess past successful innovations such as the explosion of the Internet (Alvarez & Barney, 2007). Therefore, skills of market analysis, internal analysis, innovation, creativity, sales, and bootstrapping would benefit the education of creation entrepreneurs as they seek to realize an idea, obtain necessary financing, and sell the idea to customers. Furthermore, assuring proper fit between creation entrepreneurs and skills needed for creation should enhance the quality and frequency of these innovative, world-altering offerings.

Creation entrepreneurs face several unique challenges, among them a lack of legitimacy, the lack of an existing market, skeptical sources of funding, and a general lack of understanding by key stakeholders (Aldrich & Fiol, 1994). Although newer, less studied, and taught with less frequency in our business schools vis-à-vis the discovery perspective, the creation perspective is increasingly recognized as a central process for exploiting technological progress. Indeed, educational attainment has been shown to be a significant predictor of increased venture performance (Hmieleski et al., 2015).

The Effectuation Perspective

Effectuation represents a fairly new perspective for entrepreneurship as a result of the body of work by Sarasvathy (2001). It challenges approaches of the discovery perspective most directly (also referred to as the causation perspective, Sarasvathy, 2001) in particular, by questioning the emphasis on discovery as the sole approach entrepreneurs follow in venture formation. The discovery perspective assumes a desired effect as given, and thus focuses on achieving that effect given a choice among various existing means (Sarasvathy, 2001). Effectuation, on the contrary, assumes a set of means as given (Sarasvathy, 2001), and then focuses on what effects can be reached using those means.

As a result, effectual entrepreneurs begin with their means and set a threshold for affordable loss, in contraindication to the discovery perspective's emphasis on the analysis of expected returns (Fisher, 2012; Sarasvathy, 2001). Accordingly, effectual entrepreneurs can thus fail fast (Chandler et al., 2011; Fisher, 2012) and move from one opportunity to another, attempting to generate opportunities along the way (Sarasvathy, 2003). Similarly to a related entrepreneurial literature on the process of entrepreneurial bricolage (Baker & Nelson, 2005; Fisher, 2012), effectuation stresses improvising with current means and utilizing these means to create a marketable product or service.

The effectuation perspective ties itself most closely with the risk-taking perspective of the IEO. While effectuation operates under conditions of uncertainty and not risk (Alvarez & Barney, 2007; Chandler et al., 2011; Fisher, 2012; Sarasvathy, 2001), risk-taking as defined in the IEO differs from the riskiness associated with the discovery perspective. Effectual entrepreneurs embrace this risk-taking in "taking bold actions by venturing in to the unknown, borrowing heavily and or committing significant resources to ventures in uncertain environments" (Rauch et al., 2009, p. 763).

While a relatively novel idea in the young field of entrepreneurship, effectuation has met some heavy resistance in its efforts to take its place as a bona fide perspective of entrepreneurship. Critics such as Arend, Sarooghi, and Burkemper (2015) contend that elements of the effectuation perspective have existed for decades, and argue that for the effectuation to progress it must be further distanced from related perspectives, most notably entrepreneurial bricolage (Arend et al., 2015). Fisher (2012), though, has offered persuasive evidence that despite sharing several similarities, effectuation and bricolage are also markedly distinct.

Specifically, in relation to approaches to entrepreneurial processes, and here, EPOs, the ramifications of a bricolage perspective can be fruitfully combined with the effectuation perspective due to similarities between the two perspectives. The behaviors that support effectuation appear to be theoretically similar to the skill set required for successful bricolage. For instance, entrepreneurs in both categories begin with a set of means and create something new from those means (Fisher, 2012), though the two theories then differ in regard to the role and amount of planning at the outset. The two theories also diverge on the issue of opportunities: Effectual entrepreneurs seek to create or exploit an opportunity given their available alternatives created from their means; bricoleurs ignore the opportunity to instead engage in bricolage—or the act of making do with what is at hand (Fisher, 2012).

An effectuation perspective provides an important opportunity to deviate from the more popular discovery perspective, and provides entrepreneurs with a tool to use in new markets rife with uncertainty (Fisher, 2012). Discovery and effectuation are diametrically opposed with regard to uncertainty and in their basic principles (e.g., Alsos, Clausen, & Solvoll, 2014), though both are clearly differentially effective under certain conditions (Sarasvathy et al., 2003).

The effectuation and creation perspectives present higher difficulty in terms of separating their similarities to arrive at two distinct processes. Primarily because of their conflation in past literature (e.g., Corner & Ho, 2010; Fisher, 2012; Sarasvathy et al., 2003) the two perspectives have largely been treated the same—indeed, effectuation has been treated as a potential subset of the creation process—though we propose given the above that effectuation can be considered uniquely as its own as a perspective.

In particular, while both perspectives share an objective of creating novel products and services, the skills required for effectuation diverge notably from creation. In particular, skills lending themselves more uniquely to effectuation include networking and social skills, as well as risk assessment, so as to apply the effectual boundary of affordable loss. The creation perspective for new ventures assumes no such tasks. The two perspectives do seem to share, though, a need to conduct sound internal analysis to determine available means.

While creation and effectuation have been treated as highly similar perspectives, an important distinction can be made when examining assumptions about the initial actions an entrepreneur in each perspective would take. An effectual entrepreneur looks at their means, and from those means, crafts alternatives. They thus begin with the goal of becoming an entrepreneur, and the innovative venture is a key goal. A creation entrepreneur, however, may not even begin as an entrepreneur seeking to create a venture per se, but rather as an individual with an idea that happens to take shape under the right conditions for a business to form around it. This important distinction delineates the creation perspective from both the discovery and effectuation perspectives. In total, the creation entrepreneur explores and innovates, the discovery entrepreneur analyzes, and the effectual entrepreneur assumes risk under affordable loss repeatedly until they succeed.

Although varied from the array of perspectives we examine herein (i.e., "allocation" is offered instead of effectuation), when exploring allocative, discovery, and creation views of entrepreneurship, Sarasvathy et al. (2003) stated that each perspective "is useful under different circumstances, problem spaces, and decision parameters" (p. 158). We agree, and believe this statement provides an important springboard towards a better understanding of entrepreneurship and better entrepreneurship education. Thus, teaching entrepreneurship students when and how to use each process, and moreover, determining which EPO they most embody, should improve their fit and guide them in appropriate venture creation paths.

In light of the above discussion, Table 1.1 offers a summary of how the guiding assumptions, main tenets, important skill sets, pedagogical

TABLE 1.1 Entrepreneurial Process Orientation and Guiding Perspective

	Discovery	Creation	Effectuation
Guiding Assumption	Opportunities exist and await exploitation[a,d]	Entrepreneurs must create opportunities—opportunities do not exist otherwise[a,f]	Entrepreneurs begin with existing means and craft from those means an opportunity that may or may not work—the entrepreneur will only know afterwards[b,c]
Main Tenets	Causal[a,b,c,d]	Imaginative[f] and iterative[h]	Effectual[a,b,c,d,f,g]
Important Skill Sets	Environmental analysis, planning,[d] opportunity assessment[b,c,d]	Marketing analysis,[a] internal analysis, creativity,[f] imagination,[f] and innovation[a]	Internal analysis,[b,c,d] risk assessment,[b,c,d] networking,[b,c,d,g] improvisation[b,c,d,f]
Pedagogical Implications	Business plan, business canvas map, five forces, value-chain, PESTEL analysis, etc.	Consumer and market analysis,[a] creativity,[f] and innovation,[a,e] sales,[a] bootstrapping[a]	Improvisation and remaining flexible,[b,c,d] networking,[b,c,d,g] social skills,[b,c,d] risk assessment,[b,c,d] affordable loss[b,c,d]
Behavioral Orientation	Proactiveness[a,b,c,d]	Innovativeness[a,e]	Risk-taking[b,c,d]
Entrepreneurial Process Orientation	Entrepreneurial Process Orientation-Discovery	Entrepreneurial Process Orientation-Creation	Entrepreneurial Process Orientation-Effectuation

[a] Alvarez & Barney, 2007
[b] Sarasvathy, 2001
[c] Fisher, 2012
[d] Chandler et al., 2011
[e] Hmieleski et al., 2015
[f] Lachmann, 1986
[g] Jack & Anderson, 2002
[h] Smith, Moghaddam, & Lanivich, 2019

implications, and IEO factors are theorized to differ across the perspectives. The ensuing differences in the most effective entrepreneurial process approaches for each perspective in turn support the value of a matching process orientation for the entrepreneurs.

INCORPORATING AN ENTREPRENEURIAL PROCESS ORIENTATION INTO UNDERSTANDING PERFORMANCE

The introduction of the EPO construct is consistent with fit theory in that it proposes critical dimensions for the person-side of the P-E fit, and stresses the optimal entrepreneurial process approach as the environmental feature that should be accommodated. Research remains nascent, though, on the contingencies that determine which of the three perspectives should dominate in any particular venture startup. Nevertheless, assuming a particular entrepreneurial process approach is advisable, we contend individuals differ in both their interest and skill set to pursue that appropriate entrepreneurial process approach, and research into identifying this EPO will advance both our knowledge and pedagogy.

As a first step, we theorize in the section below that IEO configurations may help identify the EPO-Discovery, EPO-Creation, and EPO-Effectuation entrepreneurs. Follow-up research could test whether self-identified EPOs are then associated with higher performance on tasks associated with entrepreneurial orientations. For instance, returning to Table 1.1, we would expect that the subsample highest on proactiveness, associated with an EPO-Discovery designation, would outperform their EPO-Creation and EPO-Effectuation peers in environmental analysis tasks. By grouping entrepreneurs into their EPO (typified here by ratings on the IEO scale), and then fitting them with process tasks associated with their EPO approach, it is expected the matched entrepreneurs would outperform their mismatched peers. Subsequent field research could explore whether eventual venture success positively relates to higher fit entrepreneurs, based on determinations of the optimal processes for a particular startup. Figure 1.1 illustrates our conceptual model.

Entrepreneurship is often conceptualized and studied as an individual-level phenomenon. Aligning our thinking with past important work done on fit at the individual level, we propose management-relevant performance relationships exist from entrepreneurs and the fit they exhibit with their venturing processes. Furthermore, we believe that in aligning cognitive traits (here represented by reference to IEO traits) with the associated

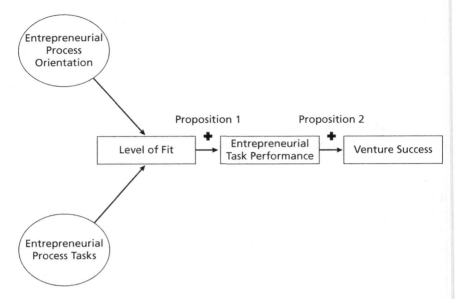

Figure 1.1 Model of entrepreneurial process orientation and entrepreneurial process fit.

entrepreneurial process, greater levels of fit will be achieved. Thus, we posit the following:

Proposition 1: *Higher fit between EPO and the entrepreneurial process approach tasks will be related to higher success in the tasks.*

Proposition 1a: *EPO-Discovery entrepreneurs will perform better at Discovery approach tasks than EPO-Creation or EPO-Effectuation entrepreneurs.*

Proposition 1b: *EPO-Creation entrepreneurs will perform better at Creation approach tasks than EPO-Discovery or EPO-Effectuation entrepreneurs.*

Proposition 1c: *EPO-Effectuation entrepreneurs will perform better at Effectuation approach tasks than EPO-Creation or EPO-Discovery entrepreneurs.*

In past empirical work, higher levels of fit have been associated with higher levels of performance (Brigham & De Castro, 2003). Thus, we expect the following:

Proposition 2: *Level of fit between the EPO and the entrepreneurial process pursued is positively related to entrepreneurial success.*

IMPLICATIONS FOR THEORY, RESEARCH, AND EDUCATION

In this work we seek to add to the current literature and help resolve the often-heated debate among the competing theoretical perspectives of entrepreneurship in the realm of entrepreneurship education. Entrepreneurship education tends to focus almost exclusively on the discovery perspective, though education utilizing effectuation frameworks and principles is on the rise (Mäkimurto-Koivumaa & Puhakk, 2013). The EPO construct, which we propose here may be proxied by varied configurations of the IEO, should contribute to enlarging our understanding of who can be included in the potential population of entrepreneurs, as well as how entrepreneurs differ from one another. A fully fleshed-out EPO would encompass a range of variables at the individual level, accommodating the fact that entrepreneurs can and do differ from one another. This more comprehensive EPO could expand to include several psychological instruments such as the Myers-Briggs Type Indicator and the NEO Personality Inventory, or test other personal characteristics such as decision making styles. Understanding the characteristics that differentiate entrepreneurs from one another presents a signal opportunity to create more effective educational methods for improving students' chances at success in becoming entrepreneurial. Below we discuss several implications for theory, research, and education.

Implications for Theory

The study of entrepreneurship is relatively new in the management literature, and has quickly grown to become a compelling field for inquiry. Venture creation is of substantive importance as a primary instrument of economic growth (Aghion, 2017), and thus studying how entrepreneurship is conducted and how it can be made more successful can serve as a useful driver for increased economic growth.

Entrepreneurship research has thus far, though, been primarily dominated by two central theoretical perspectives—discovery and creation. Creation has been conceptualized as incorporating several differing, though similar, methods, including effectuation and bricolage (Baker & Nelson, 2005; Fisher, 2012; Sarasvathy, 2001). We have proposed differentiating effectuation from creation and granting it an equal footing, outlining important differences between the three perspectives in their approach to the entrepreneurial process.

In particular, we pointed out that creation and effectuation perspectives are distinguishable and can be differentiated, notably in how an entrepreneur following each perspective would begin the process of venture creation. While creation entrepreneurs may not initially view themselves as having any place in entrepreneurship (or for that matter, even business at all), they nevertheless find themselves within those realms when they take their unique idea to market and iteratively try to make it succeed. Effectual entrepreneurs, in contrast, immediately view themselves as entrepreneurs by taking inventory of their available means and crafting from those means a new alternative to take to the market. They leverage their relationships and obtain pre-commitments to increase their chances of success, and apply the affordable loss principle to fail quickly and cheaply (Chandler et al., 2011; Fisher, 2012; Sarasvathy, 2001). Discovery entrepreneurs, in contrast to both creation and effectuation entrepreneurs, plan and choose from among alternatives based on expected return.

We have proposed the construct of EPO, and posited that greater fit between EPO and entrepreneurial process tasks leads to greater performance, thereby increasing an entrepreneur's chance of success. This provides an extension of fit literature, particularly in entrepreneurship, which has largely looked at limited cognitive factors to differentiate entrepreneurs from non-entrepreneurs, as well as some more narrow fit advantages between the entrepreneur and the particular opportunity/venture. The construct of EPO offers new understanding for entrepreneurship theory as it seeks to bring to light the implications of different theoretical perspectives for ensuing approaches to entrepreneurial processes.

Implications for Research

Research in entrepreneurship has a fruitful future (Alvarez et al., 2013). We add to that growth through presenting a challenge of building the new construct of EPO. We hope a validated and related construct of individual EPO can expand our understanding of different types of entrepreneurs as an initial phase in building the EPO construct. Researchers should be encouraged to use the EPO construct as a foundation for assembling studies that, alongside investigations of the IEO, could incorporate other instruments such as the Myers-Briggs Type Indicator and the NEO Personality Inventory to identify characteristics that predict higher performance in particular types of entrepreneurial tasks.

Implications for Education

This research is strongly driven by its objective of improving entrepreneurship education. By entrepreneurship's strong focus on the discovery perspective of entrepreneurship (Sarasvathy, 2001), it has possibly exacerbated issues of lower venture rates by under-represented groups (Fabian & Ndofor, 2007), and thus can be improved by adding additional theoretical perspectives. We have specifically argued for deeper and more widespread coverage of creation and effectuation processes in the classroom. If fitting EPO with entrepreneurial process tasks serves as a valid predictor of increased success, then at least some entrepreneurs are receiving a vastly incomplete education.

By learning to correctly categorize each entrepreneur before they engage in venture creation, we can train them to better implement the necessary tasks, thereby increasing the odds of survival for their ventures. Indeed, as Alvarez et al. (2013) argued, the tool an entrepreneur uses depends on the context they face, which can differ within the same venture over the life of the organization. Thus, entrepreneurs should be educated across different theoretical perspectives to increase their chance at long-term success.

CONCLUSION

We have proposed the new construct of EPO with the goal of expanding our view of the process of entrepreneurship, providing researchers with a new construct to validate, and improving entrepreneurship education. A key proposition was offered that entrepreneurs differ in their fit with different approaches to the entrepreneurial process, and this has implications for performance and inclusion of different types of entrepreneurs. The theoretical perspectives of discovery, creation, and effectuation were examined in light of possible EPO parameters. To study EPO, we proposed using IEO as a proxy, after which we hope to add to the EPO construct other instruments and facets. We concluded with implications for theory, research, and education.

REFERENCES

Aghion, P. (2017). Entrepreneurship and growth: Lessons from an intellectual journey. *Small Business Economics, 48*(1), 9–24.

Aldrich, H. E., & Fiol, C. M. (1994). Fools rush in? The institutional context of industry creation. *Academy of Management Review, 19*(4), 645–670.

Alsos, G. A., Clausen, T. H., & Solvoll, S. (2014). Towards a better measurement scale of causation and effectuation. *Academy of Management Proceedings, 2014*(1), Abstract 13785. Briarcliff Manor, NY: Academy of Management.

Alvarez, S. A., & Barney, J. B. (2007). Discovery and creation: Alternative theories of entrepreneurial action. *Strategic Entrepreneurship Journal, 1*(1–2), 11–26.

Alvarez, S. A., Barney, J. B., & Anderson, P. (2013). Forming and exploiting opportunities: The implications of discovery and creation processes for entrepreneurial and organizational research. *Organization Science, 24*(1), 301–317.

Arend, R. J., Sarooghi, H., & Burkemper, A. (2015). Effectuation as ineffectual? Applying the 3E theory-assessment framework to a proposed new theory of entrepreneurship. *Academy of Management Review, 40*(4), 630–651.

Baker, T., & Nelson, R. E. (2005). Creating something from nothing: Resource construction through entrepreneurial bricolage. *Administrative Science Quarterly, 50*(3), 329–366.

Bolton, D. L., & Lane, M. D. (2012). Individual entrepreneurial orientation: Development of a measurement instrument. *Education+Training, 54*(2/3), 219–233.

Brigham, K. H., & De Castro, J. O. (2003). Entrepreneurial fit: The role of cognitive misfit. In J. A. Katz & D. A. Shepherd (Eds.), *Cognitive approaches to entrepreneurship research* (pp. 37–71). Bingley, England: Emerald Group.

Brigham, K. H., Mitchell, R. K., & De Castro, J. O. (2010). Cognitive misfit and firm growth in technology-oriented SMEs. *International Journal of Technology Management, 52*(1/2), 4–25.

Chandler, G. N., DeTienne, D. R., McKelvie, A., & Mumford, T. V. (2011). Causation and effectuation processes: A validation study. *Journal of Business Venturing, 26*(3), 375–390.

Corner, P. D., & Ho, M. (2010). How opportunities develop in social entrepreneurship. *Entrepreneurship Theory and Practice, 34*(4), 635–659.

Covin, J. G., & Slevin, D. P. (1991). A conceptual model of entrepreneurship as firm behavior. *Entrepreneurship Theory and Practice, 16*(1), 7–26.

Eckhardt, J. T., & Shane, S. A. (2003). Opportunities and entrepreneurship. *Journal of Management, 29*(3), 333–349.

Edelman, L., & Yli-Renko, H. (2010). The impact of environment and entrepreneurial perceptions on venture-creation efforts: Bridging the discovery and creation views of entrepreneurship. *Entrepreneurship Theory and Practice, 34*(5), 833–856.

Fabian, F. H., & Ndofor, H. (2007). The context of entrepreneurial processes: One size doesn't fit all. In G. T. Lumpkin & J. A. Katz (Eds.), *Entrepreneurial strategic processes* (pp. 249–279). Oxford, England: Elsevier.

Fisher, G. (2012). Effectuation, causation, and bricolage: A behavioral comparison of emerging theories in entrepreneurship research. *Entrepreneurship Theory and Practice, 36*(5), 1019–1051.

Gaglio, C. M., & Katz, J. A. (2001). The psychological basis of opportunity identification: Entrepreneurial alertness. *Small Business Economics, 16*(2), 95–111.

Gupta, V. K., & Gupta, A. (2015). Relationship between entrepreneurial orientation and firm performance in large organizations over time. *Journal of International Entrepreneurship, 13*(1), 7–27.

Hmieleski, K. M., Carr, J. C., & Baron, R. A. (2015). Integrating discovery and creation perspectives of entrepreneurial action: The relative roles of founding

CEO human capital, social capital, and psychological capital in contexts of risk versus uncertainty. *Strategic Entrepreneurship Journal, 9*(4), 289–312.

Hsu, D. K., Burmeister-Lamp, K., Simmons, S. A., Foo, M. D., Hong, M. C., & Pipes, J. D. (2019). "I know I can, but I don't fit": Perceived fit, self-efficacy, and entrepreneurial intention. *Journal of Business Venturing, 34*(2), 311–326.

Jack, S. L., & Anderson, A. R. (2002). The effects of embeddedness on the entrepreneurial process. *Journal of Business Venturing, 17*(5), 467–487.

Kollmann, T., Christofor, J., & Kuckertz, A. (2007). Explaining individual entrepreneurial orientation: Conceptualisation of a cross-cultural research framework. *International Journal of Entrepreneurship and Small Business, 4*(3), 325–340.

Kristof, A. L. (1996). Person–organization fit: An integrative review of its conceptualizations, measurement, and implications. *Personnel Psychology, 49*(1), 1–49.

Kristof-Brown, A. L. (2000). Perceived applicant fit: distinguishing between recruiters' perceptions of person–job and person–organization fit. *Personnel Psychology, 53*(3), 643–671.

Kristof-Brown, A. L., Barrick, M. R., & Stevens, C. K. (2005a). When opposites attract: A multi-sample demonstration of complementary person-team fit on extraversion. *Journal of Personality, 73*(4), 935–958.

Kristof-Brown, A. L., Zimmerman, R. D., & Johnson, E. C. (2005b). Consequences of individuals' fit at work: A meta-analysis of person-job, person-organization, person group, and person-supervisor fit. *Personnel Psychology, 58*(2), 281–342.

Lachmann, L. M. (1986). *The market as an economic process.* Oxford, England: Wiley-Blackwell.

Lumpkin, G. T., & Dess, G. G. (1996). Clarifying the entrepreneurial orientation construct and linking it to performance. *Academy of Management Review, 21*(1), 135–172.

Mainela, T., & Puhakka, V. (2009). Organizing new business in a turbulent context: Opportunity discovery and effectuation for IJV development in transition markets. *Journal of International Entrepreneurship, 7*(2), 111–134.

Mäkimurto-Koivumaa, S., & Puhakka, V. (2013). Effectuation and causation in entrepreneurship education. *International Journal of Entrepreneurial Venturing, 5*(1), 68–83.

Markman, G. D., & Baron, R. A. (2003). Person–entrepreneurship fit: Why some people are more successful as entrepreneurs than others. *Human Resource Management Review, 13*(2), 281–301.

Miller, R. J., Munoz, L., & Hurt, K. J. (2016). Complex start-ups: A thematic analysis in entrepreneur-opportunity fit concept. *Journal of Business & Entrepreneurship, 28*(1), 1–29.

Morley, M. J. (2007). Person-organization fit. *Journal of Managerial Psychology, 22*(2), 109–117.

Neill, S., Metcalf, L. E., & York, J. L. (2017). Distinguishing entrepreneurial approaches to opportunity perception. *International Journal of Entrepreneurial Behavior & Research, 23*(2), 296–316.

Rauch, A., Wiklund, J., Lumpkin, G. T., & Frese, M. (2009). Entrepreneurial orientation and business performance: An assessment of past research and suggestions for the future. *Entrepreneurship Theory and Practice, 33*(3), 761–787.

Renko, M., & Freeman, M. J. (2017). How motivation matters: Conceptual alignment of individual and opportunity as a predictor of starting up. *Journal of Business Venturing Insights, 8*(C), 56–63.

Riedo, V., Kraiczy, N. D., & Hack, A. (2019). Applying person–environment fit theory to identify personality differences between prospective social and commercial entrepreneurs: An explorative study. *Journal of Small Business Management, 57*(3), 989–1007.

Robinson, P. B., Stimpson, D., Huefner, J., & Hunt, H. (1991). An attitude approach to the prediction of entrepreneurship. *Entrepreneurship Theory and Practice, 15*(4), 13–31.

Sarasvathy, S. D. (2001). Causation and effectuation: Toward a theoretical shift from economic inevitability to entrepreneurial contingency. *Academy of Management Review, 26*(2), 243–263.

Sarasvathy, S. D. (2003). Entrepreneurship as a science of the artificial. *Journal of Economic Psychology, 24*(2), 203–220.

Sarasvathy, S. D., Dew, N., Velamuri, S. R., & Venkataraman, S. (2003). Three views of entrepreneurial opportunity. In Z. J. Acs, & D. B. Audretsch (Eds.), *Handbook of entrepreneurship research* (pp. 141–160). New York, NY: Springer.

Semrau, T., & Sigmund, S. (2012). Networking ability and the financial performance of new ventures: A mediation analysis among younger and more mature firms. *Strategic Entrepreneurship Journal, 6*(4), 335–354.

Serviere-Munoz, L., Hurt, K. J., & Miller, R. (2015). Revising the entrepreneur opportunity fit model: Addressing the moderating role of cultural fit and prior start-up experience. *Journal of Business and Entrepreneurship, 27*(1), 59–80.

Shane, S. A. (2003). *A general theory of entrepreneurship: The individual-opportunity nexus.* Northampton, MA: Edward Elgar.

Singer, N. (2015, December 28). Universities race to nurture start-up founders of the future. *New York Times.* Retrieved from https://www.nytimes.com/2015/12/29/technology/universities-race-to-nurture-start-up-founders-of-the-future.html

Smith, A. W., Moghaddam, K., & Lanivich, S. E. (2019). A set-theoretic investigation into the origins of creation and discovery opportunities. *Strategic Entrepreneurship Journal, 13*(1), 75–92.

Venkataraman, S. (1997). The distinctive domain of entrepreneurship research: An editor's perspective. In J. Katz & R. Brockhaus (Eds.), *Advances in entrepreneurship, firm emergence and growth* (pp. 119–138). Greenwich, CT: JAI Press.

Venkataraman, S. (2019). The distinctive domain of entrepreneurship research. In J. A. Katz & A. C. Corbet (Eds.), *Seminal ideas for the next twenty-five years of advances* (pp. 5–20). Bingley, England: Emerald.

Wagener, S., Gordievsky, M., & Rijsdijk, S. (2010). Businessman or host? Individual differences between entrepreneurs and small business owners in the hospitality industry. *Service Industries Journal, 30*(9), 1513–1527.

Wiklund, J., & Shepherd, D. (2003). Knowledge-based resources, entrepreneurial orientation, and the performance of small- and medium-sized businesses. *Strategic Management Journal, 24*(13), 1307–1314.

Zhao, H., Seibert, S. E., & Lumpkin, G. T. (2010). The relationship of personality to entrepreneurial intentions and performance: A meta-analytic review. *Journal of Management, 36*(2), 381–404.

CHAPTER 2

INTERSECTION OF ENTREPRENEURSHIP AND BEHAVIORAL STRATEGY

A Literature Review Through Machine Learning

Burak Cem Konduk

ABSTRACT

This study examined the role of behavioral strategy in the entrepreneurship literature. To this end, it carried out a non-traditional literature review that analyzed a sample of articles published in the top three journals dedicated to entrepreneurship through unsupervised machine learning. Specifically, several machine-learning algorithms found out entrepreneurship literature's topics, clusters, and most frequently used terms, laying out the boundaries and terrain of the field. Most frequently used terms and their linkages showed that behavioral strategy influences the entrepreneurship literature through its behavioral or strategic roots but not both. This observation, in turn, suggested that behavioral strategy can enlarge its role in the entrepreneurship literature by coupling its otherwise decoupled roots. Additional analyses searched for

Entrepreneurship and Behavioral Strategy, pages 23–55

areas of the entrepreneurship literature where such coupling can take place. Findings indicated that researchers can combine behavioral and strategic roots of behavioral strategy in areas of the entrepreneurship literature that concern resources, decision-making, opportunity, performance, innovation, entrepreneurs, strategy, process, legitimacy, risk propensity, teams, learning, and effectuation.

INTRODUCTION

"Entrepreneurship is a process" (McMullen & Dimov, 2013, p. 1481). Although there are various accounts of this process (Moroz & Hindle, 2012), its crux consists of two main stages. In the first stage, entrepreneurs recognize, create, or discover an opportunity that can potentially generate a profit because of their prior knowledge, alertness, or external changes in the general, industry, and task environment (McCaffrey, 2014; Shane, 2000; Valliere, 2013). In the second stage, they develop or exploit (McMullen & Shepherd, 2006) the recognized opportunity by founding specific types of firms (Sarasvathy, 2004).

The behavioral strategy that "merges cognitive and social psychology with strategic management theory and practice" (Powell, Lovallo, & Fox, 2011, p. 1369) is relevant to this entrepreneurial process. The first stage of the entrepreneurial process concerns how entrepreneurs search for, represent, store, retrieve, combine, compare, process, and utilize information (Grégoire, Barr, & Shepherd, 2010) to recognize, create, or discover an opportunity under various emotional states (Cardon, Foo, Shepherd, & Wiklund, 2012). All of this calls for viable and realistic assumptions about human cognition and emotion. Behavioral strategy can provide these types of assumptions, which, for example, can acknowledge rather than rule out cognitive biases (Das & Teng, 1999). Behavioral strategy can also explain how entrepreneurs take advantage of an opportunity by drawing on strategic management literature's theories about value creation, value capture, and competitive advantage (Coff, 2010; Newbert, 2008). For example, strategic factor markets theory (Barney, 1986) can explain why and when some entrepreneurs capture value from resources that others discount and overlook.

Despite the relevance of behavioral strategy to entrepreneurship and its constituent stages, there has not been a systematic and comprehensive examination of the role and nature of behavioral strategy in the field of entrepreneurship. For example, searching for "behavioral strategy" and "entrepreneurship" in the abstracts of peer-reviewed journals from ABI/INFORM Collection retrieves merely 24 articles that include terms such as "behaviors," "behavioral," or "strategy" rather than the concept of "behavioral strategy" (Levinthal, 2011; Powell et al., 2011).

This chapter addresses this gap in our understanding by reviewing the role of behavioral strategy in the entrepreneurship literature through unsupervised machine learning algorithms such as cluster analysis and topic modeling. The next section discusses the purpose of the study. The following sections discuss the sample and method and the findings of different analyses.

PURPOSE OF THE STUDY

This chapter explores the role of behavioral strategy in the field of entrepreneurship through a non-traditional literature review that is broader and deeper than traditional reviews. Specifically, it examines a sample of articles published in the top three entrepreneurship journals through unsupervised machine learning methods. These methods document the terms that the entrepreneurship literature uses and count their frequencies, capturing the terms' relative popularity and pervasiveness. They also find out whether there is a direct or indirect association between these literature terms and calculate the strength of existing and available associations. Finding out the existence and strength of linkages between concepts captures the mind map of the researchers who have researched in the field of entrepreneurship over several decades.

The findings of these methods also produce insights for the extent of the overlap between strategy and entrepreneurship literatures, in general, and between behavioral strategy and entrepreneurship literatures, in particular. Overall, they suggest that entrepreneurship and strategy literatures use common terms, concepts, and theories. Despite this overall overlap between entrepreneurship and strategy, results also show that the role of behavioral strategy in the entrepreneurship literature is limited to its either behavioral or strategic roots. More specifically, findings show that behavioral strategy's roots in cognitive and social psychology, on the one hand, and strategic management, on the other hand, have independently interacted with the field of entrepreneurship. This result, in turn, shows that the entrepreneurship literature has been hesitant to combine these roots, a combination that is the essence of behavioral strategy.

The limited impact of behavioral strategy on the field of entrepreneurship, however, is a blessing in disguise. It endows behavioral strategy with an upside potential to influence the field of entrepreneurship. In particular, analyses point out that behavioral strategy as a field is directly relevant to 7 of the 14 identified clusters of studies in the entrepreneurship literature. Specifically, results show that behavioral strategy can play a role in clusters of studies about resources, decision making, opportunity, performance, innovation, entrepreneurs, and strategic aspects of entrepreneurship. Findings also show that behavioral strategy can enrich and guide topics like entrepreneurial process, institutional legitimacy, risk propensity, teams, entrepreneurial learning, and effectuation from the entrepreneurship literature.

In addition to improving our understanding of the role of behavioral strategy in the entrepreneurship literature, the discovered clusters and topics provide a snapshot of the state of the entrepreneurship field. This snapshot captures the relative importance of each cluster and topic through their size, showing the overall trends in the entrepreneurship literature. It also identifies not only the boundaries of the field but also potential gaps in the conceptual and theoretical space of the entrepreneurship literature. These boundaries and gaps, in turn, identify new topics, issue alerts about potential problems and limitations, and flag new research directions.

METHODOLOGY

Sample

The top three entrepreneurship journals constitute the sample. The titles of these journals are *Entrepreneurship Theory and Practice, Journal of Business Venturing,* and *Strategic Entrepreneurship Journal.* These journals adequately represent the scholarly work in the field of entrepreneurship due to their high impact and prestige. Acknowledging the high impact of these journals, the final *Financial Times* top 50 journals list (Financial Times, 2019), which is valid from 2017 and onwards, points out these journals as the top three entrepreneurship journals. Similar to the list of *Financial Times,* journal rankings of *Scimago Journal & Country Rank* place *Journal of Business Venturing, Entrepreneurship Theory and Practice,* and *Strategic Entrepreneurship Journal* in the 25th, 36th, and 59th positions, respectively, in all subject categories of business, management, and accounting (Scimago Journal & Country Rank, 2019). The absence of any other entrepreneurship journals in one of these top 59 positions once more demonstrates that the sampled journals are the most impactful journals dedicated to the field of entrepreneurship.

Some of the issues of these sampled journals were not available due to licensing restrictions. Thus, this review examined 1,012 articles published between 1985 and 2014 in *Journal Business Venturing,* 758 articles published in *Entrepreneurship Theory and Practice* between 2000 and 2016 (including the second issue), and 271 articles published between 2007 and 2019 in *Strategic Entrepreneurship Journal,* resulting in a total of 2,041 published manuscripts. Some of these manuscripts were not suitable for further analysis because databases contained their scanned pictures. These pictures were not machine-readable. Optical character recognition aimed to solve this problem. It was able to turn all but 12 of these scanned images into machine-encoded text for subsequent analysis. Thus, the final sample contained 2,029 manuscripts.

Method

Recent empirical work quantifies unstructured text data to generate insights given their importance, abundance, and richness (Gentzkow, Kelly, & Taddy, 2017). For example, researchers analyzed and quantified text to forecast stock market returns (Chen, De, Hu, & Hwang, 2014) and sales (Chevalier & Mayzlin, 2006). Also, scholars applied quantitative text analysis to the analysis of company web sites (Thorleuchter & Van Den Poel, 2012), financial statements (Loughran & McDonald, 2016), and online customer reviews (Yin, Mitra, & Zhang, 2016). Despite the growth of the quantitative text analysis and its direct applicability to literature reviews, literature reviews in the field of management have not benefitted from this state-of-the-art method. By addressing this limitation, this study mined the text of sampled journals through unsupervised machine learning (Hofmann, 2001) and explored the intersection of entrepreneurship and behavioral strategy.

This study treats text as data (Gentzkow et al., 2017). Thus, it parsed and then filtered the sampled documents (Chakraborty, Pagolu, & Garla, 2013) to quantify the text embedded in them. The process of parsing broke down the sampled text into tokens, which are meaningful units for analysis such as words (Silge & Robinson, 2017), and then kept only those tokens that are useful for further analysis. The parsing process of this study removed or ignored punctuation, numeric expressions, abbreviations, low information terms (i.e., "a," "an," "as," and "by") and certain parts of a speech (i.e., auxiliary, conjunction, determiner, interjection, infinite market, negative participle, possessive marker, preposition, pronoun, and prefix) that just introduce noise and thereby do not create value for exploratory and descriptive analysis.

Parsing also reduced related words (i.e., tasted and tasteful) to their stems (i.e., taste), grouped families of tokens with similar meanings (i.e., synonyms), and recognized different parts of speech, noun groups, and entities. The outcome of the parsing process was the production of a document-by-term matrix whose elements are the frequencies of derived tokens or terms. Thus, this matrix numerically represented text data and the corpus of terms.

This study then filtered the resulting document-by-term-matrix to resolve its high dimensionality and sparseness (Chakraborty et al., 2013). Despite its efforts to do otherwise, the process of parsing, in general, produces too many terms that belong to a handful of documents and a handful of terms that belong to too many documents. This skewness, in turn, not only adds too many columns to the matrix, producing high dimensionality, but also produces too many columns with zero frequencies, producing sparseness.

Filtering solved the high dimensionality and sparseness of the document-by-term-matrix through singular value decomposition. Specifically, it projected this matrix into a lower-dimensional space through singular value decomposition (SVD) without any weight. This study chose not to weigh the matrix, for example with the product of log frequency, a local weight, and entropy, a global weight, at the expense of increased computation time and resource requirements of subsequent analyses (Chakraborty et al., 2013). The reason for this was that the unweighted document-by-term matrix was an objective representation of the state of the field.

Filtering produced a list of spell-checked tokens. This list included both kept and dropped tokens. Additional analysis of rejected and accepted tokens investigated whether filtering kept (dropped) tokens that were relevant (irrelevant) to this study. This analysis added back relevant but initially dropped tokens but dropped irrelevant but initially included tokens. The subsequent analyses used only the kept tokens that appeared in at least 30 documents.

All of these steps produced the text data for unsupervised learning. Unsupervised learning, in general, does not require a model and a target variable because this type of learning aims pattern discovery and information retrieval rather than prediction. This study used two unsupervised learning models, which are cluster analysis and topic modeling (Liu, Tang, Dong, Yao, & Zhou, 2016), to analyze unstructured text data from the sampled journals with SAS Text Miner, which is a component of SAS Enterprise Miner.

Cluster analysis, in general, aims to associate every document with only one cluster via different algorithm options such as expectation-maximization or hierarchical. By not expecting a hierarchical relationship between terms, this study used the expectation-maximization algorithm that iterates between an expectation step that calculates cluster centers and a maximization step that assigns documents to the closest clusters until there is no improvement (Chakraborty et al., 2013). By using this algorithm, the cluster analysis assigned the sampled documents to naturally occurring, mutually exclusive, and exhaustive clusters (James, Witten, Hastie, & Tibshirani, 2013) and identified 50 keywords that had the closest association with each cluster (SAS Institute Inc., 2017).

Cluster analysis, in general, can produce different numbers of clusters. The exploratory nature of this study prevented pre-specification of the exact number of clusters. Thus, the analysis initially limited the maximum number of clusters to the default value of 40 and then examined the number of clusters that expectation-maximization algorithm produced for a various number of SVD dimensions under the default low resolution of SAS Text Miner (SAS Institute Inc., 2017). The examination of these clusters, their members, and associated keywords guided the selection of the number of clusters that eventually analyzed the text data.

The second unsupervised learning model, which is topic modeling (Liu et al., 2016), extracted topics from the sampled documents. To this end, it detected either direct co-occurrence of words in a document or indirect co-occurrence of words across documents through their shared linkage with a third word. Unlike cluster analysis that limited the association of a given document to only one cluster, topic modeling accounted for the possibility that a document could contain more than one topic. Topic modeling also found out the keywords that had the most substantial connection with a particular topic and ranked the documents in terms of the strength of their association with a particular topic (SAS Institute Inc., 2017).

Although it is possible to extract orthogonal or correlated topics, this study preferred correlated topics to orthogonal topics for two reasons. First, correlated topics improve the alignment between keywords and topics (SAS Institute Inc., 2017), facilitating better interpretation of topic content. Second, there is an association among the topics of the entrepreneurship literature because this literature looks at different components and elements of the very same process (McMullen & Dimov, 2013).

Since it was difficult to know the appropriate number of topics in advance, this study modeled a different number of topics and then selected the model with the highest number of topics that did not overlap with one another. Such an approach neither conflated distinct topics nor broke up the same topics, increasing their precision and coverage of the entrepreneurship literature.

In addition to cluster analysis and topic modeling, concept links captured the associations between identified terms and the strength of those associations with a hyperbolic tree. Concept links, in general, can capture direct and indirect associations at various levels as the depth of the tree can extend. Thus, they were useful to understand the strength of the relationships between terms that were critical to this study (Chakraborty et al., 2013).

RESULTS

The analyses produced a term list from the studied documents. Table 2.1 contains the top 50 terms or concepts. These terms are rank ordered by the number of documents that contain them. This table shows that the term "process" appears in the highest number of documents. This finding is consistent with the conceptualization of entrepreneurship as a process

TABLE 2.1	Top 50 Literature Terms		
Ranking	**Term**	**Frequency**	**Number of Documents**
1	process	26,760	1,859
2	opportunity	30,789	1,782
3	strategy	22,697	1,779
4	resource	33,491	1,761
5	issue	10,376	1,756
6	decision	21,757	1,756
7	strategic	30,433	1,687
8	performance	33,109	1,664
9	information	18,117	1,646
10	social	36,129	1,605
11	individual	18,841	1,601
12	group	12,796	1,600
13	product	22,903	1,587
14	capital	26,474	1,574
15	knowledge	24,701	1,570
16	experience	18,113	1,565
17	risk	13,585	1,521
18	financial	12,483	1,519
19	innovation	17,445	1,411
20	technology	15,199	1,401
21	advantage	7,281	1,378
22	attention	4,415	1,366
23	investment	18,683	1,349
24	recognize	4,120	1,294
25	competitive	7,801	1,286
26	policy	6,711	1,226
27	network (noun)	18,940	1,199
28	new venture	10,997	1,178
29	motivation	5,991	1,139
30	capability	9,924	1,114
31	uncertainty	7,558	1,082
32	survival	5,064	1,074
33	asset	6,420	1,012
34	competition	3,760	993
35	learning	8,576	962
36	institutional	9,646	952

(continued)

TABLE 2.1	Top 50 Literature Terms (Continued)		
Ranking	Term	Frequency	Number of Documents
37	innovative	4,106	924
38	investor	11,908	887
39	environmental	5,274	881
40	capacity	3,557	879
41	evolution	2,415	868
42	institution	5,542	861
43	cognitive	7,383	840
44	behavioral	2,737	791
45	cultural	3,738	783
46	equity	6,512	779
47	leadership	3,072	758
48	location	3,418	755
49	psychology	3,098	742
50	expertise	2,618	734

(McMullen & Dimov, 2013). Zooming in on this term to find its relationships and place in the literature through a conceptual link shows that the terms "cognition," "cognitive," "behavioral," "decision making," "knowledge," "entrepreneurial process," "entrepreneurial opportunity," and "exploitation" have the closest linkages.

For example, approximately 98% of the documents that contain the term "cognitive" or "behavioral" or "exploitation" or "decision making" also contain the term "process." Similarly, approximately 99% of the documents that contain the term "entrepreneurial opportunity" or "cognition" also include the term "process." The strong and direct relationship between "entrepreneurial opportunity" and "process," on the one hand, and between "exploitation" and "process," on the other hand, lends credence to the aforementioned view that the process of entrepreneurship contains opportunity recognition and exploitation stages.

Another takeaway from Table 2.1 is the overlap between strategy and entrepreneurship literatures. Among the 2,029 studied manuscripts, 1,779 documents use the term "strategy," and 1,687 documents use the term "strategic." Table 2.1 also shows that the entrepreneurship literature frequently refers to core strategy terms like "resource," "asset," "capability," "performance," "competitive," "competition," "information," "experience," "knowledge," "learning," "innovation," "risk," "institutional," "evolution," "environmental," "policy," and "network." The high overlap between these two fields is not surprising and comes from both the work of eminent strategy scholars in the field of entrepreneurship (Venkataraman,

1997) and this field's frequent citation of strategy scholars (Ferreira, Reis, & Miranda, 2015).

The high overlap between the strategy and entrepreneurship literatures also implies an overlap between behavioral strategy and entrepreneurship as the behavioral strategy is a branch of the strategy literature. Table 2.2 shows the extent of the overlap between behavioral strategy and entrepreneurship as it contains the terms that are relevant to behavioral strategy but extracted from the sampled entrepreneurship literature. For example, Table 2.2 makes repeated references to cognition that is central to behavioral strategy.

TABLE 2.2 The Overlapping Literature Terms Between Behavioral Strategy and Entrepreneurship

Ranking	Term	Frequency	Number of Documents
1	cognitive	7,383	840
2	behavioral	2,737	791
3	psychology	3,098	742
4	affect (noun)	2,929	717
5	bias	1,360	639
6	decision making	2,082	629
7	personality	2,059	550
8	cognition	3,208	481
9	mental	1,349	479
10	judgement	1,780	453
11	emotional	1,874	377
12	heuristics	1,325	282
13	personality	773	282
14	intuition	1,088	221
15	emotion	2,258	221
16	memory	935	218
17	affective	1,516	214
18	mindset	599	202
19	intuitive	478	188
20	tacit knowledge	482	182
21	cognitive process	378	177
22	social psychology	218	152
23	decision-making process	225	149
24	schema	843	146
25	decision process	338	145

(continued)

TABLE 2.2   The Overlapping Literature Terms Between Behavioral Strategy and Entrepreneurship (Continued)

Ranking	Term	Frequency	Number of Documents
26	strategic decision making	165	136
27	strategic orientation	407	135
28	venture strategy	292	135
29	cognitive perspective	228	131
30	personality trait	329	130
31	behavioral research	138	128
32	analogy	324	127
33	individual characteristic	199	121
34	heuristic	513	120
35	social construction	183	120
36	cognition	255	115
37	cognitive bias	326	112
38	overconfidence	590	108
39	sensemaking	354	99
40	psychological characteristic	144	97
41	cognitive factor	147	95
42	cognitive mechanism	126	90
43	behavioral theory	159	84
44	mental model	272	83
45	psychological	91	75
46	counterfactual	530	75
47	social cognition	136	72
48	cognitive theory	100	71
49	cognizant	77	68
50	cognition research	162	67
51	positive affect	555	63
52	personality characteristic	112	62
53	cognitive psychology	106	60
54	hubris	172	58
55	entrepreneurial perception	81	58
56	counterfactual thinking	288	58
57	bounded rationality	123	58
58	cognitive structure	106	56
59	cognitive approach	75	56
60	perceptual measure	78	55

(continued)

TABLE 2.2 The Overlapping Literature Terms Between Behavioral Strategy and Entrepreneurship (Continued)

Ranking	Term	Frequency	Number of Documents
61	psychological basis	57	54
62	cognitive ability	74	54
63	stereotype	185	54
64	overconfident	178	54
65	cross cultural cognition	53	53
66	behavioral science	54	52
67	cognitive science	113	51
68	social cognitive theory	106	51
69	anger	207	49
70	pessimistic	80	49
71	fast strategic decision	46	46
72	psychology literature	59	46
73	negative emotion	360	46
74	groupthink	75	46
75	cognitive style	211	45
76	achievement motivation	102	44
77	reference point	91	43
78	intrinsic motivation	184	43
79	mindful	57	41
80	sensemaking	65	41
81	growth aspiration	212	41
82	positive emotion	204	40
83	cognitive resource	132	40
84	survivor bias	48	39
85	organizational psychology	46	39
86	reference group	47	38
87	prospect theory	106	38
88	unlearn	81	37
89	cognitive dimension	119	37
90	cognitive framework	58	36
91	decision making process	42	36
92	decision theory	68	35
93	feeling	57	35
94	behavioral model	43	35
95	managerial decision	43	34

(continued)

TABLE 2.2 The Overlapping Literature Terms Between Behavioral Strategy and Entrepreneurship (Continued)

Ranking	Term	Frequency	Number of Documents
96	psychological trait	53	34
97	systematic bias	37	33
98	strategic thinking	42	32
99	management decision	43	32
100	hubris theory	42	32
101	social cognitive perspective	30	30
102	affective state	95	30
103	cognition-base	39	30
104	psychological theory	37	30

Specifically, it contains terms like "heuristics," "schema," "memory," "intuition," and different types of "biases" like "overconfidence," "hubris," and "survivor bias." Table 2.2 also refers to "affect" and "emotion," which are either negative or positive, disciplines like "psychology," and theories like "prospect theory" or "social cognitive theory" that behavioral strategy draws on. More to the point, Table 2.2 contains vital terms from behavioral strategy like "sense-making," "bounded rationality," "reference point," and "reference group."

Table 2.2 also shows that the entrepreneurship literature directly uses the term "behavioral" as an adjective in 791 documents, corresponding to approximately 39% of studied documents. This term is actually one of the top 50 terms that the entrepreneurship literature uses according to Table 2.1. The entrepreneurship literature also deploys this term as a component of a noun group. For example, while 128 documents use the term "behavioral research," 35 documents refer to "behavioral model" according to Table 2.2. Similarly, 84 studies contain the term "behavioral theory."

Evidence also shows that the entrepreneurship literature, like the behavioral strategy literature, associates cognition and social psychology with the umbrella term "behavioral." For example, 73% of the sampled documents that refer to social psychology also refers to the term "behavioral" in the entrepreneurship literature. Likewise, 68% of the documents that discuss cognition also use the term "behavioral."

The allusion of the entrepreneurship literature to the behavioral strategy terms and its extensive usage of the term "behavioral" either as an adjective or as a component of a noun group show that there is a role for behavioral strategy to play in the entrepreneurship literature. However, this role has been somewhat limited and partial because behavioral strategy's distinct roots in cognitive and social psychology, and strategic management rather than the integration of these roots, which is the essence of behavioral strategy, influence the entrepreneurship literature. Specifically, unlike behavioral strategy, the field of entrepreneurship does not connect cognitive or social psychology with "strategic management theory and practice" (Powell et al., 2011, p. 1369) according to concept links.

For example, the analysis showed that cognition is highly associated with venture creation, schema, nascent entrepreneur, psychology, and opportunity discovery in the entrepreneurship literature. Also, social psychology is strongly connected with self-efficacy, affect, cognition, psychology, and personality in the field of entrepreneurship. Nevertheless, neither of these terms has a strong linkage with theories and practice from strategic management. The entrepreneurship literature thereby fails to link strategic management practice and theories with cognitive and social psychology, a link that is the essence of behavioral strategy.

Examining this issue from the other side of the same coin leads to the same conclusion. Specifically, data show that strategic management concepts and theories diffuse into the entrepreneurship literature but without links to cognitive and social psychology. For example, examination of the linkages of the term "strategy" with other terms shows that this term is strongly associated with terms like "environmental," "business strategy," "resource-base," "capability," "competitive advantage," "competitor," "competitive," or "strategic" in the entrepreneurship literature. The terms that connect to "strategy," however, do not directly connect to cognitive and social psychology or any related terms. The lack of such connection shows that although the entrepreneurship literature borrows terms and concepts from the strategy literature, it does not take the additional step of merging them with cognitive and social psychology to study issues relevant to entrepreneurship.

All of this suggests that entrepreneurship literature uses concepts and ideas from strategic management and cognitive and social psychology. However, it does not combine them. This lack of combination, in turn, limits the role of behavioral strategy in the entrepreneurship literature to its either behavioral or strategic roots. Behavioral strategy, however, can make a significant contribution to the entrepreneurship literature as this literature contains its ingredients. Further analyses aimed to find out and specify the extent of such potential contribution. To this end, cluster analysis and topic modeling produced detailed maps of the entrepreneurship literature for the behavioral strategy to find its way into this literature. Specifically, these analyses aimed to identify the clusters or topics relevant to behavioral strategy and produce insights for how researchers can incorporate behavioral strategy into these relevant clusters or topics.

Cluster analysis produced 14 clusters. This number was the dominant vote among several cluster analyses that set the maximum number of SVD dimensions to 100, 200, 300, 400, and 500 respectively. Apart from the default value of 100, all other maximum SVD values (i.e., 200, 300, 400, and 500) produced 14 clusters, which were similar to one another. The following discussion analyzes the information from the cluster analysis that allowed for a maximum number of 300 SDV dimensions. Table 2.3 summarizes the findings of this analysis. Specifically, it provides cluster numbers, terms that most frequently appear in clusters, and frequency and the approximate percentage of clusters.

TABLE 2.3 Cluster Number, Descriptive Terms, Frequency, and Percentage

Cluster Number	Descriptive Terms	Frequency	Percentage
1	social capital, sociology, social, trust, cultural, social network, embeddedness, social structure, nonfamily, institution, legitimacy, family business, network	261	13%
2	networking, network, weak tie, strong tie, network structure, structural hole, network theory, personal network, network-base, networks, network tie, entrepreneurial network, social network, embeddedness	72	4%
3	strategic entrepreneurship, corporate entrepreneurship, experimentation, business strategy, strategic decision, entrepreneurial orientation, innovate, competitive advantage, leadership, innovativeness	147	7%
4	investor, equity, capitalist, venture capital, financing, venture capitalist, finance, funding, capital investment, capitalist, capital firm, investment, capital industry, investment decision, syndication, capital fund	213	10%
5	resource-based view, firm resource, resources, human resource, resource-base, resource, intangible asset, competitive advantage, competency, nonfamily, firm growth, social capital, survive	166	8%
6	decision maker, heuristics, decision making, decision, judgment, rational, experiment, cognitive, investment, rationality, cognitive process, risk, psychology, behavioral, cognition, bias	240	12%
7	franchisee, franchising, franchise contract, franchise system, business format, trademark, brand name, advertising, intangible asset, contract, vertical integration, opportunism, agency theory, antitrust law	44	2%
8	board, outside director, corporate governance, governance structure, shareholder, governance mechanism, agency theory, ownership structure, family ownership, agency problem, managerial behavior	43	2%

(continued)

TABLE 2.3 Cluster Number, Descriptive Terms, Frequency, and Percentage (Continued)

Cluster Number	Descriptive Terms	Frequency	Percentage
9	personality, self-employment, self-efficacy, entrepreneurial intention, entrepreneurial career, entrepreneurial experience, emotion, psychologist, psychology, venture creation, prior experience	175	9%
10	discovery, entrepreneurial opportunity, recognition, alertness, prior knowledge, entrepreneurial discovery, cognitive process, effectuation, opportunity identification	127	6%
11	firm performance, performance, performance measure, financial performance, organizational performance, venture performance, profitability, market share, ownership structure, entrepreneurial firm	138	7%
12	product, market share, manufacturer, rival, competitor, product development, advertising marketing, manufacture, brand name, new product, manufacturing, new market, license, differentiation	125	6%
13	alliance partner, alliance formation, alliance activity, alliances, strategic alliance, interorganizational, joint venture, biotechnology industry, interfirm, high-technology industry, collaborative	30	1%
14	transfer, technology, innovation, new knowledge, commercialization, absorptive, absorptive capacity, innovate, technological innovation, collaboration, intellectual, tacit, tech, technology-base, new technology	248	12%

Cluster 1 includes 261 articles, making it the largest cluster in terms of the number of documents that it contains. Specifically, approximately 13% of the studied articles belong to the first cluster. This cluster focuses on social ties, relations, and thereby, capital across family and non-family firms (Discua, Howorth, & Hamilton, 2013; Lester & Cannella, 2006). It also studies culture, trust, and legitimacy because of their association with social capital. The dominance of this cluster suggests that whom you know matters the most in the context of entrepreneurship.

Cluster 2 contains 72 articles. This cluster is one of the smaller clusters as it contains 4% of the sampled articles. Although both Cluster 1 and Cluster 2 broadly examine social relations, Cluster 2 differs from Cluster 1 because of its specific emphasis on the structure, shape, and form of these relationships (Hite, 2005). Specifically, the studies from Cluster 2 investigate networks and their structural properties like tie strength and structural holes. This cluster also looks at different types of networks like social networks, entrepreneurial networks (Vissa & Bhagavatula, 2012), or formal business networks (Parker, 2008). The studies in this cluster predominantly use theories like network theory (Sullivan & Ford, 2014) that are more specific than theories that dominate Cluster 1 to develop their ideas and hypotheses.

Cluster 3 includes 147 documents, corresponding to 7% of the sampled documents. This cluster concerns strategic aspects of entrepreneurship. Specifically, it focuses on strategic decisions, strategic conduct, and different types and levels of strategy (McDougall, 1989). For example, studies in this cluster examine strategic entrepreneurship (Wright & Hitt, 2017), corporate entrepreneurship (Hornsby, Kuratko, & Zahra, 2002; Sorrentino & Williams, 1995), strategic experimentation (Nicholls-Nixon, Cooper, & Woo, 2000), and strategic decisions (Kisfalvi, 2002).

Given that studies in this cluster capture the strategic aspects of entrepreneurship, the behavioral strategy is inherently relevant to this sixth largest cluster. Behavioral strategy can be a part of this cluster if researchers combine the studied strategic aspects of entrepreneurship with cognitive and social psychology. Such combination, for example, can empower researchers to find out the appropriate mindset and the strategy types that can shape the environment rather than be shaped by it, especially in the case of uncertainty, contributing to the concept of effectuation (Palmié, Huerzeler, Grichnik, Keupp, & Gassmann, 2019) in the entrepreneurship literature.

Cluster 4 contains 213 documents, constituting 10% of the studied documents. This cluster is the fourth largest cluster. The crux of this cluster is investment and financing. In particular, it focuses on financing (Orser, Riding, & Manley, 2006; Schwienbacher, 2007), venture capitalist (Manigart, 1994), syndication (Cumming & Dai, 2013), venture capital industry (Bruno & Tyebjee, 1985; Gupta & Sapienza, 1992), and capital funds (Robinson, 1987). Investment and financing decisions that this cluster covers are prone to errors that derive from human cognition, emotion, and biases. Thus, this cluster is relevant to behavioral strategy. However, behavioral finance (Shefrin, 2000) is better positioned than behavioral strategy to contribute to this cluster because of its specialized expertise for analyzing and understanding the behavioral roots of financing decisions.

Cluster 5 includes 166 documents. Documents in this cluster constitute approximately 8% of the sampled documents, making it the sixth most significant cluster. The gist of this cluster is resources (Chandler & Hanks, 1994; De Clercq, Lim, & Oh, 2013). The documents in this cluster thereby use the resource-based view (Westhead, Wright, & Ucbasaran, 2001) as the central theoretical perspective and examine competencies and different types of resources like human resources (Symeonidou & Nicolaou, 2018) and social capital (Wu, Wang, Chen, & Pan, 2008). This cluster also studies various outcomes of resources (Jarillo, 1989) such as survival and competitive advantage (Miller, Spann, & Lerner, 1991), which can mainly derive from intangible resources.

Given that the resource-based view is one of the essential perspectives in the strategy literature, the behavioral strategy can serve this fifth largest cluster. For example, researchers can use theories and ideas from the resource-based view and cognitive psychology to study creative and novel use of resources especially in the face of scarcity, contributing to the concept of bricolage (Welter, Mauer, & Wuebker, 2016) from the entrepreneurship literature.

Cluster 6 contains 166 documents, corresponding to approximately 12% of the sampled documents. This cluster is the third largest among the 14 clusters. It is all about decision making (Dew, Read, Sarasvathy, & Wiltbank, 2009). This cluster uses psychology and cognitive approaches (Mitchell et al., 2007) to study decisions, judgment, rationality, and biases (Burmeister & Schade, 2007; Busenitz & Barney, 1997; Townsend, Busenitz, & Arthurs, 2010). Cluster 6 is relevant to behavioral strategy because of its disciplinary roots and incorporation of strategic decision making. Actually, behavioral strategy currently plays a role in this cluster. For example, 136 sampled documents discuss strategic decision making and 32 documents refer to strategic thinking as indicated in Table 2.2 from predominantly a cognitive perspective.

Cluster 7 contains 44 documents, comprising approximately 2% of the sampled documents. The main concern of this rather small cluster is franchising. Whether franchising is an entrepreneurial act has been a contentious issue (Ketchen, Short, & Combs, 2011). The small size of this cluster may be due to this debate. The studies that belong to this cluster examine integration or de-integration decisions (Michael, 1996) that lead to franchise contracts and systems (Vincent, 1998) that have implications for trademarks, brand names, and advertising. This cluster also focuses on the conflict of interest between franchisee and franchisor (Kidwell, Nygaard, & Silkoset, 2007; Spinelli & Birley, 1996) which are the subject matters of agency theory (Gillis, McEwan, Crook, & Michael, 2011) and antitrust law (Vincent, 1998).

Cluster 8 contains 43 documents. Similar to Cluster 7, this cluster includes roughly 2% of the sampled documents, making it one of the smaller clusters. Corporate governance is the primary subject matter of this cluster. The size of this cluster suggests that corporate governance is not one of the central issues in the academic domain of entrepreneurship. This cluster studies board composition, types of directors like outside directors, and ownership structure that mainly concerns shareholder and family ownership (Arregle, Naldi, Nordqvist, & Hitt, 2012; Daily & Dalton, 1992). Given that this cluster focuses on the alignment of the interests of shareholders with those of managers, it frequently alludes to agency theory.

Cluster 9 contains 175 documents. This cluster is the fifth largest cluster, corresponding to 9% of all sampled articles. This cluster approaches an entrepreneur as an individual. Thus, documents in this cluster study entrepreneurial intention (Douglas, 2013), career (Lee & Wong, 2004), self-efficacy (Chen, Greene, & Crick, 1998; Wilson, Kickul, & Marlino, 2007), experience (Eesley & Roberts, 2012; Ucbasaran, Westhead, Wright, & Flores, 2010), and emotion (Cardon et al., 2012). Psychology is the leading guide of the studies in this cluster. This cluster thereby is a potential target for behavioral strategy. Injecting ideas, theories, and concepts from the strategic management literature into this cluster can strengthen the role of behavioral strategy in the entrepreneurship literature.

Cluster 10 has 127 documents, constituting 6% of the analyzed documents. This cluster focuses on opportunities. In particular, studies in this cluster examine cognitive processes (Baron, 2004) of opportunity discovery (Murphy, 2011), recognition (McCline et al., 2000), evaluation (Keh et al., 2002), creation (Goss & Sadler-Smith, 2018), co-creation (Sun & Im, 2015), and identification (Ardichvili, Cardozo, & Ray, 2003) through prior knowledge and alertness (McCaffrey, 2014; Valliere, 2013). Studies in this cluster thereby underscore the first stage of the entrepreneurial process and do not emphasize the exploitation of opportunity. The dominance of cognitive perspectives in this cluster makes it another important target for behavioral strategy.

However, this cluster's limited attention to opportunity exploitation constrains the impact of behavioral strategy that is concerned with performance, which, in turn, is more likely to derive from exploitation of an opportunity rather than its discovery, recognition, or evaluation. Also, the entrepreneurship literature already borrows heavily from cognitive and social psychology to study opportunity recognition, limiting the contribution of behavioral strategy to this cluster. For example, Grégoire et al. (2010) use a well-established theory of analogical reasoning to study opportunity recognition.

Cluster 11 consists of 138 documents and thereby almost cover 7% of the studied documents. The central theme of this cluster is performance. Work by Zahra (1991), Singal and Singal (2011), and Durand and Coeurderoy (2001) illustrates the studies that belong to this cluster. The performance orientation of this cluster relates it to behavioral strategy as the broader field of strategic management has an innate performance orientation. For example, Gaba and Bhattacharya (2012) use the behavioral theory of the firm as the central perspective to shed new light on innovation performance. Entrepreneurship (strategy) scholars can directly import (export) behavioral strategy to contribute to this cluster.

Cluster 12 is composed of 125 documents. This cluster thereby includes approximately 6% of studied documents. Products are the focus of this cluster. In particular, studies in this cluster explain the development (Plambeck, 2012), manufacturing (Abetti & Phan, 2004), and launch of new products (Simon & Shrader, 2012). They also discuss competition and rivalry through the order and timing of new products (Srivastava & Lee, 2005) and their positioning (Boone, Wezel, & Van Witteloostuijin, 2013).

Cluster 13 contains merely 30 studies. This cluster is the smallest cluster. Approximately 1% of sampled studies pertain to this cluster. The studies in this cluster are about alliances. Specifically, the studies in this cluster describe and explain alliance formation (Moghaddam, Bosse, & Provance, 2016) and activities (Leiblein & Reuer, 2004; Li, 2013) in especially technology industries (Leiblein & Reuer, 2004) like biotechnology industry (Coombs, Mudambi, & Deeds, 2006). The extensive study of alliances in other fields like strategy may be the reason for the small size of this cluster. The small size of this cluster can also be due to the possibility that entrepreneurs use social capital more frequently than alliances to obtain needed resources.

Cluster 14, the final cluster, has 248 articles, making it the second largest cluster. The large size of this cluster is not surprising because this cluster examines and studies innovation (Baron & Tang, 2011; Penney & Combs, 2013), which is critical to entrepreneurship. Specifically, studies in this cluster explore technological innovation (Kelley & Rice, 2001) and thereby new technologies (Julien, 1995; Roy, Lampert, & Stoyneva, 2018) and their commercialization and transfer (Shane, 2002). Due to its subject matter, studies in this cluster frequently adopt absorptive capacity (Zahra, Filatotchev, & Wright, 2009) as the guiding perspective. By examining the absorptive capacity of entrepreneurs rather than firms, researchers can link cognitive roots of absorptive capacity to detection and commercialization of external knowledge, creating a role for behavioral strategy in this cluster.

Overall, the cluster analysis produced 14 clusters, and further examination of these clusters showed that seven of them were more relevant to behavioral strategy than others. Specifically, Cluster 3, which is about strategic aspects of entrepreneurship, Cluster 5, which studies resources, Cluster 6, which examines decision making, Cluster 9, which studies entrepreneurs, Cluster 10, which examines opportunity, Cluster 11, which focuses on performance, and Cluster 14, which studies innovation, are relevant to behavioral strategy. Behavioral strategy can contribute to these clusters.

The aforementioned results of the cluster analysis, however, can overlook some areas of the field of entrepreneurship and thereby underrepresent the importance or relevance of behavioral strategy to the entrepreneurship literature. The reason for this stems from the fact that cluster analysis forces each document to belong to only one cluster. This constraint can, in turn, lead to the detection of fewer domains than available in the entrepreneurship literature. Topic modeling overcomes this problem by allowing each document to belong to multiple topics.

Thus, this study carried out topic modeling and examined an alternative number of topics. Among the investigated alternatives, 40 topics effectively represented the sampled documents. Table 2.4 summarizes the findings

TABLE 2.4 Topic Number, Descriptive Terms, Frequency, and Example

Topic Number	Descriptive Terms	Frequency	Example
1	knowledge, spillover, knowledge spillover, absorptive, transfer	178	Ko & Liu (2015)
2	social, social entrepreneurship, social capital, stakeholder, social entrepreneur	219	Short, Moss, & Lumpkin (2009)
3	investment, venture capital, syndication, uncertainty, capital investment	173	Jackson, Bates, & Bradford (2012)
4	decision, decision making, cognitive, judgment	195	Amit, MacCrimmon, Zietsma, & Oesch (2001)
5	performance, firm performance, venture performance, profitability, environmental	253	Chandler & Hanks (1993)
6	product, new product, competitive, advantage, competitor	210	Karakaya & Kobu (1994)
7	resource, advantage, resource-base, nascent, bricolage	212	Townsend & Busenitz (2008)
8	network, social network, networking, social capital	131	Slotte-Kock & Coviello (2010)
9	opportunity, discovery, exploitation, entrepreneurial opportunity, alertness	185	Wood & Mckinley (2017)
10	strategic, strategic entrepreneurship, corporate entrepreneurship, competitive, business model	263	Anderson, Covin & Slevin (2009)
11	innovation, innovative, innovator, innovate	163	Pérez-Luño, Wiklund, & Cabrera (2011)
12	capital, social capital, human capital, venture capital, nascent	227	Unger, Rauch, Frese, & Rosenbusch (2011)
13	process, entrepreneurial process, effectuation, nascent, creative	263	Moroz &Hindle (2012)
14	alliance, biotechnology, strategic alliance, partner, opportunism	60	Rothaermel & Deeds (2006)
15	institutional, institution, legal, cultural, legitimacy	137	Bruton, Ahlstrom, & Li (2010)
16	individual, nascent, nascent entrepreneur, entrepreneurial intention, self-efficacy	225	Levesque & Minniti (2006)
17	franchisee, contract, franchise system, franchising, competition	57	Jambulingam & Nevin (1999)
18	information, information asymmetry, survival, alertness, competitor	166	Vaghely & Julien (2010)
19	experience, team, human capital, novice, prior experience	188	Cassar (2014)

(continued)

TABLE 2.4 Topic Number, Descriptive Terms, Frequency, and Example (Continued)

Topic Number	Descriptive Terms	Frequency	Example
20	technology; transfer; license, incubator; technology	175	Harmon, Ardishvili, Cardozo, Elder, Leuthold, Parshall, Raghian, & Smith (1997)
21	risk, risk-take, emotion, risk propensity	154	Mullins & Forlani (2005)
22	strategy, competitive, competitor, differentiation, profitability	182	Ott, Eisenhardt & Bingham (2017)
23	board, shareholder; outside director; leadership	81	Gabrielsson (2007)
24	new venture, survival, legitimacy, nascent, venture performance	145	Fernhaber & Li (2010)
25	investor, financing, funding, syndication, angel investor	156	Vanacker, Manigart, & Meuleman (2014)
26	group, team, diversity, cultural, tmt	194	Lechner & Leyronas (2009)
27	trust, relational, contract, asset, legal	74	Nguyen & Rose (2009)
28	financial, asset, financing, survival, profitability	213	Brinckmann, Salomo & Gemuenden (2011)
29	capitalist, venture capital, venture capital, team, capital firm	116	Parhankangas & Landström (2006)
30	learning, organizational learning, heuristics, entrepreneurial learning	96	Cope (2005)
31	self-employment, unemployment, labor, individual, regional	60	Saridakis, Marlow, & Storey (2014)
32	family business, nonfamily, asset, stakeholder; stewardship	157	Olson, Zuiker, Danes, Stafford, Heck, & Duncan (2003)
33	capability, advantage, competitive, capacity, asset	122	Al-Aali & Teece (2014)
34	cluster; location, regional, region, competitive	98	Folta, Cooper & Baik (2006)
35	cognitive, cognition, affect, emotion, team	175	Baron & Ward (2004)
36	issue, legal, cognition, nascent, attention	182	Brown, Colborne, & McMullan (1988)
37	equity, financing, asset, security, contract	141	Cumming, (2005)
38	policy, regional, region, labor, institution	167	Minniti, (2008)
39	uncertainty, environmental, stakeholder; effectuation, effectual	158	McKelvie, Haynie, & Gustavsson (2011)
40	motivation, emotion, affect, emotional, psychology	144	McMullen, & Warnick (2015)

from these topics. Specifically, it provides descriptive terms, frequencies, and the exemplary study of a topic. Both descriptive terms and exemplary published articles are the best portrayals of identified topics because of their highest association with them (Chakraborty et al., 2013).

Comparison of Table 2.4 with Table 2.3 shows that there are more topics than clusters. This finding is not surprising because topic modeling allows documents to belong to multiple topics, leading the sum of frequencies in Table 2.4 to exceed the number of sampled documents. The results from cluster analysis and topic modeling show that clusters emphasize particular topics but neglect others. Specifically, social capital, network, strategy, investment, financing, resource-based view, decision making, franchising, corporate governance, entrepreneur, opportunity, performance, products, alliances, and innovation are the subject matters of both identified clusters and topics. As discussed above, the behavioral strategy can contribute to some of these overlapping areas like strategy, resources, decision making, entrepreneur, opportunity, performance, and innovation.

In addition to producing these topics that overlap with the results of the cluster analysis, topic modeling produces distinct and new topics that the detected clusters do not sufficiently emphasize. For example, Topic 13 (i.e., entrepreneurial process), Topic 15 (i.e., institution and legitimacy), Topic 21 (i.e., risk propensity), Topic 26 (i.e., groups and teams), Topic 30 (i.e., entrepreneurial learning), Topic 34 (i.e., clusters and competition), Topic 38 (i.e., policy and region), and Topic 39 (i.e., uncertainty and effectuation) are not central to the detected clusters. They do not define the identity of clusters.

Examination of these distinct topics that do not overlap with the results of the cluster analysis shows that behavioral strategy can assume more roles in the entrepreneurship literature than the cluster analysis showed. Specifically, behavioral strategy can contribute to Topic 13, 15, 21, 26, 30, and 39. Topic 13 relates to behavioral strategy because the strategy literature, like the entrepreneurship literature, has a process orientation. Specifically, it views strategy formulation as a process (Hax & Majluf, 1988) that has roots in cognition (Stubbart, 1989). Thus, the entrepreneurship literature can import this behavioral perspective from the strategy literature to enrich its study of the entrepreneurial process, the subject matter of Topic 13.

Institutions and institutional theories and thereby Topic 15 have always been an essential part of the strategy literature and practice. Popular and recent approaches especially emphasize the cognitive roots of institutions (Kallinikos, 1995) like neo-institutional theory (Alvesson & Spicer, 2019). The entrepreneurship literature can adopt this cognitive approach to institutions directly from the strategy literature. In that regard, it can study how entrepreneurs can use non-market strategies (Liedong, Rajwani, & Mellahi, 2017) to influence the cognitive roots of institutions and legitimize their practices.

Risk propensity and entrepreneurial learning are the other topics that should be amenable to contributions from behavioral strategy. The strategy literature has been studying risk propensity and learning at different levels of analysis. Since entrepreneurs are at the center of entrepreneurship, individual learning (Kim, 1993) and risk-taking (To, Kilduff, Ordoñez, & Schweitzer, 2018) approaches of behavioral strategy can inform the entrepreneurship literature.

Behavioral strategy can also contribute to the work on groups and teams in the entrepreneurship literature because the strategy literature has been extensively studying these topics from a cognitive perspective. For example, upper echelons theory, which is widely used and tested in the strategy literature within the context of top management teams (TMT), predicts that managers' characteristics, both observable and unobservable, influence their perceptions (Hambrick, Humphrey, & Gupta, 2015). It also asserts that moderate levels of team heterogeneity can lead to diversity in ideas, which, in turn, can spur innovation (Ferrier & Lyon, 2004), a central concept in the entrepreneurship literature. By adopting the fundamental ideas from the upper echelons perspective, the entrepreneurship literature can enrich its work on groups and teams as has been already done (Vanaelst et al., 2006).

Finally, the topic of effectuation (Palmié et al., 2019) can benefit from behavioral strategy. The purpose of effectuation is to shape the environment under uncertainty. The same purpose has been at the center of the strategic management literature long before the concept of effectuation became popular in the entrepreneurship literature. Thus, strategic management and its behavioral strategy branch can share its expertise with the entrepreneurship literature and contribute to the topic of effectuation. Especially, strategy as a practice perspective can refine the topic of effectuation due to its focus on social activities at micro-level (Whittington, 1996).

CONCLUSION

This study examined the role of behavioral strategy in the entrepreneurship literature. Specifically, it investigated entrepreneurship literature's topics, clusters, and the intersection with both strategy and behavioral strategy. To this end, it analyzed the articles published in the top three journals dedicated to entrepreneurship through unsupervised machine learning. Most frequently used terms and their linkages showed that behavioral strategy influenced the field of entrepreneurship through its either behavioral or strategic roots but not both. Also, cluster analysis and topic modeling identified the clusters or topics in which behavioral strategy has been active or could potentially play an important role.

REFERENCES

Abetti, P. A., & Phan, P. H. (2004). Zobele chemical industries: The evolution of a family company from flypaper to globalization (1919–2001). *Journal of Business Venturing, 19*(4), 589–600.

Al-Aali, A., & Teece, D. J. (2014). International entrepreneurship and the theory of the (long-lived) international firm: A capabilities perspective. *Entrepreneurship Theory and Practice, 38*(1), 95–116.

Alvesson, M., & Spicer, A. (2019). Neo-institutional theory and organization studies: A mid-life crisis? *Organization Studies, 40*(2), 199–218.

Amit, R., MacCrimmon, K. R., Zietsma, C., & Oesch, J. M. (2001). Does money matter?: Wealth attainment as the motive for initiating growth-oriented technology ventures. *Journal of Business Venturing, 16*(2), 119–143.

Anderson, B. S., Covin, J. G., & Slevin, D. P. (2009). Understanding the relationship between entrepreneurial orientation and strategic learning capability: An empirical investigation. *Strategic Entrepreneurship Journal, 3*(3), 218–240.

Ardichvili, A., Cardozo, R., & Ray, S. (2003). A theory of entrepreneurial opportunity identification and development. *Journal of Business Venturing, 18*(1), 105–123.

Arregle, J. L., Naldi, L., Nordqvist, M., & Hitt, M. A. (2012). Internationalization of family-controlled firms: A study of the effects of external involvement in governance. *Entrepreneurship Theory and Practice, 36*(6), 1115–1143.

Barney, J. B. (1986). Strategic factor markets: Expectations, luck and business strategy. *Management Science, 32*(10), 1231–1241.

Baron, R. A. (2004). The cognitive perspective: A valuable tool for answering entrepreneurship's basic "why" questions. *Journal of Business Venturing, 19*(2), 221–239.

Baron, R. A., & Ward, T. B. (2004). Expanding entrepreneurial cognition's toolbox: Potential contributions from the field of cognitive science. *Entrepreneurship Theory and Practice, 28*(6), 553–573.

Baron, R. A., & Tang, J. (2011). The role of entrepreneurs in firm-level innovation: Joint effects of positive affect, creativity, and environmental dynamism. *Journal of Business Venturing, 26*(1), 49–60.

Boone, C., Wezel, F. C., & Van Witteloostuijn, A. (2013). Joining the pack or going solo? A dynamic theory of new firm positioning. *Journal of Business Venturing, 28*(4), 511–527.

Brinckmann, J., Salomo, S., & Gemuenden, H. G. (2011). Financial management competence of founding teams and growth of new technology-based firms. *Entrepreneurship Theory and Practice, 35*(2), 217–243.

Brown, C. A., Colborne, C. H., & McMullan, W. E. (1988). Legal issues in new venture development. *Journal of Business Venturing, 3*(4), 273–286.

Bruno, A. V., & Tyebjee, T. T. (1985). The entrepreneur's search for capital. *Journal of Business Venturing, 1*(1), 61–74.

Bruton, G. D., Ahlstrom, D., & Li, H. L. (2010). Institutional theory and entrepreneurship: Where are we now and where do we need to move in the future? *Entrepreneurship Theory and Practice, 34*(3), 421–440.

Burmeister, K., & Schade, C. (2007). Are entrepreneurs' decisions more biased? An experimental investigation of the susceptibility to status quo bias. *Journal of Business Venturing, 22*(3), 340–362.

Busenitz, L. W., & Barney, J. B. (1997). Differences between entrepreneurs and managers in large organizations: Biases and heuristics in strategic decision-making. *Journal of Business Venturing, 12*(1), 9–30.

Cardon, M. S., Foo, M. D., Shepherd, D., & Wiklund, J. (2012). Exploring the heart: Entrepreneurial emotion is a hot topic. *Entrepreneurship Theory and Practice, 36*(1), 1–10.

Cassar, G. (2014). Industry and startup experience on entrepreneur forecast performance in new firms. *Journal of Business Venturing, 29*(1), 137–151.

Chakraborty, G., Pagolu, M., & Garla, S. (2013). *Text mining and analysis: Practical methods, examples, and case studies using SAS.* Cary, NC: SAS Institute.

Chandler, G. N., & Hanks, S. H. (1993). Measuring the performance of emerging businesses: A validation study. *Journal of Business Venturing, 8*(5), 391–408.

Chandler, G. N., & Hanks, S. H. (1994). Market attractiveness, resource-based capabilities, venture strategies, and venture performance. *Journal of Business Venturing, 9*(4), 331–349.

Chen, C. C., Greene, P. G., & Crick, A. (1998). Does entrepreneurial self-efficacy distinguish entrepreneurs from managers? *Journal of Business Venturing, 13*(4), 295–316.

Chen, H., De, P., Hu, Y. J., & Hwang, B. H. (2014). Wisdom of crowds: The value of stock opinions transmitted through social media. *Review of Financial Studies, 27*(5), 1367–1403.

Chevalier, J. A., & Mayzlin, D. (2006). The effect of word of mouth on sales: Online book reviews. *Journal of Marketing Research, 43*(3), 345–354.

Coff, R. W. (2010). The coevolution of rent appropriation and capability development. *Strategic Management Journal, 31*(7), 711–733.

Coombs, J. E., Mudambi, R., & Deeds, D. L. (2006). An examination of the investments in US biotechnology firms by foreign and domestic corporate partners. *Journal of Business Venturing, 21*(4), 405–428.

Cope, J. (2005). Toward a dynamic learning perspective of entrepreneurship. *Entrepreneurship Theory and Practice, 29*(4), 373–397.

Cumming, D. J. (2005). Agency costs, institutions, learning, and taxation in venture capital contracting. *Journal of Business Venturing, 20*(5), 573–622.

Cumming, D., & Dai, N. (2013). Why do entrepreneurs switch lead venture capitalists? *Entrepreneurship Theory and Practice, 37*(5), 999–1017.

Daily, C. M., & Dalton, D. R. (1992). The relationship between governance structure and corporate performance in entrepreneurial firms. *Journal of Business Venturing, 7*(5), 375–386.

Das, T. K., & Teng, B. (1999). Cognitive biases and strategic decision processes: An integrative perspective. *Journal of Management Studies, 36*(6), 757–778.

De Clercq, D., Lim, D. S., & Oh, C. H. (2013). Individual-level resources and new business activity: The contingent role of institutional context. *Entrepreneurship Theory and Practice, 37*(2), 303–330.

Dew, N., Read, S., Sarasvathy, S. D., & Wiltbank, R. (2009). Effectual versus predictive logics in entrepreneurial decision-making: Differences between experts and novices. *Journal of Business Venturing, 24*(4), 287–309.

Discua Cruz, A., Howorth, C., & Hamilton, E. (2013). Intrafamily entrepreneurship: The formation and membership of family entrepreneurial teams. *Entrepreneurship Theory and Practice, 37*(1), 17–46.

Douglas, E. J. (2013). Reconstructing entrepreneurial intentions to identify predisposition for growth. *Journal of Business Venturing, 28*(5), 633–651.

Durand, R., & Coeurderoy, R. (2001). Age, order of entry, strategic orientation, and organizational performance. *Journal of Business Venturing, 16*(5), 471–494.

Eesley, C. E., & Roberts, E. B. (2012). Are you experienced or are you talented?: When does innate talent versus experience explain entrepreneurial performance? *Strategic Entrepreneurship Journal, 6*(3), 207–219.

Fernhaber, S. A., & Li, D. (2010). The impact of interorganizational imitation on new venture international entry and performance. *Entrepreneurship Theory and Practice, 34*(1), 1–30.

Ferreira, M. P., Reis, N. R., & Miranda, R. (2015). Thirty years of entrepreneurship research published in top journals: Analysis of citations, co-citations and themes. *Journal of Global Entrepreneurship Research, 5*(1), 1–22.

Ferrier, W. J., & Lyon, D. W. (2004). Competitive repertoire simplicity and firm performance: The moderating role of top management team heterogeneity. *Managerial and Decision Economics, 25*(6–7), 317–327.

Financial Times. (2019). *50 journals used in FT research rank.* https://www.ft.com/content/3405a512-5cbb-11e1-8f1f-00144feabdc0

Folta, T. B., Cooper, A. C., & Baik, Y. S. (2006). Geographic cluster size and firm performance. *Journal of Business Venturing, 21*(2), 217–242.

Gaba, V., & Bhattacharya, S. (2012). Aspirations, innovation, and corporate venture capital: A behavioral perspective. *Strategic Entrepreneurship Journal, 6*(2), 178–199.

Gabrielsson, J. (2007). Correlates of board empowerment in small companies. *Entrepreneurship Theory and Practice, 31*(5), 687–711.

Gentzkow, M., Kelly, B. T., & Taddy, M. (2017). *Text as data.* http://dx.doi.org/10.2139/ssrn.2934001

Gillis, W. E., McEwan, E., Crook, T. R., & Michael, S. C. (2011). Using tournaments to reduce agency problems: The case of franchising. *Entrepreneurship Theory and Practice, 35*(3), 427–447.

Goss, D., & Sadler-Smith, E. (2018). Opportunity creation: Entrepreneurial agency, interaction, and affect. *Strategic Entrepreneurship Journal, 12*(2), 219–236.

Grégoire, D. A., Barr, P. S., & Shepherd, D. A. (2010). Cognitive processes of opportunity recognition: The role of structural alignment. *Organization Science, 21*(2), 413–431.

Gupta, A. K., & Sapienza, H. J. (1992). Determinants of venture capital firms' preferences regarding the industry diversity and geographic scope of their investments. *Journal of Business Venturing, 7*(5), 347–362.

Hambrick, D. C., Humphrey, S. E., & Gupta, A. (2015). Structural interdependence within top management teams: A key moderator of upper echelons predictions. *Strategic Management Journal, 36*(3), 449–461.

Harmon, B., Ardishvili, A., Cardozo, R., Elder, T., Leuthold, J., Parshall, J., Raghian, M., & Smith, D. (1997). Mapping the university technology transfer process. *Journal of Business Venturing, 12*(6), 423–434.

Hax, A. C., & Majluf, N. S. (1988). The concept of strategy and the strategy formation process. *Interfaces, 18*(3), 99–109.

Hite, J. M. (2005). Evolutionary processes and paths of relationally embedded network ties in emerging entrepreneurial firms. *Entrepreneurship Theory and Practice, 29*(1), 113–144.

Hofmann, T. (2001). Unsupervised learning by probabilistic latent semantic analysis. *Machine Learning, 42*(1–2), 177–196.

Hornsby, J. S., Kuratko, D. F., & Zahra, S. A. (2002). Middle managers' perception of the internal environment for corporate entrepreneurship: Assessing a measurement scale. *Journal of Business Venturing, 17*(3), 253–273.

Jackson, W. E. III, Bates, T., & Bradford, W. D. (2012). Does venture capitalist activism improve investment performance? *Journal of Business Venturing, 27*(3), 342–354.

Jambulingam, T., & Nevin, J. R. (1999). Influence of franchisee selection criteria on outcomes desired by the franchisor. *Journal of Business Venturing, 14*(4), 363–395.

James, G., Witten, D., Hastie, T., & Tibshirani, R. (2013). *An introduction to statistical learning.* New York, NY: Springer.

Jarillo, J. C. (1989). Entrepreneurship and growth: The strategic use of external resources. *Journal of Business Venturing, 4*(2), 133–147.

Julien, P. A. (1995). New technologies and technological information in small businesses. *Journal of Business Venturing, 10*(6), 459–475.

Kallinikos, J. (1995). Cognitive foundations of economic institutions: Markets, organizations and networks revisited. *Scandinavian Journal of Management, 11*(2), 119–137.

Karakaya, F., & Kobu, B. (1994). New product development process: An investigation of success and failure in high-technology and non-high-technology firms. *Journal of Business Venturing, 9*(1), 49–66.

Keh, H. T., Der Foo, M., & Lim, B. C. (2002). Opportunity evaluation under risky conditions: The cognitive processes of entrepreneurs. *Entrepreneurship Theory and Practice, 27*(2), 125–148.

Kelley, D. J., & Rice, M. P. (2001). Technology-based strategic actions in new firms: The influence of founding technology resources. *Entrepreneurship Theory and Practice, 26*(1), 55–71.

Ketchen, D. J., Jr., Short, J. C., & Combs, J. G. (2011). Is franchising entrepreneurship? Yes, no, and maybe so. *Entrepreneurship Theory and Practice, 35*(3), 583–593.

Kidwell, R. E., Nygaard, A., & Silkoset, R. (2007). Antecedents and effects of free riding in the franchisor–franchisee relationship. *Journal of Business Venturing, 22*(4), 522–544.

Kim, D. H. (1993). The link between individual and organizational learning. *Sloan Management Review, 33*(1), 37–50.

Kisfalvi, V. (2002). The entrepreneur's character, life issues, and strategy making: A field study. *Journal of Business Venturing, 17*(5), 489–518.

Ko, W. W., & Liu, G. (2015). Understanding the process of knowledge spillovers: Learning to become social enterprises. *Strategic Entrepreneurship Journal, 9*(3), 263–285.

Lechner, C., & Leyronas, C. (2009). Small-business group formation as an entrepreneurial development model. *Entrepreneurship Theory and Practice, 33*(3), 645–667.

Lee, S. H., & Wong, P. K. (2004). An exploratory study of technopreneurial intentions: A career anchor perspective. *Journal of Business Venturing, 19*(1), 7–28.

Leiblein, M. J., & Reuer, J. J. (2004). Building a foreign sales base: The roles of capabilities and alliances for entrepreneurial firms. *Journal of Business Venturing, 19*(2), 285–307.

Lester, R. H., & Cannella, A. A., Jr. (2006). Interorganizational familiness: How family firms use interlocking directorates to build community-level social capital. *Entrepreneurship Theory and Practice, 30*(6), 755–775.

Levesque, M., & Minniti, M. (2006). The effect of aging on entrepreneurial behavior. *Journal of Business Venturing, 21*(2), 177–194.

Levinthal, D. A. (2011). A behavioral approach to strategy—What's the alternative? *Strategic Management Journal, 32*(13), 1517–1523.

Li, D. (2013). Multilateral R&D alliances by new ventures. *Journal of Business Venturing, 28*(2), 241–260.

Liedong, T. A., Rajwani, T., & Mellahi, K. (2017). Reality or illusion? The efficacy of non-market strategy in institutional risk reduction. *British Journal of Management, 28*(4), 609–628.

Liu, L., Tang, L., Dong, W., Yao, S., & Zhou, W. (2016). An overview of topic modeling and its current applications in bioinformatics. *SpringerPlus, 5*(1), Article 1608. https://doi.org/10.1186/s40064-016-3252-8

Loughran, T., & McDonald, B. (2016). Textual analysis in accounting and finance: A survey. *Journal of Accounting Research, 54*(4), 1187–1230.

Manigart, S. (1994). The founding rate of venture capital firms in three European countries (1970–1990). *Journal of Business Venturing, 9*(6), 525–541.

McCaffrey, M. (2014). On the theory of entrepreneurial incentives and alertness. *Entrepreneurship Theory and Practice, 38*(4), 891–911.

McCline, R. L., Bhat, S., & Baj, P. (2000). Opportunity recognition: An exploratory investigation of a component of the entrepreneurial process in the context of the health care industry. *Entrepreneurship Theory and Practice, 25*(2), 81–94.

McDougall, P. P. (1989). International versus domestic entrepreneurship: New venture strategic behavior and industry structure. *Journal of Business Venturing, 4*(6), 387–400.

McKelvie, A., Haynie, J. M., & Gustavsson, V. (2011). Unpacking the uncertainty construct: Implications for entrepreneurial action. *Journal of Business Venturing, 26*(3), 273–292.

McMullen, J. S., & Dimov, D. (2013). Time and the entrepreneurial journey: The problems and promise of studying entrepreneurship as a process. *Journal of Management Studies, 50*(8), 1481–1512.

McMullen, J. S., & Shepherd, D. A. (2006). Entrepreneurial action and the role of uncertainty in the theory of the entrepreneur. *Academy of Management Review, 31*(1), 132–152.

McMullen, J. S., & Warnick, B. J. (2015). Article commentary: To nurture or groom? The parent-founder succession dilemma. *Entrepreneurship Theory and Practice, 39*(6), 1379–1412.

Michael, S. C. (1996). To franchise or not to franchise: An analysis of decision rights and organizational form shares. *Journal of Business Venturing, 11*(1), 57–71.

Miller, A., Spann, M. S., & Lerner, L. (1991). Competitive advantages in new corporate ventures: The impact of resource sharing and reporting level. *Journal of Business Venturing, 6*(5), 335–350.

Minniti, M. (2008). The role of government policy on entrepreneurial activity: Productive, unproductive, or destructive? *Entrepreneurship Theory and Practice, 32*(5), 779–790.

Mitchell, R. K., Busenitz, L. W., Bird, B., Marie Gaglio, C., McMullen, J. S., Morse, E. A., & Smith, J. B. (2007). The central question in entrepreneurial cognition research 2007. *Entrepreneurship Theory and Practice, 31*(1), 1–27.

Moghaddam, K., Bosse, D. A., & Provance, M. (2016). Strategic alliances of entrepreneurial firms: Value enhancing then value destroying. *Strategic Entrepreneurship Journal, 10*(2), 153–168.

Moroz, P. W., & Hindle, K. (2012). Entrepreneurship as a process: Toward harmonizing multiple perspectives. *Entrepreneurship Theory and Practice, 36*(4), 781–818.

Mullins, J. W., & Forlani, D. (2005). Missing the boat or sinking the boat: A study of new venture decision making. *Journal of Business Venturing, 20*(1), 47–69.

Murphy, P. J. (2011). A 2×2 conceptual foundation for entrepreneurial discovery theory. *Entrepreneurship Theory and Practice, 35*(2), 359–374.

Newbert, S. L. (2008). Value, rareness, competitive advantage, and performance: A conceptual-level empirical investigation of the resource-based view. *Strategic Management Journal, 29*(7), 745–768.

Nguyen, T. V., & Rose, J. (2009). Building trust—Evidence from Vietnamese entrepreneurs. *Journal of Business Venturing, 24*(2), 165–182.

Nicholls-Nixon, C. L., Cooper, A. C., & Woo, C. Y. (2000). Strategic experimentation: Understanding change and performance in new ventures. *Journal of Business Venturing, 15*(5–6), 493–521.

Olson, P. D., Zuiker, V. S., Danes, S. M., Stafford, K., Heck, R. K., & Duncan, K. A. (2003). The impact of the family and the business on family business sustainability. *Journal of Business Venturing, 18*(5), 639–666.

Orser, B. J., Riding, A. L., & Manley, K. (2006). Women entrepreneurs and financial capital. *Entrepreneurship Theory and Practice, 30*(5), 643–665.

Ott, T. E., Eisenhardt, K. M., & Bingham, C. B. (2017). Strategy formation in entrepreneurial settings: Past insights and future directions. *Strategic Entrepreneurship Journal, 11*(3), 306–325.

Palmié, M., Huerzeler, P., Grichnik, D., Keupp, M. M., & Gassmann, O. (2019). Some principles are more equal than others: Promotion- versus prevention-focused effectuation principles and their disparate relationships with entrepreneurial orientation. *Strategic Entrepreneurship Journal, 13*(1), 93–117.

Parhankangas, A., & Landström, H. (2006). How venture capitalists respond to unmet expectations: The role of social environment. *Journal of Business Venturing, 21*(6), 773–801.

Parker, S. C. (2008). The economics of formal business networks. *Journal of Business Venturing, 23*(6), 627–640.

Penney, C. R., & Combs, J. G. (2013). Insights from family science: The case of innovation. *Entrepreneurship Theory and Practice, 37*(6), 1421–1427.

Pérez-Luño, A., Wiklund, J., & Cabrera, R. V. (2011). The dual nature of innovative activity: How entrepreneurial orientation influences innovation generation and adoption. *Journal of Business Venturing, 26*(5), 555–571.

Plambeck, N. (2012). The development of new products: The role of firm context and managerial cognition. *Journal of Business Venturing, 27*(6), 607–621.

Powell, T. C., Lovallo, D., & Fox, C. R. (2011). Behavioral strategy. *Strategic Management Journal, 32*(13), 1369–1368.

Robinson, R. B., Jr. (1987). Emerging strategies in the venture capital industry. *Journal of Business Venturing, 2*(1), 53–77.

Rothaermel, F. T., & Deeds, D. L. (2006). Alliance type, alliance experience and alliance management capability in high-technology ventures. *Journal of Business Venturing, 21*(4), 429–460.

Roy, R., Lampert, C. M., & Stoyneva, I. (2018). When dinosaurs fly: The role of firm capabilities in the "avianization" of incumbents during disruptive technological change. *Strategic Entrepreneurship Journal, 12*(2), 261–284.

Sarasvathy, S. D. (2004). The questions we ask and the questions we care about: Reformulating some problems in entrepreneurship research. *Journal of Business Venturing, 19*(5), 707–717.

Saridakis, G., Marlow, S., & Storey, D. J. (2014). Do different factors explain male and female self-employment rates? *Journal of Business Venturing, 29*(3), 345–362.

SAS Institute Inc. (2017). *SAS® text miner 14.3: Reference help.* Cary, NC: Author. http://documentation.sas.com/api/docsets/tmref/14.3/content/tmref.pdf?locale=en

Schwienbacher, A. (2007). A theoretical analysis of optimal financing strategies for different types of capital-constrained entrepreneurs. *Journal of Business Venturing, 22*(6), 753–781.

Scimago Journal & Country Rank. (2019). *Journal rankings.* https://www.scimagojr.com/journalrank.php?area=1400

Shane, S. (2000). Prior knowledge and the discovery of entrepreneurial opportunities. *Organization Science, 11*(4), 448–469.

Shane, S. (2002). Executive forum: University technology transfer to entrepreneurial companies. *Journal of Business Venturing, 17*(6), 537–552.

Shefrin, H. (2000). *Beyond greed and fear: Understanding behavioral finance and the psychology of investing.* Boston, MA: Harvard Business School Press.

Short, J. C., Moss, T. W., & Lumpkin, G. T. (2009). Research in social entrepreneurship: Past contributions and future opportunities. *Strategic Entrepreneurship Journal, 3*(2), 161–194.

Silge, J., & Robinson, D. (2017). *Text mining with R: A tidy approach.* Sebastopol, CA: O'Reilly Media.

Simon, M., & Shrader, R. C. (2012). Entrepreneurial actions and optimistic overconfidence: The role of motivated reasoning in new product introductions. *Journal of Business Venturing, 27*(3), 291–309.

Singal, M., & Singal, V. (2011). Concentrated ownership and firm performance: Does family control matter? *Strategic Entrepreneurship Journal, 5*(4), 373–396.

Slotte-Kock, S., & Coviello, N. (2010). Entrepreneurship research on network processes: A review and ways forward. *Entrepreneurship Theory and Practice, 34*(1), 31–57.

Sorrentino, M., & Williams, M. L. (1995). Relatedness and corporate venturing: Does it really matter? *Journal of Business Venturing, 10*(1), 59–73.

Spinelli, S., & Birley, S. (1996). Toward a theory of conflict in the franchise system. *Journal of Business Venturing, 11*(5), 329–342.

Srivastava, A., & Lee, H. (2005). Predicting order and timing of new product moves: The role of top management in corporate entrepreneurship. *Journal of Business Venturing, 20*(4), 459–481.

Stubbart, C. I. (1989). Managerial cognition: A missing link in strategic management research. *Journal of Management Studies, 26*(4), 325–347.

Sullivan, D. M., & Ford, C. M. (2014). How entrepreneurs use networks to address changing resource requirements during early venture development. *Entrepreneurship Theory and Practice, 38*(3), 551–574.

Sun, S. L., & Im, J. (2015). Cutting microfinance interest rates: An opportunity co-creation perspective. *Entrepreneurship Theory and Practice, 39*(1), 101–128.

Symeonidou, N., & Nicolaou, N. (2018). Resource orchestration in start-ups: Synchronizing human capital investment, leveraging strategy, and founder start-up experience. *Strategic Entrepreneurship Journal, 12*(2), 194–218.

Thorleuchter, D., & Van Den Poel, D. (2012). Predicting e-commerce company success by mining the text of its publicly-accessible website. *Expert Systems With Applications, 39*(17), 13026–13034.

To, C., Kilduff, G. J., Ordoñez, L., & Schweitzer, M. E. (2018). Going for it on fourth down: Rivalry increases risk taking, physiological arousal, and promotion focus. *Academy of Management Journal, 61*(4), 1281–1306.

Townsend, D. M., & Busenitz, L. W. (2008). Factor payments, resource-based bargaining, and the creation of firm wealth in technology-based ventures. *Strategic Entrepreneurship Journal, 2*(4), 339–355.

Townsend, D. M., Busenitz, L. W., & Arthurs, J. D. (2010). To start or not to start: Outcome and ability expectations in the decision to start a new venture. *Journal of Business Venturing, 25*(2), 192–202.

Ucbasaran, D., Westhead, P., Wright, M., & Flores, M. (2010). The nature of entrepreneurial experience, business failure and comparative optimism. *Journal of Business Venturing, 25*(6), 541–555.

Unger, J. M., Rauch, A., Frese, M., & Rosenbusch, N. (2011). Human capital and entrepreneurial success: A meta-analytical review. *Journal of Business Venturing, 26*(3), 341–358.

Vaghely, I. P., & Julien, P. A. (2010). Are opportunities recognized or constructed?: An information perspective on entrepreneurial opportunity identification. *Journal of Business Venturing, 25*(1), 73–86.

Valliere, D. (2013). Towards a schematic theory of entrepreneurial alertness. *Journal of Business Venturing, 28*(3), 430–442.

Vanacker, T., Manigart, S., & Meuleman, M. (2014). Path-dependent evolution versus intentional management of investment ties in science-based entrepreneurial firms. *Entrepreneurship Theory and Practice, 38*(3), 671–690.

Vanaelst, I., Clarysse, B., Wright, M., Lockett, A., Moray, N., & S'Jegers, R. (2006). Entrepreneurial team development in academic spinouts: An examination of team heterogeneity. *Entrepreneurship Theory and Practice, 30*(2), 249–271.

Venkataraman, S. (1997). The distinctive domain of entrepreneurship research: An editor's perspective. In J. Katz & R. Brockhaus (Eds.), *Advances in entrepreneurship, firm emergence, and growth* (pp. 119–138), Greenwich, CT: JAI Press.

Vincent, W. S. (1998). Encroachment: Legal restrictions on retail franchise expansion. *Journal of Business Venturing, 13*(1), 29–41.

Vissa, B., & Bhagavatula, S. (2012). The causes and consequences of churn in entrepreneurs' personal networks. *Strategic Entrepreneurship Journal, 6*(3), 273–289.

Welter, C., Mauer, R., & Wuebker, R. J. (2016). Bridging behavioral models and theoretical concepts: Effectuation and bricolage in the opportunity creation framework. *Strategic Entrepreneurship Journal, 10*(1), 5–20.

Westhead, P., Wright, M., & Ucbasaran, D. (2001). The internationalization of new and small firms: A resource-based view. *Journal of Business Venturing, 16*(4), 333–358.

Whittington, R. (1996). Strategy as practice. *Long Range Planning, 29*(5), 731–735.

Wilson, F., Kickul, J., & Marlino, D. (2007). Gender, entrepreneurial self-efficacy, and entrepreneurial career intentions: Implications for entrepreneurship education. *Entrepreneurship Theory and Practice, 31*(3), 387–406.

Wood, M. S., & Mckinley, W. (2017). After the venture: The reproduction and destruction of entrepreneurial opportunity. *Strategic Entrepreneurship Journal, 11*(1), 18–35.

Wright, M., & Hitt, M. A. (2017). Strategic entrepreneurship and SEJ: Development and current progress. *Strategic Entrepreneurship Journal, 11*(3), 200–210.

Wu, L. Y., Wang, C. J., Chen, C. P., & Pan, L. Y. (2008). Internal resources, external network, and competitiveness during the growth stage: A study of Taiwanese high-tech ventures. *Entrepreneurship Theory and Practice, 32*(3), 529–549.

Yin, D., Mitra, S., & Zhang, H. (2016). When do consumers value positive vs. negative reviews? An empirical investigation of confirmation bias in online word of mouth. *Information Systems Research, 27*(1), 131–144.

Zahra, S. A. (1991). Predictors and financial outcomes of corporate entrepreneurship: An exploratory study. *Journal of Business Venturing, 6*(4), 259–285.

Zahra, S. A., Filatotchev, I., & Wright, M. (2009). How do threshold firms sustain corporate entrepreneurship? The role of boards and absorptive capacity. *Journal of Business Venturing, 24*(3), 248–260.

CHAPTER 3

THE TEMPORALITIES OF ENTREPRENEURIAL RISK BEHAVIOR

T. K. Das
Bing-Sheng Teng

ABSTRACT

Risk and risk behavior form an important segment of the entrepreneurship literature. Entrepreneurial risk behavior has been studied with both trait and cognitive approaches, but the findings do not adequately explain either how entrepreneurs differ from non-entrepreneurs, or how different types of entrepreneurs can be specified in terms of their risk behavior. This chapter is an attempt to address these issues by introducing two temporal attributes that we consider significant for understanding risk behavior, given that risk is intrinsically embedded in time. First, we discuss the notion of risk horizon, differentiating short-range risk from long-range risk. Second, we examine the risk behavior of entrepreneurs in terms of their individual future orientation, in tandem with their risk propensity. We propose a temporal framework which seeks to explain, at once, the different types of risk behavior among entrepreneurs as well as the distinction between entrepreneurs and non-entrepreneurs. The framework is also applied to networking and alliancing

Entrepreneurship and Behavioral Strategy, pages 57–87
Copyright © 2020 by Information Age Publishing

activities of entrepreneurs. Finally, a number of propositions are developed to facilitate empirical testing of the insights implicit in the temporal framework of entrepreneurial risk behavior.

INTRODUCTION

Risk is intrinsically embedded in time, and yet the temporal context continues to suffer from relative neglect in the research literature. Specifically, an individual's conception of the flow of time in the future has a significant impact on entrepreneurial risk behavior. We propose that any entrepreneurial decision with risk connotations necessarily involves, implicitly and explicitly, two particular temporal attributes. The first relates to the risk horizon, or the span of time for which the entrepreneur assesses the risk. The second is concerned with the individual future orientation of the entrepreneur. In this chapter, we develop a framework for understanding entrepreneurial risk behavior with due recognition of the role of these two temporal aspects, in conjunction with the acknowledged role of risk propensity.

Entrepreneurship has traditionally been defined as the "creation of new enterprises," and the entrepreneur as "an organizer of an economic venture, especially one who organizes, owns, manages, and assumes the risk of a business" (*Webster's Third New International Dictionary*, 1961). In recent decades, however, we have witnessed a major shift toward a firm-level orientation in entrepreneurship research (Covin & Slevin, 1991; Stevenson & Jarillo, 1990; Wales, 2016), evident in the proliferation of terms such as corporate entrepreneurship (Lerner, Zahra, & Kohavi, 2007; Stopford & Baden-Fuller, 1994), which refers to firms behaving in a proactive, innovative, and risk taking manner. It has been noted that the research focus has shifted away from the entrepreneur (Gartner, Shaver, Gatewood, & Katz, 1994; Shaver & Scott, 1991). This chapter is intended to support an interest in entrepreneurs, who supposedly behave differently from the rest of the population. Our contribution relates to an examination of the risk behavior of those who create new business ventures, and how that behavior may be better understood by incorporating two particular kinds of temporal dimensions.

In the first section that follows, we briefly review the extant literature on entrepreneurial risk behavior, noting that both the trait and cognitive approaches cannot adequately differentiate between the risk behaviors of entrepreneurs and non-entrepreneurs. We propose that the temporal elements mentioned earlier may help in this regard. In the second section, we make the case for two types of entrepreneurial risk based on the idea of risk horizon, namely, short-range entrepreneurial risk and long-range entrepreneurial risk. These two temporal types of entrepreneurial risk are then employed, in the third section, to derive different risk behaviors that typify entrepreneurs and non-entrepreneurs. In the fourth section, we examine entrepreneurial risk behavior further by including two critical personality traits, namely, individual risk propensity and individual future orientation. In the fifth section, we discuss how our proposed framework may be applied in the areas of entrepreneurial networking and alliancing. A number of propositions based on the temporal framework are also developed to facilitate empirical testing.

THE NATURE OF ENTREPRENEURIAL RISK BEHAVIOR

Risk taking appears to be one of the most distinctive features of entrepreneurial behavior, since creating new ventures is by definition a risky business. Risk is conventionally defined as substantial variances in outcomes that are of consequence (MacCrimmon & Wehrung, 1986; Yates & Stone, 1992). According to Schumpeter (1934), the entrepreneur is a person who devises new combinations and innovations of products and services. A high failure rate for such innovations has been regarded as the rule rather than the exception. Failure of new ventures also greatly affects an entrepreneur's financial well-being, career opportunity, and personal well-being (Kozan, Oksoy, & Ozsoy, 2012; Wiklund, Nikolaev, Shir, Foo, & Bradley, 2019; Wood & Rowe, 2011). On the one hand, entrepreneurial activities involve considerable investments, both financial and personal, so that a failure usually means enormous losses to the entrepreneur. On the other hand, the kind of wealth and personal fulfillment that a successful entrepreneurial attempt can bring is also much greater than normal. Given that so much is at stake in creating new ventures, it is no surprise that the subject of risk behavior should be at the heart of entrepreneurial behavior (Miller, 2007; Tipu, 2017). The literature seems to offer two main approaches to the study of entrepreneurial risk behavior, namely trait and cognitive.

The Trait Approach

The belief that entrepreneurs have distinctive personality characteristics has a long tradition in entrepreneurship studies, and research based on this premise is generally known as the trait approach. A number of psychological traits have been studied, in an attempt to differentiate entrepreneurs from non-entrepreneurs (see Brockhaus & Horwitz, 1986; Knörr, Alvarez, & Urbano, 2013; Leutner, Ahmetoglu, Akhtar, & Chamorro-Premuzic, 2014). Some of the more important ones include need for achievement (McClelland, 1965), locus of control (Mueller & Thomas, 2000), tolerance of ambiguity (Sexton & Bowman, 1985), and risk propensity (Begley & Boyd, 1987; Brockhaus, 1980; Glaser, Stam, & Takeuchi, 2016).

Regarding risk propensity, it seems a natural presumption that a high degree of dispositional risk preference exists among entrepreneurs. Since "the entrepreneurial function involves primarily *risk measurement* and *risk taking*" (Palmer, 1971, p. 38, emphasis in original), it would seem to make sense to assume that entrepreneurs are inherently risk takers. In fact, Leibenstein (1968) regards the entrepreneur as "the ultimate uncertainty and/or risk bearer" (p. 74) and Gasse (1982) states that "this distinction between creating risk and risk-bearing fundamentally distinguishes between entrepreneurs and managers" (p. 60).

In contrast to this view, McClelland (1961) has suggested that entrepreneurs actually have only a moderate level of risk propensity. The reason is that people with high need for achievement, such as entrepreneurs, would prefer to undertake tasks that are both challenging and achievable by employing their skills (McClelland, 1965). In this sense, people with moderate risk propensity are more likely to succeed in creating new businesses.

Empirical evidence relating to risk behavior has been accumulating over some period, but the results seem to be weak and contradictory (Low & MacMillan, 1988; Sexton & Bowman, 1985). On the one hand, a few studies did report a higher risk propensity of entrepreneurs compared to non-entrepreneurs (e.g., Begley & Boyd, 1987; Sexton & Bowman, 1986; Stewart & Roth, 2001). On the other hand, some studies failed to find such a difference (Brockhaus, 1980; Sexton & Bowman, 1983; Smith & Miner, 1983). McClelland's speculation that entrepreneurs are more moderate risk takers did not receive much empirical support either (Brockhaus, 1980; Litzinger, 1965).

Given such inconsistent results, one possible explanation is that many of these empirical studies are not directly comparable, since they have used different definitions of entrepreneurs (Begley, 1995; Gartner, 1989). Thus, a manager in one study could have been classified as an entrepreneur in another. Also, measures of risk propensity were far from uniform. That being the situation, more consistent research methods are clearly needed (Ginsberg & Buchholtz, 1989).

A different reaction to the inconclusive results is to suggest that there may be as much difference among entrepreneurs as between entrepreneurs and non-entrepreneurs (Gartner, 1985; Gruber & MacMillan, 2017). If so, then a typical entrepreneur may not exist and "who is an entrepreneur" may be a wrong question altogether (Gartner, 1989, p. 47). In this regard, a number of studies have proposed different entrepreneurial typologies. For instance, Webster (1977) has suggested five types of entrepreneurs (Cantillon, industry-maker, administrative, small business owner/operator, and independent), and Smith (1967) has differentiated between the craftsman entrepreneur and the opportunistic entrepreneur. Nevertheless, researchers have not adequately demonstrated how basic personality traits are linked with various entrepreneurial types (Woo, Cooper, & Dunkelberg, 1991), especially how risk behavior differs in each of these types.

The Cognitive Approach

Given the limited success with the trait approach, some researchers turned to a more cognition-oriented approach to studying entrepreneurial risk behavior (Keh, Foo, & Lim, 2002; Palich & Bagby, 1995; Peacock, 1986). The cognitive approach to risk behavior is common in management studies (Libby & Fishburn, 1977; March & Shapira, 1987, 1992; Shapira, 1995). In entrepreneurship, this approach was probably pioneered by Kirzner (1973, 1979), who advocated a theory of entrepreneurial alertness which examines entrepreneurs' unique ability to discover and exploit opportunities that others fail to see. The cognitive approach attempts to understand how perceptions (Cooper, Woo, & Dunkelberg, 1988), decision making styles (Kaish & Gilad, 1991), heuristics (Manimala, 1992), biases (Busenitz & Barney, 1997), and intentions (Bird, 1988) of entrepreneurs affect their behavior (Shaver & Scott, 1991), including entrepreneurial risk behavior.

Palich and Bagby's (1995) study exemplifies how the cognitive approach can be used to account for the risk behavior of entrepreneurs. They have reported that entrepreneurs generally are not any more disposed to taking risks than non-entrepreneurs; instead, entrepreneurs simply perceive risky situations more optimistically than others. In other words, since entrepreneurs' risk perceptions tend to be more optimistic, they are more willing to undertake those entrepreneurial efforts that others see as too risky.

While both the trait approach and the cognitive approach reveal something important about the risk behavior of entrepreneurs, a deficiency in the existing literature is that the dependent variable we wish to understand (i.e., entrepreneurial risk behavior) is perhaps too simplistic, in the sense that the dichotomy of low-risk and high-risk behaviors may not by itself yield sufficient purchase on the phenomenon. We believe that part of the deficiency in the extant approaches to understanding the full range and complexity of entrepreneurial behavior can be attributed to our failure to incorporate the critically relevant factor of time. In the next section, we will differentiate between short-range risk and long-range risk, and see how this temporal refinement helps us to initially suggest two types of entrepreneurial risk. In the section following the next, we will utilize these two types of entrepreneurial risk to propose a temporal typology of entrepreneurial risk behavior, which at once also encompasses the risk behavior of non-entrepreneurs.

TEMPORAL HORIZONS OF ENTREPRENEURIAL RISK

It is generally agreed that time plays a crucial role in risk and risk behavior (Das & Teng, 2001; Lopes, 1996; Schneider & Lopes, 1986; Strickland, Lewicki, & Katz, 1966). Risk and uncertainty are essentially about the unpredictable futures, and they are therefore plainly embedded in time. Indeed, time seems to greatly complicate the already complicated concept of risk. In the words of Lopes (1987), "The temporal element is what gives risk both savor and sting" (p. 289). Psychologists have spent many years studying this temporal dimension (e.g., Nisan & Minkowich, 1973; Shelley, 1994; Tumasjan, Welpe, & Spörrie, 2013). Researchers have often observed that several risk behaviors are related to time. The risk-taking propensities of business executives, in particular, are likely to be associated with strategies that have long-range time horizons (Das & Teng, 2001). One important finding is called discounting in time (Vlek & Stallen, 1980), which is the tendency of individuals to undertake risks when possible gains are relatively immediate and possible losses are relatively in the distant future. In addition, Strickland et al. (1966) have reported that subjects tend to be more risk-averse if a gamble is presented in an after-the-event fashion, as compared to the usual before-the-game gamble. Lopes (1996), in addition, has highlighted differences in risk behavior according to whether the gamble is to be played just once or multiple times.

While the above research findings speak to the importance of time in risk and risk behavior, we should note that time and the temporal dimension have not been adequately integrated into the conception of risk. For one thing, the bulk of the literature has not explicitly differentiated between short-range risk behavior and long-range risk behavior (Mowen & Mowen, 1991). Most studies on risk behavior implicitly cover only short-range risk (Kahneman & Tversky, 1979), while real-life risky decisions often unfold in the long run. This difference in time-spans of risk (Das, 2004) under consideration could have a profound impact on how risky alternatives are valued, as some studies have noted (e.g., Vlek & Stallen, 1980). Thus, we believe that it is important to make clear the specific temporal horizon of the risky decision.

Short-Range Risk and Long-Range Risk

Broadly defined, short-range risk refers to variances in outcomes in the near future, while long-range risk relates to variances in outcomes in the distant future (Drucker, 1972). Accordingly, short-range risk behavior is about taking or avoiding actions that may cause outcomes to vary significantly in the near future, from great gains to great losses; and long-range risk behavior is defined as taking or avoiding actions that may cause outcomes to vary significantly in the distant future. Low-risk behavior and high-risk behavior are the terms we will use to designate the two contrasting kinds of risk behavior. Thus, when people make decisions that are likely to evoke more extreme outcomes in the distant future, they are engaged in long-range risk behavior, either low-risk or high-risk. Examples of long-range risk taking may include long-term investment, not buying auto and medical insurance, smoking, and dropping out of school. Examples of short-range risk taking may include casino gambling, drinking and driving, and cheating in a test. The same individual may well exhibit low-risk behavior regarding long-range risk and high-risk behavior regarding short-range risk, or vice versa. For instance, many people take little risk with their long-term financial security, starting to save and invest early in life. The same individuals, though, could be aggressive investors in managing their personal investments in a high-risk fashion on a continuous, daily basis.

Entrepreneurial Risk Types

The time dimension has been the subject of study in a large number of disciplines (Das, 1990), and has been steadily gaining the attention of management scholars (Das, 1986; Kunisch, Bartunek, Mueller, & Huy, 2017). In keeping with this trend, fortunately, entrepreneurial research promises to play its due part (Bird, 1992; Petrakis, 2007).

Applying the temporal dimension to entrepreneurial risk, we can differentiate between short-range and long-range entrepreneurial risk. Little has been explored in this direction after Kirzner (1973) discussed the issue of the short-run and the long-run in entrepreneurship from an economics perspective. An interesting notion has been proposed by Dickson and Giglierano (1986) in terms of two types of downside risk: sinking-the-boat risk and missing-the-boat risk. While sinking-the-boat risk refers to the "probability that the venture will fail to reach a satisfactory level of performance" (p. 61), missing-the-boat risk is the risk of failing to "undertake a venture that would have succeeded" (p. 58). Thus, sinking-the-boat risk is associated with the costs of pursuing a false opportunity, and missing-the-boat risk is linked with the costs of not pursuing a genuine opportunity, or opportunity cost of not making a potentially profitable move.

While all decisions seem to involve these two types of risk, we believe that this dual conceptualization is particularly appropriate for appreciating entrepreneurial risk, because entrepreneurs are especially vulnerable to the missing-the-boat risk: Their first chance is often their last. Also, Dickson and Giglierano (1986) have stated that a critical difference between the two types of risk lies in time. Thus, this dual conceptualization can be further examined by mapping it onto the typology of short-range and long-range entrepreneurial risk.

Short-Range Entrepreneurial Risk

Certain risks involved in entrepreneurial activities are short-range in nature because they unfold rather quickly. One of such risks appears to be sinking-the-boat risk for a new venture, or the possibility that it may fail. In a new venture, sinking-the-boat risk would tend to be evident in the short run because a lack of financial slack and back-up makes new ventures particularly vulnerable to initial setbacks. Thus, if the initial performance turns out to be worse than the acceptable minimum, it would be very difficult for the entrepreneurial firm to continue its operations, whether or not the entrepreneur seeks external finance. As Dickson and Giglierano (1986) have pointed out, entrepreneurs often have only one shot in a given venture. They have suggested that sinking-the-boat risk is at its highest level at the initiation stage of a new venture, and that it starts to subside when the operations extend into a more distant future. Thus, sinking-the-boat risk will be a less intimidating prospect in the long run. In this sense, the risk of sinking the boat is particularly short-range in new ventures, as compared to more established companies. That is, established companies are less concerned about their "boat" sinking precipitously.

Long-Range Entrepreneurial Risk

Entrepreneurial activities are also exposed to risks that can be measured only in the long run. These risks may include the risk to the entrepreneurs' personal relations and psychological well-being (Liles, 1974). In addition, we argue that missing-the-boat risk may well be a critical long-range entrepreneurial risk, because the opportunity cost of not pursuing an entrepreneurial career is usually not realized until much later. Since this risk is about what one might miss in the future, it naturally takes a more long-range orientation. As in the case of not going to college, the missing of an opportunity usually amounts to larger and larger losses as the future extends. In this sense, it has been suggested that the level of missing-the-boat risk keeps going up along the future time dimension (Dickson & Giglierano, 1986). Thus, we believe that dealing with missing-the-boat risk would be the major concern in long-range entrepreneurial risk behavior. In the next section, we apply the two types of temporally based entrepreneurial risk to propose two types of entrepreneurial risk behavior, along with non-entrepreneurial risk behavior.

SHORT-RANGE AND LONG-RANGE RISK
IN ENTREPRENEURIAL RISK BEHAVIOR

So far we have discussed short-range and long-range entrepreneurial risk, and now we will apply the distinction to discuss entrepreneurial risk behavior. Entrepreneurship is widely regarded as risk taking because it is about greater gains and losses as compared to non-entrepreneurial activities. However, although risk taking may seem to differentiate entrepreneurial activities from many other activities, it does not follow that entrepreneurship is always about risk taking. In fact, not only has McClelland (1961) regarded entrepreneurial behavior as moderate risk taking, but others (e.g., Webster, 1977) also have suggested that some entrepreneurs may be more risk creators than risk takers. It seems plausible that not all entrepreneurs adopt similar risk behaviors, and that certain entrepreneurial functions actually involve risk avoiding. Indeed, it has been recognized for some time that entrepreneurial activities are of different types (Braden, 1977; Low & MacMillan, 1988). We postulate that as long as there are different types of entrepreneurship, there could be different types of entrepreneurial risk behavior, some of which may be more about short-range risk and others more about long-range risk.

Types of Entrepreneurship: Craftsman and Opportunistic

As we mentioned earlier, the literature reflects various typologies of entrepreneurs and entrepreneurship (Gartner, 1984; Webster, 1977). Braden (1977), for example, classified entrepreneurs as "caretakers" and "managers." Smith (1967) has differentiated between the craftsman entrepreneur and the opportunistic entrepreneur, and it appears to be one of the few entrepreneurial typologies that have received some empirical support (Lessner & Knapp, 1974; Peterson & Smith, 1986; Smith & Miner, 1983), although the findings are far from conclusive (Woo et al., 1991). According to Smith (1967), a craftsman entrepreneur is characterized by narrowness in education and training, and low social awareness and involvement. Essentially, craftsman entrepreneurs are those who open mom-and-pop stores around the corner. These entrepreneurs usually do not offer products and services that are truly innovative; rather, they often provide conventional products and services in areas that are under-served.

In contrast, an opportunistic entrepreneur is one who typically has breadth in education and training, as well as high social awareness and involvement. While the craftsman type of entrepreneurship involves providing conventional products/services to a new market base, the opportunistic type of entrepreneurship is associated with exploring new and novel products/services. Applying Kirzner's (1973) theory of entrepreneurial alertness, Kaish and Gilad's (1991) study found that, as compared to executives, entrepreneurs are more interested in discovering opportunities and the resources for exploiting them. These entrepreneurs seem to belong to the opportunistic type.

Smith's (1967) typology is primarily meant to distinguish different types of entrepreneurs, but it can well be extended to entrepreneurial activities. In other words, if there are different types of entrepreneurs, they would tend to behave differently, and indeed develop different kinds of entrepreneurial firms (Dunkelberg & Cooper, 1982; Smith & Miner, 1983). Adopting these two generic types[1] of entrepreneurs, we now examine how they may differ in their risk behavior, keeping in mind our earlier temporal argument.

Craftsman Entrepreneurs: Short-Range High-Risk Behavior

The craftsman entrepreneurs seem to be more associated with short-range risk taking, since they usually have "a limited time orientation" (Smith & Miner, 1983, p. 326). By definition, craftsmanship is about doing what one likes to do in the present, not so much about long-term planning such as building a successful organization (growth orientation). Such intentions are critical in determining the nature of entrepreneurial activities (Bird, 1988, 1992). Planning is not characteristic of craftsman entrepreneurs (Smith, 1967); they focus on the present time segment and are willing to take considerable risk in the short run, akin to the sinking-the-boat risk discussed earlier. Due to the nature of the businesses that craftsman entrepreneurs run (mostly standard product/service), the boat may sink rather quickly. Usually it is not about innovative products which may take a long time to reveal their potential and promise. For craftsman entrepreneurs, sinking-the-boat risk is an imminent eventuality. Thus, the willingness to take the initial high sinking-the-boat risk seems to differentiate craftsman entrepreneurs from non-entrepreneurs, especially those who also have the skills but do not dare to open their own shops in the face of this initial risk (see Figure 3.1, which, we should note here, also contains material to be developed in the next section).

Since craftsman entrepreneurs are more likely to take short-term entrepreneurial risk, such as sinking-the-boat risk, the initial risk about a new venture would tend to be very high, but this risk would also tend to go down significantly afterwards (Dickson & Giglierano, 1986). By comparison, other types of entrepreneurs, for example, the opportunistic type, are less about sinking-the-boat risk because their objectives are projected

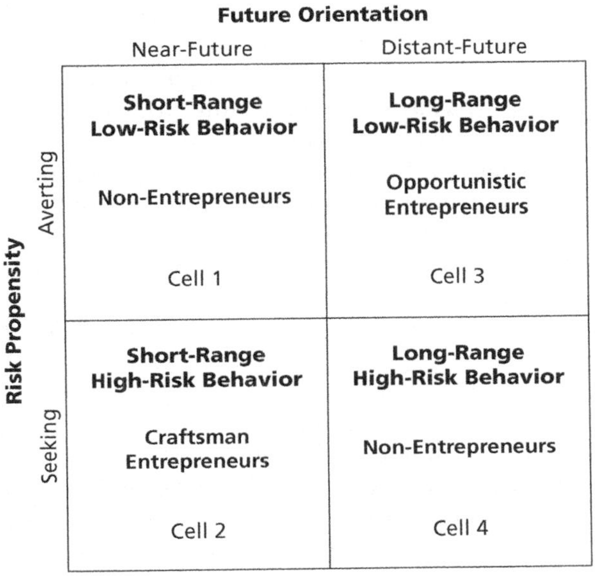

Future Orientation

	Near-Future	Distant-Future
Averting	**Short-Range Low-Risk Behavior** Non-Entrepreneurs Cell 1	**Long-Range Low-Risk Behavior** Opportunistic Entrepreneurs Cell 3
Seeking	**Short-Range High-Risk Behavior** Craftsman Entrepreneurs Cell 2	**Long-Range High-Risk Behavior** Non-Entrepreneurs Cell 4

(Risk Propensity: Averting / Seeking)

Figure 3.1 Entrepreneurial risk behavior based on risk horizon, future orientation, and risk propensity.

to be achieved over the long haul. The initial performance outcomes of craftsman entrepreneurs would reflect the type of risk they take. Thus, we propose that craftsman entrepreneurs can expect substantial performance variances in the short run. Hence:

> **Proposition 1:** *Since craftsman entrepreneurs take short-range sinking-the-boat risk, their initial performance outcomes will vary more from their goal, as compared to that of other types of entrepreneurs and of non-entrepreneurs.*

Opportunistic Entrepreneurs: Long-Range Low-Risk Behavior

According to Smith (1967), opportunistic entrepreneurs develop plans for the long run and they consciously weigh options. They are preoccupied by the need to identify and pursue opportunities in the future that others fail to see or not dare to pursue. The term "opportunistic" does not mean that they would necessarily tend to take risks. We believe that the opportunistic type of entrepreneurs would tend to have risk averse propensities and exhibit long-range low-risk behavior because it is the missing-the-boat risk that they focus on.

According to Dunkelberg and Cooper (1982, p. 4), some entrepreneurs are growth-oriented, in that they desire substantial growth of their businesses and strongly disagree that "a comfortable living is enough." These entrepreneurs are typically of the opportunistic type, as they seem to be motivated primarily by a need to avoid downside variances in terms of their personal achievement in the long run. Thus, opportunistic entrepreneurs consciously plan for a more distant future as compared to craftsman entrepreneurs (Smith, 1967). "Don't regret later because you did not try" seems to be the mindset of these entrepreneurs. Since opportunistic entrepreneurs are inclined toward action in the present in order not to regret missing the opportunity later on, they essentially eliminate or minimize missing-the-boat risk.

Although opportunistic entrepreneurs may also take higher short-range risk than non-entrepreneurs, the key characteristic that distinguishes them from others would appear to be low-risk behavior over the longer range. Research has shown that, for most people, delayed losses are discounted more than delayed gains (Shelley, 1994). As a result, substantial losses in the long run appear less intimidating, and decision makers become more daring in taking risks with delayed outcomes as compared to immediate outcomes (Mowen & Mowen, 1991). In this sense, ordinary people seem to be more accustomed to taking long-range risks, such as missing-the-boat risk. It may be argued that opportunistic entrepreneurs are simply "more missing-the-boat risk averse" (Dickson & Giglierano, 1986, p. 67).

Furthermore, according to Dickson and Giglierano (1986, p. 63), missing-the-boat risk often results from being short-sighted. Thus, opportunistic entrepreneurs would be more immune to this risk since they consciously deal with it. In fact, Kirzner's (1973, 1979) notion of entrepreneurial alertness stressed that entrepreneurship is about opportunity discovering (Kaish & Gilad, 1991). The long-term performance of opportunistic entrepreneurs will tend to reflect the risk-averting effect and show limited variances in their performance outcomes. Hence we propose:

Proposition 2: *Since opportunistic entrepreneurs avoid long-range missing-the-boat risk, their long-term performance outcomes will vary less from their goal, as compared to that of other types of entrepreneurs and of non-entrepreneurs.*

Non-Entrepreneurs: Short-Range Low-Risk Behavior and Long-Range High-Risk Behavior

By comparison, non-entrepreneurs seem to be typified by either short-range low-risk behavior or long-range high-risk behavior, depending on their respective risk propensities. Testing people's bias in the prediction of future events, Milburn (1978) found that initially negative events were seen as more likely than positive events, while the relationship was reversed in the prediction of events farther into the future. This seems to support the idea that most people are more able to perceive downside risk in the near-future. It may explain why most people feel more comfortable with avoiding short-range risk. Non-entrepreneurs are more concerned about short-term loss (Kahneman & Lovallo, 1993). They stay away from entrepreneurship since self-employment usually involves extreme outcomes (especially loss) in the immediate future. By comparison, entrepreneurs, especially crafts-man entrepreneurs, are willing to take significant short-range risk in order to do what they like to do. Thus, the short-term performance outcomes of these two groups of people would naturally differ significantly. For non-entrepreneurs, their short-term performance would not vary much from their short-term goal because they would mostly choose to play it safe. Hence:

Proposition 3: *Since non-entrepreneurs avoid short-range sinking-the-boat risk, their short-term performance outcomes will vary less from their goal, as compared to that of entrepreneurs.*

It can also be suggested that non-entrepreneurs take significant long-range risk since they may miss the boat altogether. In other words, not pursuing opportunities in the present is tantamount to taking missing-the-boat risk in the long run. Vlek and Stallen (1980) have reported that people tend to take risks involving delayed losses. Thus, it can be assumed that most people are inclined to taking long-range risk, even though it means missing out on opportunities in the long run. Consider individuals who do not save throughout their career and expect their retirement needs to be met with some kind of windfall such as winning a lottery. In that case, they take very high long-range risk because they might miss most of the boats in their lives. Regarding possible outcomes, taking long-range risk means inviting more variance from one's goal. If one takes long-term health risk by not exercising regularly, one's health condition is likely to deviate much from one's expectations in later years. For non-entrepreneurs, the idea is similar. Not willing to explore opportunities now (i.e., being opportu-nistic) often amounts to long-term performance that is far below one's expectations. Hence:

Proposition 4: *Since non-entrepreneurs take long-range missing-the-boat risk, their long-term performance outcomes will vary more from their goal, as compared to that of entrepreneurs.*

FUTURE ORIENTATION AND RISK PROPENSITY IN ENTREPRENEURIAL RISK BEHAVIOR

We have so far discussed entrepreneurial risk behavior in terms of the temporal dimension, which has enabled us to distinguish between entrepreneurial types (craftsman vs. opportunistic), as well as between entrepreneurs and non-entrepreneurs. In this section, we explore further what may be giving rise to these different types of risk behavior, that is, individual differences in their personality traits. Entrepreneurial research has traditionally emphasized the role played by personality traits in contributing to entrepreneurial behaviors (Carland, Hoy, Boulton, & Carland, 1984; Litzinger, 1965; Sexton & Bowman, 1986). Although criticism has been leveled against this approach (e.g., Gartner, 1989), it is our belief that certain personality traits do help account for behavior, and the key lies in identifying the more appropriate ones (Brockhaus & Horwitz, 1986).

To that end, we suggest that individual risk propensity (Brockhaus, 1980) and future orientation (Das, 1986) are two personality traits pertinent to entrepreneurial risk behavior. Risk propensity seems to be a trait that is naturally tied with risk behavior, and considerable evidence suggests that persistent individual differences in risk propensity do exist (Bromiley & Curley, 1992; Brown, 1970; Kogan & Wallach, 1964). Existing studies have attempted to single out risk propensity as the sole psychological determinant of entrepreneurial risk behavior, with but limited success (Low & MacMillan, 1988). Kihlstrom and Laffont (1979), for example, implicitly assumed that the less risk-averse individuals become entrepreneurs, while the more risk-averse become laborers. In a study of Chinese CEOs, Opper, Nee, and Holm (2017) confirm "the importance of risk preferences in explaining strategic choices and performance effects" (p. 1504). In our view, risk propensity (averting or seeking) alone may not provide an adequate answer to the issue, especially when entrepreneurship is no longer regarded as risk taking only.

We have already examined entrepreneurial risk behavior from one temporal perspective, namely, risk horizon. We will now introduce a further level of complexity by incorporating a second temporal variable, namely, individual future orientation. Future orientation is a personality trait that continues to be overlooked in entrepreneurial research. We will explore how the two kinds of temporal attributes jointly help determine entrepreneurial risk behavior.

Future Orientations of Individuals

Future orientation refers to individuals' psychological attribute regarding their perception of the future and the flow of time (Cottle, 1976; Das,

1986, 1987, 1991, 1993; Fraisse, 1963; Kastenbaum, 1961; Klineberg, 1968).[2] Some people are more future oriented in that they pay more attention to what may happen in a relatively distant future. Others are more present-time oriented in that they are preoccupied with the immediate future. This future time perspective tends to be fairly stable for a person, and is thus regarded as a psychological trait that reflects the person's psychological ability and focus in perceiving the flow of time. In other words, people can be differentiated by their ability to envision and "grasp" the future.

It has been found that some people are more able to "see" a distant future than others, and are comfortable envisioning what might happen far into the future (Das, 1986). To them, even events in the distant-future are psychologically possible and real in the phenomenal world of undulating time. These people are thus categorized as having a distant-future orientation. In contrast, other people are psychologically attached to present-time thinking and are not used to envisioning a distant future. To them, the immediate future means more or less all that there is in the future-time segment. Thus, instead of seeing a plethora of future events, these individuals view themselves as advancing into a relatively limited future-time segment. These individuals can be said to have a near-future orientation.

It must be noted that future orientation is about psychological time rather than clock time or calendar time (Das, 1991). While clock time and calendar time are involved in making fast decisions and expanding planning horizons, psychological time is more about the relationship of the past, present, near-future, and distant-future—all perceived in the fleeting present. Future orientation is essentially an individual's subjective experience and "grasp" of the time-flow in the future, and is minimally relevant to clock time or calendar time. Thus, it is the relative cognitive dominance of the distant-future over the near-future that characterizes a person with a distant-future orientation. In terms of the relevance of this individual future orientation, Das (1986) found a statistically significant relationship between the future orientations of business executives and their preferences for planning horizons. Distant-future oriented executives were found to be more inclined towards long-range planning than their near-future oriented compatriots in the same organization. This finding simply reinforces the general idea that behavior in the work arena finds its partial roots in personality traits. We now proceed to an examination of entrepreneurial risk behavior in relation to the two personality traits of future orientation and risk propensity.

Near-Future Orientation

When an individual has a near-future orientation and a risk propensity that tends toward averting risk, he or she is unlikely to be an entrepreneur (see Cell 1 in Figure 3.1). We argued earlier that some non-entrepreneurs are characterized by short-range low-risk behavior, or an unwillingness to take initial risks associated with entrepreneurial activities (Proposition 3). That behavior can be easily explained by their risk propensity and future orientation. First of all, since these individuals have a risk averting propensity, they would be more inclined toward low-risk behavior, that is, avoiding alternatives that may cause outcomes to vary too much from their expectations. Secondly, a near-future orientation means that these individuals would focus on short-term options, or those with short-range risks. Given a near-future orientation, these individuals would tend not to consciously ponder long-range risks, so that their risk propensity may not be operative in determining their long-range risk behavior. Since such individuals are most likely to make short-term decisions that would preclude much performance variance, an entrepreneurial career seems an unlikely choice. Thus:

Proposition 5: *Individuals with a near-future orientation and a risk averting propensity are less likely to be entrepreneurs.*

Individuals with a near-future orientation and a risk seeking propensity, however, are more likely to be craftsman entrepreneurs (Cell 2). Being near-future oriented, short-range risk is the type of risk that they would attempt to deal with. Meanwhile, due to their risk seeking propensity, it is natural that these individuals would be quite willing to take rather significant risks. As we argued earlier, craftsman entrepreneurs are characterized by short-range risk bahavior (Proposition 1), and this is in line with Smith and Miner's (1983, p. 326) observation that craftsman entrepreneurs usually have "a limited time orientation," or, in our terminology, a near-future orientation. Thus:

Proposition 6: *Individuals with a near-future orientation and a risk seeking propensity are more likely to be craftsman entrepreneurs.*

Distant-Future Orientation

Individuals with a distant-future orientation tend to be concerned more with the long run rather than the present. Thus, their personal predilection is mostly reflected in long-range risk behavior. It does not mean that these people do not take or avoid short-range risk; rather, the idea is that their risk propensity may not affect their short-range risk behavior too much due to a relative neglect of the short-run. For these individuals, their risk propensity is operative mainly in regard to long-range risk.

Thus, if the individual is risk averse, he or she would be of the long-range low-risk type (Cell 3). Our earlier discussion identified long-range risk avoiding with opportunistic entrepreneurs, since they are mostly concerned with missing-the-boat risk in the long run (Proposition 2). This is supported by Smith and Miner (1983, p. 326), who stated that opportunistic entrepreneurs exhibit "an awareness of, and orientation to, the future" (p. 326). Therefore:

Proposition 7: *Individuals with a distant-future orientation and a risk averting propensity are more likely to be opportunistic entrepreneurs.*

On the other hand, if distant-future oriented individuals have a risk seeking propensity, they are unlikely to be entrepreneurs (Cell 4). A risk seeking propensity along with a distant-future orientation lead to long-range risk taking, which we have argued to be a characteristic of non-entrepreneurs (Proposition 4), or those who are willing to put their long-term welfare at risk. The type of long-range risk that they are exposed to is mainly missing-the-boat risk. Thus,

Proposition 8: *Individuals with a distant-future orientation and a risk seeking propensity are less likely to be entrepreneurs.*

We might add that the framework can be used to predict, on the basis of the two dimensions of future orientation and risk propensity, the career alternatives of being non-entrepreneurs, craftsman entrepreneurs, or opportunistic entrepreneurs. In the case of non-entrepreneurs, Cell 1 and Cell 4 represent two different types. Individuals in Cell 1 are concerned with avoiding short-term losses, so that they would be less likely to pursue a career of self-employment. Laborers who prefer stable incomes in the short run exemplify this type. In contrast, individuals included in Cell 4 are those who would choose not to be engaged in entrepreneurial activities because they do not care much about missing opportunities in the long run, that is, those who would consciously decide to undertake a missing-the-boat risk. And, of course, craftsman entrepreneurs (Cell 2) are those who would prefer to take the immediate, sinking-the-boat risk in order to meet their relatively short-range goals, such as doing what they like to do in the present, while opportunistic entrepreneurs (Cell 3) would focus on avoiding long-range missing-the-boat risk.

Looking at the framework horizontally, we also observe that whereas opportunistic entrepreneurs (Cell 3) are able to appreciate long-range risks (being distant-future oriented) arising from not pursuing entrepreneurial activities (missing-the-boat risk), those in Cell 1 fail to perceive such long-range risks (being limited by their near-future orientation). Along similar lines, craftsman entrepreneurs (Cell 2), being near-future oriented, are likely to be attracted by an entrepreneurial career that promises to provide them with what they want in the short run (e.g., being their own boss). By comparison, some non-entrepreneurs (Cell 4), not being near-future oriented, would tend not to value such immediate outcomes.

In sum, the discussion of the characteristics of the four cells of the temporal framework, the various propositions, and the comparisons of each cell with all the others, seem in their totality to convey a coherent and comprehensive picture of the risk behaviors of entrepreneurs and non-entrepreneurs.

ENTREPRENEURIAL NETWORKING AND ALLIANCING

As an illustration of how the proposed temporal framework of entrepreneurial risk behavior can be potentially applied to different areas, we discuss its relevance to networking and alliancing activities in entrepreneurship. Cooperative linkages such as networks and strategic alliances are especially important for the entrepreneurial process, due to a lack of established internal resources (Das & He, 2006; Dubini & Aldrich, 1991). By definition, "networks are associations of individuals or groups that facilitate access to information or resources" (Holt, 1987, p. 44), while strategic alliances are defined as more integrative forms of interfirm cooperation such as joint ventures and joint R&D (Das & Teng, 1996; Golden & Dollinger, 1993). Networking and alliancing can help entrepreneurs get needed access and connections that are not available from other sources (Das & Teng, 1998a; Hansen, 1995). For example, firms in the biotechnology industry have significantly benefited in their innovation and new product development activities through interfirm cooperation (Deeds & Hill, 1996; Shan, Walker, & Kogut, 1994).

In their review article, Low and MacMillan (1988) noted that network theories are increasingly being applied to entrepreneurship research. Over the years, a considerable number of studies have been carried out in this area (Slotte-Kock & Coviello, 2010), covering topics such as informal networks (Birley, 1985; Johannisson, 1987), formal networks (Holt, 1987), strategic alliances among small firms (Borch & Huse, 1993; Larson & Starr, 1993), and entrepreneurial networking growth (Hansen, 1995) and performance (Larson, 1991). However, researchers have not so far examined the relationship between entrepreneurial risk behavior and entrepreneurial networking and alliancing. According to Golden and Dollinger (1993), different cooperative linkages may be used by different types of small firms. Using the same logic, we argue that the type of networks being used (informal vs. formal) and the involvement in strategic alliances may be examined in the light of various types of entrepreneurial risk behavior that we have discussed above.

Informal Versus Formal Entrepreneurial Networks

The literature suggests two types of entrepreneurial networks in terms of their distinctive sources: informal and formal (Birley, 1985; Johannisson, 1987). While informal entrepreneurial networks consist of personal friends, families, and business contacts, formal networks include associations with venture capitalists, banks, accountants, lawyers, creditors, and trade associations. For example, borrowing money from relatives in order to open a barber shop is informal networking, while seeking venture capital can be seen as joining a formal entrepreneurial network. The key difference is that informal networks start with personal relationships so that they are essentially trust-based organizing vehicles. In contrast, formal networks are based on business contracts and agreements, with clear rights and obligations for each involved party. Regarding the use of the two types, Birley (1985) has reported that entrepreneurs primarily used informal networks, and turned to formal networks only after their firms were in an established position.

Craftsman Entrepreneurs and Networking

Given the difference between formal and informal networks, we suggest that craftsman entrepreneurs are more likely to rely on informal networks than on formal networks. The reason is that craftsman entrepreneurs tend to take short-range risks. In our view, it is short-range risk taking if one mainly relies on personal connections to start a new business, since entrepreneurial risks would be internalized by this inner circle and not shared by external people such as venture capitalists. Furthermore, there is additional performance risk associated with informal entrepreneurial networks. Since informal networks are characterized by interpersonal trust, reciprocity, reputation, and so on (Larson, 1991, 1992), sufficient controls such as business contracts would not be used to monitor the relationships. It is generally agreed among theorists that trusting without sufficient control is equivalent to risk taking (Das & Teng, 1998b, 2004; Mayer, Davis, & Schoorman, 1995). As compared to the opportunistic type, the craftsman type would be more willing to expose themselves to this type of short-range entrepreneurial risk.

Because of the willingness to take short-range risk, when it comes to financing a new venture, craftsman entrepreneurs would tend to commit their own money, or money borrowed from family, friends, and so on, instead of raising money from venture capitalists or banks, so that they remain relatively free to do what they want. Smith (1967) described a craftsman who states: "I don't want to grow too rapidly because I can easily use up my working capital and when this is gone the banks get control" (p. 27).

This kind of resistance to formal networks seems to be characteristic of craftsman entrepreneurs.

In addition to the foregone risk aspect, another reason that craftsman entrepreneurs may rely more on informal networks is their incompetence in dealing with a broad social environment (Smith & Miner, 1983). Smith (1967) described them as having low social awareness and involvement, a fact also contributing to the reliance on informal entrepreneurial networks. Thus:

Proposition 9: *Craftsman entrepreneurs will rely more on informal networks than on formal networks.*

Opportunistic Entrepreneurs and Networking

Formal networks comprising venture capitalists and trade associations actively seek to provide support for new ideas that promise higher-than-average returns. Since opportunistic entrepreneurs also constantly look for new opportunities untapped by the market, there seems to be a fit between formal networks and opportunistic entrepreneurs. First, the types of opportunities that opportunistic entrepreneurs attempt to explore usually are not about opening a mom-and-pop store. Informal networks may not be adequately bountiful in terms of providing needed financial and knowledge resources. Second, and more importantly, in contrast to craftsman entrepreneurs, opportunistic entrepreneurs tend to engage in long-range low-risk behavior. Thus, they are highly motivated to minimize their personal risk through involving outside sources. While financing a new venture by an entrepreneur is highly risky, a sharing of this risk with formal networks makes the enterprise fairly attractive (Amit, Glosten, & Muller, 1990). Thus, opportunistic entrepreneurs often join formal networks, with strong reliance on contractual agreements and monitoring mechanisms. Hence:

Proposition 10: *Opportunistic entrepreneurs will rely more on formal networks than on informal networks.*

Entrepreneurs and Strategic Alliances

Besides networking, strategic alliances provide entrepreneurs another means to access others' resources and quickly build up their own operation. Strategic alliances are more intensive in terms of interfirm cooperation than networks, since alliance partners are expected to work together for explicit strategic objectives. Often formed by firms in the same industry, strategic alliances tend to have a relatively high level of interfirm integration. It is interesting to note that the number of entrepreneurial firms involved in strategic alliances is proportionately much less than established companies. Most of the entrepreneurial firms appear to shy away from a seemingly sensible alliancing strategy. Based on our time-risk framework, we would suggest that strategic alliances pose the kind of opportunities and threats that seem incompatible with the risk behavior of entrepreneurs (see also Das, 2006).

On the one hand, strategic alliances offer valuable opportunities to entrepreneurial firms in the short run, in that startups can always use some help from more established firms. An alliance with a prestigious firm often quickly brings about needed reputation for the startup firm itself. Considering that most startups are less than well-known, strategic alliances do serve as a stepping stone for them (Das & He, 2006). It is in this sense that strategic alliances can be viewed as a means to "buffer small firms from environmental uncertainty" (Golden & Dollinger, 1993, p. 44), and thus avoid short-range entrepreneurial risk (e.g., sinking-the-boat risk). First, by forming an alliance with a larger company, startups can significantly reduce the risk of bankruptcy in the short run. Dealership and supplier relationships are just two such examples. Second, through strategic alliances entrepreneurial firms can become more able to expeditiously capitalize on opportunities that otherwise they would have had to let go, at least in the short run. In brief, it seems that strategic alliances call for short-range low-risk behavior on the part of startup firms.

On the other hand, strategic alliances may be hazardous for entrepreneurial firms in the long run, if the alliance becomes an interim and covert cover for future acquisitions and manipulations by larger firms (Bleeke & Ernst, 1995). In fact, many established firms harbor hidden agendas when they form alliances with startups, and that is why some researchers have warned against such arrangements (Das & Teng, 1997). Over the long run, it is possible that the new startup becomes so embedded in a cooperative arrangement that it may find it difficult to survive on its own. If so, strategic flexibility may be sacrificed and long-term performance put in jeopardy (Lumpkin & Brigham, 2011). In this sense, it can be argued that strategic alliances often mean risk taking in the long run for entrepreneurial firms. As we have argued before (see Figure 3.1), entrepreneurs are more likely to exhibit short-range high-risk behavior or long-range low-risk behavior. Since strategic alliances offer two situations that are less compatible with entrepreneurial risk behavior, it is not surprising that many entrepreneurs do not pursue this option. Thus:

Proposition 11: *Entrepreneurial firms are less likely to be involved in strategic alliances than more established firms.*

CONCLUDING REMARKS

Entrepreneurial risk behavior has been examined in the literature by both the personality trait approach and the cognitive approach. Neither approach, however, has thus far yielded convincing evidence explaining entrepreneurial risk behavior in a parsimonious manner. Even the basic distinction between entrepreneurs and non-entrepreneurs does not seem to have been satisfactorily explained in terms of risk behavior. In particular, a comprehensive typology that encompasses different kinds of entrepreneurs along with non-entrepreneurs, based on risk behavior, has not been developed. In this chapter, we have proposed a framework which attempts to do this by incorporating two kinds of temporal attributes. We have based our effort in the conviction that risk is intrinsically embedded in time, coupled with the finding that the temporal context has thus far remained largely neglected (along with the lack of attention to other key dimensions of the broader entrepreneurial context, as argued by Welter, 2011; Zahra, Wright, & Abdelgawad, 2014; among others, in support of the contextualization of entrepreneurship research).

The first contribution of this chapter lies in introducing the notion of risk horizon, leading to a differentiation between short-range entrepreneurial risk and long-range entrepreneurial risk. This essentially recognizes that not all entrepreneurial risks have the same temporal context; some are more about the immediate future and others unfold only in the long run. The concepts of sinking-the-boat risk and missing-the-boat risk were used to illustrate the new insights gained from this temporal differentiation.

The second contribution is in explaining and developing different entrepreneurial types by employing their distinct risk behavior in the short run and in the long run. We have suggested that craftsman entrepreneurs can be identified by their short-range high-risk behavior, while opportunistic entrepreneurs by their long-range low-risk behavior. Along the same lines, non-entrepreneurs can be distinguished by either short-range low-risk behavior or long-range high-risk behavior. Such a framework answers directly the basic question in the literature: Are entrepreneurs more risk taking than non-entrepreneurs? Our answer, clearly, is a contingent one: It depends on the risk horizon; namely, whether it is about short-range risk or long-range risk. In other words, it helps us understand why not all entrepreneurs are about risk taking. Additionally, this temporally based risk perspective helps us better appreciate how entrepreneurial activities differ from non-entrepreneurial activities.

Thirdly, our framework also explores the role of a second temporal attribute in entrepreneurial risk behavior, namely, individual future orientation. Given that individuals may have either a risk averting or a risk seeking propensity, we have combined risk propensity with future orientation to enrich and reinforce the temporal framework with additional elements in our attempt to explain different types of entrepreneurs and to distinguish between entrepreneurs and non-entrepreneurs. Essentially, craftsman entrepreneurs would tend to be near-future oriented and have a risk seeking propensity, while opportunistic entrepreneurs would tend to be distant-future oriented and have a risk averting propensity. The non-entrepreneurs, in our framework, would be characterized by the two pairings of risk averting propensity with near-future orientation and risk seeking propensity with distant-future orientation.

It should be recognized, of course, that our framework essentially adopts the trait approach in studying entrepreneurial risk behavior. As we noted at the outset, the other major approach is cognitive, which examines the effects of cognitive biases and heuristics on entrepreneurial risk behavior. One limitation of the framework is that it leaves out the potential role of cognitive elements. For instance, differences in risk behavior between entrepreneurs and non-entrepreneurs have sometimes been attributed to differences in the perceptions of risk. It may be worthwhile to develop a more sophisticated temporal framework by incorporating both pertinent cognitive elements and insights from other disciplines (Ireland & Webb, 2007).

Finally, we have discussed how our temporal framework can be applied to the emerging topics of entrepreneurial networking and alliancing, demonstrating that this framework, and perhaps other temporal refinements of it, has the potential for the study of a wide range of topics. Thus, one direction for future research would be to apply the framework to other topics in entrepreneurship, such as long-term growth of new ventures, entrepreneurial education and training, and the intersection of risk propensity, temporal orientation, and perceived decision context among different types of entrepreneurs and non-entrepreneurs. But beyond that, we hope that our effort encourages renewed attention to contingent approaches to entrepreneurial risk behavior and its temporal context in the overall enterprise of understanding entrepreneurial behavior.

NOTES

1. It is important to note that we are adopting this typology, flawed as it is (Woo et al., 1991), for its widespread presence in the literature, as that would facilitate appreciation of the role of the time dimension (both the risk horizon aspect discussed in this section and the psychological individual future orientation to be introduced later) in understanding the postulated risk behaviors of different types of entrepreneurs as well as non-entrepreneurs. Thus, Smith's (1967) typology is used here to merely illustrate the potential role of the two temporal dimensions in studying risk behaviors; we do not attempt to critique any typology in this chapter. Obviously, an assessment of the ro-

bustness of these hitherto unexplored temporal roles in risk behavior has to await empirical investigation. We cannot resist speculating, though, that such empirical testing might help in at least partially explaining, if only as a byproduct, the lack of definitive support for the craftsman-opportunist typology, because of the possible presence of respondents who should properly be considered as non-entrepreneurs under our temporally refined framework. This "contamination" of the entrepreneurial samples, which are based on self-reported goals (e.g., Braden, 1977, p. 54) that are probably attractive to all and sundry respondents, can be eliminated by identifying and weeding out the non-entrepreneur respondents using our temporal template.

2. We should clarify that we refer to these studies as a foundation to argue for a role for individual future orientation in individual (here, entrepreneurial) risk behavior. Unfortunately, there are no empirical studies, other than Das (1986, 1987), that employ the individual future orientation construct in the management and organization area (see, for instance, the article by Thoms and Greenberger [1995]). In examining the intersection of time and entrepreneurial behavior, it is important to keep in mind the individualistic focus (hence *psychological* time) of the construct of individual future orientation. This is crucial to appreciate upfront, so that one does not expect a simplistic tie-in with the predominantly linear conception of time in the management and organization literature. It is thus important not to hark to the publications in the literature which conceive of time unquestioningly as a constant for all individuals. In this regard, we should like to suggest that researchers need to seriously consider moving away from discussing the "future" and other time topics relating to the essentially *subjective* process of human decision making in *objective*, non-problematic, constant, linear, clock-and-calendar-time terms.

ACKNOWLEDGMENT

This chapter, save some minor revisions and updating, was earlier published as Das, T. K., & Teng, B. (1997). Time and entrepreneurial risk behavior. *Entrepreneurship Theory and Practice, 22*(2), 69–88.

REFERENCES

Amit, R., Glosten, L., & Muller, E. (1990). Entrepreneurial ability, venture investments, and risk sharing. *Management Science, 36*(10), 1232–1245.

Begley, T. M. (1995). Using founder status, age of firm, and company growth as the basis for distinguishing entrepreneurs from managers of smaller businesses. *Journal of Business Venturing, 10*(3), 249–263.

Begley, T. M., & Boyd, D. P. (1987). Psychological characteristics associated with performance in entrepreneurial firms and smaller businesses. *Journal of Business Venturing, 2*(1), 79–93.

Bird, B. J. (1988). Implementing entrepreneurial ideas: The case for intention. *Academy of Management Review, 13*(3), 442–453.

Bird, B. J. (1992). The operation of intentions in time: The emergence of the new venture. *Entrepreneurship Theory and Practice, 17*(1), 11–20.

Birley, S. (1985). The role of networks in the entrepreneurial process. *Journal of Business Venturing, 1*(1), 107–117.

Bleeke, J., & Ernst, D. (1995). Is your strategic alliance really a sale? *Harvard Business Review, 73*(1), 97–105.

Borch, O. J., & Huse, M. (1993). Informal strategic networks and the board of directors. *Entrepreneurship Theory and Practice, 18*(1), 23–36.

Braden, P. (1977). *Technological entrepreneurship.* Ann Arbor: University of Michigan.

Brockhaus, R. H., Sr. (1980). Risk taking propensity of entrepreneurs. *Academy of Management Journal, 23*(3), 509–520.

Brockhaus, R. H., Sr., & Horwitz, P. S. (1986). The psychology of the entrepreneur. In D. L. Sexton & R. W. Smilor (Eds.), *The art and science of entrepreneurship* (pp. 25–48). Cambridge, MA: Ballinger.

Bromiley, P., & Curley, S. P. (1992). Individual differences in risk taking. In J. F. Yates (Ed.), *Risk-taking behavior* (pp. 87–132). Chichester, England: Wiley.

Brown, J. S. (1970). Risk propensity in decision making: A comparison of business and public school administrators. *Administrative Science Quarterly, 15*(4), 473–481.

Busenitz, L. W., & Barney, J. B. (1997). Differences between entrepreneurs and managers in large organizations: Biases and heuristics in strategic decision-making. *Journal of Business Venturing, 12*, 9–30.

Carland, J. W., Hoy, F., Boulton, W. R., & Carland, J. A. C. (1984). Differentiating entrepreneurs from small business owners: A conceptualization. *Academy of Management Review, 9*(2), 354–359.

Cooper, A. C., & Woo, C. Y., & Dunkelberg, W. C. (1988). Entrepreneurs' perceived chances for success. *Journal of Business Venturing, 3*(2), 97–108.

Cottle, T. J. (1976). *Perceiving time: A psychological investigation with men and women.* New York, NY: Wiley.

Covin, J. G., & Slevin, D. P. (1991). A conceptual model of entrepreneurship as firm behavior. *Entrepreneurship Theory and Practice, 16*(1), 7–24.

Das, T. K. (1986). *The subjective side of strategy making: Future orientations and perceptions of executives.* New York, NY: Praeger.

Das, T. K. (1987). Strategic planning and individual temporal orientation. *Strategic Management Journal, 8*(2), 203–209.

Das, T. K. (1990). *The time dimension: An interdisciplinary guide.* New York, NY: Praeger.

Das, T. K. (1991). Time: The hidden dimension in strategic planning. *Long Range Planning, 24*(3), 49–57.

Das, T. K. (1993). Time in management and organizational studies. *Time & Society, 2*(2), 267–274.

Das, T. K. (2004). Time-span and risk of partner opportunism in strategic alliances. *Journal of Managerial Psychology, 19*(8), 744–759.

Das, T. K. (2006). Strategic alliance temporalities and partner opportunism. *British Journal of Management, 17*(1), 1–21.

Das, T. K., & He, I. Y. (2006). Entrepreneurial firms in search of established partners: Review and recommendations. *International Journal of Entrepreneurial Behaviour & Research, 12*(3), 114–143.

Das, T. K., & Teng, B. (1996). Risk types and inter-firm alliance structures. *Journal of Management Studies, 33,* 827–843.

Das, T. K., & Teng, B. (1997). Sustaining strategic alliances: Options and guidelines. *Journal of General Management, 22*(4), 49–64.

Das, T. K., & Teng, B. (1998a). Resource and risk management in the strategic alliance making process. *Journal of Management, 24*(1), 21–42.

Das, T. K., & Teng, B. (1998b). Between trust and control: Developing confidence in partner cooperation in alliances. *Academy of Management Review, 23*(3), 491–512.

Das, T. K., & Teng, B. (2001). Strategic risk behavior and its temporalities: Between risk propensity and decision context. *Journal of Management Studies, 38*(4), 515–534.

Das, T. K., & Teng, B. (2004). The risk-based view of trust: A conceptual framework. *Journal of Business and Psychology, 19*(1), 85–116.

Deeds, D. L., & Hill, C. W. L. (1996). Strategic alliances and the rate of new product development: An empirical study of entrepreneurial firms. *Journal of Business Venturing, 11*(1), 41–55.

Dickson, P. R., & Giglierano, J. J. (1986). Missing the boat and sinking the boat: A conceptual model of entrepreneurial risk. *Journal of Marketing, 50*(3), 58–70.

Drucker, P. F. (1972). Long-range planning means risk-taking. In D. W. Ewing (Ed.), *Long-range planning for management* (3rd ed.; pp. 3–19). New York, NY: Harper & Row.

Dubini, P., & Aldrich, H. (1991). Personal and extended networks are central to the entrepreneurial process. *Journal of Business Venturing, 6*(5), 305–313.

Dunkelberg, W. C., & Cooper, A. C. (1982). Entrepreneurial typologies: An empirical study. In K. H. Vesper (Ed.), *Frontiers of Entrepreneurship Research: The proceedings of the Babson Conference on entrepreneurship research* (pp. 1–15). Wellesley, MA: Babson College.

Fraisse, P. (1963). *The psychology of time.* New York, NY: Harper.

Gartner, W. B. (1984). Problems in business startup: The relationships among entrepreneurial skills and problem identification for different types of new ventures. In J. A. Hornaday, F. Tarpley, J. A. Timmons, & K. H. Vesper (Eds.), *Frontiers of entrepreneurship research: The proceedings of the Babson Conference on entrepreneurship research* (pp. 496–512). Wellesley, MA: Babson College.

Gartner, W. B. (1985). A conceptual framework for describing the phenomenon of new venture creation. *Academy of Management Review, 10*(4), 696–706.

Gartner, W. B. (1989). "Who is an entrepreneur?" is the wrong question. *Entrepreneurship Theory and Practice, 13*(4), 47–68.

Gartner, W. B., Shaver, K. G., Gatewood, E., & Katz, J. A. (1994). Finding the entrepreneur in entrepreneurship. *Entrepreneurship Theory and Practice, 18*(3), 5–9.

Gasse, Y. (1982). Elaborations on the psychology of the entrepreneur. In C. A. Kent, D. L. Sexton, & K. H. Vesper (Eds.), *Encyclopedia of entrepreneurship* (pp. 57–71). Englewood Cliffs, NJ: Prentice-Hall.

Ginsberg, A., & Buchholtz, A. (1989). Are entrepreneurs a breed apart? A look at the evidence. *Journal of General Management, 15*(2), 32–40.

Glaser, L., Stam, W., & Takeuchi, R. (2016). Managing the risks of proactivity: A multilevel study of initiative and performance in the middle management context. *Academy of Management Journal, 59*(4), 1339–1360.

Golden, P. A., & Dollinger, M. (1993). Cooperative alliances and competitive strategies in small manufacturing firms. *Entrepreneurship Theory and Practice, 17*(4), 43–56.

Gruber, M., & MacMillan, I. C. (2017). Entrepreneurial behavior: A reconceptualization and extension based on identity theory. *Strategic Entrepreneurship Journal, 11*(3), 271–286.

Hansen, E. L. (1995). Entrepreneurial networks and new organization growth. *Entrepreneurship Theory and Practice, 19*(4), 7–19.

Holt, D. (1987). Network support systems: How communities can encourage entrepreneurship. In N. C. Churchill, J. A. Hornaday, B. A. Kirchhoff, O. J. Krasner, & K. H. Vesper (Eds.), *Frontiers of entrepreneurship research: The proceedings of the Babson Conference on entrepreneurship research* (pp. 44–56). Wellesley, MA: Babson College.

Ireland, R. D., & Webb, J. W. (2007). A cross-disciplinary exploration of entrepreneurship research. *Journal of Management, 33*(6), 891–927.

Johannisson, B. (1987). Anarchists and organizers: Entrepreneurs in a network perspective. *International Studies of Management and Organization, 17*(1), 49–63.

Kahneman, D., & Lovallo, D. (1993). Timid choices and bold forecasts: A cognitive perspective on risk taking. *Management Science, 39*(1), 17–31.

Kahneman, D., & Tversky, A. (1979). Prospect theory: An analysis of decisions under risk. *Econometrica, 47*(2), 262–291.

Kaish, S., & Gilad, B. (1991). Characteristics of opportunities search of entrepreneurs versus executives: Sources, interests, general alertness. *Journal of Business Venturing, 6*(1), 45–61.

Kastenbaum, R. (1961). The dimensions of future time perspective: An experimental analysis. *Journal of General Psychology, 65*(2), 203–218.

Keh, H. T., Foo, M. D., & Lim, B. C. (2002). Opportunity evaluation under risky conditions: The cognitive processes of entrepreneurs. *Entrepreneurship Theory and Practice, 27*(2), 125–148.

Kihlstrom, R. E., & Laffont, J.-J. (1979). A general equilibrium entrepreneurship theory of firm formation based on risk aversion. *Journal of Political Economy, 87*(4), 719–748.

Kirzner, I. M. (1973). *Competition and entrepreneurship.* Chicago, IL: University of Chicago Press.

Kirzner, I. M. (1979). *Perception, opportunity, and profit: Studies in the theory of entrepreneurship.* Chicago, IL: University of Chicago Press.

Klineberg, S. L. (1968). Future time perspective and the preference for delayed reward. *Journal of Personality and Social Psychology, 8*(3), 253–257.

Knörr, H., Alvarez, C., & Urbano, D. (2013). Entrepreneurs or employees: A cross-cultural cognitive analysis. *International Entrepreneurship and Management Journal, 9*(2), 273–294.

Kozan, M. K., Oksoy, D., & Ozsoy, O. (2012). Owner sacrifice and small business growth. *Journal of World Business, 47*(3), 409–419.

Kogan, N., & Wallach, M. A. (1964). *Risk taking: A study in cognition and personality.* New York, NY: Holt, Rinehart & Winston.

Kunisch, S., Bartunek, J. M., Mueller, J., & Huy, Q. N. (2017). Time in strategic change research. *Academy of Management Annals, 11*(2), 1005–1064.

Larson, A. (1991). Partner networks: Leveraging external ties to improve entrepreneurial performance. *Journal of Business Venturing, 6*(3), 173–188.

Larson, A. (1992). Network dyads in entrepreneurial settings: A study of the governance of exchange relationships. *Administrative Science Quarterly, 37*(1), 76–104.

Larson, A., & Starr, J. A. (1993). A network model of organization formation. *Entrepreneurship Theory and Practice, 17*(2), 5–15.

Leibenstein, H. (1968). Entrepreneurship and development. *American Economic Review, 58*(2), 72–83.

Lerner, M., Zahra, S. A., & Kohavi, Y. G. (2007). Time and corporate entrepreneurship. *Advances in Entrepreneurship, Firm Emergence and Growth, 10,* 187–221.

Lessner, M., & Knapp, R. R. (1974). Self-actualization and entrepreneurial orientation among small business owners: A validation study of the POI. *Educational and Psychological Measurement, 34*(2), 455–460.

Leutner, F., Ahmetoglu, G., Akhtar, R., & Chamorro-Premuzic, T. (2014). The relationship between the entrepreneurial personality and the Big Five personality traits. *Personality and Individual Differences, 63,* 58–63.

Libby, R., & Fishburn, P. C. (1977). Behavioral models of risk taking in business decisions: A survey and evaluation. *Journal of Accounting Research, 15*(2), 272–292.

Liles, P. R. (1974). *New business ventures and the entrepreneur.* Homewood, IL: Irwin.

Litzinger, W. D. (1965). The motel entrepreneur and the motel manager. *Academy of Management Journal, 8,* 268–281.

Lopes, L. L. (1987). Between hope and fear: The psychology of risk. *Advances in Experimental Social Psychology, 20,* 255–295.

Lopes, L. L. (1996). When time is of the essence: Averaging, aspiration, and the short run. *Organizational Behavior and Human Decision Processes, 65*(3), 179–189.

Low, M. B., & MacMillan, I. C. (1988). Entrepreneurship: Past research and future challenges. *Journal of Management, 14*(2), 139–161.

Lumpkin, G. T., & Brigham, K. H. (2011). Long-term orientation and intertemporal choice in family firms. *Entrepreneurship Theory and Practice, 35*(6), 1149–1169.

MacCrimmon, K. R., & Wehrung, D. A. (1986). *Taking risks: The management of uncertainty.* New York, NY: Free Press.

Manimala, M. J. (1992). Entrepreneurial heuristics: A comparison between high PI (pioneering-innovative) and low PI ventures. *Journal of Business Venturing, 7*(6), 477–504.

March, J. G., & Shapira, Z. (1987). Managerial perspectives on risk and risk taking. *Management Science, 33*(11), 1404–1418.

March, J. G., & Shapira, Z. (1992). Variable risk preferences and the focus of attention. *Psychological Review, 99*(1), 172–183.

Mayer, R. C., Davis, J. H., & Schoorman, F. D. (1995). An integrative model of organizational trust. *Academy of Management Review, 20*(3), 709–734.

McClelland, D. C. (1961). *The achieving society*. Princeton, NJ: Van Nostrand.

McClelland, D. C. (1965). Need achievement and entrepreneurship: A longitudinal study. *Journal of Personality and Social Psychology, 1*, 389–392.

Milburn, M. A. (1978). Sources of bias in the prediction of future events. *Organizational Behavior and Human Performance, 21*, 17–26.

Miller, K. D. (2007). Risk and rationality in entrepreneurial processes. *Strategic Entrepreneurship Journal, 1*(1–2), 57–74.

Mowen, J. C., & Mowen, M. M. (1991). Time and outcome valuation: Implications for marketing decision making. *Journal of Marketing, 55*(4), 54–62.

Mueller, S. L., & Thomas, A. S. (2000). Culture and entrepreneurial potential: A nine country study of locus of control and innovativeness. *Journal of Business Venturing, 16*(1), 51–75.

Nisan, M., & Minkowich, A. (1973). The effect of expected temporal distance on risk taking. *Journal of Personality and Social Psychology, 25*(3), 375–380.

Opper, S., Nee, V., & Holm, H. J. (2017). Risk aversion and *guanxi* activities: A behavioral analysis of CEOs in China. *Academy of Management Journal, 60*(4), 1504–1530.

Palich, L. E., & Bagby, D. R. (1995). Using cognitive theory to explain entrepreneurial risk-taking: Challenging conventional wisdom. *Journal of Business Venturing, 10*(6), 425–438.

Palmer, M. (1971). The application of psychological testing to entrepreneurial potential. *California Management Review, 13*(3), 32–39.

Peacock, P. (1986). The influence of risk-taking as a cognitive judgmental behavior of small business success. In R. Ronstadt, J. A. Hornaday, R. Peterson, & K. H. Vesper (Eds.), *Frontiers of Entrepreneurship Research 1986: The proceedings of the Babson Conference on entrepreneurship research* (pp. 110–118). Wellesley, MA: Babson College.

Peterson, R., & Smith, N. R. (1986). Entrepreneurship: A culturally appropriate combination of craft and opportunity. In R. Ronstadt, J. A. Hornaday, R. Peterson, & K. H. Vesper (Eds.), *Frontiers of Entrepreneurship Research 1986: The proceedings of the Babson Conference on entrepreneurship research* (pp. 1–11). Wellesley, MA: Babson College.

Petrakis, P. E. (2007). The effects of risk and time on entrepreneurship. *International Entrepreneurship and Management Journal, 3*, 277–291.

Schneider, S. L., & Lopes, L. L. (1986). Reflection in preferences under risk: Who and when may suggest why. *Journal of Experimental Psychology: Human Perception and Performance, 12*(4), 535–548.

Schumpeter, J. A. (1934). *Theory of economic development*. Cambridge, MA: Harvard University Press.

Sexton, D. L., & Bowman, N. B. (1983). Comparative entrepreneurship characteristics of students: Preliminary results. In J. A. Hornaday, J. A. Timmons, & K. H. Vesper (Eds.), *Frontiers of Entrepreneurship Research 1983* (pp. 213–232). Wellesley, MA: Babson College.

Sexton, D. L., & Bowman, N. B. (1985). The entrepreneur: A capable executive and more. *Journal of Business Venturing, 1*(1), 129–140.

Sexton, D. L., & Bowman, N. B. (1986). Validation of a personality index: Comparative psychological characteristics analysis of female entrepreneurs, managers, entrepreneurship students and business students. In R. Ronstadt, J. A. Hornaday, R. Peterson, & K. H. Vesper (Eds.), *Frontiers of Entrepreneurship Research 1986: The proceedings of the Babson Conference on entrepreneurship research* (pp. 40–51). Wellesley, MA: Babson College.

Shan, W., Walker, G., & Kogut, B. (1994). Interfirm cooperation and startup innovation in the biotechnology industry. *Strategic Management Journal, 15*(5), 387–394.

Shapira, Z. (1995). *Risk taking: A managerial perspective.* New York, NY: Russell Sage Foundation.

Shaver, K. G., & Scott, L. R. (1991). Person, process, and choice: The psychology of new venture creation. *Entrepreneurship Theory and Practice, 16*(2), 23–45.

Shelley, M. K. (1994). Gain/loss asymmetry in risky intertemporal choice. *Organizational Behavior and Human Decision Processes, 59*(1), 124–159.

Slotte-Kock, S., & Coviello, N. (2010). Entrepreneurship research on network processes: A review and ways forward. *Entrepreneurship Theory and Practice, 34*(1), 31–57.

Smith, N. R. (1967). *The entrepreneur and his firm: The relationship between type of man and type of company.* East Lansing, MI: Michigan State University.

Smith, N. R., & Miner, J. B. (1983). Type of entrepreneur, type of firm, and managerial motivation: Implications for organizational life cycle theory. *Strategic Management Journal, 4,* 325–340.

Stevenson, H. H., & Jarillo, J. C. (1990). A paradigm of entrepreneurship: Entrepreneurial management. *Strategic Management Journal, 11*(5), 17–27.

Stewart, W. H., Jr., & Roth, P. L. (2001). Risk propensity differences between entrepreneurs and managers: A meta-analytic review. *Journal of Applied Psychology, 86*(1), 145–153.

Stopford, J. M., & Baden-Fuller, C. W. F. (1994). Creating corporate entrepreneurship. *Strategic Management Journal, 15*(7), 521–536.

Strickland, L., Lewicki, R. J., & Katz, A. M. (1966). Temporal orientation and perceived control as determinants of risk taking. *Journal of Experimental Social Psychology, 2,* 143–151.

Thoms, P., & Greenberger, D. B. (1995). The relationship between leadership and time orientation. *Journal of Management Inquiry, 4*(3), 272–292.

Tipu, S. A. A. (2017). Entrepreneurial risk taking: Themes from the literature and pointers for future research. *International Journal of Organizational Analysis, 25*(3), 432–455.

Tumasjan, A., Welpe, I., & Spörrie, M. (2013). Easy now, desirable later: The moderating role of temporal distance in opportunity evaluation and exploitation. *Entrepreneurship Theory and Practice, 37*(4), 859–888.

Vlek, C., & Stallen, P. J. (1980). Rational and personal aspects of risk. *Acta Psychologica, 45,* 273–300.

Wales, W. J. (2016). Entrepreneurial orientation: A review and synthesis of promising research directions. *International Small Business Journal, 34*(10), 3–15.

Webster, F. A. (1977). Entrepreneurs and ventures: An attempt at classification and clarification. *Academy of Management Review, 2*(1), 54–61.

Webster's Third New International Dictionary. (1961). Chicago, IL: Merriam Co.

Welter, F. (2011) Contextualizing entrepreneurship: Conceptual challenges and ways forward. *Entrepreneurship Theory and Practice, 35*(1), 165–184.

Wiklund, J., Nikolaev, B., Shir, N., Foo, M.-D., & Bradley, S. (2019). Entrepreneurship and well-being: Past, present, and future. *Journal of Business Venturing, 34*(4), 579–588.

Woo, C. Y., Cooper, A. C., & Dunkelberg, W. C. (1991). The development and interpretation of entrepreneurial typologies. *Journal of Business Venturing, 6*(2), 93–114.

Wood, M. S., & Rowe, J. D. (2011). Nowhere to run and nowhere to hide: The relationship between entrepreneurial success and feelings of entrapment. *Entrepreneurship Research Journal, 1*(4), 1–41.

Yates, J. F., & Stone, E. R. (1992). The risk construct. In J. F. Yates (Ed.), *Risk-taking behavior* (pp. 1–25). Chichester, England: Wiley.

Zahra, S. A., Wright, M., & Abdelgawad, S. G. (2014). Contextualization and the advancement of entrepreneurship research. *International Small Business Journal, 32*(5), 479–500.

CHAPTER 4

ENTREPRENEURS UNDER AMBIGUITY

A Prospect Theory Perspective

Corina Paraschiv
Anisa Shyti

ABSTRACT

This chapter focuses on entrepreneurial decision making under ambiguity. Our main contribution is to insist on the importance of ambiguity in entrepreneurship, as many entrepreneurial decisions are highly strategic, unique, and mostly taken in situations with limited and imprecise information. Uncertainty, quintessential in entrepreneurship, has inspired early theoretical works and psychological analysis of decision making in the entrepreneurship literature. Past contributions have mainly focused on risk and risk preferences as determinants of entry to entrepreneurship, but the message of this literature is hardly conclusive. In this chapter, we provide a state of the art overview on a recently emerging literature on ambiguity attitudes and entrepreneurship research. Many of such recent works are based on expected utility theory and thus carry the same limitations of this theory. Our chapter emphasizes the advantage of experimental economics and the potential of prospect theory applications. We focus specifically on the weighting function

Entrepreneurship and Behavioral Strategy, pages 89–111

aspect, and theorize on how it can contribute to further our understanding of entrepreneurial behavior. Prospect theory represents a sophisticated tool that may disentangle subtle behavioral differences between entrepreneurial profiles and other decision makers.

INTRODUCTION

Entrepreneurial decisions, being at the forefront of innovation and economic development, involved with the creation or discovery processes of lucrative opportunities, are continuously subject to ambiguity (Knight, 1921; Shane & Venkataraman, 2000). Success stories in entrepreneurship are associated with many funding anecdotes. For example, in 1999, graduate students Brin and Page, founders of Google.com, offered to sell for $1 million the search engine they had developed to George Bell, CEO of Excite, who then rejected the offer. Within that year, Google.com obtained $25 million of funding, and today the company is worth $416.8 billion of market capitalization.

Embracing the unknown is intrinsic in entrepreneurship (Hayek, 1948), although not all undertakings are similar in their potential achievements and riskiness. Many entrepreneurs perish after ill-conceived market strategies, persistently trying alternative ventures, and mostly accepting losses and significant trade-offs in terms of income (Hamilton, 2000). Moreover, numerous startups flourish in Western economies, but many fail soon after inception: 50% fail within 2 years and 67% within 4 years (Geroski, 1995), a phenomenon known as "excess entry." Although the existing entrepreneurship research has advanced several explanations, as over-optimism or escalation of commitment, these observations are still considered open questions and there is no unifying theory for the entrepreneurial choice (Astebro, Herz, Nanda, & Weber, 2014). Such empirically documented observations also contradict most economic models based on expected utility theory, as these entrepreneurial choices do not appear to be wealth maximizing. Moreover, under conditions of uncertainty and ambiguity, with no probabilities available, the classical economic model is silent on behavioral predictions, let alone interpretations of observed behavior. Research in entrepreneurship, typically multidisciplinary, has developed into a stream of studies following a psychological tradition, pointing to specific traits and possible judgment biases that may influence entrepreneurial decision making. Thus far, decades of studies have investigated the degree of optimism of entrepreneurs, overconfidence, risk preferences, ambiguity perceptions, and so forth. However, these past efforts have failed to produce strong evidence of a typical "entrepreneurial profile," and whether entrepreneurs are more risk tolerant, as posited in most occupational choice theories, is yet unsettled. Additional contributions that have measured ambiguity tolerance of entrepreneurs and other decision makers, relying on psychometric scales (Dollinger, 1983; Schere, 1982) have also provided inconsistent or opposing results.

Although uncertainty is quintessential in entrepreneurship and entrepreneurial decision making, the ambiguity that characterizes most strategic and unique decisions is often neglected in management and entrepreneurial studies. With the development of theories that allow investigating ambiguity quantitatively, there is a renewed interest in addressing ambiguity attitudes in entrepreneurship research. Ambiguity refers to situations where probabilistic information is imprecise and cannot be inferred from existing statistical data (Knight, 1921). Situations of ambiguity in the business domain could refer to strategic decisions, to creation of new ventures, to choices of career paths, to resource allocation processes or other financial commitments. In situations of ambiguity estimating probabilities of success is challenging, as these decisions are often unique with no available history, are strongly dependent on contingencies and offer little opportunities for learning.

In decision contexts under ambiguity, Ellsberg (1961) in his seminal contribution predicts *ambiguity aversion*, which describes individuals' choice to refrain from options with unknown probabilities, and prefer risky options instead, with known probabilities. In fact, ambiguity in life or business generates a sort of "discomfort" that may hinder action. When considering economic decisions with no clear course of action to be taken, people may mull over expectations of possible scenarios, postpone decisions, or delay choices, in order to collect more relevant information, which may not always be available.

As an example, one could consider a developer evaluating two alternative platforms for launching his new application. Both platforms yield the same outcome in terms of profit in case of success. However, for the first platform, the developer knows that for every hundred new applications proposed, 50 succeed and 50 fail. The rates of success for the other platform are unknown. What is a sensible decision in this case? What would determine the developer's choice? Or, would he simply decide on the basis of perceptions about his own abilities to develop a successful application? The developer may be enticed to invest time and other resources in finalizing his application anyway, and decide at a later stage on the platform. He would thus be vulnerable to the ambiguity of such a decision. Maybe he overestimates the unlikely event of success, given the considerable number of other developers in his domain; or maybe he underestimates the highly likely event of failure, like many other developers did before him. How can we account for such behavioral patterns?

Advances in prospect theory have made it possible to better understand behavior under both risk and ambiguity. Very recently, emerging experimental designs in entrepreneurship are employing prospect theory to explain observed entrepreneurial behavior (Hsu, Wiklund, & Cotton, 2017; Shyti & Paraschiv, 2015). In this chapter, we offer a state of the art perspective of ambiguity theories and recent developments of experimental economics in the context of entrepreneurship. We draw insights on how we can better understand micro foundations of entrepreneurship based on behavioral theories of choice, as prospect theory.

The rest of the chapter is organized as follows. First, the chapter offers a brief review of the literature on uncertainty and ambiguity. Second, it focuses on the weighting function aspect of prospect theory. It continues by summarizing the existent literature on entrepreneurial decision making under risk and ambiguity. The chapter concludes by emphasizing the potential contributions of prospect theory and experimental economics in future developments in entrepreneurship research.

DECONSTRUCTING UNCERTAINTY: A DECISION MAKING PERSPECTIVE

The importance of uncertainty in economic activity was understood since Cantillon in 1755, when he first pointed out that the entrepreneur sustains certain costs of production while facing uncertain profits that manifest over time. Other scholars recognize that entrepreneurs are rewarded for bearing uncertainty rather than risk, which is in turn insurable (Knight, 1921; Say, 1836). In the same vein, subsequent formal theories posit that the more risk tolerant individuals self-select in entrepreneurship and hire the risk averse individuals as employees (Kihlstrom & Laffont, 1979).

However, tackling empirically uncertainty bumps into obvious operationalization difficulties. Knight (1921) offered a clear distinction between risk and uncertainty. He defined risk as a situation in which possible events (and associated consequences) are known and there is a probability distribution over the possible events. Knight (1921) defined uncertainty as a situation in which possible events are known, but there is no probability distribution available to the decision maker. This is also known as *Knightian Uncertainty*, different from Radical Uncertainty of Keynes (1921) and Shackle (1968; see Figure 4.1). Following Ellsberg (1961) the definition of ambiguity focuses on the absence of probabilities, thus locating ambiguity as an in-between situation of two extremes: the *risky* option with known probabilities on one pole, and *uncertainty*, the option with no available probabilities on the other.

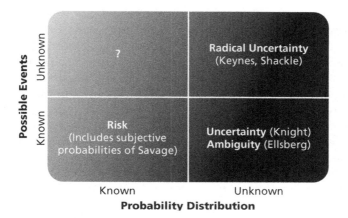

Figure 4.1 Types of uncertainty.

Situations of risk are characterized by known probabilities, and are mostly encountered in games of chance, in lotteries, or in psychological experiments. In real-life circumstances precise probabilities are rarely available. Surprisingly, past research in management has focused mainly on risk and risk perceptions of managers, investors, and other decision makers. The same trend has characterized also entrepreneurship research, in which uncertainty has been treated qualitatively (McKelvie, Haynie, & Gustavsson, 2011; McMullen & Shepherd, 2006), and often as a synonym of risk (Alvarez & Barney, 2005; Shane, 2000).

Ellsberg's Paradox

Savage (1954) is among the most prominent works in decision theory that formally represented uncertainty in individual decision making. In subjective expected utility theory, Savage (1954) introduces the notion of *subjective probability distribution* of decision makers. More precisely, uncertainty is seen as subjective and the absence of objective probabilities is considered not to affect decision making. In fact, in absence of objective probabilities, decision makers assign their subjective probabilities to any world event, and are able to evaluate economic options through the classical expected utility theory.

Ellsberg (1961) was the first to formally show that for a decision maker a risky option is not the same as an ambiguous option, which is characterized by the absence of probabilistic information. In Ellsberg's work proved that ambiguity affects decision making, as decision makers are not indifferent to it. Ellsberg (1961) shows that decision makers systematically avoid ambiguous options, and prefer risky options instead. This choice pattern causes decisions to deviate from expected utility theory predictions. Ellsberg called this phenomenon *ambiguity aversion*, which is also known as Ellsberg's Paradox.

In Ellsberg's famous two-color example, a decision maker faces two urns, each containing 100 balls. The known urn contains 50 red balls and 50 black balls. The unknown urn contains 100 balls, either red or black, but in unknown proportion. The decision maker is asked to choose one urn (known or unknown) and one color (red or black). Once he makes his choice, a ball is drawn randomly from the selected urn. If the ball is the color chosen by the decision maker, he wins a prize; otherwise, he gets nothing. The decision maker is indifferent regarding the betting color (red or black) within each urn. However, the decision maker is not indifferent between the two urns. The phenomenon that Ellsberg (1961) describes is that the decision maker, unable to assign objective probabilities to either red or black in the unknown urn, refrains from that option altogether, exhibiting *ambiguity aversion.*

Following Ellsberg's (1961) lead, two parallel streams of research developed in decision science. The first stream of research, with an axiomatic orientation, mostly produced works that model ambiguity aversion (Gilboa & Schmeidler, 1989; Schmeidler, 1989). In almost all these decision models ambiguity aversion was assumed to be an invariant feature of the decision maker's preferences. The second stream of research, with a descriptive aim, derived most of its results from experimental studies, with the objective to understand decision making under ambiguity. Experimental investigations have confirmed ambiguity aversion, but have also shown that individuals not always avoid options with unknown probabilities as in Curley and Yates (1985), Einhorn and Hogarth (1985), Fox and Tversky (1995), and Wu and Gonzalez (1999), to mention some. Studies that have addressed decision under ambiguity from a descriptive perspective include Budescu, Khun, Kramer, and Johnson (2002), Curley and Yates (1989), González-Vallejo, Bonazzi, and Shapiro (1996), and Kuhn and Budescu (1996). Other approaches have tested the impact of ambiguity on different models of behavior, most prominent works based on prospect theory including Fox and Tversky (1998), Gonzalez and Wu (1999), Hogarth and Einhorn (1990), Kilka and Weber (2001), Tversky and Fox (1995), Tversky and Wakker (1995), Wakker (2004), and Wakker (2010). Yet, another set of studies, including Cohen, Jaffray, and Said (1987), Curley and Yates (1985), and Heath and Tversky (1991), have investigated the consequences of ambiguity on choice behavior.

Operationalizing Ambiguity

Previous studies, mostly belonging to the psychological stream of research, have treated the concept of ambiguity with probability intervals

(Budescu et al., 2002; Curley & Yates, 1985; González-Vallejo et al., 1996; Smithson, 1999), a business compatible way to address ambiguity. Let's reflect on the example of the developer who considers launching the application on a commercial platform. The entrepreneur is contemplating whether he could reach one million downloads in the first semester. Imagine he seeks the opinion of a tech expert and receives an estimate of 15% rate of success. However, for the same one million downloads in the first semester, the platform owner provides an estimate of 45% rates of success. Thus, the developer is facing an interval (15%, 45%) within which may lie the rate of success of achieving one million downloads in the first semester. These estimates naturally generate a probability interval.

Another example of ambiguity represented by intervals comes from Amazon.com report in the Second Quarter 2014 Guidance stating the following:

> Net sales are expected to be between 18.1 billion and 19.8 billion, or to grow between 15% and 26% compared with second quarter 2013 and operating income (loss) is expected to be between \$(455) million and \$(55) million, compared to \$79 million in second quarter 2013.

In this example ambiguity refers to outcomes (e.g., operating income, percentage of growth, etc.), instead of probabilities. Thus, such representations of ambiguity as intervals of information may apply to other business contexts, in which experts and consultants provide their best estimates about success rates of a project, the probability of occurrence of an event, the probability of an event occurring within a time horizon, the earnings forecast of a company, and so forth.

A natural propensity of decision makers in business is to reduce uncertainty by gathering more information or seeking a third party opinion. Restricting the boundaries or noisy information allows for the application of more precise decision rules. In conditions of uncertainty, there is naturally a greater need to apply heuristics, for lack of better rules, but uncertainty also increases the potential of decision biases and errors (Kahneman, Slovic, & Tversky, 1982; Kahneman & Tversky, 1973). It emerges from dialogues with business practitioners that when they have the option to demand more information, they rarely ask probabilistic information, for instance, the probability to achieve a certain rate of return, or the probability to accomplish a project on time (Kahneman, 2011). However, this does not mean that business practitioners ignore the uncertainty of their environments and its impact on decision making.

PROSPECT THEORY FOR RISK AND AMBIGUITY

One of the most prominent modern decision theories developed to analyze uncertainty quantitatively is prospect theory (Kahneman & Tversky, 1979; Tversky & Kahneman, 1992; Wakker, 2010). This theory is the result of the devotion and work of Amos Tversky and Daniel Kahneman, the latter famous for earning the Nobel Prize in economics in 2002 and being regarded as the father of *behavioral economics*. Prospect theory was proposed as a reaction to the failure of expected utility theory to adequately explain behavior under risk. Therefore, it accounts for a large series of biases in individual decision making.

The Weighting Function

An important idea in prospect theory is the distortion of probabilities in the decision making process through a probability weighting function, $w(.)$. Consider a decision maker evaluating a risky prospect that yields an outcome X with probability p and nothing otherwise. The value of such prospect under prospect theory will depend on the importance of outcome X for the decision maker and also on his subjective perception of the probability p. Prospect theory models the fact that individuals do not behave according to the objective or given probability p, but interpret subjectively this probability by attributing more or less weight to it, through a decision weight, $w(p)$. In general, prospect theory is concerned with prospects, which evaluation is considered independent of decisions maker's total wealth. Formally, the value a decision maker attributes to the risky prospect depends on his utility function, $U(.)$, and on the probability weighting function for risk, $wr(.)$, and equals $U(X) * w_r(p)$. Under prospect theory, risk attitudes of decision makers are partially reflected in the shape of the utility function $U(.)$, and partially reflected in the shape of the weighting function for risk $w_r(.)$.

Ambiguous prospects are evaluated under prospect theory in a very similar way, meaning through a decision maker's utility function and a weighting function. When dealing with ambiguous prospects, a common approach in experimental research has consisted in assuming a different weighting function for ambiguity, $w_a(.)$. Ambiguity attitudes of decision makers reflect the differences in behavior under risk and under ambiguity. Assuming that the utility function is the same under both risk and ambiguity, ambiguity attitudes of decision makers are thus captured by the differences between weighting functions for risk, $w_r(.)$, and ambiguity, $w_a(.)$.

Experimental Evidence on Weighting Functions for Risk

Typical empirical evidence shows that decision makers exhibit risk seeking for gains with low probabilities and risk aversion for gains with high probabilities. The general interpretation of these findings in terms of the nonlinear treatment of probabilities assumed by prospect theory is that individuals overestimate small probabilities and underestimate large probabilities. Graphically the shape of $w(.)$ can be represented through an inverted S-shape probability weighting function as shown in Figure 4.2E. The idea behind the inverted S-shape probability weighting function is that the decision maker is willing to pay more to pass from an impossible event (0%) to a possible one (10%; the concave part near 0 in Figure 4.2E); as well, the decision maker is willing to pay considerable amounts to shift from a highly likely event (90%) to a sure one (100%; the convex part near 1 in Figure 4.2E). However, the decision maker's willingness to pay to improve the probability of an event from 40% to 50% is much lower.

The probability weighting function captures two distinct psychological phenomena in decision making: insensitivity and pessimism. Likelihood *insensitivity* refers to the flattened perception for changes in intermediate

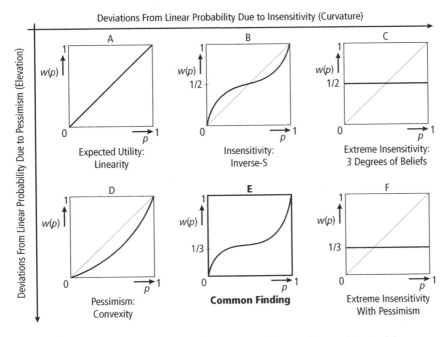

Figure 4.2 Weighting functions under prospect theory. *Source:* Adapted from Wakker (2010).

probabilities, which are perceived close to the 50% probability. This phenomenon reflects the decision makers' inability to sufficiently discriminate between probability levels. Kahneman and Tversky (1979) attribute this phenomenon to cognitive psychological causes, and assume that these distortions take place during an "editing" phase, before the decision maker attaches any value to the prospects under consideration. According to Wakker (2010), likelihood insensitivity is irrational and can be corrected through incentives and learning. *Pessimism* refers to the tendency to underestimate the chances of success and is reflected graphically by the distance of the curve from the x-axis. For gains or positive outcomes, a weighting function closer to the x-axis is associated with more pessimism, corresponding to an underweighting of probabilities. On the contrary, a weighting function further from the x-axis is associated with optimism and corresponds to inflation or overweighting of probabilities.

Empirical studies on prospect theory generally rely on functional forms to provide an overall picture on the decision maker's risk attitude. The literature offers a variety of functional forms for the weighting function (Abdellaoui, l'Haridon, & Zank, 2010; Goldstein & Einhorn, 1987; Kahneman & Tversky, 1979; Prelec, 1998), that provide the advantage of summarizing information on the decision maker's probability weighting through aggregated indexes. When information is summarized using one single index, it is difficult to establish a direct relation between the index itself and a clear psychological phenomenon. Therefore, recent literature recommends functional forms based on two indexes, related to *elevation* and *curvature* (Abdellaoui, Baillon, Placido, & Wakker, 2011). Such forms have the advantage to disentangle the two psychological phenomena discussed before: the pessimism/optimism of the decision maker captured by an elevation parameter and the sensitivity to changes in probabilities captured by a curvature parameter. One of the most commonly used functional form is Prelec's (1998) two-parameter specification, given in the equation below:

$$w(p) = \left(\exp\left(-(-\ln(p))\right)^a \right)^b \tag{2.1}$$

where a is an insensitivity index (curvature) and b is a pessimism index (elevation). When both indexes are 1, the weighting function does not present any distortion and corresponds to the 45° line. Parameter a values reflect insensitivity to changes in likelihood, with lower values corresponding to more insensitivity. Parameter b values reflect pessimism, with higher (lower) b values corresponding to higher degrees of pessimism (optimism).

While the inverse S-shaped form in Figure 4.2E with pessimism and insensitivity is the most common finding in experimental research, experiments also report substantial variation of individual behavior. Figure 4.2 depicts several possible patterns of behavior. Figure 4.2A corresponds to the expected utility model with a decision maker treating probabilities linearly, with no pessimism and no insensitivity. The other figures correspond to different combinations of insensitivity and/or pessimism: Figure 4.2B reflects pessimism; Figure 4.2C reflects extreme insensitivity, corresponding to a decision maker who has the same behavior regardless of the probabilities involved; and Figure 4.2F reflects extreme insensitivity with pessimism.

Experimental Evidence on Weighting Functions for Ambiguity

Although in the last decades the topic of decision making under ambiguity has received a lot of attention in decision theory, empirical evidence is still limited. Abdellaoui et al. (2011) is one of the first studies that tests experimentally prospect theory under ambiguity. The authors show that the inverted S-shape of the weighting function is preserved under ambiguity, but distortions are even more pronounced for extreme likelihoods. The study reports ambiguity aversion for mid-range and high likelihoods. Figure 4.3 represents the weighting function for risk, $wr(.)$, clearly different from the 45° line, as well as the weighting function for ambiguity, $wa(.)$. The line of ambiguity shows that low likelihoods are even more overweighted compared to the case of risk, and larger likelihoods are even more underweighted. Abdellaoui et al. (2011) also report that ambiguity attitudes

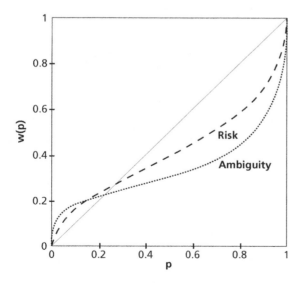

Figure 4.3 Weighting functions for risk and ambiguity. *Source:* Adapted from Abdellaoui et al. (2011).

differ according to decision contexts, for typical lottery experiments and natural sources of uncertainty (e.g., investing in the French stock market).

Taken together, these findings show that the idea of a weighting function is powerful and some key lessons emerge from the decision making literature that need to be considered in entrepreneurship research. First, a decision maker's risk and ambiguity attitudes are distinct (for a comprehensive literature review, see Camerer & Weber, 1992) and should not be treated as surrogates of each other. As individual attitudes toward risk are conceptually distinct from attitudes toward ambiguity, it's important for future research in entrepreneurship to analyze these attitudes in complement to one another. Second, risk and ambiguity attitudes are not consistent with expected utility maximization. Because the utility-maximizing argument of expected utility theory is questionable when introducing ambiguity, the experimental designs used to study ambiguity attitudes of entrepreneurs need to address the issue of probability weighting. Third, emerging evidence shows that risk and ambiguity attitudes are not invariant traits of behavior, but depend on the decision context. Experimental studies, while a valuable tool to understand ambiguity attitudes of entrepreneurs, should investigate behavior using frameworks directly related to entrepreneurial decisions. Finally, in order to assess a decision maker's behavioral responses to risk and ambiguity it is not sufficient to use only one probability point, but several questions scanning the entire probability range. This will allow to account for entrepreneurs' behavior not only for intermediate probabilities, but also for low probabilities and high probabilities.

ENTREPRENEURIAL DECISION MAKING UNDER RISK AND AMBIGUITY

The premises of decision making under ambiguity set the ground for further exploitations of prospect theory in entrepreneurship and managerial studies aimed at uncovering micro foundations of behavior in business environments.

Entrepreneurs Under Risk

An overwhelming body of literature in entrepreneurship research has considered individual risk preferences as an important determinant of entry to entrepreneurship and has employed a variety of approaches to empirically measure risk aversion. Occupational choice theories have supported the *risk tolerance* assumption of entrepreneurs (Douglas & Shepherd, 2000; Kanbur, 1979; Kihlstrom & Laffont, 1979). However, Brockhaus's (1980) efforts to measure individual risk propensities using psychometric scales in univariate investigations reported no differences between entrepreneurs and non-entrepreneurs, a result later supported by Gartner (1988). The hypothesis of *risk tolerant* entrepreneurs found some empirical validation in longitudinal surveys (Caliendo, Fossen, & Kriticos, 2009; Cramer, Hartog, Jonker, & Van Praag, 2002), which showed that the willingness to take risks increases the probability that an individual enters entrepreneurship in the future.

Risk attitudes as an entrepreneurial trait were also investigated through economic experiments with binary lotteries. Works of Elston and Audretsch (2011) and Elston, Harrison, and Rutstrom (2005) have reported that entrepreneurs are either risk neutral or slightly risk averse, but again, no specific differences were detected between entrepreneurs and other decision makers.

Clearly, such multitude of methods and variety of results do not enable to draw definitive conclusions. Typical critiques on the psychometric scales used to measure risk propensities emphasize that risk aversion or risk seeking could be conflated with over-optimism and other individual traits might influence respondents' answer patterns. Referring to the survey method, Caliendo et al. (2009) point to the difficulties and challenges of measuring risk aversion in the field. The longitudinal approach was further criticized as risk attitudes may not be stable over time. Also the experimental economics approach to investigating differences in risk attitudes of entrepreneurs and non-entrepreneurs (Elston & Audretsch, 2011; Elston et al., 2005) is not free of limitations. This approach was mostly criticized for using abstract lotteries with small-stakes, that focus on one probability point and assume expected utility theory.

Such multi-disciplinary evidence in entrepreneurship research does not allow to make clear associations of specific risk attitudes with entrepreneurial profiles (Parker, 2009). Moreover, these considerations call for more attention on the fundamental point raised by Dohmen et al. (2011) on the stability or risk attitudes across contexts and over time.

Entrepreneurs Under Ambiguity

The general inconclusiveness of risk attitudes to define entrepreneurial profiles has not discouraged research efforts to also investigate entrepreneurs' attitudes toward ambiguity.

Entrepreneurs start a new venture with a vague knowledge of their likelihood of success. In many occasions, entrepreneurs lack experience and face conflicting or insufficient statistical evidence, conditions that make it difficult to define precise predictions about the success of their business. Challenges related to estimations of likelihood of success for a new venture are also related to the aggregation that the notion of *success* incorporates.

Success can be related to surviving on a 10-year horizon, to obtaining initial funding, to achieving a 20% market share within a given time span. Most entrepreneurs believe that their fundraising campaigns will succeed and the venture capitalist decisions will be favorable for their startup. Thus, addressing how entrepreneurs perceive their chances of success in the field is challenging, as investors' feedback, market's response, or customers' appreciation may manifest in some future undefined time horizon. The initial investigations of the topic of ambiguity appeared in the 1980s, with a predominantly psychological approach. Recently, a few experimental economics contributions focus on specific aspects of entrepreneurial decision making under ambiguity. Yet, how ambiguity influences entrepreneurs' decisions is still an under-investigated topic in entrepreneurship research, despite its essential role in understanding entrepreneurial behavior.

Psychological Experiments in Entrepreneurship

Ambiguity is not new in psychological research. During the late 1940s, Frenkel-Brunswik (1949) was the first to conceive and develop a psychometric scale aimed at assessing individual perceptions to ambiguity that she named *intolerance to ambiguity*. Budner (1962) modified the original *intolerance to ambiguity* scale and its interpretation, defining an ambiguous situation as one "which cannot be adequately structured or categorized by the individual because of the lack of sufficient cues or situations characterized by novelty, complexity, or insolubility" (p. 30), with "threatening" or "avoidance" reactions to ambiguity manifesting through cognitive, emotional, and behavioral aspects. Also Mac Donald (1970) further revisited the *intolerance to ambiguity* psychometric scale switching to *ambiguity tolerance*, to convey a framing in which ambiguity was desirable.

Schere (1982), adopting a trait-approach to entrepreneurship research, investigated ambiguity perception of entrepreneurs and managers relying on applications of the ambiguity intolerance scale. Schere (1982) reported entrepreneurs to exhibit higher ambiguity tolerance compared to managers, results that confirmed his hypothesis of entrepreneurs facing highly uncertain situations, characterized as turbulent, chaotic, complex or conflicting.

Later on, Dollinger (1983) failed to replicate the same findings, and attributed such inconsistency to poor sampling. However, more recent contributions (Tajeddini & Mueller, 2009; Teoh & Foo, 1997) examine a variety of entrepreneurial personal characteristics, including the *intolerance to ambiguity* scale, with mainly inconclusive results. Generally, such psychometric scales have been subject of criticism for being unreliable, for providing piecemeal results on the psychology of ambiguity perceptions, weak links to decision making, and for lacking strong contributions to theory (McLain, 2009).

Economic Experiments in Entrepreneurship

Only very recently, a few empirical papers have addressed ambiguity attitudes of entrepreneurs, tapping in from the vast experimental literature in decision making. Hardenbol (2012) interviewed entrepreneurs, managers, and students, and reported no difference among their choice behavior. Hardenbol (2012) estimates ambiguity and risk attitudes using binary choices between lottery options, with gains up to $40. Bengtsson, Sanandaji, and Johannesson (2012) investigate ambiguity and risk for entrepreneurs and non-entrepreneurs based on a survey with 11,743 individuals from the Swedish Twin Registry. Risk attitudes are inferred through individuals' choices between a fixed and a variable salary with probability 50%. Ambiguity attitudes are determined through a single question, based on three-color Ellsberg's example (Ellsberg, 1961), in which respondents have to choose between a risky lottery and an ambiguous lottery. Bengtsson et al. (2012) findings are consistent with less risk and ambiguity aversion for entrepreneurs compared with non-entrepreneurs. Koudstaal, Sloof, and Van Praag (2014) run a large scale lab-in-the-field experiment. They gather data from a survey with 910 entrepreneurs, 397 managers, and 981 employees in Holland. This design employs tasks with multiple choice lists for both risk and ambiguity using a 50% probability. In the case of risk, the decision maker chooses between a risky option and a certain option. In the case of ambiguity, the task involves a risky option and an ambiguous option. The results of Koudstaal et al. (2014) reveal that entrepreneurs and managers are equally ambiguity averse, and slightly more ambiguity averse compared to employees. However, they report that these differences disappear when controlling for typical demographics as age, education, and income among others.

Probably the most prominent study to date on entrepreneurial behavior under uncertainty is provided by Holm, Opper, and Nee (2013) and compares 700 entrepreneurs and 200 non-entrepreneurs based in China. These authors study risk and ambiguity attitudes using several binary choices between monetary lotteries. Their main tool to determine ambiguity attitudes is a decision task in the form of a choice list with one option offering a sure outcome, and the other option offering an outcome with ambiguous probabilities between 25% and 75%, whose natural center is 50%. In another task, they use an uncertainty option (no probability information provided) instead of the ambiguous one. They observe that compared with the control group, entrepreneurs were more willing to accept situations of uncertainty involving competition and trust. As per risk and ambiguity attitudes, general results of Holm et al. (2013) report no differences between entrepreneurs and the control group.

Entrepreneurs and Prospect Theory

The above-mentioned experimental designs (Bengtsson et al., 2012; Hardenbol, 2012; Holm et al., 2013) do not sufficiently account for the existing evidence on prospect theory. They usually employ a Holt and Laury (2002) method based on expected utility, thus providing biased estimates for risk and ambiguity attitudes. Extensive empirical evidence shows that expected utility is a fallible guide in understanding decision making, as individuals consistently violate its predictions. Also, decision tasks are often based on Ellsberg-type lottery questions with relatively low stakes (Bengtsson et al., 2012; Hardenbol, 2012). Such tools, based on lotteries, are of questionable validity when used to predict behavior for business decisions as ambiguity attitudes are not constant across domains (Abdellaoui et al., 2011; Dohmen et al., 2011). Moreover, ambiguity attitudes are usually investigated for the 50% likelihood level, thus neglecting the richness of behavior that occurs at extreme likelihoods.

To the best of our knowledge, only one recent study by Shyti and Paraschiv (2014) attempts to investigate entrepreneurial behavior under ambiguity using prospect theory. Shyti and Paraschiv (2014) show that both entrepreneurs and wage earners behave according to prospect theory (Kahneman & Tversky, 1979). This is perhaps the first study that emphasizes violations to expected utility theory predictions in entrepreneurial decisions making. The paper reports the results of an online experiment aimed at comparing attitudes towards risk and towards ambiguity in occupational choice decisions for a group of entrepreneurs and a group of non-entrepreneurs. Respondents are presented with a series of potential entrepreneurial projects, differing in the degrees of risk and ambiguity, and are asked to state their wage equivalent for each project. Based on the reported wage equivalents, the authors estimate weighting function for risk, w_r, and for ambiguity, w_a. They provide evidence of inverted S-shaped weighting functions for both entrepreneurs and non-entrepreneurs, consistent with overestimation of low likelihoods and underestimation of high likelihoods under risk and under ambiguity. The use of prospect theory to analyze occupational choice decisions allows providing a very precise picture concerning behavioral differences between entrepreneurs and non-entrepreneurs. The behavior of the two groups is different, with entrepreneurs exhibiting a higher level of optimism compared to non-entrepreneurs. Overall, entrepreneurs are more risk seeking and more ambiguity averse in evaluating entrepreneurial projects. Shyti and Paraschiv (2014) report prevailing pessimism for entrepreneurs under ambiguity, consistent with entrepreneurs being more sensitive to the precision of information about the chances of success of an entrepreneurial project.

DESCRIPTIVE IMPORTANCE OF PROSPECT THEORY

Bridging experimental work in decision theory and entrepreneurship research is a challenging and not vacuous task. Besides the importance of ambiguity and uncertainty in entrepreneurship, yet very little is known regarding entrepreneurial behavior under ambiguity. Although scholars have suggested that biases influence entrepreneurial decisions, and more so under uncertainty (Busenitz & Barney, 1997; Schade & Koellinger, 2007), the specific direction of influence and the micro mechanisms of this association (i.e., whether cognitive or motivational) remain unclear. Hence, it becomes relevant to understand entrepreneurial decision making under ambiguity, and then address the role of relevant biases coupled with entrepreneurial behavioral responses. Modern behavioral theories, specifically prospect theory, may account for some of the unresolved empirical puzzles in entrepreneurship. For instance, prospect theory could offer alternative explanations for the observed over-entry in markets. Overweighting of small probabilities may contribute to risk seeking and excess entry, which may be consistent with escalation of commitment or over-investing, and may lead to high rates of entrepreneurial failure. On the other extreme of the probability range, underweighting of high probabilities may relate to underinvesting in profitable prospects. Hence, prospect theory may account for the richness of behavior that we observe empirically in the business world. However, many challenges remain, and to examine business decisions one needs to take into consideration several likelihood levels, including the extremes (e.g., very low and very high probabilities). Additionally, such theory is versatile and enables to deal with behavioral perceptions of ambiguity, the total absence of probabilities, and different degrees of ambiguity. Moreover, the enhanced descriptive power of prospect theory may allow detecting also subtle differences in decision making of entrepreneurs and non-entrepreneurs through carefully designed experiments.

CONCLUSION

This chapter contributes to the ongoing debate on the role of uncertainty in entrepreneurial decision making by focusing on ambiguity. Our main contribution is to insist on the importance of ambiguity in entrepreneurship, as many entrepreneurial decisions are taken under conditions of imprecise information. We argue that an entrepreneur is rarely in a situation with known probabilities (risk) or in a situation in which he knows nothing at all (complete ignorance or radical uncertainty), but in an intermediate state in which he has a vague idea about the chances of success. Our second message is that, in order to adequately investigate ambiguity, entrepreneurship scholars should build on modern decision theories. A considerable body of economic research in entrepreneurship is still based on expected utility theory, which is shown to be a fallible guide in understanding behavior due to its normative nature. Prospect theory can provide a better framework to study ambiguity.

Our chapter can also be seen as a state of the art of experimental economics applications to investigations of ambiguity in entrepreneurial decision making. The scant empirical evidence that has emerged so far in the entrepreneurship field confirms the challenges and constraints in addressing ambiguity in decision making. The "late" interest towards ambiguity attitudes in entrepreneurship is partly due to the complexity of models that analyze uncertainty quantitatively and partly to the difficulties to adapt experimental designs to the context of entrepreneurial decisions. The increasing number of empirical studies during the last years attests to a vivid debate on entrepreneurship research on attitudes toward ambiguity, although the message of these emerging studies is yet scattered, and does not allow to fully grasp differences in behavior or typical patterns in entrepreneurial decision making. Nonetheless, the current approach to investigating the topic of ambiguity in entrepreneurial decision making stresses the importance of economic experiments as a promising method that could further our understanding of behavior profiles of entrepreneurs and non-entrepreneurs.

However, so far many open questions remain. What do we know about ambiguity attitudes of entrepreneurs in different business contexts? Do entrepreneurs accommodate ambiguity in their decision processes and under which conditions? Do entrepreneurs differ from non-entrepreneurs and what are the factors that explain these differences? These questions call for further investigations of ambiguity based on experimental economics and behavioral decision making theories that provide the advantage to focus on particular circumstances and to assess the role of specific factors. A promising direction for future research in entrepreneurship is to explore the role of entrepreneurial experience. Two recent studies point to the importance of this factor. First, a study by Hsu et al. (2017) puts the accent on the contradicting predictions of self-efficacy theory of individuals that restart a business after experiencing failure in a previous business venture. Assuming prospect theory, Hsu et al. (2017) find experimental support for the observed entrepreneurial reentry. A second study, by Shyti and Paraschiv (2015), suggests that startup experience might reduce ambiguity aversion of entrepreneurs. Thus, serial entrepreneurs (that have more than two startup experiences) are shown to be more optimistic and less ambiguity averse than novice entrepreneurs (that have only started a business once). These findings call for further research on factors that moderate the relation between entrepreneurial experience and ambiguity attitudes, as expertise, human capital, accumulated wealth, and so forth.

In investigating behavioral differences between entrepreneurs and non-entrepreneurs, another important topic for future research might also be to refine the relation between the chosen definition of an entrepreneur (Gartner, 1988) and observed ambiguity attitudes. Potential contributions could assess ambiguity attitudes of specific types of entrepreneur, such as innovators (Schumpeter, 1934), arbitrageurs (Kirzner, 1973), or simply self-employed individuals. Future research could also focus on the degree of ambiguity, as the existence of more or less ambiguity may bear some relevance on observed behavior of entrepreneurs. Higher degrees of ambiguity might yield more prudence, which could be more pronounced for entrepreneurs than for non- entrepreneurs. Thus, higher ambiguity might be associated with higher ambiguity aversion.

ACKNOWLEDGMENT

This chapter is based on the unpublished doctoral dissertation of Anisa Shyti at HEC Paris, France (Shyti, 2014). Save some minor changes, it was earlier published as Paraschiv, C., & Shyti, A., (2016). Entrepreneurs under ambiguity: A prospect theory perspective. In T. K. Das (Ed.), *Decision making in behavioral strategy* (pp. 25–47). Charlotte, NC: Information Age.

REFERENCES

Abdellaoui, M., Baillon, A., Placido, L., & Wakker, P. P. (2011). The rich domain of uncertainty: Source functions and their experimental implementation. *American Economic Review, 101*(2), 695–723.

Abdellaoui, M., l'Haridon, O., & Zank, H. (2010). Separating curvature and elevation: A parametric probability weighting function. *Journal of Risk and Uncertainty, 41*(1), 39–65.

Alvarez, S. A., & Barney, J. B. (2005). How do entrepreneurs organize firms under conditions of uncertainty? *Journal of Management, 31*(5), 776–793.

Astebro, T., Herz, H., Nanda, R., & Weber, R. A. (2014). Seeking the roots of entrepreneurship: Insights from behavioral economics. *Journal of Economic Perspectives, 28*(3), 49–69.

Bengtsson, O., Sanandaji, T., & Johannesson, M. (2012). *Do women have a less entrepreneurial personality?* Working Paper No. 944, Research Institute of Industrial Economics, Stockholm, Sweden.

Brockhaus, R. H. (1980). Risk taking propensity of entrepreneurs. *Academy of Management Journal, 23*(3), 509–520.

Budescu, D. V., Kuhn, K. M., Kramer, K. M., & Johnson, T. R. (2002). Modeling certainty equivalents for imprecise gambles. *Organizational Behavior and Human Decision Processes, 88*(2), 748–768.

Budner, S. (1962). Intolerance of ambiguity as a personality variable. *Journal of Personality, 30*(1), 29–50.

Busenitz, L. W., & Barney, J. B. (1997). Differences between entrepreneurs and managers in large organizations: Biases and heuristics in strategic decision-making. *Journal of Business Venturing, 12*(1), 9–30.

Caliendo, M., Fossen, F. M., & Kritikos, A. S. (2009). Risk attitudes of nascent entrepreneurs–new evidence from an experimentally validated survey. *Small Business Economics, 32*(2), 153–167.

Camerer, C., & Weber, M. (1992). Recent developments in modeling preferences: Uncertainty and ambiguity. *Journal of Risk and Uncertainty, 5*(4), 325–370.

Cantillon, R. (1952). *Essai sur la nature du commerce en général.* Paris, France: INED.

Cohen, M., Jaffray, J.-Y., & Said, T. (1987). Experimental comparison of individual behavior under risk and under uncertainty for gains and for losses. *Organizational Behavior and Human Decision Processes, 39*(1), 1–22.

Cramer, J. S., Hartog, J., Jonker, N., & Van Praag, C. M. (2002). Low risk aversion encourages the choice for entrepreneurship: An empirical test of a truism. *Journal of Economic Behavior & Organization, 48*(1), 29–36.

Curley, S. P., & Yates, J. F. (1985). The center and range of the probability interval as factors affecting ambiguity preferences. *Organizational Behavior and Human Decision Processes, 36*(2), 273–287.

Curley, S. P., & Yates, J. F. (1989). An empirical evaluation of descriptive models of ambiguity reactions in choice situations. *Journal of Mathematical Psychology, 33*(4), 397–427.

Dohmen, T., Falk, A., Huffman, D., Sunde, U., Schupp, J., & Wagner, G. G. (2011). Individual risk attitudes: Measurement, determinants, and behavioral consequences. *Journal of the European Economic Association, 9*(3), 522–550.

Dollinger, M. J. (1983). Use of Budner's intolerance of ambiguity measure for entrepreneurial research. *Psychological Reports, 53*(3), 1019–1021.

Douglas, E. J., & Shepherd, D. A. (2000). Entrepreneurship as a utility maximizing response. *Journal of Business Venturing, 15*(3), 231–251.

Einhorn, H. J., & Hogarth, R. M. (1985). Ambiguity and uncertainty in probabilistic inference. *Psychological Review, 92*(4), 433–461.

Ellsberg, D. (1961). Risk, ambiguity, and the savage axioms. *Quarterly Journal of Economics, 75*(4), 643–669.

Elston, J. A., & Audretsch, D. B. (2011). Financing the entrepreneurial decision: An empirical approach using experimental data on risk attitudes. *Small Business Economics, 36*(2), 209–222.

Elston, J. A., Harrison, G. W., & Rutström, E. E. (2005). *Characterizing the entrepreneur using field experiments* (Working Paper 05–30). University of Central Florida, Orlando, FL.

Fox, C. R., & Tversky, A. (1995). Ambiguity aversion and comparative ignorance. *Quarterly Journal of Economics, 110*(3), 585–603.

Fox, C. R., & Tversky, A. (1998). A belief-based account of decision under uncertainty. *Management Science, 44*(7), 879–895.

Frenkel-Brunswik, E. (1949). Intolerance of ambiguity as an emotional and perceptual personality variable. *Journal of Personality, 18*(1), 108–143.

Gartner, W. B. (1988). Who is an entrepreneur? Is the wrong question. *American Journal of Small Business, 12*(4), 11–32.

Geroski, P. A. (1995). What do we know about entry? *International Journal of Industrial Organization, 13*(4), 421–440.

Gilboa, I., & Schmeidler, D. (1989). Maxmin expected utility with non-unique prior. *Journal of Mathematical Economics, 18*(2), 141–153.

Goldstein, W. M., & Einhorn, H. J. (1987). Expression theory and the preference reversal phenomena. *Psychological Review, 94*(2), 236–254.

Gonzalez, R., & Wu, G. (1999). On the shape of the probability weighting function. *Cognitive Psychology, 38*(1), 129–166.

González-Vallejo, C., Bonazzi, A., & Shapiro, A. J. (1996). Effects of vague probabilities and of vague payoffs on preference: A model comparison analysis. *Journal of Mathematical Psychology, 40*(2), 130–140.

Hamilton, B. H. (2000). Does entrepreneurship pay? An empirical analysis of the returns to self-employment. *Journal of Political Economy, 108*(3), 604–631.

Hardenbol, S. C. (2012). *Selection into entrepreneurship and behavioural attitudes towards situations of non-strategic uncertainty* (Unpublished master's thesis). University of Amsterdam, Amsterdam, The Netherlands.

Hayek, F. A. (1948). *Individualism and economic order.* Chicago, IL: University of Chicago Press.

Heath, C., & Tversky, A. (1991). Preference and belief: Ambiguity and competence in choice under uncertainty. *Journal of Risk and Uncertainty, 4*(1), 5–28.

Hogarth, R. M., & Einhorn, H. J. (1990). Venture theory: A model of decision weights. *Management Science, 36*(7), 780–803.

Holm, H. J., Opper, S., & Nee, V. (2013). Entrepreneurs under uncertainty: An economic experiment in China. *Management Science, 59*(7), 1671–1687.

Holt, C. A., & Laury, S. K. (2002). Risk aversion and incentive effects. *American Economic Review, 92*(5), 1644–1655.

Hsu, D. K., Wiklund, J., & Cotton, R. D. (2017). Success, failure, and entrepreneurial reentry: An experimental assessment of the veracity of self-efficacy and prospect theory. *Entrepreneurship Theory and Practice, 41*, 19–47.

Kahneman, D. (2011). *Thinking, fast and slow.* New York, NY: Farrar, Strauss, Giroux.

Kahneman, D., Slovic, P., & Tversky, A. (1982). *Judgment under uncertainty.* Cambridge, England: Cambridge University Press.

Kahneman, D., & Tversky, A. (1973). On the psychology of prediction. *Psychological Review, 80*(4), 237–238.

Kahneman, D., & Tversky, A. (1979). Prospect theory: An analysis of decision under risk. *Econometrica, 47*(2), 263–291.

Kanbur, S. M. (1979). Of risk taking and the personal distribution of income. *Journal of Political Economy, 87*(4), 769–797.

Keynes, J. (1921). *A treatise on probability.* London, England: Macmillan & Co.

Kihlstrom, R. E., & Laffont, J.-J. (1979). A general equilibrium entrepreneurial theory of firm formation based on risk aversion. *Journal of Political Economy, 87*(4), 719–748.

Kilka, M., & Weber, M. (2001). What determines the shape of the probability weighting function under uncertainty? *Management Science, 47*(12), 1712–1726.

Kirzner, I. M. (1973). *Competition and entrepreneurship.* Chicago, IL: University of Chicago Press.

Knight, F. (1921). *Risk, uncertainty, and profit.* New York, NY: Kelley and Millman.

Koudstaal, M., Sloof, R., & Van Praag, M. (2014). *Risk, uncertainty and entrepreneurship: Evidence from a lab-in-the-field experiment.* Working Paper No. 14–136/VII, Tinbergen Institute, Amsterdam, The Netherlands.

Kuhn, K. M., & Budescu, D. V. (1996). The relative importance of probabilities, outcomes, and vagueness in hazard risk decisions. *Organizational Behavior and Human Decision Processes, 68*(3), 301–317.

Mac Donald, A., Jr. (1970). Revised scale for ambiguity tolerance: Reliability and validity. *Psychological Reports, 26*(3), 791–798.

McKelvie, A., Haynie, J. M., & Gustavsson, V. (2011). Unpacking the uncertainty construct: Implications for entrepreneurial action. *Journal of Business Venturing, 26*(3), 273–292.

McLain, D. L. (2009). Evidence of the properties of an ambiguity tolerance measure: The multiple stimulus types ambiguity tolerance scale-ii (MSTAT-II). *Psychological Reports, 105*(3), 975–988.

McMullen, J. S., & Shepherd, D. A. (2006). Entrepreneurial action and the role of uncertainty in the theory of the entrepreneur. *Academy of Management Review, 31*(1), 132–152.

Parker, S. C. (2009). *The economics of entrepreneurship.* Cambridge, England: Cambridge University Press.

Prelec, D. (1998). The probability weighting function. *Econometrica, 66*(3), 497–527.

Savage, L. J. (1954). *The foundations of statistics.* New York, NY: Wiley.

Say, J. B. (1836). *A treatise on political economy: Or the production, distribution, and consumption of wealth.* Philadelphia, PA: Grigg & Elliot.

Schade, C., & Koellinger, P. (2007). Heuristics, biases, and the behavior of entrepreneurs. *Entrepreneurship, The Engine of Growth, 1,* 141–163.

Schere, J. L. (1982). Tolerance of ambiguity as a discriminating variable between entrepreneurs and managers. *Academy of Management Proceedings, 1982*(1), 404–408.

Schmeidler, D. (1989). Subjective probability and expected utility without additivity. *Econometrica, 57*(3), 571–587.

Schumpeter, J. A. (1934). *Capitalism, socialism, and democracy.* New York, NY: Harper and Row.

Shackle, G. L. S. (1968). *Uncertainty in economics and other reflections.* Cambridge, England: Cambridge University Press.

Shane, S., & Venkataraman, S. (2000). The promise of entrepreneurship as a field of research. *Academy of Management Review, 25*(1), 217–226.

Shane, S. A. (2000). *A general theory of entrepreneurship: The individual-opportunity nexus.* Northampton, MA: Edward Elgar.

Shyti, A. (2014). *Entrepreneurial decision making under ambiguity: Experimental evidence on the impact of overconfidence.* Unpublished doctoral dissertation, HEC Paris, France.

Shyti, A., & Paraschiv, C. (2014, June). *Risk and ambiguity in evaluating a new venture: An experimental study.* Paper presented at DRUID Society Conference, Copenhagen, Denmark.

Shyti, A., & Paraschiv, C. (2015). Does entrepreneurial experience affect risk and ambiguity attitudes? An experimental study. *Academy of Management Proceedings, 2015*(1), 17530.

Smithson, M. (1999). Conflict aversion: Preference for ambiguity vs. conflict in sources and evidence. *Organizational Behavior and Human Decision Processes, 79*(3), 179–198.

Tajeddini, K., & Mueller, S. L. (2009). Entrepreneurial characteristics in Switzerland and the UK: A comparative study of techno-entrepreneurs. *Journal of International Entrepreneurship, 7*(1), 1–25.

Teoh, H. Y., & Foo, S. L. (1997). Moderating effects of tolerance for ambiguity and risk taking propensity on the role conflict-perceived performance relationship: Evidence from Singaporean entrepreneurs. *Journal of Business Venturing, 12*(1), 67–81.

Tversky, A., & Fox, C. R. (1995). Weighing risk and uncertainty. *Psychological Review, 102*(2), 269–283.

Tversky, A., & Kahneman, D. (1992). Advances in prospect theory: Cumulative representation of uncertainty. *Journal of Risk and Uncertainty, 5*(4), 297–323.

Tversky, A., & Wakker, P. (1995). Risk attitudes and decision weights. *Econometrica, 63*(6), 1255–1280.

Wakker, P. P. (2004). On the composition of risk preference and belief. *Psychological Review, 111*(1), 236–241.

Wakker, P. P. (2010). *Prospect theory: For risk and ambiguity.* Cambridge, England: Cambridge University Press.

Wu, G., & Gonzalez, R. (1999). Nonlinear decision weights in choice under uncertainty. *Management Science, 45*(1), 74–85.

CHAPTER 5

DYNAMIC RESPONSES TO DISRUPTIVE BUSINESS MODEL INNOVATIONS

Rational, Behavioral, and Normative Perspectives

Oleksiy Osiyevskyy
Amir Bahman Radnejad
Kanhaiya Kumar Sinha

ABSTRACT

How should incumbent firms respond to disruptive business model innovations introduced in their industries by innovative startups, newcomers from adjacent industries, or entrepreneurial established players? Despite much discussion, the current literature provides no clear-cut answer. One view suggests establishing autonomous business units to explore disruptive business model innovations; the other approach implies ambidextrous integration of two business models in the same firm, or even ignoring the disruptive innovation to concentrate on the core business model. In this chapter, we integrate existing views in a deductively developed model of response to disruptive business model innovations in their industries, manifested in a holistic typology

Entrepreneurship and Behavioral Strategy, pages 113–145
Copyright © 2020 by Information Age Publishing

113

of response strategies. On its basis, we propose a dynamic behavioral model of incumbent firms' responses to disruptive business model innovations, describing observed behavioral patterns in disrupted industries and explaining actions and reasons why these actions might deviate from the rational path. Then, we propose a rational response model, comprising a set of testable propositions regarding the contingency factors determining optimal incumbent actions when facing a disruptive business model innovation. Finally, we supplement the insights of rational and behavioral models with the real options lens to formulate a set of normative recommendations for managers of established real-world firms having to make decisions regarding nascent or gaining momentum disruptive business models in their industries.

INTRODUCTION

Back in 2007, Garmin was on its rise in the booming GPS navigators market. The company was considered "the next Apple" by stock analysts (Leber, 2013), with excited customers, increasing sales, and skyrocketing stock price. Five years later, the momentum seems to be lost: revenues were shrinking (Leber, 2013), customers were switching to alternatives, and the market capitalization was less than a half of the one in 2007. The reason for this decline is simple: A major disruptive business model innovation is gaining momentum, taking away the market share from existing industry players (Downes & Nunes, 2013). This disruptive business model is manifested in new products, free map applications for smartphones (e.g., Google Maps or Waze).

The problems faced by Garmin are not idiosyncratic; they manifest a new and disturbing trend in today's business environment—the inability of established incumbent firms to adjust to industry change caused by disruptive innovation. The incumbents face a major two-staged problem: (a) having to foresee if the disruptive innovation will transform the industry; (b) having to come out with a proactive response strategy, even without knowing *ex ante* the answer to the first question. The long and slow demise of Kodak, notwithstanding heroic efforts of successive managers ("The Last Kodak Moment," 2012), is a vivid and identifiable example of practical significance of the topic. There are myriad of industries in which leading firms were dethroned or forced out of business by disruptive innovators: newspaper publishing disrupted by e-media (Gilbert, 2003), computer services by cloud computing (Sultan & van de Bunt-Kokhuis, 2012), steel production disrupted by mini-mills (Christensen, 1997), or photography disrupted by digital photography ("The Last Kodak Moment," 2012; Sandström, Magnusson, & Jörnmark, 2009). The other group of industries underwent a substantive change, and although most incumbents survived, they now have to adapt to new industry structure: for example, traditional airlines now having to co-exist with low-cost disruptors, or traditional stockbrokers competing with online discounters (Christensen, 2006; Markides, 2006). Lastly, there are industries where the disruptive innovations are just starting to gain momentum, and their impact is yet to be discovered: for example, traditional banking facing peer-to-peer lending, or traditional universities facing on-line models of education (Osiyevskyy & Dewald, 2018). In these cases, disruptive innovations can either completely change the existing industries, or never materialize.

The scholarly work of Clayton Christensen drew the attention of researchers and practitioners to the phenomenon of incumbent failure to adequately respond to gaining momentum disruptive innovations. Scrutinizing the issue of disruptive technology in the earlier works (Christensen, 1997; Christensen & Bower, 1996), he later extended the reasoning to disruptive business models, uniting all these notions under the umbrella term "disruptive innovation" (Christensen & Raynor, 2013; Christensen, Raynor, & McDonald, 2015). Moreover, reflecting on the further elaboration of the topic in subsequent works of strategic management scholars, Christensen (2006) explicitly emphasized the business model facet of the phenomenon ("it is a business model problem, not a technology," p. 48). Arguably, it is the evolution of disruptive business models that should receive the primary attention of researchers in this field. Indeed, "a disruptive innovation may or may not even represent a technical breakthrough. Rather, it may simply involve... the changing of a firm's business model" (Crockett, McGee, & Payne, 2013, p. 858).

How should incumbent firms respond to emerging disruptive business model innovations introduced in their industries by innovative startups, newcomers from adjacent industries, or entrepreneurial established players? Although discussed above examples of Garmin and Kodak paint a gloomy picture for established firms, in many instances incumbents can adapt successfully to protect themselves from disruptive innovations, or even to thrive on them, preserving the market leadership (Ansari & Krop, 2012; Wan, Williamson, & Yin, 2015; Yu & Hang, 2010). Even though the question of optimal response to disruptive innovation was extensively scrutinized in the management literature, it is still far from being resolved (Christensen, 2006), particularly for the case of disruptive business models rather than disruptive technologies. One view suggests establishing autonomous business units to explore disruptive business model innovations (Christensen & Raynor, 2013); the other approach implies ambidextrous integration of two business models in the same firm (O'Reilly & Tushman, 2008), ignoring the disruptive innovation to concentrate on the core business model, or even coming out with a new disruption in response (Charitou & Markides, 2003). Most of the existing models of incumbent firms' response to disruptive business model innovations are developed inductively from cases or industry data (Charitou & Markides, 2003; Christensen, 1997; Christensen

& Raynor, 2013; Habtay, 2012; Markides & Oyon, 2010). The inductive origins of these frameworks leave unanswered the question of their scope and parsimony: One cannot say for sure whether the proposed sets of actions embrace all possible responses, whether the proposed actions are not overlapping, and whether they are responses to disruption. Also, as proposed in different studies, contingency factors determining proper incumbent response must be unified in a single model. Taking into account the importance of the topic and the stage of our understanding of the disruptive business model innovations phenomenon, the further progress of the field would benefit from deductive generalizing of available theoretical insights and observed empirical regularities into a holistic theoretical model. This sets the motivation for the current chapter.

Therefore, in this chapter, we intend to address the following questions: (a) "What is the rational incumbent firm response to gaining momentum disruptive innovations?"; (b) "Which factors explain observable patterns of incumbents' behavior when faced with disruptive business model innovations?"; and (c) "What are the normative recommendations for managers of incumbent firms in such situations?"

Uniting the literature on business models and disruptive innovations, we address the listed research questions in the following way. First, we clarify the conceptualization of key terms (business model, business model innovation/change, and disruptive business model innovation), which are highly ambiguous in the current literature. From this, we discuss a holistic typology of incumbent responses to disruptive business model innovations in their industries, embracing two generic business model change strategies: explorative adoption of the disruptive business model, and exploitative strengthening of the existing business model (Osiyevskyy & Dewald, 2015a). Then, we propose a behavioral model of incumbent firms' responses to disruptive business model innovations gaining momentum in their industries; the model describes the observed behavioral patterns in disrupted industries, explaining incumbent actions and reasons why these actions might deviate from the rational path. The behavioral response model is supplemented by a rational response model, comprising a set of testable propositions regarding the contingency factors determining optimal incumbent actions when facing a disruptive business model innovation. Finally, we enhance the insights of the rational and behavioral models with the real options lens to formulate a set of normative recommendations for managers of real-world established firms having to make decisions regarding nascent or gaining momentum disruptive business model innovations in their industries. Overall, the developed models stress that the firm's response is an appropriate unit of analysis of situations of ongoing disruptive business model innovations, and that the actual responses are determined by managerial cognition, organizational context, and market factors.

RESPONSE MODEL: A TYPOLOGY

Disruptive Business Model Innovations: Clarification of the Concepts

Business Model

Before developing the theoretical models, we must first clarify the definitions of concepts used in further theoretical reasoning. The first and most important concept needing clarification is a business model, which still lacks consensual definition in existing literature, despite growing understanding of its importance (Karimi & Walter, 2016; Zott, Amit, & Massa, 2011). Authors of papers of the business model concept often study it without explicit definition, or propose competing definitions (Foss & Saebi, 2018). For instance, the essence of a business model was defined as an "articulation between different areas of activity" (Demil & Lecocq, 2010), "design or architecture" (Teece, 2010), "specific combination of resources" (DaSilva & Trkman, 2014), among other things (Zott et al., 2011). This lack of clear definition of the key construct is typical for a pre-paradigmatic stage of science, in which the literature on business models is currently situated. Yet, these conflicting definitions of the essence of a business model makes its theoretical development problematic; moreover, most of the proposed definitions (such as "architecture," "design," "conceptual tool or model") prevent conceptual linking of the business model concept with the existing body of knowledge in management studies, a necessary step for deductive development of models involving business models concept. To overcome this obstacle, we anchor on a definition of a business model that combines the essential salient features of prior conceptualizations, while at the same time providing a clear link to established management theories. Functionally, a firm's business model is an interrelated set of routines for: (a) creating economic value for firm's stakeholders, and (b) appropriating part of this value for the firm itself and its shareholders (Biloshapka & Osiyevskyy, 2018; Osiyevskyy & Zargarzadeh, 2015). In this definition, the term "interrelated set of routines" is used in the sense of the evolutionary theory of the firm (Nelson & Winter, 2009), as a complex regular behavioral pattern within a firm—used for value creation and appropriation. Notably, in line with this definition a firm can have more than one business model (if the value is created and appropriated in more than one distinct way), or have no business model at all (if no regular behavioral pattern for value creation and appropriation is established). As any other routine, a business model can become a capability underpinning the firm's competitive advantage (Casadesus-Masanell & Ricart, 2010; Markides & Charitou, 2004), provided that a set of conditions are met (e.g., the VRIN framework of Barney [1991]). Structurally, a business model as a routine comprises three major interrelated dimensions

(George & Bock, 2011; Osiyevskyy & Dewald, 2015b): *value structure* (value propositions for each stakeholder), *transactive structure* (organization and governance of exchanges within and across the firm boundaries), and *resource structure* (unique combination and organization of resources through which transactions create value (DaSilva & Trkman, 2014).

Business Model Change and Innovation

As any type of routine (Nelson & Winter, 2009), business models are in a state of constant change. Hence, a static view of business models as interrelated value, resource and transactive structures tells only half of the story; the other essential half is the dynamic, transformational view of the business model evolution (Demil & Lecocq, 2010). In line with this reasoning, *business model change* is conceptualized as any alteration of the existing business model of a firm (Osiyevskyy & Dewald, 2015a; Osiyevskyy & Zargarzadeh, 2015), either radical (major shift in one or more dimensions of a business model), or incremental (progressive refinement of individual components). In terms of novelty, the general business model change concept includes both business model innovations ("new to the world" changes introduced in the industry for the first time) and imitative business model changes ("new to the firm" changes that copy approaches of competitors or firms from other industries).

The latter distinction allows differentiating the broad term of business model change from its partial exemplar, *business model innovation* (BMI), which represents intentional, unique for the industry change of the firm business model in response to perceived opportunity to make it more effective or efficient (Osiyevskyy & Zargarzadeh, 2015). Business model innovations can be introduced by newcomers (Christensen, 1997) or diversifying entrants from adjacent industries (Tripsas, 1997), or by entrepreneurial established players (Karimi & Walter, 2016; Schumpeter, 1934). If the introduced BMI proves its potential, the remaining incumbents often learn about this, and respond by imitating and copying it (Casadesus-Masanell & Zhu, 2013). A relatively broad topology of BMIs (according to their essence) was proposed in Giesen, Berman, Bell, and Blitz (2007), distinguishing among *industry model innovations* (redefining the industry or creating a new one), *revenue model innovations* (reconfiguration of product offering and pricing), and *enterprise model innovations* (changing the role of a firm in the value chain).

Disruptive Business Model Innovations

They represent a particular type of BMI that is initially "financially unattractive for the leading incumbent to pursue, relative to its profit model and relative to other investments that are competing for the organization's resources" (Christensen, 2006, p. 49). Being perceived by incumbents and their most valued customers as inferior, the innovation seeks to find a customer base, often among price-sensitive non-consumers who cannot pay for the full-featured products or services, or among consumers who value different product or service attributes comparing to those emphasized by traditional business models (Christensen, 1997; Markides, 2006). As Christensen (1997) demonstrates, with time the prior "inferior" disruptive innovation gains momentum, develops, and ultimately surpasses the requirements of mainstream customers, who eventually switch to the new alternative. As such, disruptive BMI manifests a discovery of a fundamentally different routine for value creation and appropriation, which usually enlarges the existing market by either attracting new customers or encouraging the existing ones to consume more (Markides, 2006).

One important fact differentiates disruptive technological innovations from disruptive BMIs: Whereas the materialization of a disruptive technology in most cases leads to displacement of prior, established technology (Christensen, 1997), the rise of disruptive business models rarely eliminate prior business models in their industries (Markides, 2006). In most cases, disruptive business models gain some market share, extend the overall market, and then compete and co-exist with established ones. Indeed, "several value propositions may coexist within a specific industry" (Sabatier, Craig-Kennard, & Mangematin, 2012, p. 950), with several business models successfully co-existing.

Responses to Disruptive Business Model Innovations: Existing Approaches

When facing disruptive BMIs introduced and gaining momentum in their industries, managers of incumbent firms must make decisions regarding appropriate responses to them. As it was stressed at the beginning of the chapter, even though the question of optimal response to disruptive innovations was extensively scrutinized in the management literature (autonomy, risk-taking, and proactiveness of managers has positive association of successful adoption of disruptive BMI (Karimi & Walter, 2016), it is still far from being resolved (Christensen, 2006), particularly for the case of disruptive business models.

The early approaches suggest establishing autonomous business units (spin-offs) to explore disruptive BMIs (e.g., Christensen, 2006; Christensen & Raynor, 2013). Yet, this model implicitly assumes that incumbents should respond to every potential disruption in their industries, which is far from optimal (Markides, 2006; Markides & Charitou, 2004). Some disruptive BMIs never gain momentum, and pursuing each of them might be a waste of resources. Moreover, the discussed above fact that more than one business model can coexist in the same industry suggests other possible incumbent responses, such as ignoring the disruption and concentrating on existing business model (e.g., not all universities should switch to on-line delivery, and not all airlines should become low cost).

The action-response framework of Charitou and Markides (2003) moves the discussion much closer to a desired theoretical explanation of the optimal incumbent response to disruption. Starting with the observation that incumbents do not have to respond to every disruptive BMI by adopting it, the researchers propose a more sophisticated variation of incumbents' responses. The inductively developed action-response framework embraces five basic responses: (a) focusing on traditional business, (b) ignoring the innovation, (c) attacking back through new disruption, (d) adopting the innovation by playing both games at once, and (e) embracing the innovation and scaling it up. This work provides an important comprehensive perspective on incumbent responses, and hence represents a step towards building the theory of response to disruptive innovations. The inductive origins of the action-response framework leave unanswered the question of its scope and parsimony: One cannot say for sure whether the proposed sets of actions embrace all possible responses, whether the proposed actions are not overlapping, and whether they are responses to disruption.

Moreover, the normative implications of Charitou and Markides (2003) need further elaboration. Based on juxtaposing of only two factors (ability to respond and motivation to respond), the recommendations leave too much ambiguity: for example, in the case of high levels on both factors, we have three plausible solutions (adopt and separate, adopt and keep internal, and attack back). Additional contingencies must be taken into account to resolve these ambiguities. To some extent, these were resolved in further studies of organizational ambidexterity (O'Reilly & Tushman, 2008); yet, these separate bodies of literature are still not integrated into a holistic deductive model.

Typology of Responses

The first step in developing a model of incumbents' responses to disruptive BMIs is in clarifying the potential types of responses. Such typology provides a context from which to describe and discuss the dynamic process of responding to a BMI. On a broad level, when faced with a gaining momentum disruptive BMI, an established company can choose to respond or ignore it. The active response choice can follow two generic strategies (Osiyevskyy & Dewald, 2015a): (a) strengthening the existing business model, or (b) adopting a disruptive business model (pure imitating, or imitating some elements with adaptations to match the company's existing competencies and capabilities). This choice is consistent with the traditional distinction between the exploitation of established certainties and exploration of new opportunities in organizational learning (March, 1991), or distant and local search (Rosenkopf & Nerkar, 2001; Stuart & Podolny, 1996). Notably, these two generic response strategies are distinct, but not mutually exclusive to one another. Each strategy implies a change of the existing business model, since to match the explorative or exploitative approach, the firm has to reconsider the business model's value, transactive and resource structures (Osiyevskyy & Dewald, 2015b), including alteration of established policies, assets configuration and choice of governance (Casadesus-Masanell & Ricart, 2010).

The first generic response strategy—explorative adoption of the disruptive business model (explorative business model change)—implies imitating the disruptive business model or some of its essential elements (Osiyevskyy & Dewald, 2015a, 2018). This change is radical in nature, putting a company on a change trajectory outside linear (incremental) refinement of the existing business model. This often leads to changing the value proposition to firm customers, manifested in offering different products or services, changes in the way of delivering them, rethinking the methods of payment or price policy. In its turn, change in value proposition usually demands to reconsider the supporting transactive and resource structures of the business model (Osiyevskyy & Dewald, 2015b).

The explorative adoption of the disruptive business model has two important features. First, finding the right way to adopt the disruptive business model does not happen overnight; rather, it is a learning and experimentation process requiring significant changes with following progressive refinements to achieve internal and external consistency—among business model elements and with external environment, respectively (Demil & Lecocq, 2010; McGrath, 2010). Indeed, "an emerging dynamic perspective sees business model development as an initial experiment followed by constant revision, adaptation, and fine-tuning based on trial-and-error learning" (Sosna, Trevinyo-Rodríguez, & Velamuri, 2010, p. 384). Second, explorative adoption of the disruptive business model often implies *searching* for elements that work as a specific fit to the unique context of the existing company (peculiar assets and capabilities), rather than *mere imitation* of the disruptive approach. Pure imitation usually deprives incumbents of the first-mover advantage in the emerging market; instead, the rational response supposes coming out with original model tailored to a particular firm (Markides & Oyon, 2010).

The second strategy—exploitative strengthening of the existing business model (exploitative business model change)—implies incrementally changing the established business model (along the linear trajectory), to protect from disruptive newcomers (Osiyevskyy & Dewald, 2015a). The goal of this strategy is in creating exclusive or monopoly rents in a particular market segment (Porter, 1980) and isolating the firm from the impact of disruptors. Christensen and Bower (1996) provide an example of such strategy, a typical response of incumbents when facing a disruptive innovation: Following their most valuable customers, the firms usually migrate to a high-end market, incrementally augmenting their products or services by adding sophisticated features that up-market clients should appreciate.

Notably, the incumbents' choice of exploitative rather than explorative business model change can be a rational choice: As it was stressed before, even if a disruptive BMI gains momentum, in most cases, it does not overtake the whole market (Markides, 2006). In other words, a disruptive BMI might leave lucrative niches for incumbents to occupy, and hence exploitative strengthening of the existing business model to build strong positions in these niches might be a rational strategy.

Applying these two strategies as orthogonal axes yield the 2×2 matrix (Figure 5.1) of incumbent responses to gaining momentum disruptive BMIs (Osiyevskyy & Dewald, 2015a). The generic response strategies (with regards to a disruption) are similar to firm's positioning—with regards to competition in its industry—for example, frameworks of Porter (1980) or Miles, Snow, Meyer, and Coleman (1978), being dynamic and pre-determined by market forces and organizational characteristics.

The incumbents in Group 1 defend the existing business models without adaptations (Defiant Resistance). Examples of such response are numerous, particularly in the early stages of disruption: Consider commercial banks ignoring the peer-to-peer lending ("The Last Kodak Moment," 2012), or the U.S. public school system, mostly ignoring the online models of class delivery (Christensen, Johnson, & Horn, 2010). Companies from

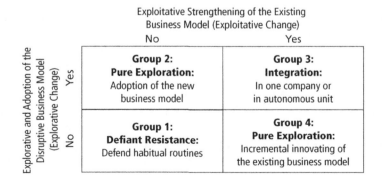

Figure 5.1 Typology of incumbent firm's responses to disruptive innovations. *Source:* Adapted from Osiyevskyy & Dewald (2015a).

this group not only decline to change their business models but also are likely to proactively resist changes, lobbying for the legislative prohibition of disruptive innovations (Dewald & Bowen, 2010). Notably, the Defiant Resistance response strategy is a natural position for firms to adopt before a disruptive innovation has proven its market potential.

Group 2 consists of firms pursuing a Pure Exploration strategy. These incumbents adopt the disruptive business model or its essential elements without the simultaneous development of the existing business model or attempting to integrate the development of both models. The adoption of a disruptive business model can be done either by switching to it entirely or by simply neglecting the existing business model, depriving it of further investment and instead focusing on developing the new one. This is a generic strategy of agents of the Schumpeterian creative destruction, either entrepreneurial incumbents or newcomers.

Group 4 includes the companies pursuing a Pure Exploitation strategy, which strengthens their existing business models without adopting any elements of the disruptive approach. Unlike members of the Defiant Resistance group, companies pursuing pure exploitation are engaged in incremental changing of their established business models. In an attempt to defend the status quo in the way business is done, and exploit the previously effective resources and capabilities possessed by the firm, managers of these firms look for incremental adjustments and refinements, such as going to upper segments of the market (protected from inferior disruptors) or differentiating (to enjoy monopoly power).

Lastly, incumbents of Group 3 (Integration) attempt to benefit from both models, simultaneously adopting the elements of the disruptive innovation and leaving the door open for other opportunities in the existing business model ("Playing Both Games at Once," in the words of Charitou and Markides [2004]). This can be achieved either through the integration of both models in the same business unit or through unrelated diversification using an autonomous business unit (spin-off). The former approach implies leveraging the synergies between business models by reinforcing their strengths. The spin-off approach, on the other hand, supposes that the new business is developed simultaneously but independently from the established one (the early recommendation proposed for responding to a technological disruption [see Christensen, 1997; Christensen & Raynor, 2013]). Nevertheless, this approach can lead to an ambidexterity challenge, which includes challenges of managing two different and conflicting business models simultaneously (Markides, 2013). The incumbent firms can overcome the challenge by aligning "complementary assets with earlier addition of the new business model and conflicting assets with an autonomous business unit for the new business model" (Kim & Min, 2015, p. 34).

BEHAVIORAL RESPONSE MODEL: A TYPICAL EVOLUTION OF A DISRUPTED INDUSTRY

Further development of the response model will proceed along two directions: behavioral and rational paths. Whereas the rational response model concentrates on the question of what incumbent firms *should do* when facing a disruptive BMI in their industries, as discussed in this section, behavioral response model studies their *actual behavior*, in terms of a typical pattern of disrupted industry's evolution.

The fundamental premise of the developed behavioral response model is considering disruption as a dynamic process rather than a one-time event. Indeed, from all disruptive BMIs that materialized (overtaking substantive part of established markets), not a single one did so overnight; rather, any nascent disruption needed time to gain momentum: "It indeed is a process, not a cataclysmic event" (Christensen, 2006, p. 50). We assert that the typical incumbent response to an emerging disruptive BMI is contingent upon the stage of disruptive innovation's development, and hence the typical established industry's response should be considered from a dynamic evolution perspective. In the majority of cases, this evolution will include three stages (Figure 5.2).

Stages of Disrupted Industry's Evolution

Stage One
In the first stage, the emerging disruptive BMI does not have the necessary momentum to become salient enough to be perceived seriously by major incumbents. Managers of incumbent firms, so as their best customers, tend to focus on inferior aspects of the disruption, making it easy to

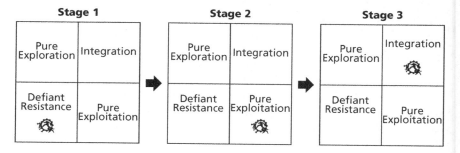

Figure 5.2 Three stages of industry evolution in reaction to disruptive business model innovation.

ignore. The disruptive offering seems to appeal to only a small subset of customers, promise insufficient financial returns and looks like a fleeting, short-term, non-serious threat. As a result, the majority of incumbents stick with the traditional business model. The rationale behind these actions is obvious: While requiring a rethinking of the whole business model, the disruptive offering is simultaneously "inferior" in terms of traditional performance measures, appeals to a different (or unknown yet) group of customers, and does not fit traditional business performance evaluation models. Therefore, on the first stage of disrupted industry's evolution, the dominant incumbent response is Defiant Resistance (akin to "Ignore the Innovation—It's Not Your Business" in Charitou and Markides, [2003]). As an example, consider the traditional book retail industry in 1995–1997, with Borders and Barnes & Noble being major specialized competitors, sharing the book market with generalist retailers like Costco and Walmart. In those days, the emergence of a pure online book retailer with totally new disruptive business model—Amazon (founded in 1995)—did not lead to any substantive reaction of incumbents (i.e., Defiant Resistance response). Barnes & Noble opened its online bookstore only in 1997 (although without a significant emphasis on it); while Borders allowed Amazon to handle its Internet sales—a mistake that would lead to fatal consequences later (Hitt, Ireland, & Hoskisson, 2016).

There are two basic mechanisms which lead to Defiant Resistance as a dominant response of most incumbents in the early stage of disruptive BMI emerging in their industry: cognitive and structural ones. On the level of managerial cognition, in the first stage of industry disruption, there is a set of factors that were shown to cause rigidity (or reduce intentions to change the business model in an explorative way) in the decision making of the managers of incumbent firms. First, the framing of the market potential for the disruptive business model is formed by managers' prior industry affiliations, beliefs, and experiences (Benner & Tripsas, 2012; Tripsas & Gavetti, 2000), biasing their search activities in favor of existing approaches and business models (Tripsas & Gavetti, 2000). Indeed, "managers of established firms, whose perspectives are deeply entrenched and largely shaped by their current experiences, tend to ignore these new low margin segments and focus on their existing customers and markets" (Crockett et al., 2013). Second, the disruptive business model is not salient enough from the point of view of managers of established businesses; hence, they perceive no major threat or opportunity from it, while these two latter factors were found to be significant drivers of explorative business model change intentions (Dewald & Bowen, 2010; Osiyevskyy & Dewald, 2015b). Finally, any nascent market sparked by a radical change, including the market of a disruptive business model, is characterized by major ambiguity and uncertainty (Benner & Tripsas, 2012). This low level of predictability also constrains the intentions to explore the new business model.

From the perspective of structural (non-cognitive) impediments for business model change on the first stage of disruption, Christensen (1997) found that incumbents rely on the advice of existing customers who do not value the specific benefits of the disruptive innovation. In addition, Charitou and Markides (2003) cite a focus on considerable prior investments in existing business (omnipresent problem of sunk costs), having more important issues to deal with in existing business, an objective need for further analysis of the situation, a lack of necessary resources for entering new business, or simply bad timing to enter as specific reasons for incumbent firms to adopt a Defiant Resistance position.

Despite the cognitive and structural barriers, the other incumbent responses are possible in the early, first stage of the disrupted industry's evolution. They may take the form of a Pure Exploration, embraced by rare incumbents that are predisposed towards the disruptive business model. An example of the latter non-dominant response is the proactive engagement of the University of Phoenix in the United States, Open University in England, and Athabasca University in Canada in online education. All these institutions were predisposed towards online education, because of the prior experience of correspondence course delivery and the emphasis on increased enrollment of diverse students from other geographical regions as an engine for further development.

Stage Two

If the disruptive BMI does not die or flatten out on the first stage and keeps on gaining momentum, with time this disruption becomes too visible for incumbents to ignore; this change manifests the beginning of the second stage of the disrupted industry's evolution. At this point, the disruptive approach starts threatening the managers of incumbent firms, requiring a proactive response. In most cases, this proactive response usually implies the dominant reaction of exploitative development of the traditional business model (Pure Exploitation), aiming at protecting from the threat posed by the disruption by increasing the customers' value to prevent the latter from switching to the disruptive alternative. This development is usually done through marginal incremental changes, rather than drastic, radical innovations (Demil & Lecocq, 2010). For instance, in traditional real estate brokerage, disrupted by discounted offerings and Internet technologies, these incremental innovations could include supplementing traditional broker's services of facilitating the transaction (search, negotiations, and legal details) with help in getting mortgage, in renovation of newly bought houses, or in preparing the real estate for sale (Osiyevskyy & Dewald, 2015b).

Prior research demonstrates that Pure Exploitation is the quadrant where the majority of industry incumbents migrate after the disruption becomes too visible to ignore (Christensen, 1997). The rationale for the Pure Exploitation response suggests that the firms protect their "premium" position from discounting newcomers through enhanced differentiation (Porter, 1980). In the case of retail bookselling, the Pure Exploitation as a dominant response in Stage 2 of the disrupted industry's evolution was manifested in the Borders' strategy in 1997–2009: indeed, while significant visible changes were happening in the industry (customers shopping for books online, growing popularity of electronic books for e-readers), "Borders invested heavily to enhance the marketing for traditional bookselling" and "tried to lure customers to its stores with promises of enriching experience" (Hitt et al., 2016, p. 3). No major attempt to explore the disruptive business model by Borders was noted; all this time, the company's online sales operations were outsourced to Amazon.

Christensen (1997) clearly described the flaws of this response, noting that at a certain point mainstream customers become "overserved" and readily switch to the less costly disruption, once it meets their minimum performance requirements ("performance overshooting"—e.g., Bergek, Berggren, Magnusson, & Hobday, [2013]). This fulfills the innovator's "dilemma." To make things worse, concentrating on strengthening the existent business model distracts managers from scrutinizing the benefits of disruptive innovation and from getting the experience of working with it.

The second stage of the industry disruption requires a proactive response from incumbents. Two main mechanisms drive the exploitation (rather than exploration or some combination) as this proactive response. From the managerial cognition perspective, the main obstacle for explorative adoption of the disruptive business model is the cognitive inability of managers of incumbent firms to understand the opportunity and value potential of the disruptive approach (Tripsas & Gavetti, 2000; Zott et al., 2011). Yet, managerial cognition is not the only obstacle; there is also a set of structural factors preventing explorative change: As Teece (2010) succinctly summarizes a large body of literature on the topic, "changing the firm's business model literally involves changing the paradigm by which it goes to market, and inertia is likely to be considerable" (p. 187). This inertia is sometimes referred to as *handicap of the incumbents* (Tripsas, 1997), when the organizational structures, routines and procedures fine-tuned for the existing business model constrain any explorative business model change.

Nevertheless, despite the hardships, some incumbents demonstrate non-dominant responses in Stage 2, of which the most important one is

Integration, embracing both explorative and exploitative changes of the firm's business model. A salient example of this strategy is that of Barnes and Noble in 1997–2009, implying integration of the established business model (brick-and-mortar retail stores) with online selling (through Barnesandnoble.com) and selling e-books (using original Nook eReader).

Stage Three

Finally, the last, third stage of the disrupted industry's evolution, starts when the disruptive business model becomes too lucrative or threatening to procrastinate or delay its adoption any more. At this time, the disruption's market potential becomes apparent, so as the performance overshooting of the traditional business model (Christensen, 1997; Crockett et al., 2013). At this time the majority of incumbents start looking for the ways to integrate both models, by pursuing the integration strategy (combination of both explorative and exploitative business model change), either through internalization of both models within one unit, or through a related diversification (spin-off or autonomous business unit for pursuing disruptive opportunity). It is in Stage 3 when the flaws of the dominant response in the prior Stage 2 become apparent, as the previously pursued pure exploitation did not allow building competences and acquiring the resources necessary for exploring the disruptive business model. Consider the case of Borders: At Stage 3 of the evolution of disrupted retail bookselling industry (in 2010–2011), it was too late to start selling books online; the chance to develop this capability was lost in 1995–2009 when these operations were outsourced to Amazon. As a result, in 2011, Borders declared bankruptcy. Barnes and Noble, on the other hand, was relatively successful pursuing the integration strategy in Stage 3 of the disrupted industry's evolution, as the potential for this was developed in Stage 2, through experimenting with the disruptive business model (through the company's online bookstore and the eBook reader).

However, the anecdotal evidence of the retail book industry does not imply that the dominant behavioral response in Stage 3—integration—is always the optimal one. Arguably, the other three response strategies (including even Defiant Resistance) could be viable for particular incumbents, contingent on their internal situation and market conditions. This issue is elaborated in detail in the next section, discussing the rational response model.

One last observation is worth noting with regards to non-dominant responses, particularly Pure Exploration. On any of the three stages of the disrupted industry's evolution, this strategy of incumbents (i.e., embracing the new business model while neglecting the old one) is highly unlikely. First, it is hard to abandon the core business model, which can still be profitable, in order to switch to something new. Secondly, this transition would require significant alteration of all aspects of business, including resource structure, processes organization, and even ways of thinking. One more important reason for not pursuing this option is strategic consideration: When making this switch, a firm will not be able to leverage the existing resources and competencies, having to build new competencies and to acquire necessary resources from scratch, without any advantage over disrupting newcomers.

Rational Determination: Critical Determinants of the Impact of Disruptive Innovations

Having provided a descriptive overview of the behavioral response patterns of incumbents in disrupted industries, in this section, we develop propositions and provide a richer understanding of rational responses to disruptive BMI, acknowledging the complexity and dynamics of change, and the cognitive and structural drivers of firms' actions.

Rational response model is intended to provide testable propositions concerning the appropriate response of an incumbent firm when facing a disruptive BMI introduced in its industry. The *unit of analysis* within the proposed model is *disruptive BMI by the company*. This statement stresses the fact that a single disruption can require heterogeneous responses from different companies (Bergek et al., 2013; Yu & Hang, 2010), as well as that a single company cannot have a unified approach towards all disruptive BMIs (Charitou & Markides, 2003). Therefore, the model links drivers of responses (innovation-related—market drivers; company-related—organizational enablers) with an optimal response strategy, formulated in terms of explorative or exploitative change of the existing incumbent's business model. The two dependent variables are expected performance outcomes of explorative and exploitative business model changes in response to disruption, reflecting the impact of embracing each of these response strategies on the long-term financial performance of an incumbent firm. Schematically, the discussed in the next section's model is presented in Figure 5.3.

The Role of Market Drivers

The innovation-related determinants of the appropriate incumbent response are summarized in the concept of market drivers.

The first determinant, *market propensity*, reflects the potential demand for the offering of the disruptive BMI (demand for its value proposition to customers), comprising the demand from prior non-consumers and the demand from part of the customers served by the existing business model who migrate to the offering of the disruptive business model. The first component of the demand for the disruptive BMI is particularly noteworthy,

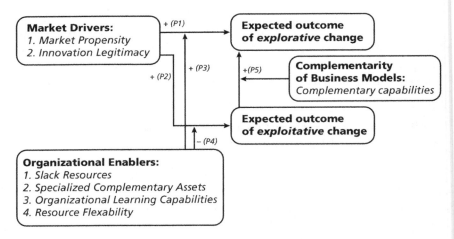

Figure 5.3 Rational response model: Expected outcomes of explorative and exploitative business model changes.

since, as it was noted before, the disruptive innovations usually expand the customer base, attracting former non-consumers (Christensen, 1997; Markides, 2006). The second component of the demand for the disruptive BMI, driven by the migration of consumers of conventional business model, is determined by the propensity of existing customers to switch to the disruptive approach. The ultimate characteristic of the market propensity is the potential for economic value appropriated by an incumbent when serving the customers using the disruptive business model, compared to the value appropriated using the existing business model. The higher the market propensity of the disruptive BMI for a particular incumbent, the higher is the expected outcome of responding to it. Market propensity, in its turn, is influenced primarily by the evolution of customer needs (in the dimensions of performance, functionality, convenience, simplicity, and price (Christensen & Raynor, 2013).

The market propensity is not the sole essential factor determining the appropriate incumbent response, as not all disruptive innovations can be exploited despite their market potential. Consider numerous disruptive innovations in healthcare (such as empowering professional nurses) that cannot be implemented despite the obvious market potential for them; these innovations first need to gain legitimacy in the eyes of powerful stakeholders in the healthcare industry. Hence, the second crucial factor, *innovation legitimacy*, determines whether the offering of the disruptive business model (value proposition to customers) is perceived as legitimate by key stakeholders in the industry. Any changes or innovations in organizational practices, forms, or policies require legitimization before being perceived as an objective reality (Tost, 2011) and being allowed to be implemented. In addition to individual-level legitimacy from the customer perspective, a disruptive BMI also often needs explicit endorsing by the institutional environment through regulatory actions (Kaplan & Tripsas, 2008), such as implicit or explicit approval by regulators, who "measure, credential, or certify innovations" (Ansari & Krop, 2012). Hence, on the most basic level, the innovation legitimacy comprises two components—subjective legitimacy (the evaluation of the innovation by important decision makers [namely, customers] and their influencers), and legal legitimacy (the endorsement of the innovation by authorities, such as government regulators or accrediting bodies).

Therefore, the combination (mathematically: interaction) of market propensity and legitimacy of the disruptive business model determines the salience of market drivers of response to the emerging innovation. A low level on either of these two components prevents the disruptive BMI from gaining momentum; moderate or high levels of components reinforce each other. *Ceteris paribus*, the higher the market drivers of the disruptive innovation for a particular incumbent firm, the higher is the expected outcome of its embracing:

Proposition 1: *Market drivers are positively associated with the expected performance outcome of the incumbent's explorative business model change in response to a disruptive business model innovation.*

However, market drivers of a disruptive BMI facilitate not only its explorative adoption. Even the incumbents who respond in an exploitative manner will still benefit from doing so when facing a disruptive BMI with high market drivers. First, as it was already argued, disruptive BMIs usually expand the industry by appealing to non-consumers, and exploitative strengthening of the existing business model can help an incumbent to benefit from this expansion. Second, if the disruptive business model gains momentum (which is more likely in the case of innovations with high market potential), an incumbent will have to compete with disruptors in the future, and exploitative strengthening of the existing business model will help to protect its market position. Therefore, all other things being equal, exploitative strengthening of the existing business model in response to a disruptive innovation with high market drivers is a rational action:

Proposition 2: *Market drivers are positively associated with the expected performance outcome of the incumbent's exploitative business model change in response to a disruptive business model innovation.*

The Role of Organizational Enablers

In the prior section, we postulated that external market drivers make a proactive business model change (explorative or exploitative) the optimal incumbent strategy when faced with a disruptive BMI. The exact nature of the best response—explorative change, exploitative change, or integration—is determined by internal organizational factors—enablers of the disruptive business model change. The latter term refers to internal contextual factors that make embracing the disruptive business model a viable option.

The first crucial organizational enabler is the availability of *slack resources* necessary for explorative business model change (Hill & Rothaermel, 2003). Explorative business model change often requires long-term investment with uncertain outcomes, and unless an incumbent possesses or can acquire the necessary resources (from existing operations or external sources), explorative change cannot be a viable option. Indeed, the high level of available slack allows an organization to take additional risks and experiment (Mone, McKinley, & Barker III, 1998). This argument is supported by the behavioral theory of the firm (Cyert & March, 1963), arguing that, "slack provides a source of funds for innovations that would not be approved in the face of scarcity but that have strong subunit support" (Cyert & March, 1963, p. 189). Moreover, slack buffers an organization from the downside risk associated with a significant change, and increases the change's legitimacy in the eyes of powerful stakeholders (Singh, 1986). In the case of explorative business model change, the slack resources can be utilized for acquiring generic complementary assets necessary for the change, and for initial launching (experimenting, refinement) of the new business model, until it becomes sustaining.

The second organizational enabler of explorative business model change is the availability of *specialized complementary assets* necessary for the new business model. Adding this enabler is justified by the assumption that BMI requires additional complementary assets (or capabilities) for its deployment in a particular company. Unlike generic complementary assets (which are freely available on the market and are not company-specific), specialized complementary assets are company-specific, and hence must be developed internally. Specialized complementary assets necessary for the disruptive business model can buffer incumbents from the competition and facilitate value appropriation from this innovation (Ansari & Krop, 2012; Teece, 1986; Tripsas, 1997). Examples of such complementary assets include, *inter alia*, specialized manufacturing capabilities and sales/service networks (Tripsas, 1997), strong brand name and corporate reputation (which will make innovation's legitimization and endorsement more easy), or unique network of partners (alliances, joint ventures) supporting the value chain activities necessary for the new disruptive business model.

An explorative business model change is possible only if an incumbent possesses the *organizational learning capabilities*, in that the proper new business model, suiting both external conditions and internal context, can rarely be apparent early on, and those organizations that are well positioned to learn and adjust are more likely to succeed (McGrath, 2010; Teece, 2010). We argue that two key organizational learning capabilities are absorptive capacity and learning orientation. Absorptive capacity (Cohen & Levinthal, 1990; Zahra & George, 2002) represents the incumbent's ability to recognize the value and essential features of the disruptive business model, to assimilate the available knowledge about it, and to apply this knowledge for planning and executing the actual explorative business model change. As such, absorptive capacity is essential for triggering the explorative business model change.

As it was argued before, explorative business model change is not only a one-time radical change but also the following process requiring continuous refinements, adjustments, and learning, as a new sustaining business model cannot be conceived and created at once. Hence, whereas the conceiving of the explorative change is facilitated by absorptive capacity, the crucially important further adjustments require an organizational commitment to learning, open-mindedness, and knowledge-questioning values—a culture of learning orientation (Baker & Sinkula, 1999; Sinkula, Baker, & Noordewier, 1997).

Finally, an explorative business model change is facilitated if an incumbent has *resource flexibility*, or the ability to redeploy the available resources for the disruptive BMI. In some cases, the lack of resource flexibility might lead to lock-in and pursuing the conventional business model. For instance, the traditional airlines might be prevented from a rapid switch to discounted models by existing union agreements, or the traditional steel plants might be stuck with the old, integrated mills technology because of the prior significant investments into the plants (which cannot be easily redeployed to pursue the disruptive mini-mills model).

In summary, the high level of organizational enablers makes explorative business model change the better option in cases of high market drivers of disruptive BMI:

Proposition 3: *Organizational enablers strengthen the positive association between market drivers and expected performance outcome of the incumbent's explorative business model change in response to a disruptive business model innovation.*

On the other hand, in case of exploitative strengthening of the existing business model in response to high market drivers of disruption, the organizational enablers (which are aimed at facilitating explorative adoption of the disruptive business model) become wasted resources, reducing the overall performance outcome. In other words, in the situations of high market drivers, the exploitative business model change becomes an appropriate proactive response only if the organizational enablers are low:

Proposition 4: *Organizational enablers weaken the positive association between market drivers and expected performance outcome of the incumbent's exploitative business model change in response to a disruptive business model innovation.*

The formal Propositions 1–4 can be briefly summarized as follows:

If the market drivers are low, the only optimal incumbent response to a disruptive business model innovation is Defiant Resistance; if the market drivers are high, the optimal response is explorative business model change (in case of high enablers) or exploitative business model change (in case of low enablers).

In other words, as the moderator (organizational enablers) changes on a continuum from low to high, the slope of the "Market Drivers → Outcome of the explorative change" line goes up (counterclockwise), while the slope of the line "Market Drivers → Outcome of the exploitative change" goes down (clockwise).

This framework ignores one important response—integration (both explorative and exploitative changes)—that becomes a viable option in the case of substantive synergy effects between existing and disruptive business models in an incumbent firm.

The Role of Synergy

Sometimes, each business model (existing and disruptive) can reinforce the performance outcome of the other one. Both models can leverage the same complementary assets and capabilities (e.g., sales and support channels, brand name, the corporate reputation of the parent company, technological expertise), achieving by this means economies of scale and scope. An example of this mechanism can be found in the airline industry, where conventional and low-cost business models can share a substantive amount of complementary capabilities (airport infrastructure, trained personnel, IT systems, etc.), leading to a synergistic effect from both explorative and exploitative business model changes. In such cases, simultaneous pursuit of both exploitative strengthening of the existing business model and explorative adoption of the disruptive business model will reinforce the positive performance outcome of both actions:

Proposition 5: *Synergy between existing and disruptive business models (achieved through exploitation of complementary capabilities) increases expected performance outcomes of both exploitative and explorative business model changes.*

Notably, provided the substantive synergy between existing and disruptive business models, the optimal incumbent response to disruptive BMI in cases of high market drivers becomes integration, comprising both explorative adoption of the disruptive business model and exploitative strengthening of the business model, regardless of the level of organizational enablers. In the case of low synergy, on the other hand, the optimal response to disruption is governed by Propositions 1–4.

The Dynamic Perspective

The whole prior argument is based on the static analysis of the determinants of the rational response of incumbents to gaining momentum disruptive innovations; in other words, the propositions are formulated without considering the temporal dimension of the disruption phenomenon. In the real world, both market drivers and organizational enablers are not time invariant. Particularly, most salient changes with time happen along the three dimensions. First, the market propensity develops, driven by the evolution of customer needs (performance, functionality, convenience, simplicity, price; Christensen & Raynor, 2003). Second, the innovation legitimacy changes over time, particularly its regulatory aspect, as sooner or later, the authorities endorse the more efficient disruptive approach. Finally, the organizational enablers are not time-invariant, in that with time, the organization might acquire or develop the necessary specialized complementary assets, needed for embracing the disruptive approach. These three types of change shift the market drivers and organizational enablers of disruptive innovation; ergo, the rational response of an incumbent can change with time. This warrants the dynamic investigation of the rational response, depending on the time-variant parameters.

NORMATIVE RECOMMENDATIONS

Real Options to Manage Contingency

Like all other models discussed in this chapter, the rational and behavioral response models have their shortcomings and limitations when providing normative recommendations for the managers of real-world companies having to choose a response strategy when facing a gaining momentum disruptive BMI. The behavioral model explains the typical response evolution within an industry as the disruption gains momentum, remaining ignorant about performance implications of particular actions. The rational model provides valuable insights regarding the optimal response but demands the ability to accurately predict the exact values of contingency factors (market drivers, organizational enablers, and synergy). As such, it can be very valuable for explaining the performance differential of heterogeneous incumbent responses *ex-post* (after the disruption gained momentum or flattened out), but has limited use for providing *ex-ante* guidance for managers of established incumbent firms. In fact, it is the rational model's unrealistic demands for available information and the decision maker's cognitive abilities that leads to prevalent patterns of incumbent actions in the behavioral model, which usually deviate from the optimal path suggested by *ex-post* rational response model's analysis.

Hence, the main problem of the rational response model for providing the normative ex ante guidance is the essential inability of humans to predict the dynamics of the industry disruption (Benner & Tripsas, 2012; Demil & Lecocq, 2010; Yu & Hang, 2010). Whereas some of the crucial contingencies (particularly organizational enablers: learning capabilities, slack resources, specialized complementary assets) can be estimated ex ante with enough accuracy, others (market drivers: market propensity and innovation legitimacy) cannot be forecasted with the precision enough for strategic decision making. Moreover, some market contingencies are dependent upon the firm's actions (such as the subjective legitimacy of an innovation going substantively up after its endorsement by a dominant incumbent), which adds complexity and dynamics to the disruption process.

Consequently, to be able to infer normative *ex-ante* recommendations based on the rational response model, it must be supplemented with an uncertainty resolution mechanism, such as a real options perspective (Hill & Rothaermel, 2003; McGrath, 2010; Raynor, 2007).

According to real options logic, investments in the development of the disruptive business model are treated as paying the premium for a real option on this approach. This allows managers of the incumbents to possess a call option on the disruptive approach—the ability to execute the option by embracing the disruptive business model and scaling it up if in the future the market drivers for the disruption turn out to be substantive (Hill & Rothaermel, 2003; McGrath, 2010), or the resolution of uncertainty turns out to be in favor of the disruption (Raynor, 2007). Moreover, additional information regarding the disruption is often collected as a by-product of experimentation and implementation of the disruptive approach; this additional information improves the incumbent managers' ability to forecast the market drivers and organizational enablers (of the rational response model), and to build the absorptive capacity with regards to the disruptive approach (Hill & Rothaermel, 2003).

Therefore, on the early stage of the evolution of the disrupted industry (when significant uncertainty still makes impossible the accurate estimation of the market potential of the disruptive approach), the incumbents should invest in both explorative and exploitative business model changes, treating these investments as payment for real options on uncertainty of the future, which limit the downside risk of the change (McGrath, 2010) and prevent the lock-out (Hill & Rothaermel, 2003). On these stages, the contingency factors of the rational response model (market drivers, organizational enablers, synergy) are not known yet; rather, they have to be treated as dimensions to build scenarios of the possible futures (Raynor, 2007). Within each scenario, the contingency factors are assumed to be certain, and the rational response model will yield the optimal response strategy, contingent upon the scenario being materialized. Since in the future, only one scenario will become a reality, and there is no way to find out *ex-ante* which one, a portfolio of real options must support this optimal strategy for each scenario. The latter will make sure that no matter which scenario of the future materializes, the incumbent is not locked out from the winning business model approach at a later stage of the disruption when all significant uncertainties are resolved.

In most cases, the real options approach implies simultaneous investment of small amounts into both explorative and exploitative business model changes; these investments with limited downside potential allow gathering the information about both approaches as the disruption gains momentum, as well as building the portfolio of real options to make sure that regardless of the actual future, the company has the ability to acquire the necessary capabilities to embrace and scale up the winning approach.

Proper Cognitive Framing of the Disruptive Innovation

In the prior section, we discuss how embracing the real options lens for analyzing the investments into exploring the disruptive innovation can remediate the uncertainty of structural factors driving the rational response. In business practice, this rational reasoning should be supplemented by proper cognitive framing of the disruptive innovation, to remove the cognitive barriers of the rational response. We suggest that from the very beginning, the disruptive innovation must be framed in terms of both threat (to existing business model) and opportunity (to profit from the disruptive change). Such dual framing of the disruption in the minds of organizational decision making will lead to cognitive resilience (Dewald & Bowen, 2010; Osiyevskyy & Dewald, 2018), a necessary precondition for experimenting with or embracing the disruptive innovation. As such, the dual threat-opportunity framing of the innovation must supplement the discussed above real options mechanisms when responding to the gaining momentum disruptive innovations.

Internalization or Autonomy

As discussed in this chapter, integration response implies the simultaneous development of two business models, existing and disruptive ones, aiming at leveraging the synergies between them. Moreover, even in the cases of Pure Exploration response (explorative adoption of the disruptive business model only), both business models have to co-exist, at least for some time, before the existing model is abandoned. This raises the question of the proper way of combining and managing the two models in the same organization. Existing extensive literature on the topic of combining multiple business models in one organization stresses two basic approaches for this: internalization of both models in one organization, or creating an autonomous business unit (spin-off) for developing the disruptive business model independently from the existing business model (Christensen & Raynor, 2013; Hill & Rothaermel, 2003; Markides, 2006; Markides & Charitou, 2004; O'Reilly & Tushman, 2008), with most recommendations inclined towards the latter approach (Crockett et al., 2013; Markides & Charitou, 2004).

The internalization approach implies tight coupling of both business models within the same organizational context (organizational structure, incentives system, a system of market information collection, organizational culture), which facilitates maximal exploitation of the synergies between business models. Indeed, keeping both models tightly coupled, as opposed to keeping them independent, facilitates more free flow of information between managers responsible for their development, as well as ensuring the necessary support of the nascent disruptive offering. With benefits, the internalization approach brings potential costs, caused by inherent conflicts between the existing and disruptive business models. These conflicts are caused by different value propositions of the two models, which result in significant incongruities in their supporting transactive and resource structures (e.g., different approaches to serving the customer bases, different cost structures, and different emphasis on activities in value chains). Some authors even argue that these conflicts are so severe and frequent, that "the simultaneous pursuit of different business models within the same organizational unit will lead to a failure to execute one or perhaps both models" (Hill & Rothaermel, 2003, p. 267).

Loose coupling of the existing and disruptive business models through establishing an autonomous business unit for the disruptive approach eliminates the conflicts (Christensen & Raynor, 2013; Hill & Rothaermel, 2003; Markides & Charitou, 2004), but also reduces the benefits from the economies of scale and scope which result from coordinated activities between the two business models.

Therefore, the optimal choice of a governance mechanism for managing two business models is contingent upon the benefits of coordinated activities, achieved within the internalization approach, and costs associated with them. As the prior literature suggests, the costs of keeping both business models in the same organizational context usually substantively exceed the benefits from synergy; hence, the most frequent solution to the innovator's dilemma is establishing a spin-off unit for pursuing disruptive opportunities (Christensen & Raynor, 2013; Hill & Rothaermel, 2003; Markides & Charitou, 2004).

DISCUSSION

Key Insights: Summary

We began the chapter by posing the question of how incumbent firms should respond to emerging disruptive BMIs introduced in their industries, and why the observable actions are usually deviant from the rational path. To provide a comprehensive answer to these broad research questions, we draw heavily on the literature streams on business models and disruptive innovations. We propose a rational response model, anchored in the Osiyevskyy and Dewald's (2015a) typology of incumbent responses (explorative adoption of the disruptive business model versus exploitative development of the existing one), supplemented by a set of testable propositions regarding contingency factors determining optimal incumbent actions when facing a disruptive BMI. We demonstrate the essential groups of contingency factors (market drivers and organizational enablers of the disruptive innovation, synergy, complementarity of the business models), which determine the expected performance outcomes of explorative and exploitative business model changes. In addition, we develop a behavioral model of incumbent firms' responses to disruptive BMIs gaining momentum in their industries, describing and explaining the typical pattern in incumbent firm response (Defiant Resistance → Pure Exploitation → Integration), contingent upon the stage of the disruptive innovation's development. Finally, we supplement the insights of rational and behavioral models with *normative recommendations* for managers of real-world established firms having to make decisions regarding nascent or gaining momentum disruptive BMIs in their industries.

Implications for Theory and Future Research

We see a set of theoretical contributions of the chapter for the nascent literature on business models (Foss & Saebi, 2018; Zott et al., 2011), as well as for the more established literature on disruptive innovations. To the former stream of literature, we add new insights regarding business model change and innovations; while for the latter stream our contribution stems from emphasizing the peculiar features of disruptive BMIs, as opposed to traditional disruptive technologies.

First, we clarify the conceptualization of the essential terms, most notably, BMI and business model change, providing a clear theoretical distinction between the two. This clarification of the key terms is necessary for further development of the BMI field.

Second, we study the complexity of the phenomenon of business model change in response to emerging disruptive innovation, showing two distinct dimensions of this process: explorative and exploitative change. Being developed deductively from existing theories (rather than inductively from the data), the proposed typology of responses is both parsimonious and all-inclusive. None of the two generic approaches is ultimately superior in all situations; rather, it is a set of contextual factors that determine the optimal response (or their combination).

Third, the developed rational response model provides a set of testable propositions (P1–P5) regarding the contextual factors determining the performance outcomes of different types of incumbent responses, uniting prior disparate studies suggesting appropriate responses into a holistic contingency-based model.

Fourth, in the developed behavioral response model, we elaborate on the question of the dynamics of the pattern of incumbent responses to disruptive BMIs introduced in their industries. First time in the literature, the model stresses the temporal aspect of a disruptive BMI process, explaining the reasons for observable behavior in different stages of the disruption.

The obtained theoretical insights open a set of future research streams. The current study stresses the importance of understanding disruptive innovations in today's business environment and the infancy of the literature on the topic, which open the rich opportunity available to researchers.

The employed typology of business model changes can be employed in further studies of business models and disruptive innovations within the descriptive and prescriptive theoretical perspectives, as a parsimonious, holistic conceptualization of the variation of business model change phenomenon.

The developed contingency-based rational responses model opens a fruitful research agenda with the potential for conceptual and empirical studies of the determinants of optimal incumbent actions when facing a disruptive BMI. Particularly promising would be conceptualizing and empirical investigating the impact of crucial contextual factors, market drivers, or organizational enablers. The richest further research agenda opens in relation to the warranted fine-grain analysis of organizational enablers of embracing the disruptive approach, which was only briefly outlined in the current chapter. Potential studies could discriminate between the impact of different types of slack (e.g., absorbed, unabsorbed, potential), or diverse types of organizational learning capabilities (e.g., learning orientation and absorptive capacity).

The other important understudied question is related to the drivers of the contingency factors, most important, what are the determinants of the market drivers (market propensity and innovation legitimacy), and how the actions of established incumbents influence these drivers? How do different aspects of innovation legitimacy (subjective, regulatory) evolve over time? How do incumbents' actions influence innovation legitimacy and market propensity? Answering these questions would make the dynamics of the disruption process more predictable.

Finally, the behavioral view of response also requires further clarification, using the multi-dimensional analysis of strategic decisions and stressing the role of cognition and decision-making in expanding the behavioral stream of strategy research. Particularly interesting is studying the few incumbents who respond to the disruption by Pure Exploration response, or by switching to the new business model without the development of the established one. We argued that such responses are very rare among established players, because of the cognitive barriers and structural inertia preventing radical business model change. Despite being rare, such companies still exist. What drives such responses, and what are their performance outcomes?

Implications for Practice

For managers of incumbent firms, the chapter provides guidance for making appropriate decisions when faced with emerging disruptive BMIs in their industries. The discussed rational response model provides specific advice regarding choosing the optimal response (with highest expected performance outcome), provided full information is available (namely, the future values of contingency factors). The proposed later real options and cognitive resilience lenses provide normative guidance when the assumption of full available information is relaxed. Notably, the dual framing of the disruptive innovation—as both an opportunity and a threat—allows removing the cognitive barriers of the appropriate response.

The other crucial for practice insight of this chapter is the emphasis on internal contingency factors (organizational enablers) when adopting a disruptive business model. We provide a comprehensive (although probably not exhaustive) list of crucial internal success factors for disruptive innovating of the firm, all being within the managerial control: slack resources, specialized complementary assets, and organizational learning capabilities. Strengthening these (most important, having the buffer of slack resources and enhancing organizational learning capabilities) opens up opportunities for real-world companies to increase the likelihood of success of the radical business model change projects.

REFERENCES

Ansari, S. S., & Krop, P. (2012). Incumbent performance in the face of a radical innovation: Towards a framework for incumbent challenger dynamics. *Research Policy, 41*(8), 1357–1374.

Baker, W. E., & Sinkula, J. M. (1999). The synergistic effect of market orientation and learning orientation on organizational performance. *Journal of the Academy of Marketing Science, 27*(4), 411–427.

Barney, J. (1991). Firm resources and sustained competitive advantage. *Journal of Management, 17*(1), 99–120.

Benner, M. J., & Tripsas, M. (2012). The influence of prior industry affiliation on framing in nascent industries: The evolution of digital cameras. *Strategic Management Journal, 33*(3), 277–302.

Bergek, A., Berggren, C., Magnusson, T., & Hobday, M. (2013). Technological discontinuities and the challenge for incumbent firms: Destruction, disruption or creative accumulation? *Research Policy, 42*(6–7), 1210–1224.

Biloshapka, V., & Osiyevskyy, O. (2018). Value creation mechanisms of business models. *The International Journal of Entrepreneurship and Innovation, 19*(3), 166–176.

Casadesus-Masanell, R., & Ricart, J. E. (2010). From strategy to business models and onto tactics. *Long Range Planning, 43*(2), 195–215.

Casadesus-Masanell, R., & Zhu, F. (2013). Business model innovation and competitive imitation: The case of sponsor-based business models. *Strategic Management Journal, 34*(4), 464–482.

Charitou, C. D., & Markides, C. (2003). Responses to disruptive strategic innovation. *MIT Sloan Management Review, 44*(2), 55–63.

Christensen, C. (1997). *The innovator's dilemma: When new technologies cause great firms to fail.* Boston, MA: Harvard Business Review Press.

Christensen, C. (2006). The ongoing process of building a theory of disruption. *Journal of Product Innovation Management, 23*(1), 39–55.

Christensen, C., & Bower, J. L. (1996). Customer power, strategic investment, and the failure of leading firms. *Strategic Management Journal, 17*(3), 197–218.

Christensen, C., Johnson, C. W., & Horn, M. B. (2010). *Disrupting class.* New York, NY: McGraw-Hill.

Christensen, C., & Raynor, M. (2013). *The innovator's solution: Creating and sustaining successful growth.* Boston, MA: Harvard Business Review Press.

Christensen, C., Raynor, M. E., & McDonald, R. (2015). What is disruptive innovation. *Harvard Business Review, 93*(12), 44–53.

Cohen, W. M., & Levinthal, D. A. (1990). Absorptive capacity: A new perspective on learning and innovation. *Administrative Science Quarterly, 35*(1), 128–152.

Crockett, D. R., McGee, J. E., & Payne, G. T. (2013). Employing new business divisions to exploit disruptive innovations: The interplay between characteristics of the corporation and those of the venture management team. *Journal of Product Innovation Management, 30*(5), 856–879.

Cyert, R. M., & March, J. G. (1963). *A behavioral theory of the firm.* Englewood Cliffs, NJ: Prentice-Hall.

DaSilva, C. M., & Trkman, P. (2014). Business model: What it is and what it is not. *Long Range Planning, 47*(6), 379–389.

Demil, B., & Lecocq, X. (2010). Business model evolution: In search of dynamic consistency. *Long Range Planning, 43*(2–3), 227–246.

Dewald, J., & Bowen, F. (2010). Storm clouds and silver linings: Responding to disruptive innovations through cognitive resilience. *Entrepreneurship Theory and Practice, 34*(1), 197–218.

Downes, L., & Nunes, P. F. (2013). Big bang disruption. *Harvard Business Review, 91*(3), 44–56.

Foss, N. J., & Saebi, T. (2018). Business models and business model innovation: Between wicked and paradigmatic problems. *Long Range Planning, 51*(1), 9–21.

George, G., & Bock, A. J. (2011). The business model in practice and its implications for entrepreneurship research. *Entrepreneurship Theory and Practice, 35*(1), 83–111.

Giesen, E., Berman, S. J., Bell, R., & Blitz, A. (2007). Three ways to successfully innovate your business model. *Strategy & Leadership, 35*(6), 27–33.

Gilbert, C. (2003). The disruption opportunity. *MIT Sloan Management Review, 44*(4), 27–33.

Habtay, S. R. (2012). A firm-level analysis on the relative difference between technology-driven and market-driven disruptive business model innovations. *Creativity and Innovation Management, 21*(3), 290–303.

Hill, C. W. L., & Rothaermel, F. T. (2003). The performance of incumbent firms in the face of radical technological innovation. *Academy of Management Review, 28*(2), 257–274.

Hitt, M. A., Ireland, R. D., & Hoskisson, R. E. (2016). *Strategic management: Concepts and cases: Competitiveness and globalization.* Boston, MA: Cengage Learning.

Kaplan, S., & Tripsas, M. (2008). Thinking about technology: Applying a cognitive lens to technical change. *Research Policy, 37*(5), 790–805.

Karimi, J., & Walter, Z. (2016). Corporate entrepreneurship, disruptive business model innovation adoption, and its performance: The case of the newspaper industry. *Long Range Planning, 49*(3), 342–360.

Kim, S. K., & Min, S. (2015). Business model innovation performance: When does adding a new business model benefit an incumbent? *Strategic Entrepreneurship Journal, 9*(1), 34–57.

Leber, J. (2013, March 8). A shrinking Garmin navigates the smartphone storm. *MIT Technology Review.* Retrieved from https://www.technologyreview.com/s/511786/a-shrinking-garmin-navigates-the-smartphone-storm/

March, J. G. (1991). Exploration and exploitation in organizational learning. *Organization Science, 2*(1), 71–87.

Markides, C. (2006). Disruptive innovation: In need of better theory. *Journal of Product Innovation Management, 23*(1), 19–25.

Markides, C. (2013). Business model innovation: What can the ambidexterity literature teach us? *Academy of Management Perspectives, 27*(4), 313–323.

Markides, C., & Charitou, C. D. (2004). Competing with dual business models: A contingency approach. *Academy of Management Perspectives, 18*(3), 22–36.

Markides, C., & Oyon, D. (2010). What to do against disruptive business models (when and how to play two games at once). *MIT Sloan Management Review, 51*(4), 25–32.

McGrath, R. G. (2010). Business models: A discovery driven approach. *Long Range Planning, 43*(2), 247–261.

Miles, R. E., Snow, C. C., Meyer, A. D., & Coleman, H. J. (1978). Organizational strategy, structure, and process. *Academy of Management Review, 3*(3), 546–562.

Mone, M. A., McKinley, W., & Barker, V. L., III (1998). Organizational decline and innovation: A contingency framework. *Academy of Management Review, 23*(1), 115–132.

Nelson, R. R., & Winter, S. G. (2009). *An evolutionary theory of economic change.* Cambridge, MA: Harvard University Press.

O'Reilly, C. A., III, & Tushman, M. L. T. (2008). Ambidexterity as a dynamic capability: Resolving the innovator's dilemma. *Research in Organizational Behavior, 28*, 185–206.

Osiyevskyy, O., & Dewald, J. (2015a). Explorative versus exploitative business model change: The cognitive antecedents of firm-level responses to disruptive innovation. *Strategic Entrepreneurship Journal, 9*(1), 58–78.

Osiyevskyy, O., & Dewald, J. (2015b). Inducements, impediments, and immediacy: Exploring the cognitive drivers of small business managers' intentions to adopt business model change. *Journal of Small Business Management, 53*(4), 1011–1032.

Osiyevskyy, O., & Dewald, J. (2018). The pressure cooker: When crisis stimulates explorative business model change intentions. *Long Range Planning, 51*(4), 540–560.

Osiyevskyy, O., & Zargarzadeh, A. (2015). Business model design and innovation in the process of the expansion and growth of global enterprises. In A. A. Camillo (Ed.), *Global enterprise management* (pp. 115–133). New York, NY: Palgrave Macmillan.

Porter, M. E. (1980). Industry structure and competitive strategy: Keys to profitability. *Financial Analysts Journal, 36*(4), 30–41.

Raynor, M. E. (2007). *The strategy paradox: Why committing to success leads to failure (and what to do about it).* New York, NY: Doubleday.

Rosenkopf, L., & Nerkar, A. (2001). Beyond local search: Boundary-spanning, exploration, and impact in the optical disk industry. *Strategic Management Journal, 22*(4), 287–306.

Sabatier, V., Craig-Kennard, A., & Mangematin, V. (2012). When technological discontinuities and disruptive business models challenge dominant industry logics: Insights from the drugs industry. *Technological Forecasting and Social Change, 79*(5), 949–962.

Sandström, C., Magnusson, M., & Jörnmark, J. (2009). Exploring factors influencing incumbents' response to disruptive innovation. *Creativity and Innovation Management, 18*(1), 8–15.

Schumpeter, J. A. (1934). *The theory of economic development: An inquiry into profits, capital, credit, interest, and the business cycle.* New Brunswick, NJ: Transaction.

Singh, J. V. (1986). Performance, slack, and risk taking in organizational decision making. *Academy of Management Journal, 29*(3), 562–585.

Sinkula, J. M., Baker, W. E., & Noordewier, T. (1997). A framework for market-based organizational learning: Linking values, knowledge, and behavior. *Journal of the Academy of Marketing Science, 25*(4), 305–318.

Sosna, M., Trevinyo-Rodríguez, R., & Velamuri, S. (2010). Business model innovation through trial-and-error learning: The Naturhouse case. *Long Range Planning, 43*(2), 383–407.

Stuart, T. E., & Podolny, J. M. (1996). Local search and the evolution of technological capabilities. *Strategic Management Journal, 17*(S1), 21–38.

Sultan, N., & van de Bunt-Kokhuis, S. (2012). Organisational culture and cloud computing: Coping with a disruptive innovation. *Technology Analysis & Strategic Management, 24*(2), 167–179.

Teece, D. J. (1986). Profiting from technological innovation: Implications for integration, collaboration, licensing and public policy. *Research Policy, 15*(6), 285–305.

Teece, D. J. (2010). Business models, business strategy and innovation. *Long Range Planning, 43*(2–3), 172–194.

The Last Kodak Moment. (2012, January 14). *Economist.* https://www.economist.com/business/2012/01/14/the-last-kodak-moment

Tost, L. P. (2011). An integrative model of legitimacy judgments. *Academy of Management Review, 36*(4), 686–710.

Tripsas, M. (1997). Unraveling the process of creative destruction: Complementary assets and incumbent survival in the typesetter industry. *Strategic Management Journal, 18*(S1), 119–142.

Tripsas, M., & Gavetti, G. (2000). Capabilities, cognition, and inertia: Evidence from digital imaging. *Strategic Management Journal, 21*(10–11), 1147–1161.

Wan, F., Williamson, P. J., & Yin, E. (2015). Antecedents and implications of disruptive innovation: Evidence from China. *Technovation, 39–40,* 94–104.

Yu, D., & Hang, C. C. (2010). A reflective review of disruptive innovation theory. *International Journal of Management Reviews, 12*(4), 435–452.

Zahra, S. A., & George, G. (2002). Absorptive capacity: A review, reconceptualization, and extension. *Academy of Management Review, 27*(2), 185–203.

Zott, C., Amit, R., & Massa, L. (2011). The business model: Recent developments and future research. *Journal of Management, 37*(4), 1019–1042.

CHAPTER 6

BEHAVIORAL STRATEGY AND INTERNATIONAL ATTENTION

Theory and Evidence From Dutch Small- and Medium-Sized Enterprises

Jiasi Fan
Gjalt de Jong
Hans van Ees

ABSTRACT

It has often been observed that real-world managers make strategic decisions that are not in line with the standard assumptions of individual rationality. In part, this empirical anomaly is due to the unrealistic assumptions concerning human behavior in economic models. Our study aims to offer new foundations for the strategic decision making behavior of managers of small and medium-sized enterprises (SMEs). This chapter investigates how export-related factors shape the international attention of SME managers. Based on unique survey data from Dutch SME exporters, our research reveals three important insights. First, there are goal-directed processes in which the international attention of SME managers is determined by a firm's export experience and export diversity. Second, there are stimulus-driven processes in which the in-

Entrepreneurship and Behavioral Strategy, pages 147–177
Copyright © 2020 by Information Age Publishing
All rights of reproduction in any form reserved.

ternational attention of SME managers is determined by export market turbulence. Third, the relationship between export market turbulence and the international attention of SME managers hinges on the presence or absence of an export department within a SME. In so doing, we open the black box of international attention of SME managers and contribute to a growing field of behavioral strategy and entrepreneurship research that aims to strengthen the empirical relevance and practical usefulness of strategy and entrepreneurship research.

INTRODUCTION

Internationalization is a key strategic decision of managers. Despite all efforts, however, an in-depth understanding of variations in internationalization is still lacking to date. We argue that behavioral perspectives are helpful in the understanding of internationalization strategy. Economic theory assumes that economic agents such as managers are rational and that they all behave in the same way. Empirical evidence concerning internationalization and experimental economics show that these assumptions are not in line with real-world strategic decisions—such as internationalization—for firms in general and for small and medium-sized enterprises (SMEs) in particular. We therefore align with behavioral strategy that suggests applying cognitive and social perspectives to management challenges in order to overcome the empirical contradictions (see, e.g., Das [2014] for some perspectives in the recent literature). In line with behavioral strategy scholars, we aim to bring realistic assumptions about the internationalization strategy of SMEs. We study the underlying behavioral mechanisms and determinants of variations in international attention of SME managers. In so doing, this chapter contributes to this relatively new but fast growing research tradition of behavioral strategy and entrepreneurship.

Research on behavioral mechanism underlying firm strategy has attracted considerable interests (Greve, 2008; Joseph & Wilson, 2017). Although the behavioral strategy theory of the firm presumes that firm growth varies with the focus and limits of managerial attention, the actual role played by managerial attention has remained largely implicit. The attention-based view (ABV) is a useful lens through which to investigate this issue. International attention is a key concept in ABV and is defined as "the extent to which top executives invest time and effort in activities, communications, and discussions in order to improve their understanding of the global marketplace" (Bouquet, Morrison, & Birkinshaw, 2009, p. 108). Bouquet and Birkinshaw (2011) discuss how international attention matters for the global strategy and success of large multinationals. International attention is different from a related construct—global mindset. The latter represents "a highly complex cognitive structure . . . and the cognitive ability . . ." (Levy,

Beechler, Taylor, & Boyacigiller, 2007, p. 244). Simply put, a global mindset is about cognitive structures of managers, while international attention is concerned with their practices.

Despite the insights provided by this pioneer work, it tends to consider managerial attention as a prerequisite for a firm's internationalization and performance (Bouquet et al., 2009), ignoring the fact that managerial attention may evolve with a firm's international efforts. The ABV has explained that managerial attention can be determined by immediate contexts and prevailing structures (Ocasio, 1997). Venturing internationally entails environmental (i.e., contextual) changes that enhance or inhibit a firm's competitive advantage, demand organizational (i.e., structural) adaptations in response to various international opportunities and threats, and thus may affect managerial attention.

This chapter explicitly considers the underlying processes that determine international attention. Specifically, we distinguish between goal-directed processes (in which attention is driven by internal goals and incentives; Kanfer & Ackerman, 1989) and stimulus-driven processes (in which attention is driven by external stimuli; Hansen & Haas, 2001). We offer four contributions to the literature. First, we investigate the effects of firm-level export experience and export diversity on international attention as goal-directed processes. Export experience generates a strong belief about the relevance of current operations on the anticipated goal (i.e., internationalization) and therefore may reduce the incentives that encourage managers to pay attention to new international opportunities and information. Export diversity, on the other hand, is likely to increase a manager's international attention in the sense that spreading activities across a large number of export markets not only reinforces the primacy of foreign sales and markets in a firm's business goals but also requires more effort to coordinate.

Second, we examine two specific stimulus-driven processes as attention drivers: export competitive intensity and export market turbulence. Both characterize important and relevant aspects of the export environment and address the point emphasized by Ocasio (1997) that managers pay attention only to salient, important, and relevant aspects. By doing so, we respond to a call for considering goal-directed and stimulus-driven processes simultaneously when studying managerial attention (Ocasio, 2011).

Third, our theoretical arguments are developed in the context of SMEs. While large global companies may provide an appropriate domain for exploring the subject of international attention, it can be argued that developing international attention is particularly imperative for SMEs. SMEs now operate in a world where a firm's core competitive advantage depends on its ability to develop internationally (Lu & Beamish, 2001). International expansion offers SMEs numerous benefits, for example, getting access to a larger customer base, achieving economies of scale, spreading business risks, and so forth (Knight, 2000). Yet SMEs are underrepresented in the international marketplace (OECD, 2008). Among the various barriers encountered, a lack of knowledge about international opportunities and foreign markets acts as a major impediment to SMEs' internationalization (for a review, see Arteaga-Ortiz & Fernández-Ortiz, 2010). Such challenges require a high level of international attention on the part of SME managers. However, there has been little consideration in the literature about how an SME manager's international attention is shaped in these processes.

Fourth, we also examine whether and how the presence of an export department moderates the stimulus-driven processes of international attention. Prior studies on the role of organizational units in shaping managerial attention often assume that different units could hold distinct and sometimes conflicting perspectives, and thus have to compete for managerial attention (Bouquet & Birkinshaw, 2008). This is particularly relevant for large corporations comprising multiple organizational levels and subunits. However, it is also possible that departmentalization in SMEs increases functional specialization in a SME organization and eases a manager's workload. In this respect, SMEs offer a relevant research context as these firms normally have simple structures, with an individual at the top contributing all the attention until some delegation of responsibilities emerges in the firm. An export department can take over certain responsibilities from a manager, including keeping track of changes in the international marketplace. We therefore theorize and test how the effects of environmental stimuli on the international attention of SME managers vary according to the presence/absence of an export department.

The outline of this chapter is as follows. Section two presents the theoretical foundations and hypotheses of our research. Section three presents the data collection and measurement of constructs. The empirical results are in section four. Section five concludes the chapters and offers avenues for future research.

THEORY AND HYPOTHESES

The behavioral theory of the firm was developed by Cyert and March (1963) and has since then inspired a great deal of work on behavioral organization studies and behavioral strategy. In its original formulation, the firm is understood as a problem-solving entity with limited attentional capacity (see Ocasio, 2011). Multiple and perhaps conflict goals among organizational units and members of the firm's political coalition compete for managerial attention (March, 1962). Managerial attention can also be shaped by organizational experience with existing decisions, which determine certain patterns of attention and automatic responses accordingly

(Ocasio, 2011). When failing to meet aspiration levels, problematic search and organizational learning will be triggered in response to performance shortfalls (Greve, 2008). We suggest that managerial attention is driven by organizational goals.

A stimulus-driven attentional process is usually lacking in the behavioral studies of strategy (Ocasio, 2011). However, in an ABV of the firm, the environment provides stimuli for managers to attend to and to make decisions upon (Ocasio, 1997). Attentional processes can be goal-directed (e.g., goals and schemas) and stimulus-driven (e.g., situational and environmental factors; Ocasio, 2011). As such, the ABV can be considered as a specific extension of the behavioral strategy of entrepreneurship, with its emphasis on the interplay among structures, environmental influences, individual, and organization attention. Building upon the ABV, we therefore develop a set of hypotheses that include goal-directed and stimulus-driven processes of international attention. While most behavioral studies of strategy have treated attentional processes implicitly, we bring managerial attention and its foundational processes to the forefront.

Goal-Directed Processes of International Attention

Research into goal-directed processes links attention to incentives (Kanfer & Ackerman, 1989; Ocasio, 2011). In goal-directed processes managerial attention can be driven by knowledge (Swan, 1997), resources and capabilities (Barreto & Patient, 2013), and more straightforwardly, goals (Cyert & March, 1963) or interests (Dutton, Fahey, & Narayanan, 1983). In this chapter, we focus on two firm-level goal-related factors: experience (manifesting knowledge, resources, and capabilities) and strategy (manifesting goals and interests). Experience represents accumulated knowledge and capabilities, which constitute an important base for a firm's competitive advantage. However, experience as such often leads to a strong belief about the relevance of existing knowledge and capabilities for achieving an expected goal, simultaneously reducing incentives for new paradigms or information (Levinthal & March, 1993). As March and Simon (1958) argue, managers often rely on a learned pattern of responses which is structurally reinforced instead of employing new search efforts. Here we draw on learning theory to support our argument (on the relationship between export experience and managers' international attention) as experience reflects a firm's past learning. International attention differs from the concept of learning. For example, learning involves inferences from information (Levinthal & March, 1993), but attention does not. Given this myopia (Levinthal & March, 1993) and inertia (i.e., routine rigidity; Gilbert, 2005), we argue that a firm's export experience may discourage a manager's international attention. A firm's dominant strategy embodies its expectations, interests, and current goals, and will therefore encourage a manager to focus attention in a specific direction (De Clercq, Sapienza, & Zhou, 2014; Ocasio, 2011). We argue that a diversified international market strategy (i.e., export diversity) not only reinforces the importance of foreign sales and markets but also increases the complexity of and demand for coordination efforts, thereby enhancing a manager's international attention.

Export Experience and International Attention

Export experience demonstrates a firm's knowledge with respect to doing business in foreign markets (Kaleka, 2002). Such experience can be an important source in guiding a firm's actions to achieve certain goals in international markets. SMEs with export experience are likely to understand foreign markets better and perceive less uncertainty in their export activities (Tesfom & Lutz, 2006). In addition to knowledge about specific foreign markets, experience also brings about firm-wide routines and procedures resulting from repeated engagement. The latter constitutes an organization's knowledge about how to organize international operations, which has important implications for its future behavior (Eriksson, Johanson, Majkgard, & Sharma, 1997). Routines are also expected to improve task performance by increasing reliability and speed (Bingham & Eisenhardt, 2011). As a firm develops relevant routines, the incentives for its manager to search for a broader range of action alternatives may weaken however. Considering it a contradiction in the entrepreneur's information processing, Zahra, Korri, and Yu (2005) suggest that extensive international experience might prevent managers from identifying new international opportunities, as the experience encourages a rigid focus on familiar areas at the cost of ignoring new information. Similarly, Kaleka (2002) argues that firms could become inflexible as their experiential knowledge increases, maintaining a presence in current markets without further exploration. To that end, we argue that experienced SME managers are less likely to seek new information about international markets constantly. This echoes the view that experience-based attention tends to be narrow, centering on current activities (Gavetti & Levinthal, 2000).

On the contrary, less experienced exporters lack sufficient knowledge about export operations. As Fernhaber and Li (2013) note, a manager's focus of attention varies with information demand at different stages of a venture. New ventures typically pay attention to a broad range of information from their external environments to ensure survival and success. Older ventures, on the other hand, focus attention on specific information that helps gain competitive advantage. In a similar vein, we argue that less experienced exporters require more general knowledge about international markets compared to experienced exporters, in order to be able to address the liabilities of newness and foreignness. Managers of less-experienced exporters have stronger incentives to gather information about local environments, develop a network of overseas contacts and carefully plan export-marketing programs. Therefore, we propose the following:

Hypothesis 1: *Export experience will be negatively associated with the international attention of SME managers.*

Export Diversity and International Attention

Export diversity, often measured by the number of country-markets served, has been used to indicate the degree of market expansion of a firm's export strategy (Dhanaraj & Beamish, 2003; Lee & Yang, 1990). Export diversity reflects a firm's intention to pursue export sales, representing a mode of operation deployed to fulfill the firm's goals in international markets. As such, export diversity reflects a goal-directed process of international attention. As Ocasio (1997) notes, corporate strategy can be understood as a pattern of organizational attention—the distinct focus of a firm's (and its manager's) time and effort on a particular set of issues and factors that are central to the purpose of the firm. The empirical work of De Clercq et al. (2014), for example, shows that an entrepreneurial strategic posture is positively related to a firm's learning efforts in foreign markets. As a firm expands into a larger number of different country-markets, foreign sales and markets become increasingly important to the business goal, thereby motivating the manager to pay more attention to the international marketplace.

It could be argued that a firm's entry into multiple countries might not arise entirely from internal motives but can be triggered by external stimuli (e.g., exchange rates, tax incentives). It is beyond the scope of this study to discuss how such diversity emerges. However, in either case, we argue that the increased task demand associated with diversity is likely to promote a manager's international attention. Specifically, a high level of diversity increases the complexity of a firm's export activities and the ensuing coordination efforts. From an information-processing perspective (Thomas & McDaniel, 1990), managers have to attend to many variables when a firm's strategy involves high levels of diversity and complexity. SMEs that export to large numbers of foreign countries are confronted with various cross-national differences associated with for instance legal frameworks, culture, and customer behavior (Cieślik, Kaciak, & Welsh, 2012). Managing these cross-national differences consumes a manager's time and effort. Therefore, the larger the number of foreign countries a SME serves the more international attention the manager will exhibit. In cases where export diversity is treated as a component of experience (i.e., the geographic scope of export experience; Erramilli, 1991), our theory suggests that the length of export experience and the geographic scope of export experience differ in their effects on a manager's international attention. Taken together, we hypothesize the following:

Hypothesis 2: *Export diversity will be positively associated with the international attention of SME managers.*

Stimulus-Driven Processes of International Attention

Research into stimulus-driven processes centers on how the characteristics of relevant stimuli determine a manager's attention (Hansen & Haas, 2001). A firm's environment provides constant flows of stimuli competing for the manager's attention (Ocasio, 1997). Among the various stimuli, managers tend to allocate attention to those with greater salience, importance, and relevance (Ocasio, 1997). Therefore, environments featured by strong cues in the form of high levels of uncertainty (i.e., manifesting salience; Daft, Sormunen, & Parks, 1988; Garg, Walters, & Priem, 2003) will gain the attention of managers.

Compared with the general environment (e.g., political, economic, and technological), the specific environment of the firm (e.g., competitors and customers) is characterized by higher rates of change, greater complexity and can affect firm performance on a daily basis manifesting importance and relevance (Daft et al., 1988). This is also true for exporters, as Kaleka and Berthon (2006) have observed, noting that competitive intensity and market turbulence are of particular importance to a firm's acquisition of export market information. We therefore focus on two key players in the export environment of the firm: competitors and customers. We argue that uncertainties pertaining to these two players, termed export competitive intensity and export market turbulence, will draw the international attention of managers.

Export Competitive Intensity and International Attention

Competitive intensity concerns the extent of rivalry behaviors among competitors (Jaworski & Kohli, 1993). A hypercompetitive environment features frequent and unpredictable changes in competitors' actions, preventing managers from developing a clear and comprehensive understanding of a situation (Nadkarni & Barr, 2008). While such challenges can make it difficult for managers to identify future competitors (Yu, Wang,

& Brouthers, 2015), certain efforts are needed to maintain a firm's competitive position, for example, to focus on current competitors and track relevant information. In contrast, managers are rarely challenged in an environment characterized by weak competition, and are less prone to refine their knowledge about competitors and the competition. The stability and predictability of a weak competitive environment allow managers to use established knowledge to manage a firm's activities in international markets. As such, we anticipate the following:

Hypothesis 3: *Export competitive intensity will be positively associated with the international attention of SME managers.*

Export Market Turbulence and International Attention

Market turbulence refers to the stability in the composition of a firm's customers and their preferences (Jaworski & Kohli, 1993). In turbulent markets, customers' needs and preferences change constantly. Firms feel the pressure of ambiguity and uncertainty regarding customer behaviors (Sinkula, 1994). Some researchers therefore conclude that strategic planning in this case may no longer be productive as the market is changing at the same time the planning occurs (Sarasvathy, 2009). However, we argue that market turbulence requires actions, for example, to modify products/services and marketing strategies to meet emerging customer needs (Kaleka & Berthon, 2006). Managerial attention can be focused when participating in such actions (Ocasio, 1997). This is also in line with the research on export market orientation, which is different from international attention. The latter represents market-oriented behaviors at the firm level, see Cadogan, Diamantopoulos, & Siguaw, 2002), insofar as that firms operating in turbulent markets experience a greater need to be market-oriented to keep track of emerging changes in markets and to update their understanding and interpretation of markets (Cadogan et al., 2002). Thus, we expect the following:

Hypothesis 4: *Export market turbulence will be positively associated with the international attention of SME managers.*

The Moderating Effect of an Export Department

Researchers have studied the relationship between units in organizations and managerial attention (Bouquet & Birkinshaw, 2008; Dutton & Ashford, 1993; Dutton, Ashford, O'Neill, & Lawrence, 2001). The existing research tends to focus on the competition between (business) units for managerial attention. The main argument set out by the research is that separate business units may have divergent interests and have to compete for the limited managerial attention in order to satisfy these interests in the wider organizational context. While acknowledging this competition perspective on attention, we develop an alternative view which discusses the possibility that functional departmentalization in SMEs may relieve a SME manager's workload, including certain attention efforts.

Organizational design research indicates that the number of departments in a firm usually increases with environmental uncertainty (Daft, 2007). For example, many companies develop research and development (R&D) departments to handle technological change. Similarly, an export department, with its own functionalities, can help monitor and formulate responses to uncertainties emerging in the export environment (Katsikeas, 1994). As such, we argue that the effects of environmental stimuli on the international attention of managers could vary depending on whether an export department is present or not.

This is especially the case for SMEs. Typically, small firms are simple-configured (Mintzberg, 1979), being low in specialization and formalization but high in centralization, as one individual is responsible for all activities (Burton, Obel, & DeSanctis, 2011). Managers in SMEs tend to expend most of their attention alone, until some functional distribution occurs, for example by bringing together relevant staff and resources into a separate department that operates the firm's export activities. The establishment of an export department increases the division of labor (i.e., the distribution of tasks) and thus the functional specialization within the firm (Becker & Murphy, 1992). An export department is responsible for gathering information about foreign markets, locating prospective customers, organizing export activities, delivering export sales reports, and managing business relationships in export markets (Katsikea, Theodosiou, Perdikis, & Kehagias, 2011). Managers do not have to stretch their limited attention to oversee the export environment, since the responsibility is delegated to the specific department. To this end, we posit the following:

Hypothesis 5a: *The presence of an export department will moderate the positive relationship between export competitive intensity and the international attention of SME managers, such that the relationship becomes less positive in the presence of an export department.*

Hypothesis 5b: *The presence of an export department will moderate the positive relationship between export market turbulence and the international attention of SME managers, such that the relationship becomes less positive in the presence of an export department.*

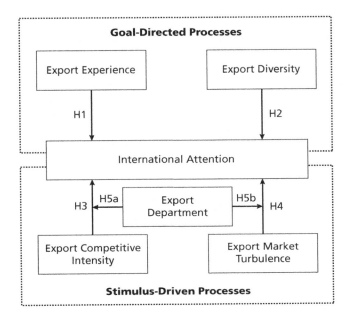

Figure 6.1 Conceptual framework of international attention.

Figure 6.1 presents the hypotheses of this study. Note that we tested and found that there are no significant moderating effects between variables connected to goal-directed and stimulus-driven processes.

METHODS

Sample and Data Collection

To test the hypotheses, we collected new survey data from SME exporters in the Netherlands. The Netherlands offers a suitable context for this study, given that more than 99% of Dutch firms are classified as SMEs according to the definition of the European Union. The exporting Dutch SMEs offer a relevant research context because they show incentives for internationalization (Hessels, 2005).

We employed the Orbis database (Bureau van Dijk, 2014) for our sampling process. To be included in our sample, a firm must: (a) be an SME as defined by the European Union, (b) be engaged in exports—since the export-related features are the main variables of interest, and (c) be independently owned so that the manager's international attention would not be influenced by a parent firm. We identified 1,574 relevant SME companies that met these criteria. From this, we selected a random sample of 750 SME companies and managers to whom we sent our questionnaire.

The data were collected via a structured questionnaire mailed to the owner-manager or the managing director of each of the targeted SME companies. Most of the questions and items used in the survey were adapted from previous studies complemented with questions and items relevant for the specific context of our research. Researchers adept at SME surveys were invited to review the initial instrument. A pilot test through in-depth semi-structured interviews conducted with five SME managers with different export volumes was performed to ensure the quality of the survey. The final tested questionnaire was translated into Dutch following the usual forward-backward translation process (Brislin, 1970). Considering that the empirical data derives from a single survey instrument, we took precautions at this stage to control for common method bias. Following the recommendations of Podsakoff, MacKenzie, Lee, and Podsakoff (2003), we used multi-item constructs. The items for each construct were distributed over different sections of the questionnaire. We also collected archival data whenever possible, as an integrated part of the data collection effort, and used this to cross-validate some of the measures.

The survey was administered with an initial mailing followed by two reminders. A total of 158 responses were obtained from 716 questionnaires that were delivered successfully. After eliminating incomplete questionnaires, a valid sample of 135 responses was obtained representing an effective response rate of approximately 19%. According to Harzing (1997), this is appropriate for a business mail survey.

Measures

Dependent Variable

We used the modified version of the scale of Bouquet et al. (2009) to measure international attention. International attention was operationalized as a high-order construct, which includes three components: international scanning, overseas communications, and internationalization discussions. The specific items corresponding to each component were adapted to and complemented with additional items tailor-made to our SME research setting. All items included in our measure focus on the practices of individual decision makers rather than top management teams, which are usually absent in SMEs. Respondents were asked to indicate the extent to which they behaved in the manner described for each item on a seven-point Likert scale ranging from 1 (very rarely) to 7 (very frequently).

International scanning denotes the environmental surveillance activities through which a manager senses stimuli emerging in the international marketplace. Four items were used to measure this component of international attention: (IA1) collect strategic information (on e.g., customers, competitors, price, promotion, distribution, or the general environment) from around the world; (IA2) organize and/or participate in marketing research (e.g., mail surveys or telephone interviews) to analyze international market developments; (IA3) use public information sources (e.g., the Internet, government programs, or publications) to discover international opportunities; and (IA4) routinely compare the company against key competitors worldwide. Items IA1 and IA4 were drawn directly from Bouquet's original scale. Considering the common tools and assistance used by SMEs in collecting foreign market information (e.g., Hart & Tzokas, 1999; Souchon & Diamantopoulos, 1999), items IA2 and IA3 replacing Bouqet's item (that is, "the use of business intelligence software to analyze global market development").

Overseas communications are defined here as information exchange between SME managers and their overseas contacts. This is motivated by evidence that SME managers tend to rely on personal contacts to acquire market information (Andersen, 2006). To measure this component, we replaced Bouqet's items (which concern media richness and meeting rotation adopted by large multinationals) by three new items: (IA5) attend international trade fairs, exhibitions, and so forth; (IA6) visit foreign contacts on a regular basis; and (IA7) involve foreign contacts in key decision making processes. The final item derives from Bouquet's questionnaire: (IA8) the amount of time spent traveling abroad yearly. It can be expected that managers of international SMEs allocate time to travelling and visiting foreign markets (Andersson & Florén, 2011).

Internationalization discussions are in-house talks and meetings in which SME managers share and discuss important information and decisions regarding their firms' internationalization. While research tends to consider internationalization of SMEs as a random process lacking formal decision making, it has been argued that managers of international SMEs devote more time and effort to formal discussions on internationalization decisions than managers of domestic SMEs do (Andersson & Florén, 2011). We used the following items to measure this component: (IA9) have informal talks with other staff in the firm concerning internationalization decisions; (IA10) make internationalization decisions after a free and open exchange of ideas within the company; (IA11) make internationalization decisions alone (reverse coded); and (IA12) the proportion of total meeting time in a year spent discussing internationalization decisions. All of Bouqet's items pertaining to this dimension of international attention were retained (i.e., items IA9, IA10, and IA11) but the wording was changed to avoid the focus on top management teams. Item IA12 was new and added following the logic that more extensive discussion implies greater international attention (Sonpar & Golden-Biddle, 2008; Tuggle, Schnatterly, & Johnson, 2010).

Independent Variables

The export experience variable was measured by the total number of years a firm has been involved in exporting (He, Brouthers, & Filatotchev, 2013). The variable export diversity was measured by the total number of countries to which a firm exports (Dhanaraj & Beamish, 2003; He et al., 2013). We used the scales of Cadogan, Paul, Salminen, Puumalainen, and Sundqvist, (2001)—which were adapted from Jaworski and Kohli's (1993)—to measure export competitive intensity and export market turbulence. For export competitive intensity, we asked the respondents to indicate on a seven-point Likert scale—ranging from 1 (*strongly disagree*) to 7 (*strongly agree*)—the extent to which they agreed with the following three items: (CI1) there are many promotion wars in our export markets; (CI2) others can match easily whatever one competitor can offer on the market; and (CI3) price competition is a hallmark of our export markets. Export market turbulence was measured with a similar seven-point Likert scale using the following three items: (MT1) our export customers' product/service preferences change quite a bit over time; (MT2) new export customers tend to have different product/service needs from those of our existing export customers; and (MT3) we are witnessing changes in the type of products/services demanded by our export customers.

Moderator

We used a dummy to measure the existence of an export department. A value of 1 was coded if the SME had a separate export department; otherwise a value of 0 was coded.

Control Variables

We used three sets of control variables in the analysis. The first set of control variables accounts for variations in managerial background. We controlled for manager age and manager education. Both have been identified as indicators of a manager's tendency to take risks and his or her capability to understand new knowledge (Hitt, Tihanyi, Miller, & Connelly, 2006), and therefore might determine the manager's international attention. We asked managers to provide their age in years. We measured the manager's education with a list of Dutch education levels and coded them in the following manner: 1 primary school or below; 2 secondary education; 3 secondary vocational education; 4 higher vocational education; and 5 university education. Research has also shown that a manager's international experience potentially has a significant effect on their ability to effectively attend to international stimuli (e.g., Nummela, Saarenketo, & Puumalain-en, 2004). We therefore included a manager's international experience as a control variable, measured by the number of years that a manager had worked, studied, or lived outside the Netherlands.

Firm size has been widely recognized as an indicator of a firm's resources and capabilities to pursue international opportunities (Dhanaraj & Beamish, 2003), thereby influencing the manager's international attention. We controlled for this size effect by including the natural logarithm of a firm's number of employees in the analysis (note that we did not control for firm age because many Dutch SMEs had started exporting since their inception, meaning that including firm age and years of export experience at the same time would risk collinearity).

We finally controlled for potential industry-specific effects. We used the two-digit NACE Rev. 2 industry classification (2008) and classified the sample firms into (A) agriculture, forestry, and fishing; (C) manufacturing; (F) construction; (G) wholesale and retail trade; and (H) transportation and storage. Four industry dummies were created (with the wholesale trade sector as the base case in our analysis).

Common Method and Non-Response Bias Assessment

Since our dependent and explanatory variables were measured with data collected from the same respondent, a risk of common method bias may exist. In addition to the ex ante approaches employed during the questionnaire design, we performed ex post statistical analyses to test for the risks of common method bias (Podsakoff et al., 2003). We first performed a Harman's single-factor test—loading all of the survey variables into an exploratory factor analysis—and examined whether any single factor would emerge from the analysis. We found a seven-factor solution with the first factor (with an eigenvalue of 5.97) accounting for 24.87% of the variance, and a cumulative variance of 66.88% explained by all seven factors. Alternatively, we conducted a confirmatory factor analysis (CFA) to investigate whether all the survey items were loaded on a common "method" factor. The CFA analysis yielded poor model fit to the data (χ^2 [252, $n = 135$] = 759.06, $p < 0.001$, RMSEA = 0.12, GFI = 0.68, NNFI = 0.70, CFI = 0.78). Taken together, these results indicate that the risk of common method bias in our data is relatively low.

To estimate the likelihood of non-response bias, we examined whether the responding and non-responding firms differed significantly with respect to firm age and number of employees. We chose these variables because the data for the variables were available for both groups. No significant differences between these groups for these variables were found ($t = -0.61$, $p = 0.54$ for firm age; and $t = 0.69$, $p = 0.49$ for firm size). We also examined whether there are differences between the early respondents (who replied to the first mailing) and late respondents (who replied to the follow-up mailings), as the latter could be analogous to non-respondents (Armstrong & Overton, 1977). The two groups were compared on firm age ($t = 0.52$, $p = 0.60$), number of employees ($t = -0.52$, $p = 0.61$), exporting experience ($t = 0.24$, $p = 0.81$), and export diversity ($t = -0.01$, $p = 1.00$). The results suggest no significant differences between the early and late respondents offering confidence in the quality of our data.

EMPIRICAL RESULTS

Measurement Assessment

Table 6.1 shows the CFA results for the measure of international attention. In the analysis, item IA8 was dropped due to correlated errors with item IA6 and a low factor loading (0.37). Item IA11 was also dropped due to a low factor loading (0.09). In an exploratory factor analysis, both of two items show high cross-loadings on other items. The final factor structure and measure of international attention provides a good fit to the data (χ^2 [32, $n = 135$] = 36.71, $p = 0.26$, RMSEA = 0.03, GFI = 0.95, NNFI = 0.99, CFI = 1.00). The Cronbach's alpha of the final measure of international attention was 0.89, exceeding the benchmark value of 0.70 as recommended by Nunnally (1978). All items loaded significantly on their respective factors/components (with factor loadings > 0.50). Composite reliability scores ranged from 0.75 to 0.95, higher than the benchmark value of 0.60 recommended by Fornell and Larcker (1981). The values of average variance extracted (AVE) were well above 0.50 in all cases, providing support for convergent validity.

Following Bouquet et al. (2009), we compared the three-factor model of international with two alternatives: (a) a one-factor model that incorporates all items into a single factor, and (b) a two-factor model in which the component of internationalization discussions was retained while the other two components (i.e., international scanning and overseas communications) were combined into one. Both the one-factor model (χ^2 [35, $n = 135$] = 68.94, $p < 0.01$, RMSEA = 0.09, GFI = 0.91, NNFI = 0.97, CFI = 0.98) and the two-factor model (χ^2 [35, $n = 135$] = 67.23, $p < 0.01$, RMSEA = 0.08, GFI = 0.91, NNFI = 0.97, CFI = 0.98) reported a poor fit with the data. The Chi-square difference tests ($\Delta\chi^2$ = [68.94 − 36.71] = 32.23, $p < 0.001$; $\Delta\chi^2$ = [67.23 − 36.71] = 30.52, $p < 0.001$) further allowed us to conclude that international attention is best measured as a higher-order

TABLE 6.1   Confirmatory Factor Analysis of International Attention[a]

Construct/Indicator	Standardized Loadings[b]		CR	AVE
International scanning			0.84	0.56
IA1	0.74			
IA2	0.67	(7.42)		
IA3	0.80	(8.80)		
IA4	0.78	(8.67)		
Overseas communications			0.75	0.51
IA5	0.64			
IA6	0.64	(6.30)		
IA7	0.84	(7.71)		
IA8[c]				
Internationalization discussions			0.75	0.51
IA9	0.81			
IA10	0.76	(8.91)		
IA11[d]		(5.93)		
IA12	0.53			
International attention			0.95	0.87
International scanning	0.88	(8.27)		
Overseas communications	0.98	(7.53)		
Internationalization discussions	0.93	(9.56)		

[a] Seven-point scale ranging from 1 (*very rarely*) to 7 (*very frequently*) unless otherwise indicated; Path coefficients for the leading indicators were set to 1.00 to establish scales; CR = Composite Reliability; AVE = Average Variance Extracted.
[b] *t*-values are in parentheses, with values above 2.33 indicating factor loadings significant at the 0.01 level.
[c] The item was dropped due to correlated errors with item IA6 and low factor loading (0.37).
[d] The item was dropped due to very low factor loading (0.09).

construct with three first-order components. To create an additive measure of international attention that is used in the regression analyses, we first calculated the three component-scores by adding and averaging the corresponding items for each component. The final measure of international attention was obtained by subsequently adding and averaging the values for each of the three components.

Table 6.2 shows the CFA results for the various measurements of the SME firm's export environment. The Cronbach's alpha values exceed the threshold value of 0.70 for both measures (0.86 for the export competitive intensity; and 0.80 for the export market turbulence). The composite reliability values for both measures are above the threshold of 0.60 suggested by

TABLE 6.2 Confirmatory Factor Analysis of Export Environment Uncertainty[a]

Construct/Indicator	Standardized Loadings[b]		CR	AVE
Competitive Intensity			0.86	0.68
CI1	0.81	(10.61)		
CI2	0.76	(9.88)		
CI3	0.90	(12.27)		
(Cronbach's alpha = 0.86)				
Market Turbulence			0.80	0.56
MT1	0.79	(9.60)		
MT2	0.76	(9.19)		
MT3	0.72	(8.61)		
(Cronbach's alpha = 0.80)				

[a] Seven-point scale ranging from 1 (*strongly disagree*) to 7 (*strongly agree*). CR = Composite Reliability. AVE = Average Variance Extracted.
[b] *t*-values are in parentheses, with values above 2.33 indicating factor loadings significant at the 0.01 level.

Fornell and Larcker (1981). The measurement model of these two factors provides a good fit to the data (χ^2 [8, n = 135] = 6.08, p = 0.64; RMSEA = 0.00; GFI = 0.99; NNFI = 1.00; CFI = 1.00). The mean score for each measure was calculated from the items per measure and used to estimate the effects of export competitive intensity and export market turbulence in the regression analyses.

Tests of Hypotheses

Table 6.3 presents the means, standard deviations, and correlations for the variables. To test the hypotheses, we adopted an hierarchical ordinary least squares (OLS) regression estimation technique. Since variables in our models were measured using different scales, all continuous variables were standardized prior use in the regression analyses. To test the interaction effects, product terms were created and included in the models (Aguinis, 2004; Baron & Kenny, 1986).

Before running the regression analyses, we performed the usual tests to assess our data (Hair, Black, Babin, Anderson, & Tatham, 2006). The Breusch-Pagan heteroskedasticity test had a significance level far above 0.1, indicating no evidence of heteroskedasticity (χ^2 [15, n = 135] = 12.26, p = 0.66). The Jarque-Bera test showed non-normality, satisfied at the 0.1 level (χ^2 [2, n = 135] = 3.28, p = 0.19). We tested for collinearity among variables by calculating the variance inflation factor (VIF) for each of the

TABLE 6.3 Descriptive Statistics and Correlations[a]

Variable	Mean	SD	1	2	3	4	5	6	7	8	9	10
International Attention	3.25	1.24	1.00									
Firm Size[b]	18.84	11.24	0.13	1.00								
Manager Age	51.47	9.54	-0.09	-0.08	1.00							
Manager Education	3.57	1.03	0.27	0.07	-0.17	1.00						
Manager International Experience	1.28	4.01	0.26	-0.10	0.13	0.19	1.00					
Export Experience	20.46	14.84	-0.13	0.09	0.12	-0.11	0.09	1.00				
Export Diversity	13.83	17.46	0.35	0.21	-0.05	0.11	0.09	0.40	1.00			
Export Competitive Intensity	3.92	1.52	0.10	-0.07	-0.10	-0.01	-0.04	0.09	-0.02	1.00		
Export Market Turbulence	3.78	1.28	0.22	-0.02	-0.06	-0.10	-0.11	-0.07	-0.02	0.29	1.00	
Export Department	0.13	0.33	0.21	0.14	-0.05	0.03	0.09	0.01	0.30	0.01	0.03	1.00

[a] $N = 135$; values of correlations larger than $|0.17|$ are significant at the 0.05 level, and those larger than $|0.21|$ are significant at the 0.01 level; for presentation purposes, industry dummies are not included and the maximum value of their correlations with all the other variables is $|0.33|$.

[b] The natural logarithm is used for correlations, but the actual values are reported for the descriptive statistics.

regression coefficients in our full model. VIF values ranged from a low of 1.12 to a high of 1.50, well below the cut-off of 10 recommended by Hair et al. (2006). Following Wooldridge's (2015) suggestion, we used robust standard errors in our analysis.

Table 6.4 shows the regression results. Model 1 is the baseline model, which includes the control variables. We added the export experience and export diversity variables in Models 2 and 3, respectively. In Models 4 and 5, we entered the export competitive intensity and export market turbulence variables, respectively. We examined the interaction effects between the two stimulus variables and the presence of an export department in Models 6 and 7. Model 8 presents the full model, which includes all the variables and the interaction effects. The various fit parameters show that our model fits the data increasingly well. The adjusted R-square improves significantly from 10% in Model 1 to 33% in Model 8. The estimates remain robust in terms of signs and significance levels. We focus our discussions on the results obtained from Model 8. The results of the control variables are in line with expectations and indicate that manager education and international experience each have a significant impact on international attention.

For our main variables of interest, Model 8 shows that export experience has a negative and statistically significant relationship with a manager's international attention ($b = -0.37$, $p < 0.001$). Hypothesis 1 is therefore supported. The positive and statistically significant coefficient for export diversity confirms its positive relationship with international attention ($b = 0.48$, $p < 0.001$). Hence, Hypothesis 2 is also supported.

The main effect of export competitive intensity is not significant. Hypothesis 3 is therefore not supported. In contrast, Model 8 shows that export market turbulence is positively related to international attention ($b = 0.34$, $p < 0.001$). Therefore, Hypothesis 4 is supported.

Contrary to our expectations, the presence of an export department does not influence the relationship between export competitive intensity and international attention ($b = -0.31$, not significant). Hypothesis 5a is therefore not supported. However, Model 8 shows that the effect of export market turbulence on international attention becomes less positive in the presence of an export department with a significant negative parameter estimate for this interaction effect ($b = -0.80$, $p < 0.05$). Hypothesis 5b is therefore supported. We plot this moderating effect in Figure 6.2 following Dawson's (2014) suggestion. Figure 6.2 shows that the slope between export market turbulence and international attention becomes negative in the presence of an export department. One possible explanation for this could be that managers are more likely to delegate relevant responsibilities to an export department to free up their attention when they are under excessive pressure caused by high levels of market turbulence. In contrast, when market turbulence is low, managers may feel less stressed and choose

TABLE 6.4 Regression Results: Exporting and International Attention in Dutch SMEs[a]

Variable	Model 1	Model 2	Model 3	Model 4	Model 5	Model 6	Model 7b	Model 8b
Constant	2.53 (0.45)***	2.62 (0.46)***	2.78 (0.39)***	2.75 (0.38)***	2.66 (0.38)***	2.61 (0.37)***	2.65 (0.37)***	2.61 (0.37)***
Agriculture[c]	-0.32 (0.28)	-0.32 (0.28)	-0.20 (0.24)	-0.13 (0.24)	-0.13 (0.22)	-0.12 (0.22)	-0.15 (0.22)	-0.14 (0.22)
Manufacturing[c]	-0.23 (0.25)	-0.25 (0.25)	-0.33 (0.24)	-0.27 (0.24)	-0.29 (0.24)	-0.29 (0.24)	-0.39 (0.24)	-0.38 (0.24)
Construction[c]	-0.11 (0.28)	-0.18 (0.28)	-0.01 (0.32)	0.14 (0.33)	-0.02 (0.39)	-0.03 (0.37)	-0.19 (0.34)	-0.19 (0.33)
Transportation[c]	0.02 (0.59)	-0.12 (0.56)	-0.09 (0.54)	-0.15 (0.60)	-0.19 (0.56)	-0.25 (0.54)	-0.18 (0.58)	-0.19 (0.59)
Firm Size	0.16 (0.10)	0.18 (0.10)†	0.09 (0.09)	0.11 (0.09)	0.11 (0.09)	0.10 (0.09)	0.10 (0.08)	0.10 (0.08)
Manager Age	-0.08 (0.10)	-0.06 (0.10)	-0.00 (0.10)	0.02 (0.10)	0.02 (0.09)	0.03 (0.09)	0.03 (0.09)	0.03 (0.09)
Manager Education	0.24(0.11)*	0.22 (0.11)*	0.17 (0.10)†	0.17 (0.09)†	0.20 (0.09)*	0.21 (0.09)*	0.20 (0.09)*	0.21 (0.09)*
Manager International Experience	0.28 (0.08)***	0.31 (0.08)***	0.27 (0.07)***	0.28 (0.07)***	0.30 (0.07)***	0.29 (0.06)***	0.28 (0.07)***	0.28 (0.06)***
Export Experience		-0.18 (0.09)*	-0.39 (0.11)***	-0.42 (0.10)***	-0.39 (0.10)***	-0.39 (0.10)***	-0.36 (0.10)***	-0.37 (0.10)***
Export Diversity			0.53 (0.10)***	0.55 (0.10)***	0.53 (0.10)***	0.51 (0.11)***	0.47 (0.11)***	0.48 (0.11)***
Export Competitive Intensity				0.18 (0.10)†	0.09 (0.10)	0.11 (0.10)	0.04 (0.09)	0.07 (0.10)
Export Market Turbulence					0.28 (0.09)**	0.27 (0.09)**	0.35 (0.09)***	0.34 (0.09)***
Export Department						0.20 (0.33)	0.30 (0.28)	0.31 (0.28)
Department × Competitive Intensity						-0.20 (0.40)		-0.31 (0.29)
Department × Market Turbulence							-0.75 (0.33)*	-0.80 (0.35)*
F	5.13***	5.27***	8.84***	8.86***	10.74***	9.88***	9.23***	8.51***
R2	0.15	0.17	0.31	0.33	0.38	0.38	0.40	0.41
ΔR^2		0.02*	0.14***	0.02†	0.05**	0.00	0.02*	0.03*
Adjusted-R2	0.10	0.11	0.26	0.27	0.32	0.31	0.33	0.33

[a] $N = 135$; robust standard errors are in parentheses; † $p < 0.1$, * $p < 0.05$, ** $p < 0.01$, *** $p < 0.001$; all continuous variables are standardized.

[b] The ΔR^2 values of Model 7 is calculated based on Model 5; The ΔR^2 values of Model 8 is calculated based on Model 6.

[c] The base industry is wholesale trade.

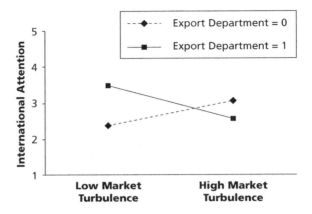

Figure 6.2 Export department, export market turbulence, and international attention.

to pay personal attention to international markets, despite the availability of a dedicated export department.

Robustness Analyses

We performed additional tests to examine the robustness of our findings. Table 6.5 presents these results. First, we examined whether our results remain robust with an alternative measure for the dependent variable—international attention—using the factor scores instead of the average score for the three components. Panel A in Table 6.5 shows that this does not affect our results.

Second, we tested the hypothesized relationships for each of the three components of international attention independently. Panel B in Table 6.5 shows that the main effects of export experience, export diversity, and export market turbulence remain robust for all three models. The results for the moderating effect of an export department remain consistent with the hypotheses with "international scanning" and "overseas communications" as a dependent variable. The moderation effect is not supported for "internationalization discussions" as a dependent variable. The negative sign of the coefficient suggests that the effect of export market turbulence on internationalization discussions does become less positive in the presence of an export department, albeit that the moderating effect is not as strong as for the other two components of international attention.

TABLE 6.5 Exporting and International Attention: Robustness Analyses[a]

Variable	Panel A	Panel B		
	IA Measured by Factor Scores	International Scanning	Overseas Communications	Internationalization Discussions
Constant	-0.38 (0.22)†	2.20 (0.46)***	3.37 (0.44)***	2.24 (0.39)***
Agriculture[b]	-0.08 (0.13)	0.17 (0.27)	-0.07 (0.29)	-0.51 (0.26)*
Manufacturing[b]	-0.23 (0.14)	-0.33 (0.28)	-0.48 (0.27)†	-0.33 (0.27)
Construction[b]	-0.09 (0.20)	-0.13 (0.42)	-0.65 (0.38)†	0.21 (0.35)
Transportation[b]	-0.14 (0.35)	-0.05 (0.99)	-0.45 (0.67)	-0.06 (0.44)
Firm size	0.06 (0.05)	0.04 (0.10)	0.12 (0.11)	0.14 (0.10)
Manager age	0.02 (0.06)	0.10 (0.13)	-0.03 (0.11)	0.02 (0.10)
Manager education	0.13 (0.05)*	0.26 (0.11)*	0.14 (0.11)	0.24 (0.10)*
Manager international experience	0.16 (0.04)***	0.19 (0.15)	0.38 (0.07)***	0.26 (0.09)**
Export experience	-0.22 (0.06)***	-0.49 (0.10)***	-0.40 (0.13)**	-0.22 (0.11)†
Export diversity	0.29 (0.06)***	0.50 (0.12)***	0.52 (0.13)***	0.41 (0.12)***
Export competitive intensity	0.04 (0.06)	0.04 (0.12)	0.13 (0.12)	0.04 (0.11)
Export market turbulence	0.20 (0.06)***	0.34 (0.11)**	0.35 (0.12)**	0.32 (0.10)**
Export department	0.20 (0.17)	0.29 (0.29)	0.29 (0.35)	0.36 (0.36)
Department × Competitive intensity	-0.19 (0.17)	-0.33 (0.27)	-0.63 (0.38)	0.02 (0.34)
Department × Market turbulence	-0.48 (0.21)*	-0.76 (0.31)*	-1.13 (0.43)**	-0.51 (0.44)
F	8.36***	6.76***	6.97***	5.57***
R2	0.40	0.31	0.37	0.33
Adjusted-R2	0.32	0.23	0.29	0.25

[a] $N = 135$; robust standard errors are in parentheses; † $p < 0.1$; * $p < 0.05$, ** $p < 0.01$, *** $p < 0.001$; all continuous variables are standardized.

[b] The base industry is wholesale trade.

DISCUSSION

Strategic decisions of SMEs are taken by managers who, unlike what mainstream economics postulates, are not completely rational and who each make their own decisions that inherently are different. This results in variations of outcomes such as, in our case, variations in international attention. We therefore argue that behavioral strategy offers important guidelines to understand real-world variations in outcomes of strategic decision making processes. We translate this view in our focus on international attention of SME managers as the dependent variable. We also incorporate a behavioral strategy view by incorporating goal-directed and stimulus processes that each determine variations in international attention of SME managers. That is, this chapter investigated how the international attention of SME managers is determined by goal-directed and stimulus-driven processes. The results obtained from 135 Dutch SME exporters offer convincing support for the majority of our hypotheses. For goal-directed processes, we found strong evidence that the international attention of SME managers is influenced by a firm's export experience and export diversity. For stimulus-driven processes, we found that export market turbulence determines the international attention of SME managers. Our study shows that the presence of an export department moderates the relationship between export market turbulence and the international attention of SME managers. Contrary to our expectations, export competitive intensity has no significant impact on the international attention of SME managers. Taken together, we offer new theoretical insights and empirical evidence for a behavioral strategy of SME international attention. The following contributions are worthwhile highlighting.

First, studies of international attention as a strategy focus are far and in between. Our study is among the first to explain variations in international attention for SMEs. The few available studies in strategy and management research, uses managerial attention or related constructs (such as managerial mindsets) as a dependent variable, that is, to account for variations in a firm's internationalization or other strategy outcomes. We are among the first to use international attention as the dependent variable and developed a set of hypotheses to understand variations in the international attention of SME managers. The unique focus on SMEs and on international attention is the first contribution of our study. Given the newness of our study, we present and test simple and direct causal relationships between the various goal-directed and stimulus-response variables and international attention. It opens doors for more dynamic and complex relationships between managerial attention and a firm's international venturing in future research for which this study offers points of departure.

Second, the few studies that also have examined the determinants of managerial attention focused largely on goal-directed issues only (Ocasio, 2011). Our study contributes to this literature by developing dual attention-shaping processes that embrace both goal-directed and stimulus-driven factors in order to understand how SME managers allocate attention to the international marketplace. In so doing, our study offers a more generic theory of SME international attention. This is the second contribution of our research.

Third, our findings regarding the moderating effect of an export department offer contributions to an relatively underdeveloped area of research in SME strategy studies: The impact of organizational structures on strategy and behavior of SME managers. In the presence of an export department, our study shows that increased export market turbulence is less likely to gain the international attention of SME managers. Small firms are usually simply structured organizations in which often many strategic and decision making responsibilities are taken by one individual (Miocevic & Crnjak-Karanovic, 2011). However, even SMEs tend to organize themselves and we show that variations in such SME organizational structures matter for understanding variations in the international attention of SME managers. For the same reason, departmentalization and delegation in these firms can largely alleviate attention demands placed on the individual manager. This is also in line with organizational-design thinking (Daft, 2007), in the sense that a certain structure is required to manage environmental challenges. This is the third important contribution of our research.

Finally, we make a contribution to the behavioral strategy and ABV literature by developing our understanding of international attention of SME managers. Prior research focuses exclusively on large companies (Bouquet & Birkinshaw, 2008; Bouquet et al., 2009; Ocasio, 1997). Our research complements these studies by analyzing managerial international attention in SMEs, by collecting new data and by developing a measurement of international attention tailor-made for the research context of SME managers. Our study therefore presents a conceptualization and a measurement of the international attention of SME managers, which offers various promissory future research opportunities including an international comparison of our Dutch context to other contexts.

Managerial Implications

Our study provides various implications for SME managers. First, evidently we show that exporting and the associated goal-associated factors and external stimuli could affect a manager's international attention. Years of experience in exporting may be valuable in improving a firm's responsiveness to market changes. Our findings, however, also suggest that this firm-wide experience may cause myopia in, for example, a manager's international searching efforts. Managers therefore need to be vigilant about such myopia and be attentive to the international marketplace.

Second, it is also evident that SME managers can rely on export strategies to sustain their international attention. A diversified strategy in market expansions can remind managers of the salience and importance of foreign sales and resources, and thus continuously focus their attention on the international marketplace.

Third, the insights generated in this research could help managers design appropriate organizational structures to cope with information overabundance, ambiguity, and uncertainty, and improve the chances of allocating their attention to the issues of utmost importance. SME managers who implicitly or explicitly delegate tasks to exporting personnel or organize activities into a subunit may experience less export market turbulence compared to managers who choose to take all responsibilities. Delegation or organizational structures may therefore be important for SME firms that have ambitions to foster the international position of their firms.

Limitations and Directions for Future Research

No study is perfect and ours is no exception. This study is subject to limitations, which open avenues for future research. First, we controlled for potential country effects by limiting our sample to Dutch SME exporters. An international study of SME international attention offers an opportunity to cross-validate the findings of our research and to test the generalizability of our findings to SME exporters outside the Netherlands.

Second, we used a dummy variable to indicate the presence or absence of an export department. While this is an important first step towards detecting the moderation effect of organizational SME structures on behavioral strategy relationships, the measure is not sufficiently nuanced to capture specific features and characteristics (e.g., size or age) of such organizational SME units. These characteristics may offer a more in-depth perspective of the international attention of SME managers. Future research could extend our work by developing measurements that allow for analyzing attention variations among SMEs with an export or other departments, depending on the specific characteristics of that department.

Third, our model is estimated with cross-sectional data thereby limiting the analyses of more time-varying dynamic relationships. Although this is common in strategy research, there might be dynamic features underlying the relationships between the international attention of SME managers and its determinants. For example, it can be argued that the adaptation of a firm's export strategy and the evolution of the international attention of the SME manager may not be independent from each other, but develop simultaneously in co-evolutionary processes. Future research could use our research and construct dynamic models using time-series or panel data. Panel data or comprehensive longitudinal case studies permit tracing changes in managerial attention and its root causes over time.

Finally, our thinking is guided by the presumption that international attention of SME managers is a crucial element for the ongoing international success of SMEs. However, having international attention perhaps is a necessary but sufficient condition for successful international SME leadership. Future research could address related but new questions such as how individual international attention can be integrated into firm-level capabilities. It would also be interesting to study how other behavioral dimensions such as personality traits or leadership of culturally different team attributes affect the impact of the international attention of SME managers on SME firm performance.

REFERENCES

Aguinis, H. (2004). *Regression analysis for categorical moderators*. New York, NY: Guilford Press.

Andersen, P. H. (2006). Listening to the global grapevine: SME export managers' personal contacts as a vehicle for export information generation. *Journal of World Business, 41*(1), 81–96.

Andersson, S., & Florén, H. (2011). Differences in managerial behavior between small international and non-international firms. *Journal of International Entrepreneurship, 9*(3), 233–258.

Armstrong, J. S., & Overton, T. S. (1977). Estimating nonresponse bias in mail surveys. *Journal of Marketing Research, 14*(3), 396–402.

Arteaga-Ortiz, J., & Fernández-Ortiz, R. (2010). Why don't we use the same export barrier measurement scale? An empirical analysis in small and medium-sized enterprises. *Journal of Small Business Management, 48*(3), 395–420.

Baron, R. M., & Kenny, D. A. (1986). The moderator-mediator variable distinction in social psychological research: Conceptual, strategic, and statistical considerations. *Journal of Personality and Social Psychology, 51*(6), 1173–1182.

Barreto, I., & Patient, D. L. (2013). Toward a theory of intraorganizational attention based on desirability and feasibility factors. *Strategic Management Journal, 34*(6), 687–703.

Becker, G., & Murphy, K. M. (1992). The division of labor, coordination costs, and knowledge. *Quarterly Journal of Economics, 107*(4), 1137–1160.

Bingham, C. B., & Eisenhardt, K. M. (2011). Rational heuristics: The "simple rules" that strategists learn from process experience. *Strategic Management Journal, 32*(13), 1437–1464.

Bouquet, C., & Birkinshaw, J. (2008). Weight versus voice: How foreign subsidiaries gain attention from corporate headquarters. *Academy of Management Journal, 51*(3), 577–601.

Bouquet, C., & Birkinshaw, J. (2011). How global strategies emerge: An attention perspective. *Global Strategy Journal, 1*(3–4), 243–262.

Bouquet, C., Morrison, A., & Birkinshaw, J. (2009). International attention and multinational enterprise performance. *Journal of International Business Studies, 40*(1), 108–131.

Brislin, R. W. (1970). Back-translation for cross-cultural research. *Journal of Cross-Cultural Psychology, 1*(3), 185–216.

Burton, R. M., Obel, B., & DeSanctis, G. (2011). *Organizational design: A step-by-step approach.* Cambridge, England: Cambridge University Press.

Bureau van Dijk (2014). *Orbis company information around the globe.* Brussels, Belgium: Author.

Cadogan, J. W., Diamantopoulos, A., & Siguaw, J. A. (2002). Export market-oriented activities: Their antecedents and performance consequences. *Journal of International Business Studies, 33*(3), 615–626.

Cadogan, J. W., Paul, N. J., Salminen, R. T., Puumalainen, K., & Sundqvist, S. (2001). Key antecedents to "export" market-oriented behaviors: A cross-national empirical examination. *International Journal of Research in Marketing, 18*(3), 261–282.

Cieślik, J., Kaciak, E., & Welsh, D. H. B. (2012). The impact of geographic diversification on export performance of small and medium-sized enterprises (SMEs). *Journal of International Entrepreneurship, 10*(1), 70–93.

Cyert, R. M., & March, J. G. (1963). *A behavioral theory of the firm.* Englewood Cliffs, NJ: Prentice Hall.

Daft, R. L. (2007). *Understanding the theory and design of organizations.* Nashville, TN: South-Western.

Daft, R. L., Sormunen, J., & Parks, D. (1988). Chief executive scanning, environmental characteristics, and company performance: An empirical study. *Strategic Management Journal, 9*(2), 123–139.

Das, T. K. (Ed.). (2014). *Behavioral strategy: Emerging perspectives.* Charlotte, NC: Information Age.

Dawson, J. F. (2014). Moderation in management research: What, why, when, and how. *Journal of Business and Psychology, 29*(1), 1–19.

De Clercq, D., Sapienza, H. J., & Zhou, L. (2014). Entrepreneurial strategic posture and learning effort in international ventures: The moderating roles of operational flexibilities. *International Business Review, 23*(5), 981–992.

Dhanaraj, C., & Beamish, P. W. (2003). A resource-based approach to the study of export performance. *Journal of Small Business Management, 41*(3), 242–261.

Dutton, J. E., & Ashford, S. J. (1993). Selling issues to top management. *Academy of Management Review, 18*(3), 397–428.

Dutton, J. E., Ashford, S. J., O'Neill, R. M., & Lawrence, K. A. (2001). Moves that matter: Issue selling and organizational change. *Academy of Management Journal, 44*(4), 716–736.

Dutton, J. E., Fahey, L., & Narayanan, V. K. (1983). Toward understanding strategic issue diagnosis. *Strategic Management Journal, 4*(4), 307–323.

Eriksson, K., Johanson, J., Majkgard, A., & Sharma, D. D. (1997). Experiential knowledge and cost in the internationalization process. *Journal of International Business Studies, 28*(2), 337–360.

Erramilli, M. K. (1991). The experience factor in foreign market entry behavior of service firms. *Journal of International Business Studies, 22*(3), 479–501.

Fernhaber, S. A., & Li, D. (2013). International exposure through network relationships: Implications for new venture internationalization. *Journal of Business Venturing, 28*(2), 316–334.

Fornell, C., & Larcker, D. F. (1981). Structural equation models with unobservable variables and measurement error: Algebra and statistics. *Journal of Marketing Research, 18*(3), 382–388.

Garg, V. K., Walters, B. A., & Priem, R. L. (2003). Chief executive scanning emphases, environmental dynamism, and manufacturing firm performance. *Strategic Management Journal, 24*(8), 725–744.

Gavetti, G., & Levinthal, D. (2000). Looking forward and looking backward: Cognitive and experiential search. *Administrative Science Quarterly, 45*(1), 113–137.

Gilbert, C. G. (2005). Unbundling the structure of inertia: Resource versus routine rigidity. *Academy of Management Journal, 48*(5), 741–763.

Greve, H. R. (2008). A behavioral theory of firm growth: Sequential attention to size and performance goals. *Academy of Management Journal, 51*(3), 476–494.

Hair, J. F., Black, W. C., Babin, B. J., Anderson, R. E., & Tatham, R. L. (2006). *Multivariate data analysis* (6th ed.). Upper Saddle River, NJ: Pearson Prentice Hall.

Hansen, M. T., & Haas, M. R. (2001). Competing for attention in knowledge markets: Electronic document dissemination in a management consulting company. *Administrative Science Quarterly, 46*(1), 1–28.

Hart, S., & Tzokas, N. (1999). The impact of marketing research activity on SME export performance: Evidence from the UK. *Journal of Small Business Management, 37*(2), 63–75.

Harzing, A.-W. (1997). Response rates in international mail surveys: Results of a 22-country study. *International Business Review, 6*(6), 641–665.

He, X., Brouthers, K. D., & Filatotchev, I. (2013). Resource-based and institutional perspectives on export channel selection and export performance. *Journal of Management, 39*(1), 27–47.

Hessels, J. (2005). *Internationalisation of Dutch SMEs.* Working Paper No. M200507, Economisch Instituut Midden en Klein Bedrijf, Zoetermeer, The Netherlands.

Hitt, M. A., Tihanyi, L., Miller, T., & Connelly, B. (2006). International diversification: Antecedents, outcomes, and moderators. *Journal of Management, 32*(6), 831–867.

Jaworski, B. J., & Kohli, A. K. (1993). Market orientation: Antecedents and consequences. *Journal of Marketing, 57*(3), 53–70.

Joseph, J., & Wilson, A. J. (2017). The growth of the firm: An attention-based view. *Strategic Management Journal, 39*(6), 1779–1800.

Kaleka, A. (2002). Resources and capabilities driving competitive advantage in export markets: Guidelines for industrial exporters. *Industrial Marketing Management, 31*(3), 273–283.

Kaleka, A., & Berthon, P. (2006). Learning and locale: The role of information, memory and environment in determining export differentiation advantage. *Journal of Business Research, 59*(9), 1016–1024.

Kanfer, R., & Ackerman, P. L. (1989). Dynamics of skill acquisition: Building a bridge between intelligence and motivation. In R. Sternberg (Ed.), *Advances in the psychology of human intelligence* (Vol. 5, pp. 83–134). Hillsdale, NJ: Erlbaum.

Katsikea, E., Theodosiou, M., Perdikis, N., & Kehagias, J. (2011). The effects of organizational structure and job characteristics on export sales managers' job satisfaction and organizational commitment. *Journal of World Business, 46*(2), 221–233.

Katsikeas, C. S. (1994). Export competitive advantages: The relevance of firm characteristics. *International Marketing Review, 11*(3), 33–53.

Knight, G. (2000). Entrepreneurship and marketing strategy: The SME under globalization. *Journal of International Marketing, 8*(2), 12–32.

Lee, C. S., & Yang, Y. S. (1990). Impact of export market expansion strategy on export performance. *International Marketing Review, 7*(4), 41–51.

Levinthal, D. A., & March, J. G. (1993). The myopia of learning. *Strategic Management Journal, 14*(2), 95–112.

Levy, O., Beechler, S., Taylor, S., & Boyacigiller, N. A. (2007). What we talk about when we talk about "global mindset": Managerial cognition in multinational corporations. *Journal of International Business Studies, 38*(2), 231–258.

Lu, J. W., & Beamish, P. W. (2001). The internationalization and performance of SMEs. *Strategic Management Journal, 22*(6/7), 565–586.

March, J. G. (1962). The business firm as a political coalition. *Journal of Politics, 24*(4), 662–678.

March, J. G., & Simon, H. A. (1958). *Organizations.* New York, NY: Wiley.

Mintzberg, H. (1979). *The structuring of organizations.* Englewood Cliffs, NJ: Prentice Hall.

Miocevic, D., & Crnjak-Karanovic, B. (2011). Cognitive and information-based capabilities in the internationalization of small and medium-sized enterprises: The case of Croatian exporters. *Journal of Small Business Management, 49*(4), 537–557.

Nadkarni, S., & Barr, P. S. (2008). Environmental context, managerial cognition, and strategic action: An integrated view. *Strategic Management Journal, 29*(13), 1395–1427.

Nummela, N., Saarenketo, S., & Puumalainen, K. (2004). A global mindset – a prerequisite for successful internationalization? *Canadian Journal of Administrative Sciences, 21*(1), 51–64.

Nunnally, J. (1978). *Psychometric theory.* New York, NY: McGraw-Hill.

Ocasio, W. (1997). Towards an attention-based view of the firm. *Strategic Management Journal, 18*(S1), 187–206.

Ocasio, W. (2011). Attention to attention. *Organization Science, 22*(5), 1286–1296.

OECD. (2008). *Removing barriers to SME access to international markets.* Paris, France: Author.

Podsakoff, P. M., MacKenzie, S. B., Lee, J.-Y., & Podsakoff, N. P. (2003). Common method biases in behavioral research: A critical review of the literature and recommended remedies. *Journal of Applied Psychology, 88*(5), 879–903.

Sarasvathy, S. D. (2009). *Effectuation: Elements of entrepreneurial expertise.* London, England: Edward Elgar.

Sinkula, J. M. (1994). Market information processing and organizational learning. *Journal of Marketing, 58*(1), 35–45.

Sonpar, K., & Golden-Biddle, K. (2008). Using content analysis to elaborate adolescent theories of organization. *Organizational Research Methods, 11*(4), 795–814.

Souchon, A. L., & Diamantopoulos, A. (1999). Export information acquisition modes: Measure development and validation. *International Marketing Review, 16*(2), 143–168.

Swan, J. (1997). Using cognitive mapping in management research: Decisions about technical innovation. *British Journal of Management, 8*(2), 183–198.

Tesfom, G., & Lutz, C. (2006). A classification of export marketing problems of small and medium-sized manufacturing firms in developing countries. *International Journal of Emerging Markets, 1*(3), 262–281.

Thomas, J. B., & McDaniel, R. R. (1990). Interpreting strategic issues: Effects of strategy and the information-processing structure of top management teams. *Academy of Management Journal, 33*(2), 286–306.

Tuggle, C. S., Schnatterly, K., & Johnson, R. A. (2010). Attention patterns in the boardroom: How board composition and processes affect discussion of entrepreneurial issues. *Academy of Management Journal, 53*(3), 550–571.

Wooldridge, J. (2015). *Introductory econometrics: A modern approach.* Boston, MA: Cengage Learning.

Yu, C. L., Wang, F., & Brouthers, K. D. (2015). Competitor identification, perceived environmental uncertainty, and firm performance. *Canadian Journal of Administrative Sciences, 33*(1), 21–35.

Zahra, S. A., Korri, J. S., & Yu, J. (2005). Cognition and international entrepreneurship: Implications for research on international opportunity recognition and exploitation. *International Business Review, 14*(2), 129–146.

CHAPTER 7

PARTNERING WITH WHOM AND HOW?

Institutional Transition and Entrepreneurial Team Formation in China

Chenjian Zhang
Guido Möllering

ABSTRACT

Extant literature suggests that entrepreneurs tend to form a team with their existing committed ties. However, contextual influence on entrepreneurial team formation remains underexplored. We offer a contextual- and process-oriented study by examining entrepreneurial team formation in the context of institutional transition. Based on the comparative analysis of two groups of Chinese entrepreneurs' teaming behaviors, this study finds that a founding institutional environment defines the nature and degree of political risk and market risk and the degree of resource munificence at the macro environmental level, and further through its effects on entrepreneurs' use of prior experience and venturing demands at the individual and organizational level, it impacts how entrepreneurs compose teams and develop trust. Based on these findings, our study provides an institutional perspective on entrepreneurial team formation processes.

Entrepreneurship and Behavioral Strategy, pages 179–207

INTRODUCTION

In entrepreneurship literature, accumulated evidence has demonstrated that team-founded ventures achieve better performance than individually founded ventures (Birley & Stockley, 2000; Doutriaux, 1992; Klotz, Hmieleski, Bradley, & Busenitz, 2014). Research from interpersonal attraction theory explained that individuals are attracted to those they have more exposure and proximity to and those who share similarity in many ways (Huston & Levinger, 1978), thus entrepreneurs are naturally inclined to draw team members from their close circles such as family members, relatives, friends, and previous colleagues and business associates because of prior shared experience and familiarity about members' knowledge, skills, and personal characteristics and partnering with those ties requires less effort to develop team cohesion (Ensley, Pearson, & Amasone, 2002; Kamm & Nurick, 1993; Katz, 1982; Ruef, Aldrich, & Carter, 2003). However, other studies find that teaming up with new partners could facilitate access to diverse resources and expertise and enhance venture performance (Grandi & Grimaldi, 2003; Hmieleski & Ensley, 2007; Shrader & Siegel, 2007). Despite these insights, questions related to the team formation process—how and why entrepreneurs seek venture partners, where they look, what criteria they use for selection and how they develop trust—have been insufficiently addressed (Kamm, Shuman, Seeger, & Nurick, 1990).

Entrepreneurial team formation is featured with the process of scrutinizing, communicating, and bonding (Ucbasaran, Lockett, Wright, & Westhead, 2003; Vyakarnam, Jacobs, & Handelberg, 1999). This exchanging behavior is likely to be affected by a venture's founding environment. Venture context provides "situational opportunities and constrains that affect the occurrence and meaning of organizational behavior" (Johns, 2006, p. 386). In particular, a venture's founding environment functions as "a surrogate for environmental stimuli" and affects entrepreneurs' economic and social relationships (Johns, 2006, p. 392). Studies have shown a founding environment such as environmental uncertainty, social structure, resources availability affects entrepreneurs' decision making, opportunity development, and performance (Chrisman, Bauerschmidt, & Hofer, 1998; Eisenhardt & Schoonhoven, 1990; Ravasi & Turati, 2005). However, the role of a founding environment has not been sufficiently explored, taking it into account could "yield a more interpretable and theoretically interesting pattern" (Rousseau & Fried, 2001, p. 4) for understanding entrepreneurial teaming behaviors.

Our study examines the role of a founding environment on an entrepreneur's team formation by focusing on a venture's founding institutional environment. In our context, entrepreneurial team is defined as the team consists of members taking part in venture creation and early development and having financial interest and influence in strategic decisions (Ensley

et al., 2002; Gartner, Shaver, Gatewood, & Katz, 1994). A founding institutional environment creates "a bundle of stimuli" (Johns, 2006, p. 388)
that structures opportunities and constrains and shapes entrepreneurs'
meaning-making and response patterns. Formal institutions consist of policies and laws that regulate market exchange. Informal institutions such as
norms, values, and beliefs delineate roles and expectations that guide entrepreneurial behaviors (Jennings, Greenwood, Lounsbury, & Suddaby, 2013;
Puffer, McCarthy, & Boisot, 2010; Scott, 2008). Prior research has shown
a founding institutional environment affects entrepreneurs' resource acquisition (Martens, Jennings, & Jennings, 2007), legitimacy seeking (Lounsbury & Glynn, 2001), and networks (Puffer et al., 2010; Zhang, Tan, &
Tan, 2016). Recent research has paid increasing attention to understand
how institutional change might affect and change these behaviors (Beckert, 1999; Sine & David, 2003), in particular in the context of transitional
economies (Guo & Miller, 2010; Peng, 2003; Smallbone & Welter, 2012).
However, it remains underexplored regarding the effects of a founding institutional environment and the process of entrepreneurial team formation
in the context of institutional change. Thus we ask: "How do entrepreneurs
form their teams under different founding institutional environments during the institutional transition?"

To answer this question, we conducted a comparative study of two groups
of Chinese entrepreneurs who started their ventures under different founding environments during the market-oriented institutional transition since
1992. Based on rich qualitative data, our study discovered the effects of a
founding institutional environment on entrepreneurial team formation: At
the macro level, different founding institutional environments define the nature and degree of political risk and market risks as well as degree of resource
munificence, and further through its effect on entrepreneurs' use of prior
experience and venturing features at the micro level, it impacts how entrepreneurs compose teams and develop trust relationships. Our study provides
an institutional perspective that enables future exploration of the impacts
of a founding environment, entrepreneurs' experience, and venturing demands and their interaction on the process and strategy of team formation.

THEORETICAL BACKGROUND

Institutional Environment and Exchange Relationship

As "rules of the game" (North, 1990, p. 3), institutions reduce uncertainty, facilitate the shared understanding of acceptable behaviors, and encourage trustworthy behaviors between exchange partners (Nguyen & Rose,
2009; Zucker, 1986). In particular, institutional environment shapes how

actors configure ties and develop trust with their exchange partners. First, institutional environment shapes with whom the actor forms an exchange relationship, in particular, it shapes to what extent actors feel secure about exchange with unfamiliar others. If the institutional context is uncertain or does not effectively reduce uncertainties and risks, it reinforces the existing relationships and impedes adding new ties (Beckman, Haunschild, & Phillips, 2004; Möllering & Stache, 2010). Second, institutional environment influences how actors develop trust (Möllering, 2006a, 2006b). For example, in an environment where institutional-based trust (Zucker, 1986)—a set of shared expectations derived from formal social structures and system—is weak, process-based trust (Zucker, 1986)—trust produced based on past or expected exchanges between specific actors—might become more important. Child and Möllering (2003) find that in China, where the institutional foundation for trust remains underdeveloped, active trust development is particularly valuable for exchange relationships between foreign managers and local staff. Nguyen and Rose (2009) show that in Vietnam, where the market institutions are underdeveloped, entrepreneurs actively build trust with new business partners by establishing rapport and sharing business information and practice.

Entrepreneurial Team Formation in Transitional Economies

The institutional environment of transitional economies has been featured with high environmental uncertainty and risks because of weak property rights protection and underdeveloped market structure (Nee, 1992; Peng & Heath, 1996). Studies have shown sweeping institutional transition has a profound impact on entrepreneurs' entry rates, resource acquisition, opportunity development, legitimation activities, and business networks (Ahlstrom & Bruton, 2002; Estrin, Meyer, & Bytchkova, 2005; Manolova, Eunni, & Gyoshev, 2008; Peng, 2003; Smallbone & Welter, 2001; Webb, Tihanyi, Ireland, & Sirmon, 2009). However, we know little about how institutional transition—featured with different institutional environments at different periods—affects and diverges entrepreneurs' team formation process.

Nevertheless, prior literature drawing from a network perspective provides clues to understand how institutional environment influences business tie formation and trust development. For example, during the early transition in Russia and Ukraine, dysfunctional institutions and ill-conceived rules discourage trust in strangers and limit business exchanges to existing ties (Guseva & Rona-Tas, 2001; Radaev, 2002). Researchers expect that the development of regulative institutions would encourage developing ties and trust in unfamiliar others who could provide diverse resources and opportunities (Cook, Rice, & Gerbasi, 2004; Peng & Zhou, 2005).

Research with a China focus has contributed to understanding why business relationships and trust are formed in an underdeveloped institutional environment and how they are subject to change during the transition. For example, Tan, Yang, and Veliyath (2009) find that during China's transition from a centrally planned economy to a market economy, entrepreneurs of small- and medium-sized enterprises (SMEs) tend to develop business relationships and trust with strangers in the market. The trust literature has categorized two types of trust: *affective trust* as a mode of trust emphasizes emotional bond and obligation and *cognitive trust* as a mode of trust focuses on knowledge about each other's resources, capabilities, and reliability (McAllister, 1995; Smith & Lohrke, 2008). Chua and his colleagues (Chua, 2012; Chua, Morris, & Ingram, 2009) find that, with China's globalization process, cognitive trust becomes increasingly important for conducting international business. These studies focus on understanding how entrepreneurs and managers develop ties and trust with external business ties, yet we know little about how entrepreneurs compose their teams and develop trust relationships in the context of institutional transition.

Taken together, although extant research provides insights into how institutional environment affects entrepreneurs' behaviors and external networks, it offers little knowledge about how entrepreneurs form teams during the institutional transition. Although research drawing from the network perspective provides some clues about external network formation and trust development in transitional economies, entrepreneurial team formation is distinctive as it involves more cautious tie selection and swift partnering process and requires stronger trust and closer working relationships (Klotz et al., 2014) that fit into environment and ventures to facilitate partner's contribution. Given this research gap, we ask: "How do entrepreneurs form their teams under the different founding institutional environments during the institutional transition?"

RESEARCH METHODS

Research Site and Sampling

The large-scale, unprecedented changes during China's institutional transition provide an opportunity to study entrepreneurial team formation behavior and its variance. Recognizing its "phase transition" characteristics, researchers have demarcated China's institutional transition into different periods, of which two are widely recognized as critical for private entrepreneurship (Peng, 2003; Tan, 2007). The 1992–2001 period marks the early stage of market-oriented transition. After the 1989 Tiananmen Incident, the central government set back its economic liberalization measures. In 1992, Deng Xiaoping's Southern Tour reinvigorated the reform process. In 1989, there were only 1,071 registered private enterprises with a gross output of 50 million RMB (SUFEP, 2008). In a single year of 1992, the registered number of private enterprises in Shanghai grew by 84.1% compared to 1991 (*Shanghai Municipal Statistical Bureau*, 1994). The period after 2002 marks the deepening of the market-oriented transition. In 2002, the Communist Party modified its constitution to encourage, support, and guide the development of the private sector. We selected Shanghai as our research site as its private entrepreneurship development well reflects China's institutional transition. After China obtained WTO membership in 2002, Shanghai's integration into the global economy accelerated. The number of private enterprises doubled, increased from 224,662 in 2002 to 498,900 in 2007 (SUFEP, 2008, pp. 4–12).

Our study employed a qualitative approach to address the research question. In particular, we adopted a comparative research design to explore and explain potential variations among studied entrepreneurial populations (Lewis & Nicholls, 2014). We sampled two groups of entrepreneurs based on the time they started up their ventures. The first group of entrepreneurs started up their ventures in the period of early market-oriented transition 1992–2001 (P1), they are labeled as "early entrepreneurs" (EEs). The second group started up their ventures in the period of deepening market-oriented transition 2002–2009 (P2, this study was conducted in 2009), labeled as "new entrepreneurs" (NEs). The comparative design allowed us to identify potential variations of teaming behaviors and explain their underlying mechanisms.

Data Collection

The fieldwork was conducted by the first author in Shanghai from May through October, 2009. We identified potential respondents via personal contacts and organizational recommendations. Because age effect might induce different teaming behaviors, we selected entrepreneurs who started their ventures when they were 20–35 years of age. Given our comparative design, respondents were selected to reflect their diversity (Lewis & Nicholls, 2014). Thus we did not restrict the selection to a particular industry. This enables us to examine the differences both within and across entrepreneur groups (Eisenhardt & Graebner, 2007). We identified 16 EEs and 17 NEs and conducted semi-structured interviews with them.

Interview questions consisted of three parts. First, we asked respondents about their background, prior experience, and perception and interpretation of their founding institutional environment. Second, employing an open-ended format (Turner, 2010), we asked why they started up their ventures, what challenges they faced during the emergence stage, with whom they discussed venturing ideas, and whether they started up alone or with someone else. Third, we followed up with questions to identify how they selected partners and developed trust with them. The interviews ranged from 90 to 120 minutes, and they were recorded by the first author and transcribed by research assistants.

Data Analysis

Data analysis followed three main steps. Figure 7.1 illustrates the analytical process and data structure emerged from this inductive study. First, we used an open coding technique (Corbin & Strauss, 1998, pp. 101–121) to identify properties and dimensions of concepts relevant to entrepreneurial team formation and its contextual influence. These codes typically described whether a focal entrepreneur formed a team, and if so, from where she found team members, and how she developed trust with them. These codes were then grouped into themes of "team composing" and "trust developing" as two major processes of team formation. We further coded data to identify the contextual influence. For example, we identified "political risk," "market risk," and "resource munificence," which depict entrepreneurs' understanding of their founding institutional environment. We also identified entrepreneurs' "prior experience," which includes "existing ties" and "interactive experience," and "venturing demands," which includes "resource needs" and the need to reduce "relational risk" and/or "performance risk." These codes depict individual and organizational factors that are relevant to team formation.

Second, we adopted an axial coding technique to identify relationships among coded concepts and themes (Corbin & Strauss, 1998, pp. 123–142). We moved back and forth between data, themes, and emerging patterns until we obtained adequate understanding (Eisenhardt, 1989) of the relationship between a founding institutional environment and team formation process. We began to see patterns and mechanisms by which the two groups differ in the team formation process.

Third, we used a selective coding technique to search for a more focused answer to our research question by reassembling coded data and integrating themes to form theoretical explanations (Corbin & Strauss, 1998, pp. 143–161). The analysis involved continuous movement between data and theory to refine constructs, validate explanations, explain variations, and trim excess ones (Corbin & Strauss, 1998, p. 156). Based on our analysis, we theorized

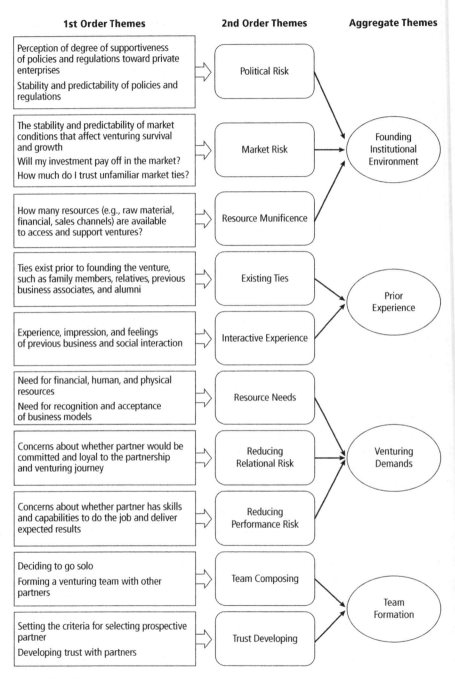

Figure 7.1 Exploratory data analysis for entrepreneurial team formation.

that a founding institutional environment generates macro environmental impact, and its influence on team formation is mediated through entrepreneurs' responses by taking into account micro factors such as prior experience and venturing demands. Below, we describe entrepreneurs' distinctive team formation patterns and explain the underlying mechanisms.

RESULTS

In our quest to explore how entrepreneurs form early teams under different institutional environments during the institutional transition, we compared two groups of Chinese entrepreneurs who founded their ventures in the early market-oriented transition period (P1) and deepening market oriented transition period (P2). Based on inductive analysis, we uncovered how entrepreneurs compose teams and develop trust relationships that suit their founding environment and venturing demands. The outcome of the analysis is the model that is presented in Figure 7.2 and elaborated throughout the results section.

As the first element in the model, we identified the role of founding institutional environments in shaping the nature and degree of environmental risk—political risk and market risk—and the degree of resource munificence. Political risk refers to politically generated circumstances and changes which may constrain business activities (Fitzpatrick, 1983; Kobrin, 1982). Market risk refers to the unforeseen condition affecting size, growth, and accessibility of market (Parhankangas, 2007; Ruhnka & Young, 1991). Resource munificence refers to the extent to which resources are plentiful or scarce to support ventures (Anderson & Tushman, 2001; Koka, Madhavan, & Prescott, 2006). The macro effect of a founding institutional environment shapes the propensity of going solo or forming teams—to what extent entrepreneurs are willing and able to find new team partners.

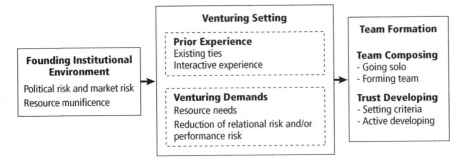

Figure 7.2 Founding institutional environment and entrepreneurial team formation.

Embedded in a different founding institutional environment, team formation is also affected by a venturing setting which includes an entrepreneur's prior experience and venturing demands. We find that during the team formation, how entrepreneurs consider and use their prior experience such as existing ties and interactive experience for team partnership also hinges on their understanding of their founding environment. Venturing demands depict a venture's resource needs and the necessity and urgency to reduce relational risk and/or performance risk. Relational risk addresses "the probability and consequences of a partner not fully committing to a relationship and not acting in the manner expected" and performance risk concerns the probability and consequences of not being able to achieve goals due to certain constraints such as a lack of competence and expertise (Das & Teng, 1996; Das & Teng, 2004, p. 101). The consideration of these two types of collaborative risk affects an entrepreneur's search scope (i.e., team composing) and trust developing strategies. The following section elaborates the model and findings in detail.

EARLY ENTREPRENEURS' (EEs') TEAM FORMATION

Team Composing

In the early stage of market transition, EEs perceived discriminatory policies and regulations towards private enterprises. Although the government started to reduce intervention into market and business, to a great extent, resources such as financial capital, raw materials, and sale channels were still largely controlled by government agencies and affiliated entities. The underdeveloped market factors and interwoven relationship between business and government created a high degree of market risk and political risk and low degree of resource munificence, leading EEs to go solo or team up with existing ties.

Going Solo: Exploiting Political Ties to Facilitate Venture Emergence
Under the condition of low resource munificence, existing ties with government officials could mitigate this limitation and facilitate new venture emergence. Some EEs ($N = 4$) received significant help from their friends, schoolmates, students, and former colleagues who were working in government agencies, and thus became solo entrepreneurs. For example, EE-8 and EE-6 both worked in government departments before founding their own ventures. When the government launched reforms to separate administrative functions from enterprise management, political ties helped them transform those entities into private business (see Table 7.1, II.1). EE-1 helped his schoolmate commercialize safety products when he was lecturing at a local public security college. Meanwhile, his former students who

TABLE 7.1   Early Entrepreneurs (N = 16)* : Team Formation

Major Pattern	Team Composing[a] and Trust Developing[b]	The Role of Founding Institutional Environment and Entrepreneurs' Response	Illustrative Quotes
Going solo (N = 6)	Exploiting political ties to facilitate venture emergence[a] Entrepreneurs (N = 4) obtained business opportunities from friends, schoolmates, students, and previous colleagues who were working in government departments.	The underdeveloped market condition and interwoven relationship between business and government created high political risk and relational risk, leading to solo entrepreneurship.	II.1 "At that time, the State-owned Enterprises were undergoing system reform. Enterprise needed to be separated [from administration]. So I asked them [government officials] if they could hand over the advertisement department to me and let me to run it. They really handed it to me, because we were very familiar with each other. Then I started up a firm and stripped the administrative relationship from the Planning and Construction Bureau." (EE-8)
Teaming up with existing ties (N = 10) Source: Family members, relatives, friends, alumni, schoolmates, and former colleagues.	Engaging familiar ties to secure commitment [a] Entrepreneurs formed teams with familiar ties to protect against potential opportunistic behaviors and secure commitment to nascent ventures.	The unstable and unconducive policy environment, underdeveloped market system, and low resource munificence affected entrepreneurs in forming teams with existing ties to reduce market risk and relational risk.	II.2 "At that time, two of them and I had very good relationships at colleges. We were all members of the Student Union. There was another one, we grown up together….We started up together. This is a low cost and effective way of teaming up. As classmates, we know each other very well. (EE-15)

(continued)

TABLE 7.1 Early Entrepreneurs (N = 16)[a]: Team Formation (Continued)

Major Pattern	Team Composing[a] and Trust Developing[b]	The Role of Founding Institutional Environment and Entrepreneurs' Response	Illustrative Quotes
	Affective filtering: using interpersonal matching leads to "somewhere"[b] Entrepreneurs selected partners by checking and confirming match in personality and social values. Interpersonal matching led entrepreneurs to form teams before business idea was elaborated.	In the context of high market risk and low resource munificence, entrepreneurs were mainly concerned about relational risk. Teaming up with existing ties through affective filtering could secure resource access and reduce relational risk.	II.3 "Business investment looked like this. When you just gradually developed, nobody wanted to invest in your business. These [companies] wanted investment were generally very big...I didn't have much resources; however, I didn't do what may cause me to lose my share....A previous roommate from my school, he made fortune by doing clothing business. He had some resources to initiate our business....As college classmates, we knew each other very well. He supported me because he appreciated some of my qualities. He was willing to contribute, I then started collecting some money and tried to do this business." (EE-16)
	Affective consolidating: Sharing joys and hardships to nourish devotion[b] Entrepreneurs consolidated affective trust by expressing care and concerns and sharing joys and hardship to strengthen emotional attachment and resource contribution.	Early reform created market turbulence and posed challenges and investment unpredictability. Through affective consolidating, entrepreneurs reinforce partners' commitment and contribution, thus reducing relational risk.	II.4 "It was a hard time. However, we endured all hardships. We discussed together and worked on small things. We started from disassembling and loading parts, then gradually involved sales...Gradually, we involved in purchase, production, quality control, etc." (EE-15)

worked in the public security office helped him open the product market and soon he embarked on his own business. These solo entrepreneurs exploited such opportunities and understood that political ties embedded in the context of high political risk entailed high relational risk: Turnover of government officials would cause business turbulence and disclosure of such informal exchange would lead both parties into trouble. In order to reduce the relational risk, they went solo and did not form a team to share this type of connection and business opportunities.

Teaming Up: Engaging Familiar Ties to Secure Commitment

The majority of EEs ($N = 10$) drew team members from their existing ties such as family members, relatives, alumni, former colleagues, and business associates. To their observation, the policies and regulations toward private business were uncertain and unfavorable, the nascent market lacked variety and dynamics of resources such as financial capital, raw materials, and labor, and there were only a few people engaged in private business. These conditions engendered high market risk as venture investment payoffs were uncertain, which caused EEs' concern about the relational risk. For example, EEs faced the difficulties of getting bank loans and they were concerned that if they teamed up with someone they did not know well, they might be taken advantage of and not able to secure sustained resource commitment. EEs realized that only familiar ties would take the risk to invest in these nascent ventures and offer timely financial, labor, and emotional support. Thus, EEs initiated and co-started ventures with these ties who could provide resources and offer protection against relational risk, as EE-15 described it as an "effective solution" (II.2). Similarly, EE-2 faced the difficulties of getting venturing resources, thus he teamed up with his brother-in-law to secure resource access:

> I suffered a lot in Shenzhen [in getting a bank loan and running business]. So I felt it was very important to have a platform. Therefore, I returned to Shanghai and we formed a company. My brother-in-law and me. He was asked to take the role as the director of Pudong Private Entrepreneur Association. He was doing the similar business. At that time, not so many people were involved in private business. I got married very late, at around 40. I was frowned upon by other people. They didn't run private business.

Trust Developing

Although existing ties were generally associated with familiarity, EEs still consolidated attachment to invoke their willingness to undertake market risk and devote resources to the nascent ventures. EEs were mainly engaged in "affective filtering" to find personal match and "affective consolidating" to cultivate partner dedication, thus reducing relational risk in partnership.

Affective Filtering: Using Interpersonal Matching to Lead to "Somewhere"

In the early market-oriented transition period, new ventures were challenged by the condition of low resource munificence and high market risk; entrepreneurs needed timely help to fulfil the gaps in financial capital and human capital. When teaming up with prospective partners from their existing circle, EEs put little emphasis on specific competence requirements; instead, they emphasized on finding a good match in personality and behavioral styles. This interpersonal matching was used to check, demonstrate, and confirm whether both an entrepreneur and potential partner had the quality of integrity, generosity, and benevolence, which were regarded by EEs as the foundation for teaming up. For example, EE-16 was concerned that introducing investment and partnership from unfamiliar parties was likely to cause business uncertainty and the risk of losing control. He started his health products sale business with his previous college roommate because of mutual understanding and validation of personal qualities (II.3).

A common pattern shows that in the emergence stage, entrepreneurs did not have a clear idea about how a particular business might work out, but after validating interpersonal match with their selected familiar ties, they formed teams, tried out, and developed business ideas. In other words, business followed *after* familiarity and trust were in place. For example, EE-14 had two friends working in different industries, it was their good personal relationship that pulled them together to co-start the business. He was not very sure what the exact business might look like, but his team believed this partnership would lead to "somewhere." With this belief, they gradually developed business ideas and achieved business success. As he said:

> At the beginning, it's just like a couple of good friends wanted to do something. We never thought that our company was developing so fast and we never thought about our sales [were so good]. We just thought that if we could survive for 6 years, the company would be matured.

Affective Consolidating: Sharing Joys and Hardships to Nourish Devotion

Under the context of market turbulence during the market transition, EEs further consolidated affective attachment to reinforce partners' commitment and devotion to the new ventures. Their typical activities included expressing care and concerns and sharing joys and hardship together (II.4). Back in 1997, EE-10 was working as a dean of a state-owned research institute. He realized that the market turbulence caused by institutional reform was going to affect his subordinates' work and life. He felt a sense of obligation to take care of his colleagues and provide a shelter from the massive reorganization and layoffs, as he said, "We needed to overcome the difficulties all together." He thus called upon several of his subordinates to start up their own business and strengthened the emotional attachment to consolidate their trust and devotion to the new venture:

> We [with colleagues] discussed secretly: How large we wanted to make, how to get the money, and how to get the customers . . . We wanted to make money all together, making profit alone is not interesting. We needed to overcome the difficulties all together. Then a group of younger men followed me. Our former head who was old and retired knew that we were doing our own business, he came and said to me: "I want to join in."

NEW ENTREPRENEURS' (NEs') TEAM FORMATION

Team Composing

To NEs' understanding, their founding environment was conducive to their venturing. From 2002, the Chinese government encouraged entrepreneurship and innovation, enacted new laws to protect private property rights and amended laws to comply with WTO obligations. NEs spotted and developed business ideas from their understanding of market gaps and customer needs. Political risk was not a major concern for them. They noticed that starting up your own business had become a fashion among Chinese younger generation. NEs appreciated a dynamic flow of financial capital, business information, and human resources and they found many people and organizations were available to communicate and explore business opportunities. The major challenges NEs faced were the lack of recognition of their novel business models and increasing market competition, leading to a perception of high market risk. They were concerned that if they could not find partners who can provide business validation, resources, and expertise, their venturing effort would be all in vain. NEs' observation of policy conduciveness, high degree of resource munificence, and high degree of market risk led them to form teams by mixing existing and new ties.

Mixing Existing and New Members: Stabilizing Team and Exploring Resources

It is common that NEs co-founded ventures with former colleagues and business associates, alumni, and family members and relatives. For example, NE-14 teamed up with a previous business partner and his MBA classmate based on his evaluation of the complementarity of their experience.

However, NEs did not limit their search scope within the existing circle. They ($N = 9$) also actively searched and selected new members from the market, thus adding new ties to their team or being added to others' founding teams. In the emergence period, teaming up through open recruiting had become trendy for NEs. NE-7 and NE-9 shared similarities in this process. Both worked as venture capitalists (VC) in their previous companies, they searched for opportunities to team up with industry peers to start up their own VC companies, finally they found their partners through recruiting. After initial contact, they met face-to-face with the potential partners and discussed their investment philosophies. After that, they decided to join the teams and became the co-founders of nascent VC firms. Another typical scenario was that entrepreneurs invited new partners to their newly founded teams, which were composed by existing ties (Table 7.2, II.5). In these mixed teams, team members were from diverse functional backgrounds, such as technology, finance, marketing, and management. For instance, NE-6 described why he recruited a new partner to his team:

> This is why I invited Vincent to join our team. He previously worked as a senior executive at Microsoft. He also started up a business and had led a team. Actually, we share many similarities in ideas and vision. After we discovered these, we began to discuss the developmental strategies. Then we moved forward step by step.

Teaming up with existing ties they were familiar with helped stabilize new teams and increased cohesiveness, adding new partners provided new expertise and resources and granted access to their external networks.

Going Solo: Cognitive Scrutinizing Before Jumping on Board

Entrepreneurs ($N = 3$) who had bad experience at their previous work would rather start up their business alone. NE-2 and NE-5, previously worked as a division manager in a state-owned enterprise and a senior manager in a private firm respectively, complained about how particularistic relationships within the organizations obscured their outstanding performance by unfairly promoting other employees. NE-11 reflected on conflicts among previous team members in a start-up firm and concluded that the misfit of the management style and values had impaired the team cooperation (II.6). They described their negative experiences and the consequences in a cognitive tone instead of complaining about affective disappointment. Their negative experience did not lead them to lose confidence in trusting new others. They became more cautious, and emphasized the importance of evaluating potential team members' capabilities, business values, and external networks before committing to a partnership. As NE-11 reflected:

TABLE 7.2 New Entrepreneurs (N = 17): Team Formation			
Major Pattern	Team Composing[a] and Trust Developing[b]	The Role of Founding Institutional Environment and Entrepreneurs' Response	Illustrative Quotes
Mixing existing ties and new ties ($N = 9$) *Source:* former colleagues and business associates, alumni, relatives, and family members; new partners in the market	*Stabilizing team and exploring resources*[a] Entrepreneurs mixed team members with diverse functional backgrounds. Teaming up with existing ties helped stabilize team while teaming up with new partners provided new expertise and diverse resources.	Entrepreneurs who perceived conducive policy orientation, high market risk, and high resource munificence were prone to mix existing ties and new ties to stabilize new team and explore diverse resources.	II.5 "I am the person who wishes to have a pure working environment and do something consistent with my vision. That is to say, I was looking for such an environment, and then tried to achieve my goals. I am the person who seeks the ideal. I was very luck to know Mr. Tian....Then I knew he was going to start up his own company. There were another two who also knew Mr. Tian from previous projects, they also joined...Our company also looked and added other team members from the market." (NE-1)
Going solo ($N = 5$)	*Cognitive scrutinizing before jumping on board*[b] Entrepreneurs having conflicts with team members in previous work decided to go solo. They emphasized scrutinizing potential team members' capabilities, resources, and values before committing to partnership ($N = 3$).	Negative team experience led to solo entrepreneurship and delayed partnership. High resource munificence and high performance risk led entrepreneurs to be open and cautious about the new partnership.	II.6 "In the early stage, the team members didn't know each other very well. Therefore the communication problem arose. Everyone's way of doing things, management style and values were actually very different. These impaired the cooperation really a lot!" (NE-11)

(continued)

TABLE 7.2 New Entrepreneurs (N = 17)*: Team Formation (Continued)

Major Pattern	Team Composing[a] and Trust Developing[b]	The Role of Founding Institutional Environment and Entrepreneurs' Response	Illustrative Quotes
Teaming up, including with existing, new and mixed ties (N = 11)	*Cognitive filtering; letting business determine partnership[b]* Entrepreneurs focused on cognitive evaluation and selected those who were proved to be trustworthy, capable, and resourceful during previous interactions.	Perceiving high market risk and high resource munificence, entrepreneurs had an open mind for partnership, but they filtered capable and resourceful partners from a potential pool to reduce performance risk.	II.7 "The component of a team, for me, the most important thing is its complementarity...I met my partner in the previous company. Another one is my MBA classmate. We thought that our team is very stable based on our firm friendship. He [the first partner] has a strong management capability and very good market sense...Another one [the MBA classmate] has worked in this industry for many years and knows it pretty well. So we discussed and established our team, and then further developed our ideas." (NE-14)
	Cognitive resonating; Formulating a shared vision to get "there"[b] Entrepreneurs focused on constructing and formulating a shared vision to solidify with team members who had different interactive experience and diverse backgrounds.	Perceiving high market risk, entrepreneurs motivated partners to form a shared vision to reduce performance risk and relational risks.	II.8 "We need to evaluate whether we have the same common vision. I mean, for example, whether we have a common language, common vision in our career and company development....In this case, we share the common view. I think it is the background for later cooperation." (NE-6)

It's like "once bitten, twice shy." I became very prudent. Is he really suitable for being a partner? What types of capabilities and networks he has to contribute to the growth of my firms? I won't make decision until I think these things over.

Trust Developing

Starting up ventures in the period of deepening market-oriented transition, NEs observed high market risk due to the intensified competition. In addition, because of a lack of market recognition of new business models, they faced a high degree of performance risk: If partners were not carefully selected to engage in market creation and development, teams might not deliver expected results. They were also concerned with a medium degree of relational risk: Partners with different backgrounds might not cooperate in the desired manner because of style and value differences. These concerns led to their focus on "cognitive filtering" to determine partnership and "cognitive resonating" to cultivate a shared vision.

Cognitive Filtering: Letting Business Determine Partnership
During the team member identification process, NEs scrutinized whether the prospective partners had rich market experience, diverse networks, and capable technology and management skills through prior interaction, potential team members' reputation, and face-to-face negotiations. Although NEs formed teams with their existing ties with whom they had developed affective attachments, they only teamed up with those they cognitively evaluated as trustworthy, capable, and resourceful (II.7). Recall that some NEs first chose their partners and then developed business ideas, for NEs, this would be almost the reverse: Prior experience lays foundation for new partnership, however, only after passing the evaluation of the initial business idea and each members' potential contribution, prospective members could then enter the partnership. For example, NE-3 said:

> We have been working with each other for many years. Everybody is talking in the same language. These people are very important to me, such as my partners, shareholders, and investors. They are all speaking the same language. The customers notice that, and they bestow the trust in our organizational and managerial team. In this aspect, we are all professional in corporate management and personal management. From the auditor's point of view, they recognize that our company is very professional and has standard governance structures.

When searching for new team members, NEs sought to obtain the information about prospective partner's capability and compatibility through observing in the market and/or through knowing their reputation from industry peers. NE-6 exemplified combining both ways in recruiting a new team member. After having observed Vincent's market performance and venturing experience, and after receiving a very positive evaluation of Vincent from other industry peers, NE-6 then invited him to join his team.

Cognitive Resonating: Formulating a Shared Vision to Get "There"

Our early analysis shows that EEs emphasized on matching personality and behavioral styles and they commonly founded teams before the business ideas were well formulated. In contrast, NEs regarded partnership as a means to an end—using partnership to achieve planned business goals. When teaming up with their existing ties who had diverse functional backgrounds, EEs strived to construct a shared vision for the future business to reduce potential performance risk and relational risk. For instance, when founding a financial service firm with his former colleagues, NE-3 and his teammates not only spoke a "shared language" and tackled tasks from a similar business perspective but also developed a shared vision about how they could develop their financial service model. They resonated value and vision to improve coordination and intra-team trust. This resonation also sent signals to the market that they were an effective team.

Cognitive resonating was even more salient in mixed teams as members from diverse backgrounds needed some common grounds to work effectively. For example, NE-7 contacted a VC and exchanged information about each other's project experience and vision for future venturing. Although some business and collaborating details needed to be elaborated, resonating in vision and strategy made him feel "the partnership was very promising," therefore he joined the founding team. NE-6's team comprised existing ties and new members. He emphasized the role of cultivating a common vision for the business development (II.8). He regarded disagreements and hustles as normal elements of the team process. However, in order to reduce performance risk and relational risk, he sought to unite the team by envisioning and conveying a common goal that could benefit all team members:

> We [founding team members] have become managers. Now I am a leader, an innovator, a revolutionist, an inspirator, like a flag of the company...From the mission perspective, I am doing this for the benefits of everybody. However, if there are disagreements, critics, and hustle, let it be...This is a very normal process...An entrepreneur needs to realize company's maximum value. He needs to lead a team towards the goal. He needs to help team members and let them follow you. With this leadership and spirit, we can achieve higher effectiveness.

DISCUSSION AND CONCLUSION

An Institutional Perspective on Entrepreneurial Team Formation

Research on venture team formation has found that entrepreneurs are naturally inclined to draw team members from their existing circles because of shared experience and familiarity (Ensley et al., 2002; Kamm & Nurick, 1993; Katz, 1982; Ruef et al., 2003). However, little is known about how ventures' founding environment might affect and differ entrepreneurs' team formation behaviors. Drawing on an inductive and comparative study, our research develops an institutional perspective on entrepreneurial team formation by shedding light on the impacts of a founding institutional environment and how entrepreneurs founded ventures in different institutional environment respond differently in team composing and trust developing processes. Our study contributes to the literature in the following aspects.

First, prior research focusing on transitional economies has shown that regulative, market, and cultural forces and their changes affect entrepreneurs' business opportunities, resource acquisition, legitimation activities, and business networks (Ahlstrom & Bruton, 2002; Estrin et al., 2005; Peng, 2003; Smallbone & Welter, 2001; Webb et al., 2009). However, these studies have paid little attention to how they affect entrepreneurial team formation. Drawing on an institutional perspective on exchange relationships (Möllering, 2006a; Zucker, 1986) and network studies of entrepreneurship in transitional economies (Guseva & Rona-Tas, 2001; Radaev, 2002; Tan et al., 2009), we explore the effects of a founding institutional environment on entrepreneurial team formation. We uncover that a founding institutional environment shapes the nature and degree of political risk and market risk and determines the degree of resource munificence at a macro level. It further affects micro-level factors and processes such as entrepreneurs' propensity of using prior experience and consideration of venturing demands. These macro-micro effects define the search scope—to what extent entrepreneurs feel necessary and secure about partnering with unfamiliar others—and shapes trust developing strategies—what kinds of trust developing approaches could consolidate partnership and commitment that fit into their founding conditions. These effects create a divergent path for entrepreneurs who found ventures in different institutional environments and differ in teaming behaviors. Our findings show that when perceiving high political risk and market risk (i.e., investment uncertainty) and low resource munificence, entrepreneurs tend to rely on existing ties for partnership, while perceiving high market risk (i.e., lack of business model recognition and intensifying competition) and high resource munificence, entrepreneurs tend to mix existing ties and new ties in founding teams.

Second, our study further contributes to the process-oriented understanding of entrepreneurial team formation (Clarysse & Moray, 2004; Hoang & Antoncic, 2003), in particular, its trust developing process. Studies have found that active trust building compensates the weak legal framework and less efficient market institutions in transitional economies (Child & Möllering, 2003; Nguyen & Rose, 2009). Actors are expected to put less effort in process-based trust building as the institutional development advances trust in the social-economic system (Bachmann & Inkpen, 2011; Luhmann, 1979; Zucker, 1986). Our study shows that active trust developing is always crucial for new venture teams and institutional transition does not negate active trust building process but directs trust developing strategies. For example, early entrepreneurs use affective filtering and consolidating to work with existing ties to reduce relational risk embedded in the early transitional period; new entrepreneurs adopt cognitive filtering and resonating to find new partners and solidify diverse teams with the major concern to reduce performance risk. Thus, our study also goes beyond the simple distinction of affective and cognitive trust in existing literature (McAllister, 1995; Smith & Lohrke, 2008) by shedding light on *how* and *why* entrepreneurs adopt different trust developing strategies with their venturing partners.

Third, our study sheds light on how micro factors such as entrepreneur prior experience and venturing demands—shaped by institutional environment—affect team formation. Previous studies have shown personal attraction and interactive experience lead entrepreneurs to form a team with existing ties (Aldrich & Kim, 2007; Kamm & Nurick, 1993; Kamm et al., 1990; Ruef et al., 2003). Our study finds that these factors should not be considered independently from the founding environment. We show that when the external environmental risk (i.e., political risk and market risk) and relational risk are high, entrepreneurs tend to form teams with existing ties and those they had interactive experience with. However, when the market risk (lack of market recognition and legitimacy) and performance risk are high, new entrepreneurs actively search partners with unfamiliar ties.

Considering entrepreneurs' industry engagement and venture form are likely to evolve with institutional change to increase probability of survival and growth (Aldrich & Ruef, 2006; Baum & Oliver, 1992; Hannan & Carroll, 1992), we do not restrict our comparison within a single industry. We instead compare entrepreneurs across different industries, which allows us to explore similarities and variations among studied entrepreneurial populations. We find entrepreneurs' industrial engagement and business models are evolving with China's market-oriented transition and these factors, to a certain degree, are reflected in the variation of ventures' resource needs. Although engaged in different industries, EEs mainly need financial and labor resources during the emergence stage while NEs need diverse resources such as financial resource, market recognition and legitimacy, technology expertise and management competence. The former leads to adding existing ties to the early team while the latter leads to mixing existing and new members who have diverse functional experience and capabilities to the team. Our analysis of ventures' resource needs during institutional change provides fine grained understanding of how organizational factors, embedded in an institutional environment, affect team formation and its variation.

Limitations and Future Research Direction

This study has several limitations that suggest future research directions. First, this study mainly focuses on team composing and trust building during a venture's early stage, the retrospective design raises potential recall bias. It is possible that affective trust building was more salient for early entrepreneurs than for new ones since team members with strong affective attachment are more likely to be reported. In addition, our study mainly presented and explained the dominant trust developing strategies of two groups of entrepreneurs. However, the relative weight of cognitive and affective elements in teams shifts over time (Smith & Lohrke, 2008). It would be intriguing to study how early entrepreneurs and their teams respond to increasing demands for expertise and competences during the institutional transition and whether new entrepreneurial teams develop more affective attachment over time, and if so, how they might differ from the early entrepreneurs.

Second, we did not systematically control variables such as industry, business model, and function of team members. However, we examined venture resource needs as an indication of the variation of industrial and business models and we suggest that this variation is a natural process inherent in institutional change (Aldrich & Ruef, 2006; Hannan & Carroll, 1992). Nevertheless, entrepreneurs' team formation process and the effects of institutional environment and venturing features could be better understood by controlling these variables when a large longitudinal dataset becomes available.

Third, future studies could examine how team composition and trust development affect venture performance. A possible venue is to investigate which type of team composition (i.e., the percentage of existing ties, new ties, and mixed ties) and trust developing strategy (affective or cognitive) could better contribute to venture performance at a different venturing stage and under a different context. Fourth, our results are drawn from a small sample of private entrepreneurs in Shanghai, therefore there is a generalizability concern. Future studies could verify our findings with larger samples in other contexts, such as other transitional economies. Abundant research has studied entrepreneurs' opportunities generation and venturing strategies in transitional economies, leaving entrepreneurial teaming behavior an underexplored topic. We expect that researchers will discover additional patterns and new practices in those contexts, which will provide new evidence and theorizing opportunities.

CONCLUSION

The current study develops understanding of the impacts of a founding institutional environment and the process of entrepreneurial team formation during the institutional transition. Our study is among the first in entrepreneurship literature to theorize the relationship between the founding environment and teaming behaviors and discover the underlying mechanisms. This study challenges the previous literature which suggests entrepreneurs are naturally inclined to draw team members from their existing circle by showing that entrepreneurs would recruit new members and actively develop trust in an environment that encourages and requires partnership with diverse and new team members. This study opens up a research venture on the founding environment, venturing setting, and their interaction on entrepreneurial team formation and dynamics.

ACKNOWLEDGMENTS

The authors gratefully acknowledge the comments and suggestions provided by Dimo Dimov, Tao Wang, Weiwen Li, Xin Zheng, and Zhujun Ding.

REFERENCES

Ahlstrom, D., & Bruton, G. D. (2002). An institutional perspective on the role culture in shaping strategic actions by technology-focused entrepreneurial firms in China. *Entrepreneurship Theory and Practice, 26*(4), 53–70.

Aldrich, H., & Ruef, M. (2006). *Organizations evolving* (2nd ed.). London, England: SAGE.

Aldrich, H. E., & Kim, P. H. (2007). Small worlds, infinite possibilities? How social networks affect entrepreneurial team formation and search. *Strategic Entrepreneurship Journal, 1*(1–2), 147–165.

Anderson, P., & Tushman, M. L. (2001). Organizational environments and industry exit: The effects of uncertainty, munificence and complexity. *Industrial and Corporate Change, 10*(3), 675–711.

Bachmann, R., & Inkpen, A. C. (2011). Understanding institutional-based trust building processes in inter-organizational relationships. *Organization Studies, 32*(2), 281–301.

Baum, J. A. C., & Oliver, C. (1992). Institutional embeddedness and the dynamics of organizational populations. *American Sociological Review, 57*(4), 540–559.

Beckert, J. (1999). Agency, entrepreneurs, and institutional change. The role of strategic choice and institutionalized practices in organizations. *Organization Studies, 20*(5), 777–799.

Beckman, C. M., Haunschild, P. R., & Phillips, D. J. (2004). Friends or strangers? Firm-specific uncertainty, market uncertainty, and network partner selection. *Organization Science, 15*(3), 259–275.

Birley, S., & Stockley, S. (2000). Entrepreneurial teams and venture growth. In D. L. Sexton & H. Landstrom (Eds.), *Blackwell handbook of entrepreneurship* (pp. 287–307). Oxford, England: Blackwell.

Child, J., & Möllering, G. (2003). Contextual confidence and active trust development in the Chinese business environment. *Organization Science, 14*(1), 69–80.

Chrisman, J. J., Bauerschmidt, A., & Hofer, C. W. (1998). The determinants of new venture performance: An extended model. *Entrepreneurship Theory & Practice, 23*(1), 5–29.

Chua, R. Y. J. (2012). Building effective business relationships in China. *Mit Sloan Management Review, 53*(4), 27–33.

Chua, R. Y. J., Morris, M. W., & Ingram, P. (2009). Guanxi vs networking: Distinctive configurations of affect- and cognition-based trust in the networks of Chinese vs American managers. *Journal of International Business Studies, 40*(3), 490–508.

Clarysse, B., & Moray, N. (2004). A process study of entrepreneurial team formation: The case of a research-based spin-off. *Journal of Business Venturing, 19*(1), 55–79.

Cook, K., Rice, E., & Gerbasi, A. (2004). The emergence of trust networks under uncertainty: The case of transitional economies-insights form social psychological research. In J. Kornai, B. Rothstein, S. Rose-Ackerman, & C. Budapest (Eds.), *Creating social trust in post-socialist transition* (pp. 193–212). New York, NY: Palgrave Macmillan.

Corbin, J., & Strauss, A. (1998). *Basics of qualitative research: Procedures and techniques for developing grounded theory.* Thousand Oaks, CA: SAGE.

Das, T. K., & Teng, B. (1996). Risk types and inter-firm alliance structures. *Journal of Management Studies, 33*(6), 827–843.

Das, T. K., & Teng, B. (2004). The risk-based view of trust: A conceptual framework. *Journal of Business and Psychology, 19*(1), 85–116.

Doutriaux, J. (1992). Emerging high-tech firms—how durable are their comparative start-up advantages. *Journal of Business Venturing, 7*(4), 303–322.

Eisenhardt, K. M. (1989). Building theories from case study research. *Academy of Management Review, 14*(4), 532–550.

Eisenhardt, K. M., & Graebner, M. E. (2007). Theory building from cases: Opportunities and challenges. *Academy of Management Journal, 50*(1), 25–32.

Eisenhardt, K. M., & Schoonhoven, C. B. (1990). Organizational growth—Linking founding team, strategy, environment, and growth among United States semiconductor ventures, 1978–1988. *Administrative Science Quarterly, 35*(3), 504–529.

Ensley, M. D., Pearson, A. W., & Amasone, A. C. (2002). Understanding the dynamics of new venture top management teams – cohesion, conflict, and new venture performance. *Journal of Business Venturing, 17*(4), 365–386.

Estrin, S., Meyer, K. E., & Bytchkova, M. (2005). Entrepreneurship in transition economies. In M. Casson, A. Basu, B. Yeung, & N. Wadeson (Eds.), *Oxford handbook of entrepreneurship* (pp. 693–725). Oxford, England: Oxford University Press.

Fitzpatrick, M. (1983). The definition and assessment of political risk in international-business—a review of the literature. *Academy of Management Review, 8*(2), 249–254.

Gartner, W. B., Shaver, K. G., Gatewood, E., & Katz, J. A. (1994). Finding the entrepreneur in entrepreneurship. *Entrepreneurship Theory and Practice, 18*(3), 5–10.

Grandi, A., & Grimaldi, R. (2003). Exploring the networking characteristics of new venture founding teams: A study of Italian academic spin-off. *Small Business Economics, 21*(4), 329–341.

Guo, C., & Miller, J. K. (2010). Guanxi dynamics and entrepreneurial firm creation and development in China. *Management and Organization Review, 6*(2), 267–291.

Guseva, A., & Rona-Tas, A. (2001). Uncertainty, risk, and trust: Russian and American credit card markets compared. *American Sociological Review, 66*(5), 623–646.

Hannan, M. T., & Carroll, G. (1992). *Dynamics of organizational populations: Density, legitimation, and competition.* New York, NY: Oxford University Press.

Hmieleski, K. M., & Ensley, M. D. (2007). A contextual examination of new venture performance: Entrepreneur leadership behavior, top management team heterogeneity, and environmental dynamism. *Journal of Organizational Behavior, 28*(7), 865–889.

Hoang, H., & Antoncic, B. (2003). Network-based research in entrepreneurship—A critical review. *Journal of Business Venturing, 18*(2), 165–187.

Huston, T. L., & Levinger, G. (1978). Interpersonal-attraction and relationships. *Annual Review of Psychology, 29*, 115–156.

Jennings, P. D., Greenwood, R., Lounsbury, M. D., & Suddaby, R. (2013). Institutions, entrepreneurs, and communities: A special issue on entrepreneurship. *Journal of Business Venturing, 28*(1), 1–9.

Johns, G. (2006). The essential impact of context on organizational behavior. *Academy of Management Review, 31*(2), 386–408.

Kamm, J. B., & Nurick, A. J. (1993). The stages of team venture formation: A decision-making model. *Entrepreneurship Theory and Practice, 17*(2), 17–27.

Kamm, J. B., Shuman, J. C., Seeger, J. A., & Nurick, A. J. (1990). Entrepreneurial teams in new venture creation: A research agenda. *Entrepreneurship Theory and Practice, 14*(4), 7–17.

Katz, R. (1982). The effects of group longevity on project communication and performance. *Administrative Science Quarterly, 27*(1), 81–104.

Klotz, A. C., Hmieleski, K. M., Bradley, B. H., & Busenitz, L. W. (2014). New venture teams: A review of the literature and roadmap for future research. *Journal of Management, 40*(1), 226–255.

Kobrin, S. J. (1982). *Managing political risk assessment: Strategic response to environmental change.* Berkeley: University of California Press.

Koka, B. R., Madhavan, R., & Prescott, J. E. (2006). The evolution of interfirm networks: Environmental effects on patterns of network change. *Academy of Management Review, 31*(3), 721–737.

Lewis, J., & Nicholls, C. M. (2014). Design issues. In J. Ritchie, J. Lewis, C. M. Nicholls, & R. Ormston (Eds.), *Qualitative research practice: A guide for social science students and researchers* (pp. 48–76). London, England: SAGE.

Lounsbury, M., & Glynn, M. A. (2001). Cultural entrepreneurship: Stories, legitimacy, and the acquisition of resources. *Strategic Management Journal, 22*(6–7), 545–564.

Luhmann, N. (1979). *Trust and power.* New York, NY: Wiley.

Manolova, T. S., Eunni, R. V., & Gyoshev, B. S. (2008). Institutional environments for entrepreneurship: Evidence from emerging economies in Eastern Europe. *Entrepreneurship Theory and Practice, 32*(1), 203–218.

Martens, M. L., Jennings, J. E., & Jennings, P. D. (2007). Do the stories they tell get them the money they need?: The role of entrepreneurial narratives in resource aquisition. *Academy of Management Journal, 50*(5), 1107–1132.

McAllister, D. J. (1995). Affect-based and cognition-based trust as foundations for interpersonal cooperation in organizations. *Academy of Management Journal, 38*(1), 24–59.

Möllering, G. (2006a). Trust, institutions, agency: Towards a neoinstitutional theory of trust. In R. Bachmann & A. Zaheer (Eds.), *Handbook of trust research* (pp. 355–376). Cheltenham, England: Edward Elgar.

Möllering, G. (2006b). *Trust: Reason, routine, reflexivity.* Amsterdam, The Netherlands: Elsevier.

Möllering, G., & Stache, F. (2010). Trust development in German–Ukrainian business relationships: Dealing with cultural differences in an uncertain institutional context. In N. K. Saunders, D. Skinner, G. Dietz, N. Gillespie, & R. J. Lewicki (Eds.), *Organizational trust: A cultural perspective* (pp. 205–226). Cambridge, England: Cambridge University Press.

Nee, V. (1992). Organizational dynamics of market transition: Hybrid forms, property rights, and mixed economy in China. *Administrative Science Quarterly, 37*(1), 1–27.

Nguyen, T. V., & Rose, J. (2009). Building trust-evidence from vietnamese entrepreneurs. *Journal of Business Venturing, 24*(2), 165–182.

North, D. C. (1990). *Institutions, institutional change and economic performance.* Cambridge, England: Cambridge University Press.

Parhankangas, A. (2007). An overview of research on early stage venture capital: Current status and future directions. In H. Landström (Ed.), *Handbook of research on venture capital* (pp. 253–280). Cheltenham, England: Edward Elgar.

Peng, M. W. (2003). Institutional transitions and strategic choices. *Academy of Management Review, 28*(2), 275–296.

Peng, M. W., & Heath, P. S. (1996). The growth of the firm in planned economies in transition: Institutions, organizations, and strategic choice. *Academy of Management Review, 21*(2), 492–528.

Peng, M. W., & Zhou, J. Q. (2005). How network strategies and institutional transitions evolve in Asia? *Asia Pacific Journal of Management, 22*(4), 321–336.

Puffer, S. M., McCarthy, D. J., & Boisot, M. (2010). Entrepreneurship in Russia and China: The impact of formal institutional voids. *Entrepreneurship Theory & Practice, 34*(3), 441–467.

Radaev, V. (2002). Entrepreneurial strategies and the structure of transaction costs in Russian business. *Problems of Economic Transition, 44*(12), 57–84.

Ravasi, D., & Turati, C. (2005). Exploring entrepreneurial learning: A comparative study of technology development projects. *Journal of Business Venturing, 20*(1), 137–164.

Rousseau, D. M., & Fried, Y. (2001). Location, location, location: Contextualizing organizational research. *Journal of Organizational Behavior, 22*(1), 1–13.

Ruef, M., Aldrich, H. E., & Carter, N. M. (2003). The structure of founding teams: Homophily, strong ties, and isolation among US entrepreneurs. *American Sociological Review, 68*(2), 195–222.

Ruhnka, J. C., & Young, J. E. (1991). Some hypotheses about risk in venture capital investing. *Journal of Business Venturing, 6*(2), 115–133.

Scott, W. R. (2008). *Institutions and organizations: Ideas and interests* (3rd ed.). Los Angeles, CA: SAGE.

Shanghai Municipal Statistical Bureau. (1994). *Shanghai statistical yearbook 1994.* Shanghai, China: Chinese Statistics Publishing House of the City of Shanghai's Statistical Bureau.

Shrader, R., & Siegel, D. S. (2007). Assessing the relationship between human capital and firm performance: Evidence from technology–based new ventures. *Entrepreneurship Theory and Practice, 31*(6), 893–908.

Sine, W. D., & David, R. J. (2003). Environmental jolts, institutional change, and the creation of entrepreneurial opportunity in the US electric power industry. *Research Policy, 32*(2), 185–207.

Smallbone, D., & Welter, F. (2001). The distinctiveness of entrepreneurship in transition economies. *Small Business Economics, 16*(4), 249–262.

Smallbone, D., & Welter, F. (2012). Entrepreneurship and institutional change in transition economies: The commonwealth of independent states, Central and Eastern Europe and China compared. *Entrepreneurship & Regional Development, 24*(3–4), 215–233.

Smith, D. A., & Lohrke, F. T. (2008). Entrepreneurial network development: Trusting in the process. *Journal of Business Research, 61*(4), 315–322.

SUFEP. (2008). *Shanghai private economy yearbook 2008.* Shanghai, China: Shanghai University of Finance and Economics Press.

Tan, J. (2007). Phase transitions and emergence of entrepreneurship: The transformation of Chinese SOEs over time. *Journal of Business Venturing, 22*(1), 77–96.

Tan, J., Yang, J., & Veliyath, R. (2009). Particularistic and system trust among small and medium enterprises: A comparative study in China's transition economy. *Journal of Business Venturing, 24*(6), 544–557.

Turner, D. W. (2010). Qualitative interview design: A practical guide for novice investigators. *The Qualitative Report, 15*(3), 754–760.

Ucbasaran, D., Lockett, A., Wright, M., & Westhead, P. (2003). Entrepreneurial founder teams: Factors associated with member entry and exit. *Entrepreneurship Theory and Practice, 28*(2), 107–128.

Vyakarnam, S., Jacobs, R., & Handelberg, J. (1999). Exploring the formation of entrepreneurial teams: The key to rapid growth business? *Journal of Small Business and Enterprise Development, 6*(2), 153–165.

Webb, J. W., Tihanyi, L., Ireland, R. D., & Sirmon, D. G. (2009). You say illegal, I say legitimate: Entrepreneurship in the informal economy. *Academy of Management Review, 34*(3), 492–510.

Zhang, C., Tan, J., & Tan, D. (2016). Fit by adaptation or fit by founding? A comparative study of existing and new entrepreneurial cohorts in China. *Strategic Management Journal, 37*(5), 911–931.

Zucker, L. G. (1986). Production of trust: Institutional sources of economic structure, 1840–1920. In B. M. Staw & L. L. Cummings (Eds.), *Research in organizational behavior* (pp. 53–111). Greenwich, CT: JAI Press.

CHAPTER 8

BUILDING STRATEGIC ALLIANCES IN NEW AND SMALL VENTURES

A Review of Literature and Integrative Framework

Alice Comi
Martin J. Eppler

ABSTRACT

In order to reap the advantages associated with strategic alliances, entrepreneurial ventures need to develop an organization-wide capability to establish, structure, and manage such alliances. Yet the entrepreneurship literature has developed separately from alliance research, leaving new and small ventures with little advice on how to develop and thrive through strategic alliances. To close this gap, we review the alliance literature by taking the perspective of entrepreneurial ventures operating in highly competitive and knowledge-intensive industries. While keeping the focus on new and small ventures, we develop our literature review in connection with the broader literature on strategic alliances, covering a total of 105 peer-reviewed articles. We organize

Entrepreneurship and Behavioral Strategy, pages 209–242

the collected articles according to an input-process-output framework. After reviewing the antecedents and the outcomes of alliance formation in new and small ventures, we take a closer look at the processes entailed by involvement in the alliance itself (i.e., alliance structuring, alliance management, and capability building). Our primary contribution consists of consolidating research on strategic alliances in entrepreneurial ventures with reference to the broader literature on strategic alliances. From a managerial perspective, we elaborate on the key success factors of strategic alliances in entrepreneurial ventures, and provide a roadmap for new and small ventures to develop an alliance capability. We conclude by identifying research themes that need further exploration, and by suggesting theoretical perspectives that may be suitable for the exploration of such themes.

INTRODUCTION

New and small ventures are receiving increasing attention by both policy makers and researchers, since they represent a major source of economic growth and innovation (Acs, 2006; Wennekers & Thurik, 1999; Wong & Autio, 2005). However, entrepreneurial ventures have high failure rates due to a "liability of smallness" and a "liability of newness," which involve scarcity of in-house resources, lack of reputation in the final market, and uncertainty about internal operations (Baum, Calabrese, & Silverman, 2000; Stinchcombe, 1965). The formation of strategic alliances may enable entrepreneurial ventures to overcome such liabilities, as well as to avoid the pitfalls associated with the earliest stages of venture development (Narula, 2004). As argued by Baum et al. (2000, p. 270), "by forming strategic alliances, start-ups can potentially access social, technical, and commercial competitive resources that normally require years of operating experience to acquire."

Yet strategic alliances are risky endeavors, and failure may be particularly consequential at the start-up stage, when in-house resources are stretched to the limit (Baum et al., 2000; Minshall, Mortara, Elia, & Probert, 2008; Narula, 2004). To reap the advantages associated with strategic alliances, entrepreneurial ventures need to develop an organization-wide capability to establish, structure and manage alliances (Draulans, DeMan, & Volberda, 2003). However, the entrepreneurship literature has developed separately from research on strategic alliances (Ariño, Ragozzino, & Reuer, 2008; Das & He, 2006). The few publications discussing strategic alliances in entrepreneurial ventures are scattered across different theoretical perspectives, ranging from the resource-based view to the network perspective. Unavoidably, this leads to a fragmented picture of the challenges and experiences encountered by entrepreneurial ventures that set out to form, manage, and learn from strategic alliances.

In this chapter, we contribute to bridging this gap, by reviewing the literature on strategic alliances from the viewpoint of entrepreneurial ventures operating in knowledge-intensive and high-technology sectors. From a search of business and management journal collections, we selected a total of 105 peer-reviewed articles, drawn from the literature on strategic alliances and the literature on entrepreneurial ventures. We organize the collected articles according to an input-process-output framework: After reviewing the antecedents and the outcomes of alliance formation in new and small ventures, we take a closer look at the processes entailed by involvement in the alliance itself (i.e., alliance structuring, alliance management, and capability building). From a managerial perspective, we elaborate on the key success factors of strategic alliances in entrepreneurial ventures, and provide a roadmap for new and small ventures to develop an alliance capability. We conclude by identifying five research themes that need further exploration, and by suggesting theoretical perspectives that may be suitable for the exploration of such themes.

Our primary contribution consists of consolidating research on strategic alliances in new and small ventures, by drawing connections with the broader literature on strategic alliances. In particular, our literature review makes an attempt not to compare theoretical perspectives, but rather to cull out research themes that cut across theoretical perspectives on strategic alliances in new and small ventures.[1] By so doing, we intend to suggest an agenda for future research and to provide a resource of intelligence for entrepreneurial ventures that wish to engage in strategic alliances.

METHODOLOGY

In this section, we define the central constructs of our review and outline the methodological approach adopted for gathering and analyzing articles on strategic alliances in entrepreneurial ventures. A "strategic alliance" is broadly defined as a collaborative agreement whereby two or more companies team up in order to share reciprocal inputs, while maintaining their own organizational identities (De Man & Duysters, 2005). By the term "entrepreneurial venture," we refer to new and small ventures that operate in highly-technological and knowledge-intensive sectors (Baum et al., 2000; Narula, 2004). With this definition, we wish not to make distinctions between new and small ventures, but rather to consider the two types of firms jointly. This is consistent with a literature tradition which "generally use 'start-ups' and 'small start-ups' and 'entrepreneurial firms' interchangeably, and use data collected from young and small firms in high tech industries to address entrepreneurial issues" (Das & He, 2006, p. 120).

212 ■ A. COMI and M. J. EPPLER

The strategic alliances undertaken by entrepreneurial ventures can be classified into three broad categories, based on the partner's position along the industry value chain (Colombo, Grilli, & Piva, 2006; Faems, Van Looy, & Debackere, 2005; Forrest, 1990; George, Zahra, Wheatley, & Khan, 2001). New and small ventures may constitute strategic alliances with *downstream partners* closer to commercial and marketing channels, with *horizontal partners* in a similar position along the value chain, or with *upstream partners* conducting basic or applied research. For example, a biotech start-up may undertake downstream alliances with pharmaceutical companies to leverage their brands, sales force, and distribution channels (Alvarez & Barney, 2001; Powell, Koput, & Smith-Doerr, 1996); and at the same time pool resources with horizontal and upstream partners for exploring an untested research field (Baum et al., 2000). As our literature review will make clear, the distinction between *downstream, upstream, and horizontal alliances* brings along relevant implications for alliance management in entrepreneurial ventures.

In order to select articles on strategic alliances in entrepreneurial ventures, we performed an extensive search of electronic databases—ABI Inform, JSTOR, Science Direct, and Springer Link—looking for the keywords "entrepreneurial venture" (or synonyms) and "strategic alliance" (or synonyms) in the title or abstract. As synonyms, we selected the keywords "new venture," and "start-up," followed by "partnership" and "inter-organizational collaboration" for "strategic alliance." We performed crossed searches of the above said keywords, and limited results to scholarly journals included in business and management collections (29 articles). We then extended our literature search to include contributions on small enterprises ("SMEs") that set out to form strategic alliances in highly-technological and knowledge-intensive sectors (18 articles).

Furthermore, we broadened our literature search to articles on entrepreneurial networks (8 articles), recognizing that the network perspective provides relevant insights for the study of dyadic alliances. As suggested by Inkpen and Tsang (2005), the value creation logic in alliance networks is conceptually the same as in dyadic alliances, although involving greater managerial complexity. As a result, we gathered a total of 55 peer-reviewed, scholarly articles on strategic alliances in entrepreneurial ventures (i.e., new and small ventures).

Given our intent to bridge the entrepreneurship and the alliance literature, we simultaneously made an attempt to get a picture of the state of the art as regards the broader literature on strategic alliances. To this end, we consulted literature reviews on strategic alliances (e.g., Barringer & Harrison, 2000; Ireland, Hitt, & Vaidyanath, 2002) and screened the references of our literature collection in search for highly cited articles on strategic alliances (50 articles). These articles are relevant for representing the backdrop against which the literature on strategic alliances in entrepreneurial ventures develops. Furthermore, this extension of the literature search enabled comparing the development of the literature on strategic alliances in entrepreneurial ventures against the development of the wider literature on strategic alliances. As displayed in Table 8.1, we gathered a total of 105 articles, drawn from the entrepreneurship literature and from research in strategic alliances.

Following an inductive analysis of the articles collected, we identified four literature themes—*alliance formation, structuring, management,* and *capability*

TABLE 8.1 Literature Overview		
Life Cycle Phase	**Alliance Literature on Entrepreneurial Ventures**	**General Alliance Literature**
Alliance Formation	BarNir & Smith (2002)[b]	Ahuja (2000)
	Baum & Silverman (2004)[a]	Barringer & Harrison (2000)
	Baum et al. (2000)[c]	Chung et al. (2000)
	Calabrese et al. (2000)[a]	Das & Teng (2000b)
	Chen & Li (1999)[a]	De Man & Duysters (2005)
	Colombo et al. (2006)[a]	Faems et al. (2005)
	Colombo et al. (2009)[a]	Gulati (1998)
	Deeds & Hill (1996)[a]	Ireland et al. (2002)
	Eisenhardt & Schoonhoven (1996)[a]	Muller & Välikangas (2002)
	Elfring & Hulsink (2003)[c]	Powell et al. (1996)
	Elfring & Hulsink (2007)[c]	Stuart (1998)
	Hara & Kanai (1994)[a]	Vanhaverbeke et al. (2007)
	Hoang & Antoncic (2003)[c]	Willoughby & Galvin (2005)
	Lee (2007)[b]	Zineldin & Dodourova (2005)
	Lee et al. (2001)[a]	
	Leiblein & Reuer (2004)[a]	
	McGee et al. (1995)[a]	
	Park et al. (2002)[a]	
	Shan (1990)[a]	
	Shan et al. (1994)[a]	
	Shane & Cable (2002)[a]	
	Silverman & Baum (2002)[a]	
	Steier & Greenwood (2000)[c]	
	Stuart et al. (1999)[a]	
	Van Gils & Zwart (2004)[b]	
	Walker et al. (1997)[c]	
Alliance Structuring	Alvarez & Barney (2001)[a]	Bierly & Gallagher (2007)
	Ariño et al. (2008)[a]	Brouthers et al. (1995)
	Das & Hea	Das & Teng (1996)
	Forrest (1990)[b]	Das & Teng (2000a)
	Gomes-Casseres (1997)[b]	Hitt et al. (2000)
	Hoffmann & Schlosser (2001)[b]	Holmberg & Cummings (2009)
	Narula (2004)[b]	Joskow (1985)
	O'Dwyer & O'Flynn (2005)[b]	Kogut (1991)
	Street & Cameron (2007)[b]	Lorange & Roos (1993)
		Mowery et al. (1996)

(continued)

TABLE 8.1   Literature Overview (Continued)

Life Cycle Phase	Alliance Literature on Entrepreneurial Ventures	General Alliance Literature
Alliance Management	Beecham & Cordey-Hayes (1998)[b]	Anderson et al. (2006)
	Doz (2002)[b]	Brachos et al. (2007)
	Faems et al. (2010)[b]	Das & Teng (1998)
	Huiskonen & Pirttilä (2002)[b]	Das & Teng (2001)
	Larson (1991)[a]	Deeds and Hill (1999)
	Larson (1992)[a]	Duysters et al. (1999)
	Maurer & Ebers (2006)[c]	George et al. (2001)
	Miles et al. (1999)[b]	Kelly et al. (2002)
	Senker & Sharp (1997)[b]	Kumar & Andersen (2000)
	Slowinski et al. (1996)[b]	Lane & Lubatkin (1998)
	Standing et al. (2008)[a]	Nicholls Nixon & Woo (2003)
	Yli-Renko et al. (2001)[c]	Simonin (1999)
	Yli-Renko et al. (2002)[a]	Uzzi (1997)
		Vlaar et al. (2006)
Alliance Capability Building	Almeida et al. (2003)[a]	Anand & Khanna (2000)
	Beugelsdijk et al. (2003)[b]	Brockelman & Cucci (2000)
	Davenport et al. (1998)[b]	De Man (2005)
	Minshall et al. (2008)[a]	Draulans et al. (2003)
	Minshall et al. (2010)[a]	Harbison & Pekar (1997)
	Rothaermel & Deeds (2006)[a]	Heimeriks & Duysters (2007)
	Walter et al. (2006)[a]	Heimeriks & Reuer (2006)
		Heimeriks et al. (2009)
		Hoang & Rothaermel (2005)
		Kale & Singh (2007)
		Kale et al. (2002)
		Mascarenhas & Koza (2008)

[a] Articles focusing primarily on new ventures
[b] Articles focusing primarily on small ventures
[c] Articles with a network perspective

building—which can be organized within an input-process-output framework. The first theme covers the inputs and outputs of strategic alliances, whereas the remainder themes explore different processes entailed by strategic alliances. Research on alliance structuring and management is concerned with the relationship between the alliance partners, whereas research in alliance capability building shifts attention towards the internal processes of the alliance partner. In Figure 8.1, we provide an overview of the four literature themes, which will be deepened in the remainder of the chapter.

The advantage of adopting an input-process-output framework is two-fold: First, this framework cuts across theoretical perspectives, therefore enabling the classification and integration of articles scattered across a variety of theoretical perspectives. For example, our review of alliance formation synthesizes results from the resource based view, transaction cost, and social network perspectives. Second, the input-process-output framework is

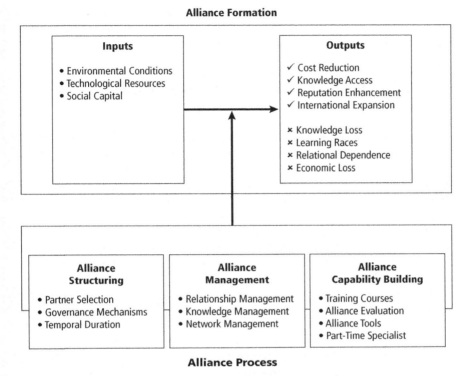

Figure 8.1 Input-process-output framework of strategic alliances in entrepreneurial ventures.

applicable to all types of organizations, and is therefore useful to facilitate comparisons between the literature on strategic alliances in entrepreneurial ventures and the broader literature on strategic alliances. At the same time, the classes are of a broad nature and hence do not suppress the organizational specificities that are discussed within each literature stream.

ALLIANCE FORMATION IN NEW AND SMALL VENTURES

This literature stream is concerned primarily with understanding the antecedents of strategic alliances (inputs), while also outlining the relative consequences in terms of advantages and disadvantages (outputs). As suggested in Table 8.1, the theme of alliance formation is covered extensively by the broad literature on strategic alliances, and receives considerable attention also within the narrower perspective on entrepreneurial ventures. While the general literature provides an overarching framework for understanding alliance formation, the entrepreneurship literature sheds further light on the distinctive motivations, advantages, and challenges for new and small ventures engaging in strategic alliances.

Inputs for Alliance Formation in Entrepreneurial Ventures

According to several scholars (Colombo et al., 2006; Freeman, 1991; Gomes-Casseres, 1997; McGee, Dowling, & Megginson, 1995; Shan, 1990), entrepreneurial ventures facing adverse environmental conditions are especially inclined to establish strategic alliances. As pointed out by Eisenhardt and Schoonhoven (1996), new and small ventures in highly competitive markets suffer from vulnerable strategic positions, because the margins are low and product differentiation is difficult. In this context, the incentive to alliance making is particularly high, since "strategic alliances can reduce the likelihood of competitive threats...and offer a mechanism for exploiting new market opportunities" (Park, Chen, & Gallagher, 2002, p. 528).

However, entrepreneurial ventures vary considerably in their resource endowment, therefore presenting a different ability to tap into interorganizational networks and to sustain long-term performance (Baum et al., 2000). Ahuja (2000), Eisenhardt and Schoonhoven (1996), and Park et al. (2002) have shown that new and small ventures with valuable resources—in terms of technology, manufacturing, and finances—are better able to bring about alliances in highly volatile markets. On the contrary, resource-poor ventures are less likely to secure alliances, even though they would profit the most from tapping into a network of external resources (Stuart, 1998). In this case, the very condition which provides an incentive to form alliances—that is, resource scarcity—acts as a barrier against the ability to form alliances. Eisenhardt and Schoonhoven (1996) note the "fundamental irony of alliancing" (p. 137), observing that strategic alliances are set up to access external resources, yet internal resources are needed to set up strategic alliances.

Besides resource endowment, the social capital of a new venture—defined in terms of the network ties of the founding team—was found to facilitate alliance making (Eisenhardt & Schoonhoven 1996; Shan, Walker, & Kogut, 1994; Vanhaverbeke, Beerkens, & Duysters, 2007; Walker, Kogut, & Shan, 1997). A study by BarNir and Smith (2002) on small ventures showed that the social ties of senior executives account for a substantial amount of variance in the formation of horizontal and vertical alliances (11% and 22%, respectively). Elfring and Hulsink (2003, 2007) further showed that alliance formation is best supported by a mix of strong and weak ties. On the one hand, strong ties (i.e., close relationships) are associated with the exchange of tacit knowledge, and with the provision of crucial resources on the part of actors close to the founding team. On the other hand, weak ties (i.e., loose relationships) provide access to innovative knowledge combinations, while also offering connections to contacts outside of the entrepreneur's close network (BarNir & Smith, 2002; Chung, Singh, & Lee, 2000; Hoang & Antoncic, 2003).

In summary, the foremost inputs for the formation of strategic alliances in new and small ventures are a combination of environmental conditions, technological resources, and social capital. Whereas environmental conditions provide the strategic rationale for new and small ventures' engagement in strategic alliances, technological and social capitals represent the primary enablers of alliance formation. In the next section, we turn to the outputs of alliance formation, by taking a closer look at the advantages as well as the disadvantages that strategic alliances pose to entrepreneurial ventures. In effect, alliance formation has uncertain effects on venture development, since the characteristics of entrepreneurial ventures amplify both the benefits and the risks that are entailed by strategic alliances.

OUTPUTS OF ALLIANCE FORMATION IN ENTREPRENEURIAL VENTURES

Favorable Outputs

A wide body of research suggests that the formation of strategic alliances has the potential to sustain the development of entrepreneurial ventures (Chen & Li, 1999; Lee, 2007; Shan et al., 1994; Stuart, Hoang, & Hybels, 1999; Van Gils & Zwart, 2004; Willoughby & Galvin, 2005). As we will review below, strategic alliances can deliver a number of favorable outcomes to entrepreneurial ventures, by reducing the economic cost of operations, providing access to knowledge assets, and enhancing their reputation and expansion in international markets.

The economic advantages of alliance formation are particularly beneficial for new and small ventures confronted with resource constraints in high-tech and hyper-competitive sectors (Narula, 2004). To a certain extent, strategic alliances provide the security of a reversible investment, since limited damage is inflicted to the primary operations of a partner company, in case of project failure or alliance dissolution. At the same time, strategic alliances can lower the risks inherent to large projects, by spreading costs across a number of partners, while also securing funding to bring forth the innovation process. Teaming up with competent partners might also result in a reduction in lead times, an aspect of particular relevance in high-tech sectors with a shortened product life-cycle (Faems et al., 2005; De Man & Duysters, 2005).

In addition to providing economic advantages, alliance formation enables new and small ventures to sustain innovation and new product development by accessing, absorbing, and creating knowledge. A specific reason why alliance formation fosters innovation consists in the provision of a "radar function" for accessing knowledge in the external environment (De Man & Duysters, 2005). Such function is particularly germane to entrepreneurial ventures—permitting to scan the alliance network for relevant knowledge, without incurring the cost of investing in a particular technology or infrastructure (Narula, 2004). Alliance formation also enables new and small ventures to absorb knowledge from the partner company, and therefore to further reduce the newcomers' disadvantage (Faems et al., 2005; Lane & Lubatkin, 1998; Simonin, 1999). Such a process of knowledge absorption, in turn, sustains the creation of new knowledge within the scope of the collaborative venture (Baum et al., 2000; Muller & Välikangas, 2002).

Besides providing access to knowledge assets, strategic alliances can enhance the reputation of new and small ventures, by providing status transfer from prominent partners (Baum et al., 2000). By leveraging the reputation of alliance partners, an entrepreneurial venture can improve its position in the competitive domain and attract capital for its investments (Stuart et al., 1999). This is especially the case in high-tech sectors, where scientific uncertainty about a product's viability leads investors to assess a venture by looking at its network relationships (Baum et al., 2000; Shane & Cable, 2002; Stuart et al., 1999). In particular, Baum and Silverman (2004) found that formation of downstream (rather than upstream) alliances is positively correlated to the obtainment of financing from venture capitalists. Downstream alliances, in fact, are an indicator of a venture's access to commercial channels, and signal the confidence of established firms in the technical soundness, and commercial viability of its products. Conversely, venture capitalists may interpret upstream alliances as an indication that the venture lacks critical resources and remains in an exploratory phase far from product commercialization. In this regard, upstream alliances may be subject to ambiguous interpretation on the part of venture capitalists, despite providing access to cutting-edge knowledge essential for new product development.

A further advantage of alliance formation consists in the possibility of improving an entrepreneurial venture's position in the global market, by expanding operations across geographically dispersed locations (Hara & Kanai, 1994; Leiblein & Reuer, 2004; Kuemmerle, 1999; Yli-Renko, Autio, & Tontti, 2002). As suggested by Narula (2004), international alliances permit to overcome barriers to foreign market entry and to leverage the market expertise of local partners for product adaptation and commercialization. Moreover, international alliances enable to access location-specific assets, and to tap into technological systems located in the most innovation-intensive regions of the global industry (Colombo, Grilli, Murtinu, Piscitello, & Piva, 2009). However, resource constraints make new ventures less capable than large companies to take advantage of international relations (Leiblein & Reuer, 2004; Narula, 2004). In effect, the formation of international alliances involves complex coordination and demands substantial commitment in terms of financial, managerial, and administrative resources.

Unfavorable Outputs

Since they bring along considerable challenges for both established and new ventures, strategic alliances are often dissolved without achieving the desired results (Das & Teng, 2000b; De Man & Duysters, 2005). Alliance failure brings heightened risks for small and new ventures, which often lack the financial resources to recover from economic losses and find alternative partners (Draulans et al., 2003; Zineldin & Dodourova, 2005). While a number of factors contribute to the instability of strategic alliances, the primary reason for failure is the lack of binding mechanisms, combined with the presence of both performance and relational risks. Whereas relational risks pertain to the relationship between the partners (e.g., opportunistic behavior), performance risks encompass intrinsic difficulties in achieving the objectives of the alliance (Das & Teng, 2000b).

As "incomplete contracts" (Anand & Khanna, 2000, p. 295), strategic alliances often lack a clear definition of responsibility allocation, and of the property rights associated with the collaborative outputs. Due to the lack of binding mechanisms, alliance partners may fear opportunistic behavior from the counterpart, and hence withhold resources at the expense of the collaboration (Das & Teng, 2000b). For example, fear of helping a competitor in developing a new technology may be an incentive to hold back in the alliance, by protecting research results or hiding the best people (De Man & Duysters, 2005). Ultimately, intra-alliance rivalry may deteriorate into a "learning race," where the partners attempt to absorb external knowledge as much as possible, while divulging internal knowledge as little as possible (Baum et al., 2000, p. 271). New and small ventures are particularly vulnerable to the risks of a learning race, possessing a limited technological portfolio, while also lacking the financial resources to enforce control mechanisms (Colombo et al., 2006; Narula, 2004). The phenomenon of learning races is fiercest in horizontal alliances, since partners with similar positioning are more likely to reduce knowledge transfer in order to prevent competition (Baum et al., 2000; Silverman & Baum, 2002). In turn, the negotiation, contractual, and administrative costs incurred for dealing with appropriation concerns in horizontal alliances can be overwhelming for new and small ventures (Colombo et al., 2006).

Even when alliance partners do not engage in learning races, their collaborative activity may face severe barriers, as the process of integrating knowledge across organizational boundaries is fraught with inherent complexity. On the one hand, knowledge transfer may be obstructed by substantial differences in terms of knowledge bases, organizational cultures, and operational infrastructures.[2] On the other hand, knowledge recombination may be prevented by the inability to successfully retain and exploit the knowledge transferred by the partner company (Baum et al., 2000; Szulanski, 1996; Willoughby & Galvin, 2005). The retention barrier may represent a major challenge for entrepreneurial ventures, which usually lack previous expertise in absorbing knowledge from partner companies. Absorptive capacity, in fact, is enhanced by repeated involvement in collaborative relations, which expose the firm to a broad repertoire of experiences (Anand & Khanna, 2000; Lane & Lubatkin, 1998).

PROCESSES OF ALLIANCE MAKING IN NEW AND SMALL VENTURES

Having synthesized the literature on the inputs and outputs of alliance formation, in this section we take a closer look at the contributions that outline the processes involved in strategic alliances. As suggested in Figure 8.1, we have identified three processes of alliance making and corresponding literature streams—that is, alliance structuring, management, and capability building. While alliance structuring is concerned with defining the structural design of strategic alliances (Das & Teng, 2000b), alliance management deals with governing day-to-day alliance relationships (Ireland et al., 2002). Finally, the literature on alliance capability building shifts attention towards the internal processes of alliance partners, arguing for the need to build up an organizational-wide capability to manage strategic alliances (Draulans et al., 2003).

Alliance Structuring

This research stream covers the foremost stages of alliance making, when a company sets out to define the overall structure of a strategic alliance. Alliance structuring involves the selection of suitable partners, the design of governance mechanisms, and the definition of the temporal horizon for the strategic alliance. As evident in Table 8.1, this theme has received considerable attention in both the alliance and the entrepreneurship literatures, even though the focus on new and small ventures could be further developed.

The selection of an appropriate partner is considered to be the foremost requirement for realizing the potential benefits of a strategic alliance (Bierly & Gallagher, 2007; Hitt, Dacin, Levitas, Arregle, & Borza, 2000; Hoffmann & Schlosser, 2001; Holmberg & Cummings, 2009). In selecting partners, new and small ventures should be even more careful than established ones, since they have fewer possibilities to eventually recover from alliance failure (Narula, 2004). The most suitable arrangement is between partners with complementary competences, compatible objectives and a cooperative attitude (Baum et al., 2000; Brouthers, Brouthers, & Wilkinson, 1995; Hitt et al., 2000). Lane and Lubatkin (1998) add that alliance partners should present relatively similar knowledge bases in order to effectively integrate knowledge. In fact, sharing a common ground fosters the alliance partners' capability to recognize, assimilate, and ultimately deploy the combined knowledge.

As a confirmation of the importance of partner selection for entrepreneurial ventures, it is worth noticing the development of a stand-alone research stream discussing the viability of strategic alliances with larger companies (Das & He, 2006). According to Brouthers et al. (1995), strategic alliances work better when the partners present a symmetric configuration in terms of organizational dimensions, financial resources, and managerial style. By contrast, more recent research has revealed that "asymmetric partnerships" may deliver considerable advantages to entrepreneurial ventures (Alvarez & Barney, 2001; O'Dwyer & O'Flynn, 2005; Minshall et al., 2008). A strategic alliance with a large company, in fact, may provide an entrepreneurial venture with the resources necessary to bring its technology to the market, and may eventually increase its reputation via status transfer.

Yet such advantages are achieved at the price of heightened risks. Often, most of the economic value created by the strategic alliance is appropriated by the large company, with severe threats for the survival of the entrepreneurial venture. To a large extent, such a disparity in wealth appropriation is caused by a difference in the learning rate, with the large company being in a position to absorb knowledge at a faster pace. A further reason lies in the ease of appropriation of the different competences: While the organizational competences of an established company are usually embedded within organizational routines, the technology developed by the entrepreneurial venture is embodied in discrete processes—and as such is made accessible through the alliance itself. After learning about the entrepreneurial venture's technology, the large company has an incentive to underinvest in the relationship, by shifting resources towards alternative activities (Alvarez & Barney, 2001; Das & He, 2006).

The literature advises new and small ventures to put in place protective measures, by performing due diligence on the large firm under consideration, and by carefully crafting the alliance contract (Minshall et al., 2008; Minshall, Mortara, Valli, & Probert, 2010). Above all, entrepreneurial ventures should pursue a diversified technology development strategy, by bringing a bundle of potentially valuable technologies to the strategic alliance. As pointed out by Alvarez and Barney (2001), "The inventive capability—a capability that large firms usually value but cannot develop or imitate—makes it possible for entrepreneurial firms to create value and appropriate wealth through alliances with large firms" (p. 147). Das and He (2006) further advise entrepreneurial ventures seeking established partners to outline compatible objectives for the alliance, to secure access to manufacturing and marketing functions, to involve middle managers of both firms from the very beginning, to create a dedicated task force and to define detailed plans of action.

After conclusion of the partnering process, the next task of alliance partners consists of defining governance mechanisms for the strategic alliance (Barringer & Harrison, 2000; Das & Teng, 1996, 2000b; Gulati, 1998; Ireland et al., 2002). This involves making choices among a variety of arrangements, ranging from non-equity to equity arrangements (Lorange & Roos, 1993). On the one side, non-equity alliances entail a loose interaction among partners and result in a flexible framework allowing to control risks, limit commitment, and exit easily. On the other side, equity alliances formally lay out the relationships among partners and provide the vertical integration necessary to enforce control, align incentives, and distribute residuals. As such, equity alliances are more likely to be observed when a cooperative attitude cannot be taken for granted (Das & Teng, 1996) and partners face greater ambiguity in codifying knowledge—as is the case in research-intensive collaborations (Anand & Khanna, 2000; Mowery, Oxley, & Silverman, 1996). While defining governance mechanisms, the alliance partners must concurrently align their perceptions and expectations regarding the time horizon of the strategic alliance (Das & Teng, 1996, 2000b; Joskow, 1987; Kogut, 1991). A short-term orientation (i.e., exploitation propensity) provides assurance against failure risks, enabling an incremental approach to the collaborative engagement, and avoiding excessive burdens on corporate partners. Conversely, a long-term orientation (i.e., exploration propensity) contributes to align the partners' incentives, by providing a base for a durable relationship and discouraging opportunistic behavior.

The definition of governance mechanisms therefore depends on the scope of the strategic alliance (Lorange & Roos, 1993), the risks entailed by the collaborative relationship (Das & Teng, 1996), and the temporal horizon of the alliance itself (Das, 2004, 2006; Das & Teng, 2000b). While these factors determine the initial design of governance mechanisms, the dynamic nature of strategic alliances inevitably involves a need of adapting such mechanisms over time (Ariño et al., 2008; Ireland et al., 2002).[3] Ex post contractual renegotiations are necessary in order to accommodate for unexpected requirements from alliance partners, as well as to correct the inefficiencies generated by governance misalignments—occurring when excessive control is enforced for relatively undemanding collaborations, or scarce control is put in place for commitment-intensive alliances. In a study of alliance dynamics, Ariño et al. (2008) found that entrepreneurial ventures are less likely than established companies to adapt alliances in the face of changing conditions. The lack of collaboration expertise, financial resources, and administrative capabilities for contractual renegotiation explains new and small ventures' low responsiveness to governance misalignments. Furthermore, entrepreneurial ventures often fail to add safeguard mechanisms in their contractual agreements, when making transaction-specific investments in strategic alliances. As a result, they are subject to the risk of alliance lock-in, since transaction-specific assets cannot be easily put to other uses in case of alliance breakdown (Ariño et al., 2008).

Alliance Management

This literature stream takes a dynamic perspective on strategic alliances, by shifting attention from the alliance structure to the on-going relationship between the alliance partners. Besides aspects of relationship building, particular attention is paid to managing the knowledge bases of the alliance partners, as well as to addressing the relational and performance risks that are entailed by strategic alliances. As suggested in Table 8.1, the alliance management perspective still needs to gain momentum in the entrepreneurship literature, even though a few authors have started discussing the unique challenges encountered by new and small ventures.

As a foremost consideration, this literature stream suggests that the appropriate structuring of a strategic alliance does not provide—by itself—a direct way to success (Ireland et al., 2002; Lane & Lubatkin, 1998; Nicholls-Nixon & Woo, 2003). As pointed out by Standing, Standing, and Lin (2008, p. 789), "Complementarity, compatibility, and relational capital are the basis for forming an alliance . . . but after an alliance has been formed, a key issue is managing and guiding the alliance through the various stages of its lifecycle." Yet, small ventures tend to underestimate the amount of managerial effort required to make the alliance work (Beecham & Cordey-Hayes, 1998).

According to various scholars, one of the main reasons for alliance failure can be found in the managers' inability to address relational problems arising after the contractual agreement (Anderson, Christ, & Sedatole, 2006; Das & Teng, 1996, Doz, 2002; Kelly, Schaan, & Joncas, 2002, Vlaar, Van den

Bosch, & Volberda, 2006). As put by Beecham and Cordey-Hayes (1998), "The initial agreements emphasize strategic complementarity as a source of value for the partnership, but take subsequent strategic convergence as given. Cultural distance, uncertainties and misunderstandings as well as hidden agendas make such a convergence difficult, unless it is truly desired by the top management of both partners and is actively managed" (p. 194).

Recognizing that such challenges may be particularly threatening for new and small ventures, Larson (1991) and Senker and Sharp (1997) advise their executives to envision a *trial-and-error phase* in alliance management. The trial period ensures the reversibility of decisions, by providing the occasion for the alliance partners to renegotiate their contractual agreement in the case that unforeseen circumstances hinder collaboration progress. During this period, the alliance partners set up the relationship, and concurrently lay out rules, norms and procedures for interaction. At the end of the trial period, trust should be established as a guiding principle for the collaboration, and the partners can accordingly move on to the *operating phase* of the strategic alliance.

While the trial stage involves an incremental process of relationship building, the operating stage is characterized by a steady investment in the collaboration, and entails a tight integration of the partner organizations (Larson, 1991). To ease the operational stage, the collaborating parties may set up an alliance management team in charge of coordinating information, resources, and tasks across organizational boundaries (Standing et al., 2008). The appointed team should act as boundary spanning agents between alliance partners, take responsibility for the implementation of the alliance operations, and manage to resolve emerging conflict (Huiskonen & Pirtillä, 2002).

This literature stream also points to the importance of managing knowledge assets, which represent the foremost source of competitive advantage for entrepreneurial ventures (Colombo et al., 2006; Lane & Lubatkin, 1998). As mentioned above, strategic alliances are a mixed blessing, providing an occasion to access knowledge in the external network, while at the same time posing the threat of losing proprietary knowledge. The management function is thus required to reconcile divergent objectives, namely to protect partners against unintended knowledge spillover, while also ensuring knowledge sharing within the scope of the strategic alliance.

As regards the objective of preventing knowledge spillover, Faems, Janssens, and Van Looy (2010) identified three management strategies that entrepreneurial ventures could possibly adopt. Firstly, partners can reduce the need to share sensitive information by partitioning the alliance activities in partner-specific task domains and working at the interfaces between the diverse modules. Secondly, partners may subdivide the intellectual property rights in different knowledge domains, which reflect their technological competence. Thirdly, partners may agree to exploit the knowledge developed within the alliance in different commercial domains, so to avoid the hazard of future competition. Yet these strategies are not without constraints: In fact, the definition of partner-specific tasks may lead to duplications and at the same time hinder the possibility of jointly solving unexpected problems. Moreover, the definition of knowledge and commercial domains is possible only if the partners operate with different technological focuses, and if the product can be exploited in different domains.

As regards the objective of sustaining knowledge sharing, Yli-Renko, Autio, and Sapienza (2001) suggest investing in the development of relational capital—defined in terms of goodwill, trust and reciprocal obligations between the alliance partners. Brachos, Kostopoulos, Soderquist, and Prastacos (2007) underscore the relevance of creating a "social space" between alliance partners in order to foster reciprocal trust, and increase individual motivation to share knowledge. Social activities such as visits to the partner's facilities help build a solid relational foundation, and motivate engagement in a fine-grained interaction conducive to knowledge transfer (Faems et al., 2010). Slowinski, Seelig, and Hull (1996) showed that the buildup of relational capital between alliance managers ensures greater continuity in asymmetric alliances with established companies. A trustworthy relationship in fact is more effective in deterring opportunistic behavior than contractual agreements (Deeds & Hill, 1999; Larson, 1991, 1992).

Yet, Yli-Renko et al. (2001) found that relational capital may inhibit the process of knowledge sharing in the alliance itself, since a very high level of trust may subtly instill the expectation that the partner will provide information when needed. In their words, "As relationship quality or trust reaches a very high level, the perceived need to monitor diminishes, decreasing the level of conflict and of intense processing of information . . . While lowered monitoring and bargaining may reduce the cost of knowledge exchange, they may also lower the amount of new knowledge acquired" (pp. 607–608). In addition, excessive trust may subjugate the entrepreneurial venture to the threat of competitive abuse from the partner organization, even though the investment in relational capital was initially intended to deter opportunistic behavior. The over-commitment to a strategic alliance in fact involves the risk of relational dependence, and leaves the entrepreneurial venture with few possibilities of considering exit strategies or forming other alliances (Miles, Preece, & Baetz, 1999; Standing et al., 2008). Particularly in asymmetric partnerships, failure to leave the door open to alternative alliance options may put the entrepreneurial venture into a weaker negotiating position with respect to the partner.

In other words, investing all resources into a single relationship entails excessive risk for new and small ventures, given the high instability and failure rate of strategic alliances (Das & Teng, 2000b). Uzzi (1997) added that close ties with the alliance partner bring along the risk of over-embeddedness with respect to the wider network of external relationships. While acting as conduits of knowledge sharing within the dyadic relationship, close ties may in fact insulate the entrepreneurial venture from external sources of knowledge. Thus, new and small ventures are advised to manage their dyadic alliance in connection with the broader network, by developing a diversified portfolio of collaborative relationships (George et al., 2001). Yet this recommendation raises the critical issue of how entrepreneurial ventures with constrained resources can set out to successfully manage a constellation of network relationships, while being involved in a dyadic alliance.

Maurer and Ebers (2006) advise entrepreneurial ventures to pursue specialization in alliance management, with each member of the management team cultivating diverse alliances within the firm's network. For example, a manager in a biotech start-up may specialize in strategic alliances with venture capitalists, research laboratories, or business consultants. In turn, such specialization requires the entrepreneurial venture to devise integrating mechanisms (such as formal meetings) whereby managers can share information and know-how flowing from the diverse alliances. While posing additional challenges, coordinating network alliances provides a safety net against the relational risks involved in dyadic alliances, and exposes the new venture to multiple sources of knowledge (BarNir & Smith, 2002; Maurer & Ebers, 2006).

Alliance Capability Building

This literature stream shifts attention towards the internal processes of alliance partners, suggesting the build-up of an "alliance capability" as a way of increasing the likelihood of alliance success. As visible in Table 8.1, alliance capability is a growing research stream, but has not yet received substantial attention from alliance scholars focusing on entrepreneurial ventures. This literature gap is surprising, since companies with limited experience of strategic alliances—such as new and small ventures—tend to be less successful in alliance management (Anand & Khanna, 2000).

Alliance capability is broadly defined as the capability to effectively establish, structure, and manage strategic alliances (Beugelsdijk, Noordehaven, & Koen, 2003; Draulans et al., 2003; Walter, Auer, & Ritter, 2006). Rothaermel and Deeds (2006) argue that the development of an alliance capability is crucial for entrepreneurial ventures, given their limited resources to cope with alliance failure. In particular, new and small ventures need to develop different capabilities in order to address the requirements posed by upstream and downstream alliances. Upstream alliances with research laboratories demand a large amount of knowledge management capabilities, given the tacitness, ambiguity, and complexity of the knowledge being shared (Rothaermel & Deeds, 2006). Downstream alliances with larger companies mainly require relationship management capabilities to deal with substantial differences in the organizational structures of the alliance partners (Alvarez & Barney, 2001).

An organization's ability to manage alliances is suggested to be path-dependent—that is, it is expected to increase gradually with repeated engagement into strategic alliances (Anand & Khanna, 2000; Heimeriks & Duysters, 2007; Rothaermel & Deeds, 2006; Standing et al., 2008). However, learning-by-doing has inherent limitations (Hoang & Rothaermel, 2005; Draulans et al., 2003), particularly for entrepreneurial ventures lacking initial experience in alliance management (Rothaermel & Deeds, 2006). A study by Deeds and Hill (1996) on biotech start-ups, in fact, showed that engagement in strategic alliances has a positive impact on new product development, but the relationship exhibits diminishing returns as the number of alliances increases. From a study of 86 semiconductor start-ups, Almeida, Dokko, and Rosenkopf (2003) concluded that even larger start-ups may not be mature enough to learn from their strategic alliances.

As suggested by De Man (2005), "Learning-by-doing is the first step for building an alliance capability, [but] it is not sufficient. Companies also need to focus on mechanisms that formalize lessons learned and transfer alliance best practices inside companies" (p. 316). Taking a disciplined approach to capability building in fact creates a platform for repeatable success, enable managers to proactively respond to unforeseen circumstances and eventually leads to superior growth via strategic alliances (Brockelman & Cucci, 2000; De Man, 2005; Draulans et al., 2003; Harbison & Pekar, 1997; Kale, Dyer, & Singh, 2002; Kale & Singh, 2007; Heimeriks & Duysters, 2007; Heimeriks & Reuer, 2006; Mascarenhas & Koza, 2008). The need to systematically invest in building up an alliance capability is even more prominent in new and small ventures: "[Alliance] management capabilities may be limited in small innovative firms which are focused on turning science and ideas into a usable product. This creates the need to increase management's business acumen or acquire additional management resources" (Standing et al., 2008, p. 789). The literature on capability building suggests various techniques to institutionalize alliance-related knowledge within the firm, such as training in alliance management, the implementation of alliance evaluations, the use of frameworks for alliance management, and the appointment of an alliance specialist (within or outside the firm).

Draulans et al. (2003) showed that training in alliance management does foster alliance performance, with companies adopting such a technique outperforming the non-adopters by 10% in their alliance success rate. Taught either by in-company specialists or external consultants, training courses are particularly useful to new and small ventures lacking previous experience in alliance making (Heimeriks, Klijn, & Reuer, 2009; Harbison & Pekar, 1997; Heimeriks & Reuer, 2006). Minshall et al. (2008) found that high-tech start-ups are able to learn from the others' experience through participation in multi-company workshops, involvement in a community of practice, and access to web-based reading materials. In an action research project, Minshall et al. (2010) documented best practices in the management of asymmetric alliances, and accordingly disseminated results among start-ups in the Cambridge high-tech business cluster. The research project concluded with the development of a public website (www.managing-partnerships.net) for broader dissemination of background knowledge on asymmetric alliances.

In combination with alliance training, the evaluation of previous alliances contributes to develop an alliance capability by providing an occasion to learn from experience, and to cull out lessons of wider applicability (Draulans et al., 2003; Harbison & Pekar, 1997). Draulans et al. (2003) draw a distinction between individual and cross-alliance evaluation— the latter requiring the comparison of multiple alliances. Whereas alliance-experienced companies take advantage of crossed evaluations, alliance-inexperienced companies benefit the most from individual evaluations. For alliance-inexperienced companies, even simple evaluation methods contribute to the build-up of alliance know-how (while complex evaluation methods may be cumbersome to apply). The rate of alliance success in inexperienced companies increases significantly when individual alliance evaluation is applied with respect to a number of evaluation criteria, ranging from relationship quality to financial performance (Draulans et al., 2003).

Furthermore, use of alliance frameworks—such as process-support guidelines, decision-support protocols, and performance-evaluation templates—was found to facilitate the management of day-to-day alliance operations (De Man, 2005; Heimeriks et al., 2009). In general, an alliance framework contains codified knowledge related to different stages of the alliance life-cycle, thus supporting the alliance manager along with the evolution of the collaborative relationship. According to Standing et al. (2008), alliance tools are particularly useful to entrepreneurial ventures, providing clear guidance to alliance managers with limited first-hand experience. Standing et al. (2008) further developed a holistic framework for biotech start-ups to manage diverse aspects of alliance making, ranging from partner selection, to product development, to virtual teamwork. Minshall et al. (2010) found that high-tech start-ups benefit from the use of technology roadmaps whereby they can document non-confidential aspects of their business models for communication with potential partners. Used in the context of face-to-face meetings, technology roadmaps also enable the partners to identify opportunities to jointly develop technological innovations (Duysters, Kok, & Vaandrager, 1999).

In addition to the techniques mentioned above, the appointment of an alliance specialist significantly increases the success rate of strategic alliances (Draulans et al., 2003; De Man, 2005). The designation of such an alliance specialist, however, is a difficult and risky task for entrepreneurial ventures, as resources and know-how are scarce and most efforts must go into product development and customer relations. Nevertheless, new and small ventures may implement this important function by taking advantage of business angels, start-up incubators or venture capitalists as part-time alliance specialists (Steier & Greenwood, 2000). Davenport, Davies, and Grimes (1998) further suggest that governmental institutions may act as "honest brokers" of strategic alliances for high-tech ventures, while also supporting the development of alliance management capabilities. For example, *Europe Innova* is a collaborative policy program of the European Union providing high-tech start-ups with specialized expertise in the set-up of technology alliances for innovation development.

DISCUSSION AND DIRECTIONS FOR FUTURE RESEARCH

Critical Success Factors for Strategic Alliances in Entrepreneurial Ventures

In this section, we further elaborate on the reviewed literature with a view of formulating managerial recommendations for new and small ventures to thrive by engaging in strategic alliances. To this end, we propose a conceptual diagram (Figure 8.2) which suggests a course of action for entrepreneurial ventures to address the many challenges encountered in structuring, managing, and learning about strategic alliances. This conceptual diagram provides a synoptic overview of managerial recommendations, and concurrently makes an attempt to connect the research streams on new ventures and strategic alliances.

The cyclical pathway describes the course of action that entrepreneurial ventures should follow to succeed in strategic alliances, while the edged shape represents the factors which act against this endeavor. The three stars represent supportive activities (i.e., manage network relations, strengthen internal capabilities, and connect with start-up incubators) that new and small ventures should carry out at all stages in order to increase chances of success.

Ideally, it is possible to envision a learning trajectory, by which entrepreneurial ventures first gather general information via alliance training, and subsequently enter a number of strategic alliances. As suggested by the starting point in Figure 8.2, entrepreneurial ventures should first acquire basic knowledge about strategic alliances, by engaging in training programs. The training activity will establish the ground for alliance structuring, by

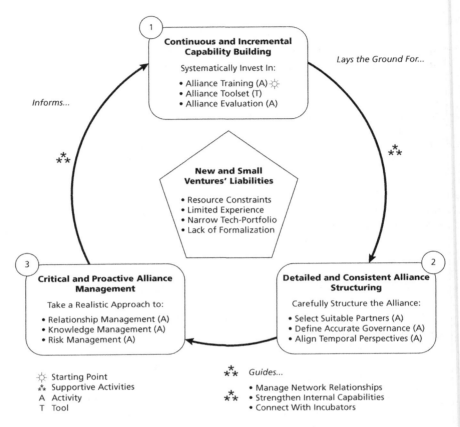

Figure 8.2 Critical success factors for strategic alliances in entrepreneurial ventures.

providing practical guidance on selecting partners, defining governance mechanisms, and aligning perspectives. In turn, the accurate structuring will guide alliance management, which requires a critical and proactive approach to building up the relationship with the alliance partner, creating the conditions for knowledge sharing, and dealing with multiple risks.

New and small ventures' managers should undertake an individual assessment of any concluded alliance in order to derive managerial lessons of wider applicability. At the time when practical experience will have produced a basic alliance capability, the management team should further invest in formal approaches to alliance learning. For example, entrepreneurial ventures may acquire a tailored toolset to support the diverse stages of alliance making. In this way, they should be able to gradually scale up in alliance capability according to their learning curve, and to accommodate for other developmental necessities.

Our review of literature revealed that relational dependence, over-embeddedness and knowledge appropriation represent the most severe risks for entrepreneurial ventures involved in strategic alliances. While being engaged in a dyadic alliance, new and small ventures should simultaneously manage their broader network of relationships, in order to take advantage of multiple ties and to avoid the risk of relational lock-in. The business network of an entrepreneurial venture—defined as a set of strong and weak ties—will expose the new venture to innovative combinations of knowledge, and at the same time provide the milieu for the formation of new strategic alliances.

Besides looking at the broader network of relationships, a new venture should invest in the development of internal capabilities, and expand its technological portfolio in order to profit the most from interorganizational collaboration. In fact, technological competences interact with external linkages in determining the economic performance of a new venture (Lee, Lee, & Pennings, 2001) and are of essence to attract valuable partners (Eisenhardt & Schoonhoven, 1996) as well as to mitigate risks in asymmetric alliances (Alvarez & Barney, 2001). In addition, technological competences—together with collaborative linkages—influence a new venture's ability to pursue expansion in highly competitive global industries (Leiblein & Reuer, 2004).

As a means to overcome impediments to successful alliance making, new and small ventures may request the support of business incubators. A prominent role is emerging for incubators to train tenants in alliance making, and to facilitate the identification of suitable partners (Baum et al., 2000; Europe Innova, 2008). First, incubators may act as *sources of expertise*, by providing entrepreneurial ventures with the knowledge and resources necessary for building up an alliance capability. In this view, incubators are expected to disseminate knowledge, by providing alliance consultancy, training courses, and evaluation frameworks to large communities of new and small ventures. Second, incubators may act as *linking devices*, and foster the constitution of successful alliances by means of connecting ventures with complementary competences and resources. In the long run, incubators may build up an international forum whereby tenants get access to innovation systems located in other countries, thus meeting the challenges of internationalization.

Nevertheless, the support activity of incubators encounters considerable barriers, since the available research is relatively under-organized, and ultimately fails to provide actionable advice on building strategic alliances in the start-up phase. As recognized in a review on incubator policies in European countries, strategic alliances represent a priority issue for new and small ventures, yet a practical methodology is lacking to guide tenants in the constitution, management, and evaluation of collaborative relationships

(OECD, 2002). The following section thus highlights the current gaps in the literature in order to provide a starting point for future research to be carried out in the domain of alliance making in new and small ventures.

Directions for Future Research

As suggested in our literature review, research on strategic alliances in entrepreneurial ventures is relatively underdeveloped, and lags behind the broader literature on strategic alliances. While providing some insights into the formation and structuring of strategic alliances in new and small ventures, the reviewed literature fails to develop a focused outlook on the ensuing processes of alliance management and capability building. This gap is surprising, since entrepreneurial ventures direly need to become skillful in alliance management, having fewer possibilities to recover from alliance failure. Therefore, researchers should advance the exploration of strategic alliances while taking into consideration the unique features of entrepreneurial ventures. In this section, we identify research themes that have been discussed only marginally in the reviewed literature, and suggest theoretical perspectives that are suitable to begin the exploration of such themes.

Dyadic Versus Network Level

The literature streams on dyadic and network alliances have developed separately, although considerable benefits may derive from an integrated perspective (see Inkpen & Tsang, 2005). In our literature review, we have favored a dyadic perspective on alliance formation, while also making an attempt to understand how dyadic alliances should be managed within the broader network. Future research should take this agenda a step further, by exploring in greater detail the managerial practices emerging at the interfaces between dyadic alliances and the broader network. As an example, a prospect study may attempt to uncover whether network ties give shape to the dyadic alliance, by exerting an influence on the strategic choices of the alliance partners. Previous research in business-to-business networks suggests that a business affects and in turn is affected by the network of business relations in which it is embedded (Håkansson, Ford, Gadde, Snehota, & Waluszewski, 2009). However, the nature of mutual influences between network ties and strategic alliances has not yet been studied systematically, either in the general literature on strategic alliances or in the literature focused on entrepreneurial ventures.

Micro Level of Analysis

Current research on strategic alliances favors a macro perspective of analysis, to a large extent neglecting the interpersonal relationships involved in alliance management (Stock, 2006). Most knowledge processes still take place in interpersonal groups—such as alliance management teams—formed at the intersection between the alliance partners (Soekijad & Andriessen, 2003). This is particularly the case in new and small ventures, where the management style tends to be informal and based on relational aspects. In such ventures, the success of a collaborative endeavor is likely to rely heavily on communication exchanges taking place at the interpersonal level (Brachos et al., 2007; Nonaka & Takeuchi, 1995; Szulanski, 1996). Nevertheless, communication barriers arising in interpersonal relationships may hinder knowledge sharing between alliance partners. Team members may encounter considerable difficulties in conveying complex insights to each other, especially when different cultures, expertise, and backgrounds are at play. When they lack motivation, trust, and learning orientation, team members may engage in defensive routines, therefore limiting their efforts in providing, or receiving knowledge (Mengis & Eppler, 2008). Future research should adopt an interactionist or communicative perspective, in order to uncover the dynamics underlying knowledge sharing and development in the social space between the alliance partners. In doing so, it should be possible to uncover the micro-processes of alliance making, and to accordingly derive workable advice on creating a fertile context for knowledge sharing and development. The emergent literature on knowledge communication may provide a promising perspective, focusing on improving communication dynamics for facilitating knowledge processes (Mengis & Eppler, 2008). In such a close-up approach to strategic alliances in new and small ventures, one should not neglect consideration of the role of industry factors, of the national context, and of the scope of the strategic alliance—which in turn give way to other future research areas.

Industry Factors

As indicated at the outset of the chapter, this literature review is focused on knowledge-intensive industries and high-tech ventures operating in highly competitive markets. However, entrepreneurial ventures and their proneness to form strategic alliances may differ substantially based on the network structure of their core industry (Eisenhardt & Schoonhoven, 1996). Some industries may consist of highly connected players, as is the case of the information technology industry where private equity firms can act as bridge builders between entrepreneurial and established ventures. Other industries may be configured by a set of isolated players and thus require a more autonomous approach to alliance structuring, management, and learning. Furthermore, entrepreneurial ventures operating in sensitive sectors such as military technology may have to take secrecy requirements into consideration and accordingly face a higher path dependency in their alliance learning. Another aspect that is related to industry characteristics is the ease at which alliances can be formed and dismissed. Whereas some industries such as the business-to-consumer service industry may allow for rapid strategic alliance formation and discontinuation in case of failure, other industries, such as the biotech, pharmaceutical or medical devices sectors, may require more careful and thus lengthy strategic alliance deliberations (also due to regulatory demands).

Cultural and National Factors

Next to the industry logic, national and cultural factors may also affect the alliance making attitudes of new ventures (Baker, Gedajlovic, & Lubatkin, 2005). In some countries with high uncertainty avoidance and low social capital (generic trust), strategic alliance formation may require a less frequent approach, as it contains many uncertain eventualities (Hofstede, Hofstede, & Minkov, 1997). Cross-national, comparative research in this area could thus be a further promising research area. A cultural perspective may also lead to insights regarding international alliances of entrepreneurial ventures that are "born global" (Knight & Cavusgil, 2004).

CONCLUSION

The primary contribution of this literature review consists of organizing, integrating, and consolidating the literature on strategic alliances in new and small ventures, in connection with the broader literature on strategic alliances. We have gathered a relatively large collection of articles, and adopted an input-process-output framework to integrate the findings of the two literature streams. We have then offered a synopsis of current research on the inputs and outputs of alliance formation in entrepreneurial ventures, as well as on the associated processes of alliance structuring, management, and capability building.

Future research should intensify research on strategic alliances in new and small ventures, while also beginning the exploration of different lines of inquiry: First, to integrate the dyadic and the network perspectives; second, to explore patterns of interaction and communication; and, third, to derive tailored recommendations for entrepreneurial ventures to manage and build up an alliance capability. Such recommendations should take into consideration factors related to the industry, as well as the cultural and national context of the strategic alliance. Formulating evidence-based, tailored, and pragmatic advice is a key requirement to unlock the innovation potential of entrepreneurial ventures through strategic alliances.

NOTES

1. For excellent reviews of theoretical perspectives on alliance making, see Barringer and Harrison (2000), Ireland et al. (2002), and Street and Cameron (2007).
2. This is particularly relevant in international alliances, where cultural diversity may prevent reciprocal understanding, and eventually result in inter-partner conflict over values, beliefs, and norms (Kumar & Andersen, 2000).
3. The dynamic perspective on contractual negotiations represents an original contribution within the strategy literature, which usually favors a static perspective on alliance making.

ACKNOWLEDGMENTS

This work was partially funded by the Swiss National Science Foundation (SNSF) grant no. PBTIP1_140022. The authors would like to thank Francesco Chirico and Philipp Sieger for their comments on an earlier version of this manuscript. This chapter, save some minor changes, was earlier published as Comi, A., & Eppler, M. J. (2015). Building strategic alliances in new and small ventures: A review of literature and integrative framework. In T. K. Das (Ed.), *Strategic alliances for SME development* (pp. 61–94). Charlotte, NC: Information Age.

REFERENCES

Acs, Z. (2006). How is entrepreneurship good for economic growth? *Innovations, 1*(1), 97–107.

Ahuja, G. (2000). The duality of collaboration: Inducements and opportunities in the formation of interfirm linkages. *Strategic Management Journal, 21*(3), 317–343.

Almeida, P., Dokko, G., & Rosenkopf, L. (2003). Startup size and the mechanisms of external learning: Increasing opportunity and decreasing ability? *Research Policy, 32*(2), 301–315.

Alvarez, S. A., & Barney, J. B. (2001). How entrepreneurial firms can benefit from alliances with large partners. *Academy of Management Executive, 15*(1), 139–148.

Anand, B. N., & Khanna, T. (2000). Do firms learn to create value? The case of alliances. *Strategic Management Journal, 21*(3), 295–315.

Anderson, S. W., Christ, M. H., & Sedatole, K. L. (2006). *Managing strategic alliance risk: Survey evidence of control practices in collaborative inter-organizational settings.* Altamonte Springs, FL: Institute of Internal Auditors Research Foundation.

Ariño, A., Ragozzino, R., & Reuer, J. J. (2008). Alliance dynamics for entrepreneurial firms. *Journal of Management Studies, 45*(1), 147–168.

Baker, T., Gedajlovic, E., & Lubatkin, M. (2005). A framework for comparing entrepreneurship processes across nations. *Journal of International Business Studies, 36*, 492–504.

BarNir, A., & Smith, K. A. (2002). Interfirm alliances in the small business: The role of social networks. *Journal of Small Business Management, 40*(3), 219–232.

Barringer, B. R., & Harrison, J. S. (2000). Walking a tightrope: Creating value through interorganizational relationships. *Journal of Management, 26*(3), 367–403.

Baum, J. A. C., Calabrese, T., & Silverman, B. S. (2000). Don't go it alone: Alliance network composition and startups' performance in Canadian biotechnology. *Strategic Management Journal, 21*(3), 267–294.

Baum, J. A. C., & Silverman, B. S. (2004). Picking winners or building them? Alliance, intellectual, and human capital as selection criteria in venture financing and performance of biotechnology startups. *Journal of Business Venturing, 19*, 411–436.

Beecham, M. A., & Cordey-Hayes, M. (1998). Partnering and knowledge transfer in the U.K. motor industry. *Technovation, 18*(3), 191–205.

Beugelsdijk, S., Noorderhaven, N. G., & Koen, C. I. (2003). *Organizational culture, alliance capabilities and social capital.* Working paper No. 27/2003, University of Tilburg, Tilburg, The Netherlands.

Bierly, P. E., & Gallagher, S. (2007). Explaining alliance partner selection: Fit, trust and strategic expediency. *Long Range Planning, 40*(2), 134–153.

Brachos, D., Kostopoulos, K., Soderquist, K. E., & Prastacos, G. (2007). Knowledge effectiveness, social context and innovation. *Journal of Knowledge Management, 11*(5), 31–44.

Brockelman, S., & Cucci, A. (2000). *Institutionalizing alliance capabilities. A platform for repea*table *success.* Washington, DC: Corporate Executive Board.

Brouthers, K. D., Brouthers, L. E., & Wilkinson, T. J. (1995). Strategic alliances: Choose your partners. *Long Range Planning, 28*(3), 18–25.

Calabrese, T., Baum, J. A. C., & Silverman, B. S. (2000). Canadian biotechnology start-ups, 1991–1997: The role of incumbents' patents and strategic alliances in controlling competition. *Social Science Research, 29*, 503–534.

Chen, R., & Li, M. (1999). Strategic alliances and new product development: An empirical study of the US Semiconductor start-up firms. *Advances in Competitiveness Research, 7*(1), 35–61.

Chung, S., Singh, H., & Lee, K. (2000). Complementarity, status similarity and social capital as drivers of alliance formation. *Strategic Management Journal, 21*(1), 1–22.

Colombo, M. G., Grilli, L., & Piva, E. (2006). In search of complementary assets: The determinants of alliance formation of high-tech start-ups. *Research Policy, 35*(8), 1166–1199.

Colombo, M. G., Grilli, L., Murtinu, S., Piscitello, L., & Piva, E. (2009). Effects of international R&D alliances on performance of high-tech start-ups: A longitudinal analysis. *Strategic Entrepreneurship Journal, 3*(4), 346–368.

Das, T. K. (2004). Time-span and risk of partner opportunism in strategic alliances. *Journal of Managerial Psychology, 19*(8), 744–759.

Das, T. K. (2006). Strategic alliance temporalities and partner opportunism. *British Journal of Management, 17*(1), 1–21.

Das, T. K., & He, I. Y. (2006). Entrepreneurial firms in search of established partners: Review and recommendations. *International Journal of Entrepreneurial Behaviour & Research, 12*(3), 114–143.

Das, T. K., & Teng, B. (1996). Risk types and inter-firm alliance structures. *Journal of Management Studies, 33*, 827–843.

Das, T. K., & Teng, B. (1998). Resource and risk management in the strategic alliance making process. *Journal of Management, 24*(1), 21–42.

Das, T. K., & Teng, B. (2000a). A resource-based theory of strategic alliances. *Journal of Management, 26*(1), 31–61.

Das, T. K., & Teng, B. (2000b). Instabilities of strategic alliances: An internal tensions perspective. *Organization Science, 11*(1), 77–101.

Das, T. K., & Teng, B. (2001). A risk perception model of alliance structuring. *Journal of International Management, 7*(1), 1–29.

Davenport, S., Davies, J., & Grimes, C. (1998). Collaborative research programmes: Building trust from difference. *Technovation, 19*(1), 31–40.

De Man, A. (2005). Alliance capability: A comparison of the alliance strength of European and American companies. *European Management Journal, 23*(3), 315–323.

De Man, A., & Duysters, G. (2005). Collaboration and innovation: A review of the effects of mergers, acquisitions and alliances on innovation. *Technovation, 25*(12), 1377–1387.

Deeds, D. L., & Hill, C. W. L. (1996). Strategic alliances and the rate of new product development: An empirical study of entrepreneurial biotechnology firms. *Journal of Business Venturing, 11*(1), 41–55.

Deeds, D. L., & Hill, C. W. L. (1999). An examination of opportunistic action within research alliances: Evidence from the biotechnology industry. *Journal of Business Venturing, 14*(2), 141–163.

Doz, Y. (2002). Technology partnerships between larger and smaller firms: Some critical issues. In F. J. Contractor & P. Lorange (Eds.), *Cooperative strategies in international business: Joint ventures and technology partnerships between firms* (pp. 317–338). Oxford, England: Elsevier Science.

Draulans, J., DeMan, A., & Volberda, H. W. (2003). Building alliance capability: Management techniques for superior alliance performance. *Long Range Planning, 36*(2), 151–166.

Duysters, G., Kok, G., & Vaandrager, M. (1999). Crafting successful strategic technology partnerships. *R&D Management, 29*(4), 343–351.

Eisenhardt, K. M., & Schoonhoven, C. B. (1996). Resource-based view of strategic alliance formation: Strategic and social effects in entrepreneurial firms. *Organization Science, 7*(2), 136–150.

Elfring, T., & Hulsink, W. (2003). Networks in entrepreneurship: The case of high-technology firms. *Small Business Economics, 21*(4), 409–422.

Elfring, T., & Hulsink, W. (2007). Networking by entrepreneurs: Patterns of tie formation in emerging organizations. *Organization Studies, 28*(12), 1849–1872.

Europe Innova. (2008). *Do's and don'ts for biotech cluster development: The results of NetBioClueE.* Milan, Italy: NetBioCluE.

Faems, D., Janssens, M., & Van Looy, B. (2010). Managing the co-operation–competition dilemma in R&D alliances: A multiple case study in the advanced materials industry. *Creativity and Innovation Management, 19*(1), 3–22.

Faems, D., Van Looy, B., & Debackere, K. (2005). Interorganizational collaboration and innovation: Toward a portfolio approach. *Journal of Product Innovation Management, 22*(3), 238–250.

Forrest, J. E. (1990). Strategic alliances and the small technology-based firm. *Journal of Small Business Management, 28*(3), 37–45.

Freeman, C. (1991). Networks of innovators: A synthesis of research issues. *Research Policy, 20*(5), 499–514.

George, G., Zahra, S. A., Wheatley, K. K., & Khan, R. (2001). The effects of alliance portfolio characteristics and absorptive capacity on performance: A study of biotechnology firms. *Journal of High Technology Management Research, 12*(2), 205–226.

Gomes-Casseres, B. (1997). Alliance strategies of small firms. *Small Business Economics, 9*(1), 33–44.

Gulati, R. (1998). Alliances and networks. *Strategic Management Journal, 19*(4), 293–317.

Håkansson, H., Ford, D., Gadde, L. E., Snehota, I., & Waluszewski, A. (2009). *Business in networks.* Chichester, England: Wiley.

Hara, G., & Kanai, T. (1994). Entrepreneurial networks across oceans to promote international strategic alliances for small businesses. *Journal of Business Venturing, 9*(6), 489–507.

Harbison, J. J., & Pekar, P. (1997). *Institutionalizing alliance skills: Secrets of repeatable success.* New York, NY: Booz-Allen & Hamilton.

Heimeriks, K. H., & Duysters, G. (2007). Alliance capability as a mediator between experience and alliance performance: An empirical investigation into the alliance capability development process. *Journal of Management Studies, 44*(1), 25–49.

Heimeriks, K. H., Klijn, E., & Reuer, J. J. (2009). Building capabilities for alliance portfolios. *Long Range Planning, 42*(1), 96–114.

Heimeriks, K. H., & Reuer, J. J. (2006). *How to build alliance capabilities.* SMG Working paper No. 17/2006, Copenhagen Business School, Copenhagen, Denmark.

Hitt, M. A., Dacin, M. T., Levitas, E., Arregle, J.-L., & Borza, A. (2000). Partner selection in emerging and developed market contexts: Resource-based and organizational learning perspectives. *Academy of Management Journal, 43*(3), 449–467.

Hoang, H. T., & Antoncic, B. (2003). Network-based research in entrepreneurship: A critical review. *Journal of Business Venturing, 18*(2), 165–187.

Hoang, H. T., & Rothaermel, F. T. (2005). The effect of general and partner-specific alliance experience on joint R&D project performance. *Academy of Management Journal, 48*(2), 332–345.

Hoffmann, W. H., & Schlosser, R. (2001). Success factors of strategic alliances in small and medium-sized enterprises: An empirical survey. *Long Range Planning, 34*(3), 357–381.

Hofstede, G., Hofstede, G. J., & Minkov, M. (1997). *Cultures and organizations.* New York, NY: McGraw-Hill.

Holmberg, S. R., & Cummings, J. L. (2009). Building successful strategic alliances. *Long Range Planning, 42*(2), 164–193.

Huiskonen, J., & Pirttilä, T. (2002). Lateral coordination in a logistics outsourcing relationship. *International Journal of Production Economics, 78*, 177–185.

Inkpen, A. C., & Tsang, E. W. K. (2005). Social capital, networks, and knowledge transfer. *Academy of Management Review, 30*, 146–165.

Ireland, R. D., Hitt, M. A., & Vaidyanath, D. (2002). Alliance management as a source of competitive advantage. *Journal of Management, 28*(3), 413–446.

Joskow, P. (1987). Contract duration and relationship-specific investments: Empirical evidence from coal markets. *American Economic Review, 77*(1), 168–185.

Kale, P., Dyer, J. H., & Singh, H. (2002). Alliance capability, stock market response, and long-term alliance success: The role of the alliance function. *Strategic Management Journal, 23*(8), 747–767.

Kale, P., & Singh, H. (2007). Building firm capabilities through learning: The role of the alliance learning process in alliance capability and firm-level alliance success. *Strategic Management Journal, 28*(10), 981–1000.

Kelly, M. J., Schaan, J.-L., & Joncas, H. (2001). Managing alliance relationships: Key challenges in the early stages of collaboration. *R&D Management, 32*(1), 11–22.

Knight, G. A., & Cavusgil, S. T. (2004). Innovation, organizational capabilities, and the born-global firm. *Journal of International Business Studies, 35*, 124–141.

Kogut, B. (1991). Joint ventures and the option to expand and acquire. *Management Science, 37*(1), 19–33.

Kuemmerle, W. (1999). The drivers of foreign direct investment into research and development: An empirical investigation. *Journal of International Business Studies, 30*(1), 1–24.

Kumar, R., & Andersen, P. H. (2000). Inter firm diversity and the management of meaning in international strategic alliances. *International Business Review, 9*(2), 237–252.

Lane, P. J., & Lubatkin, M. (1998). Relative absorptive capacity and interorganizational learning. *Strategic Management Journal, 19*(5), 461–477.

Larson, A. (1991). Partner networks: Leveraging external ties to improve entrepreneurial performance. *Journal of Business Venturing, 6*(3), 173–188.

Larson, A. (1992). Network dyads in entrepreneurial settings: A study of the governance of exchange relationships. *Administrative Science Quarterly, 37*(1), 76–104.

Lee, C. W. (2007). Strategic alliances influence on small and medium firm performance. *Journal of Business Research, 60*(7), 731–741.

Lee, C., Lee, K., & Pennings, J. M. (2001). Internal capabilities, external networks, and performance: A study on technology-based ventures. *Strategic Management Journal, 22*(6–7), 615–640.

Leiblein, M. J., & Reuer, J. J. (2004). Building a foreign sales base: The roles of capabilities and alliances for entrepreneurial firms. *Journal of Business Venturing, 19*(2), 285–307.

Lorange, P., & Roos, J. (1993). *Strategic alliances: Formation, implementation, and evolution.* Oxford, England: Blackwell.

Mascarenhas, B., & Koza, M. P. (2008). Develop and nurture an international alliance capability. *Thunderbird International Business Review, 50*(2), 121–128.

Maurer, I., & Ebers, M. (2006). Dynamics of social capital and their performance implications: Lessons from biotechnology start-ups. *Administrative Science Quarterly, 51*(2), 262–292.

McGee, J. E., Dowling, M. J., & Megginson, W. L. (1995). Cooperative strategy and new venture performance: The role of business strategy and management experience. *Strategic Management Journal, 16*(7), 565–580.

Mengis J., & Eppler, M. J. (2008). Understanding and managing conversations from a knowledge perspective: An analysis of the roles and rules of face-to-face conversations in organizations. *Organization Studies, 29*(10), 1287–1313.

Miles, G., Preece, S. B., & Baetz, M. C. (1999). Dangers of dependence: The impact of strategic alliance use by small technology-based firms. *Journal of Small Business Management, 37*(2), 20–29.

Minshall, T., Mortara, L., Elia, S., & Probert, D. (2008). Development of practitioner guidelines for partnerships between start-ups and large firms. *Journal of Manufacturing Technology Management, 19*(2), 391–406.

Minshall, T., Mortara, L., Valli, R., & Probert, D. (2010). Making "asymmetric" partnerships work. *Research Technology Management, 53*(3), 53–63.

Mowery, D. C., Oxley, J. E., & Silverman, B. S. (1996). Strategic alliances and interfirm knowledge transfer. *Strategic Management Journal, 17*(S2), 77–91.

Muller, A., & Välikangas, L. (2002). Extending the boundary of corporate innovation. *Strategy and Leadership, 30*(3), 4–9.

Narula, R. (2004). R&D collaboration by SMEs: New opportunities and limitations in the face of globalisation. *Technovation, 24*(2), 153–161.

Nicholls-Nixon, C. L., & Woo, C. Y. (2003). Technology sourcing and output of established firms in a regime of encompassing technological change. *Strategic Management Journal, 24*(7), 651–666.

Nonaka, I., & Takeuchi, H. (1995). *The knowledge-creating company: How Japanese companies create the dynamics of innovation.* New York, NY: Oxford University Press.

O'Dwyer, M., & O'Flynn, E. (2005). MNC–SME strategic alliances: A model framing knowledge value as the primary predictor of governance modal choice. *Journal of International Management, 11*(3), 397–416.

OECD (2002). *Small and medium enterprises outlook.* Paris, France: Author.

Park, S. H., Chen, R., & Gallagher, S. (2002). Firm resources as moderators of the relationship between market growth and strategic alliances in semiconductor start-ups. *Academy of Management Journal, 45*(3), 527–545.

Powell, W. W., Koput, K. W., & Smith-Doerr, L. (1996). Interorganizational collaboration and the locus of innovation: Networks of learning in biotechnology. *Administrative Science Quarterly, 41*(1), 116–145.

Rothaermel, F. T., & Deeds, D. L. (2006). Alliance type, alliance experience and alliance management capability in high-technology ventures. *Journal of Business Venturing, 21*(4), 429–460.

Senker, J., & Sharp, M. (1997). Organizational learning in cooperative alliances: Some case studies in biotechnology. *Technology Analysis & Strategic Management, 9*(1), 35–51.

Shan, W. (1990). An empirical analysis of organizational strategies by entrepreneurial high-technology firms. *Strategic Management Journal, 11*(2), 129–139.

Shan, W., Walker, G., & Kogut, B. (1994). Interfirm cooperation and startups innovation in the biotechnology industry. *Strategic Management Journal, 15*(5), 387–394.

Shane, S., & Cable, D. (2002). Network ties, reputation, and the financing of new ventures. *Management Science, 48*(3), 364–381.

Silverman, B. S., & Baum, J.A.C. (2002). Alliance-based competitive dynamics. *Academy of Management Journal, 45*(4), 791–806.

Simonin, B. L. (1999). Ambiguity and the process of knowledge transfer in strategic alliances. *Strategic Management Journal, 20*(7), 595–623.

Slowinski, G., Seelig, G., & Hull, F. (1996). Managing technology-based strategic alliances between large and small firms. *S.A.M. Advanced Management Journal, 61*(2), 42–47.

Soekijad, M., & Andriessen, E. (2003). Conditions for knowledge sharing in competitive alliances. *European Management Journal, 21*(5), 578–587.

Standing, S., Standing, C., & Lin, C. (2008). A framework for managing knowledge in strategic alliances in the biotechnology sector. *Systems Research and Behavioral Science, 25*(6), 783–796.

Steier, L., & Greenwood, R. (2000). Entrepreneurship and the evolution of angel financial networks. *Organization Studies, 21*(1), 163–192.

Stinchcombe, A. L. (1965). Social structure and organizations. In J. G. March (Ed.), *Handbook of organizations* (pp. 142–193). Chicago, IL: Rand McNally.

Stock, M. (2006). Interorganizational teams as boundary spanners between supplier and customer companies. *Journal of the Academy of Marketing Science, 34*(4), 588–599.

Street, C. T., & Cameron, A. (2007). External relationships and the small business: A review of small business alliance and network research. *Journal of Small Business Management, 45*(2), 239–266.

Stuart, T. E. (1998). Network positions and propensities to collaborate: An investigation of strategic alliance formation in a high-technology industry. *Administrative Science Quarterly, 43*(3), 668–698.

Stuart, T. E., Hoang H., & Hybels, R. C. (1999). Interorganizational endorsements and the performance of entrepreneurial ventures. *Administrative Science Quarterly, 44*, 315–349.

Szulanski, G. (1996). Exploring internal stickiness: Impediments to the transfer of best practice within the firm. *Strategic Management Journal, 17*(S2), 27–43.

Uzzi, B. (1997). Social structure and competition in interfirm networks: The paradox of embeddedness. *Administrative Science Quarterly, 42*(2), 35–67.

Van Gils, A., & Zwart, P. (2004). Knowledge acquisition and learning in Dutch and Belgian SMEs: The role of strategic alliances. *European Management Journal, 22*(6), 685–692.

Vanhaverbeke, W., Beerkens, B., & Duysters, G. (2007). *Technological capability building through networking strategies within high-tech industries* (Working paper No. 2007/018). United Nations University, Maastricht, The Netherlands.

Vlaar, P. W. L., Van den Bosch, F. A. J., & Volberda, H. W. (2006). Coping with problems of understanding in interorganizational relationships: Using formalization as a means to make sense. *Organization Studies, 27*(11), 1617–1638.

Walker, G., Kogut, B., & Shan, W. (1997). Social capital, structural holes and the formation of an industry network. *Organization Science, 8*(2), 109–125.

Walter, A., Auer, M., & Ritter, T. (2006). The impact of network capabilities and entrepreneurial orientation on university spin-off performance. *Journal of Business Venturing, 21*(4), 541–567.

Wennekers, S., & Thurik, R. (1999). Linking entrepreneurship and economic growth. *Small Business Economics, 13*(1), 27–56.

Willoughby, K., & Galvin, P. (2005). Inter-organizational collaboration, knowledge intensity, and the sources of innovation in the bioscience-technology industries. *Knowledge, Technology, & Policy, 18*(3), 56–73.

Wong, P. K., Ho, Y. P., & Autio, E. (2005). Entrepreneurship, innovation and economic growth: Evidence from GEM data. *Small Business Economics, 24*(3), 335–350.

Yli-Renko, H., Autio, E., & Sapienza, H. J. (2001). Social capital, knowledge acquisition, and knowledge exploitation in young technology-based firms. *Strategic Management Journal, 22*(6–7), 587–613.

Yli-Renko, H., Autio, E., & Tontti, V. (2002). Social capital, knowledge, and the international growth of technology-based new firms. *International Business Review, 11*(3), 279–304.

Zineldin, M., & Dodourova, M. (2005). Motivation, achievements and failure of strategic alliances: The case of Swedish auto-manufacturers in Russia. *European Business Review, 17*(5), 460–470.

CHAPTER 9

THE ROLE OF INSIGHT IN ENTREPRENEURIAL ACTION

A Preliminary Exploration

Lincoln Brown
Joan L. Brown

ABSTRACT

In this chapter we extend the conceptualization of the insight moment in the dynamic entrepreneurial process following an experienced affective event. Using a qualitative exploratory design, we examine the subjective entrepreneurial process of entrepreneurs to shift the focus of extant insight research from the laboratory to the field. Entrepreneurs continually face real-world problems that require adjustments in strategy and action to solve. Based on those findings, we develop a framework that includes the role and impact of insight in the entrepreneurial process. In our proposed model, we attempt to more accurately reflect what entrepreneurs actually do in response to experienced affective events.

Entrepreneurship and Behavioral Strategy, pages 243–262
Copyright © 2020 by Information Age Publishing

INTRODUCTION

Researchers in entrepreneurship, economics, and strategic management have given considerable attention to the dynamic entrepreneurial process. From an individual perspective, aspects of the entrepreneurial process involve a complex process of identifying and disseminating relevant signals emanating from an ever-changing environment (Grégoire, Barr, & Shepherd, 2010a) that is fraught with uncertainty (Packard, Clark, & Klein, 2017) and requires frequent refinement based on an equally dynamic entrepreneurial judgment process (Brown, Packard, & Bylund, 2018; McMullen, 2015; McMullen & Dimov, 2013). Companys and McMullen (2007) concluded individuals are generally in the habit of maximizing utility based on their current situation, and are relatively unmotivated to search for alternatives without the experience of personally significant environmental or contextual change. Given the propensity to maintain status quo, what is it that signals the need to embark in and sustain this highly dynamic, uncertain activity called entrepreneurship?

The preponderance of extant research related to time (Bluedorn & Martin, 2008; Casson & Wadeson, 2007; McMullen & Dimov, 2013), and the acquisition of experience over time (Baron & Ensley, 2006; Gielnik, Zacher, Wang, & Chen, 2018; Morris, Kuratko, Schindehutte, & Spivack, 2012) bespeaks the complexity inherent in explaining the entrepreneurial process, but to date, little clarity has emerged regarding the mechanisms responsible for directing the process. While the moment of insight has received passing consideration, we suggest insight has not been properly understood as the gatekeeper of said process. Insight research contends that restructuring occurs through the unconscious action of bisociation (Koestler, 1964) which is a cognitive process used in problem solving. The restructuring process is believed to be incremental, where progress is made step by step as the individual gets closer to the moment where insight manifests (Durso, Rea, & Dayton, 1994; Gruber, 1995; Kounios & Beeman, 2009). The moment of insight is the conscious realization of a new association (Weisberg, 1995), which can be positive, suggesting the entrepreneurial process should advance, or negative, indicating revision of or perhaps abandonment of the process is warranted.

The purpose of this chapter is to examine the role of insight within the entrepreneurial process and explicate the implications of what strategic insight may entail. This study shifts attention to consider insight following the experience of personally significant affective events. Closely aligned with insight, the mechanism responsible for an urgent need to discover new answers, the mental itch, is introduced to the entrepreneurial process discussion. Previous research has focused on individual differences as a way to explain why certain people engage in entrepreneurship, while others do not (Baron & Ensley, 2006; Choi & Shepherd, 2004; Grégoire et al., 2010a, 2010b; Shane, 2000). Experienced entrepreneurs use cognitive alignment or pattern recognition to connect the dots between prior knowledge and new markets or technologies (Baron, 2006; Baron & Ensley, 2006; Grégoire et al., 2010a). Prior knowledge has also been linked to the recognition of new opportunities (Corbett, 2005; Dimov, 2007; Fiet, 1996; Shane, 2000; Shepherd & DeTienne, 2005). The structural relationships developed while acquiring prior knowledge are useful for interpreting new ambiguous information, and the process is enhanced when the current challenge has emotional significance (Blanchette & Dunbar, 2001). When an experienced entrepreneur notices similarities between new stimuli and previous structural alignments, brain activation is heightened, which can produce a mental leap (Holyoak & Thagard, 1995). The mental leap allows information from unrelated domains to crossover and become useful in another.

In spite of significant progress, the inner workings of the entrepreneurial process have not been adequately theorized to explain the phenomenon. Central to the notion of entrepreneurship is providing solutions to problems that have the potential to enhance economic growth and societal well-being (Audretsch, Keilbach, & Leman, 2006; Baumol, 1986; Bylund & McCaffrey, 2017; Schumpeter, 1934). Here, we advocate for an increased consideration of the problem solving, insight literature as a means of explaining the gatekeeper function of the entrepreneurial process. We employ an exploratory qualitative design as a step toward a theory of the entrepreneurial process (Suddaby, Bruton, & Si, 2015) that incorporates the role of insight in directing the entrepreneurial process following the experience of personally significant affective events. Drawing on affective events theory, we argue that the occurrence of insight serves the individual by bringing a sense of closure or resolution to the mental itch. The contributions provide an enhanced view of how the entrepreneurial process achieves orientation and direction.

THEORETICAL BACKGROUND

Affective Events Theory and Insight

In spite of the time between the experienced problem and the eventual moment of insight, consensus among researchers exists that the experience of insight for the individual is perceived as sudden, surprising, and seemingly coming from some unknown place (DeYoung, Flanders, & Peterson, 2008; Hill & Kemp, 2018; Jarman, 2014, 2016; Weisberg, 2015). Insight is often preceded by an emotionally charged triggering event, where the individual experiences some unexpected, unsettling, often aversive stimuli, which results in creative stress (Koestler, 1964), creative tension (Ludwig, 1995), or felt tension (Csikszentmihalyi, 1996) because no immediate solution is available. A common experience prior to an insight moment is impasse (Ohlsson, 2011; Perkins, 2000) which occurs because no immediate solution presents itself following the experienced event. Conversely, Fleck and Weisberg (2004) found that insight does not always require impasse. What is important to note about the Fleck and Weisburg (2004) findings is that producing an insight experience in a laboratory is not able to capture adequately what actually occurs following a real-world experience. Triggering events that result in impasse result in a new set of needs (Brown, 2016) because of the novelty of the experience and activate a mental itch (Jarman, 2016).

The mental itch is the mechanism responsible for the imperative to respond to the triggering event, and is only scratched when a solution is discovered. The triggering event or events can be positive or negative and both have the potential to produce a mental itch. It may be more intuitive to think of a negative triggering event as one leading to a mental itch; however, a positive triggering event is often accompanied with a new problem or set of problems. For example, having a baby or receiving an inheritance may be viewed as positive; however, these events may also introduce new challenges and the need to acquire new solutions.

Affective events theory (AET) elucidates how experienced events produce affective states that affect behavior (Weiss & Beal, 2005; Weiss & Cropanzano, 1996). The central tenet of AET is that an individual's response to experienced events is based on their emotional and cognitive judgments, attitudes, and mood. Life is replete with events; some expected and planned for, while others are the result of exogenous factors completely outside a person's control. Desjarlais (1997) suggests significant events can occur independently or as part of an ongoing series of events. Understanding the effect events elicit is a complex process that depends on a number of individual factors (Csikszentmihalyi, 1990). Implicit meaning is derived as the individual processes and encodes perceptual, sensory, and affective information, and is ultimately determined by the personal significance or meaning attributed to the event. How an individual experiences an event, and the lasting effects the event has, is determined by the affective state that emerges from the event (e.g., thoughts, feelings, and emotions; Throop, 2003).

Events are experienced as temporal in that they are quickly assessed to determine significance and meaning. Significance and meaning are determined by the event's dissimilarity with previous experiences as well as the surprise or shock value of the event (Morris, Kuratko, Schindehutte, & Spivack, 2012). When an event is perceived to be disruptive to the norm, it is considered meaningful or significant, and worthy of additional processing (Bruner, 1986). Significant events transcend cognition to include emotional, physical, and perceptual realities (Ortony, Norman, & Revelle, 2005).

Weiss and Beal (2005) contend that events are appraised in two stages: first, as positive or negative regarding well-being, and second, for context and potential consequences. As an event is experienced information enters conscious awareness and processing begins in order to make sense of the incoming stimuli (Epstein, Pacini, Denes-Raj, & Heier, 1996). When events produce unexpected or conflicting information that cannot be linked to prior knowledge, the process adjusts, and attempts begin to renegotiate or reconstruct information in new ways, which is the cognitive activity of problem solving using insight (Weisberg, 1995).

Weisberg's integrated theory of insight (2015) incorporates redistribution theory (Ohlsson, 2011), breakthrough thinking (Perkins, 2000), and analytic thinking (Fleck & Weisberg, 2004; Weisberg, 2006a, 2006b), in an attempt to gain a more complete understanding of the insight process. Analytic thinking involves three stages: (a) solution through transfer, (b) solution through heuristics, and (c) solution through restructuring. When an individual progresses through the stages of analytic thinking without finding a solution, they reach impasse. In order to progress beyond impasse, they must consider alternative ways to structure the problem. Similarly, impasse is reached in redistribution theory (Ohlsson, 2011), and is followed by a rejection of the old ways of thinking about the problem. For Ohlsson, a solution is either creative (based on insight), or it is not.

Perkins (2000) described breakthrough thinking as "a decisive break from the past." He implies that most if not all truly novel ideas come through the use of breakthrough thinking. Breakthroughs are the result of a series of events that are similar to Gestalt psychologists' insight sequence. In breakthrough thinking, the sequence includes a long search, where the individual makes multiple attempts to find a solution. The second event is the impasse, which happens when no appropriate solution is found. Then the person experiences some form of a precipitating event. Precipitating events can be external or mental and cause the person to think about problems in a different way. The fourth event is the cognitive snap or ah-hah moment when the solution suddenly appears, seemingly out of nowhere. The final event is transformation. In transformation, breakthrough thinking has permanently altered how the person relates to their world. Perkins (2000) suggested breakthrough thinking is required to deal with problems that previous logic would not be capable of answering. These problems would be considered unreasonable to previous logic, and therefore would require thinking unreasonably.

Mental Itch

Hennessey and Amabile (2010) asserted that intrinsic motivation is the factor most prevalent for general creativity. It is widely accepted that creativity and insight is more common when the person finds the problem interesting and personally significant. Where creativity and insight differ is that insight typically follows an unsettling state resulting in creative or felt tension (Csikszentmihalyi, 1996; Ludwig, 1995) or creative stress (Koestler, 1964). Proulx and Inzlicht (2012) found that the experience of an unsettling or arousal state in one domain is related to enhanced creativity in another domain.

The present research describes the arousal state as the triggering event or events that serve to activate a mental itch (Jarman, 2016). The mental itch results in an imperative to reduce the arousal state, and is only scratched when the problem is solved. Despite the strong desire to alleviate the mental itch, the triggering event or events can be positive or negative. In instances where the triggering event is positive, the event may heighten the desire to create something novel and this mental itch is scratched when the solution is discovered or the new artifact is produced. The obsessive need to alleviate the mental itch increases activation of cognitive resources required to make new connections of previously stored semantic information, which increases the likelihood that an insight will occur (Jarman, 2016).

Complex problems often require a series of insights in order to acquire an adequate solution (Sawyer, 2012). In AET, a highly charged emotional or personally significant triggering event or events result in higher magnitude mental itch states. This is due to a heightened cognitive activation that follows, in part, from an obsessive passion (Vallerand et al., 2007) for solving the problem. This obsession increases the time and cognitive resources that can be allocated towards solving the problem. The heightened cognitive activation also changes the fundamental pattern of connections between cognitively stored semantic information, leading to a cognitive state of heightened semantic interdependence and criticality from which radical insights are more likely to occur.

METHOD

Participants and Procedures

We employ a qualitative, inductive design to delineate the insight moment within the entrepreneurial process. As a subjective experience, the entrepreneurial process is unique to the individual (Packard, 2017). In his call for an interpretivist lens from which to explore the subjective nature of entrepreneurship, Packard (2017) argues that "such an approach may be most appropriate to the individualists' nature of entrepreneurship" (p. 536). Rather than attempt to target a representative sample of the general population, we target a purposive sample consisting of entrepreneurs with varying backgrounds, experience levels, industries, and localities across the United States. The design employs two studies: one from an undergraduate student population completing a venture creation assignment, and the second, from actual entrepreneurs.

Study One

The objective of the study was to examine the use and role of insight in the entrepreneurial process. Participants were undergraduate students enrolled in an introduction to entrepreneurship class. In week one of class, students were given a four-part assignment. Part 1 required recalling an experienced event that had personal meaning or significance for them. The event selected was to be novel in that it presents challenges to previous thought and actions. Part 2 was to write a one-half page reflection paper describing the event and how it made them feel. In Part 3, students were asked to think of an entrepreneurial business that would address or provide a solution to the challenge introduced by the experienced event and write a one-page paper describing the business and how it would address or solve their challenge.

Following submission of their entrepreneurial business, students spent the remainder of the semester developing that business by completing a number of activities ultimately concluding with a written executive summary and formal pitch of the business. Three weeks prior to the conclusion of the semester, students were given an assignment where they indicated whether they had any insight experiences while thinking of or developing their business. Students were to select from one of six categories that best described their experience: (a) those who recalled a personally significant event and experienced one insight moment during the completion of the assignment, (b) those who recalled a personally significant event but did not experience insight during the completion of the assignment, (c) those who recalled a personally significant event and experienced more than one insight moment during the completion of the assignment, (d) those who did not recall a personally significant event and did not experience an insight moment while completing the assignment, (e) those who did not recall a personally significant event but experienced an insight moment during the completion of the assignment, and (f) those who did not recall a personally significant event but experienced more than one insight moment during the completion of the assignment. One student from each group was randomly selected and invited to participate in the qualitative interview. The qualitative interviews were semi-structured, designed to capture the nature of the insight experience, and whether or not it was experienced as a one time, or multiple time occurrence.

Analysis

We began our examination of the data using content analysis as a sense-making effort to obtain understanding of the key meanings (Patton, 2002). The goal of content analysis is to discover patterns and themes. Thematic analysis is a commonly accepted method for the identification of global themes (patterns), and finer grained organizing themes (Creswell & Plano Clark, 2011). Once the interviews were completed and transcribed, the coding process began by spending time with the data, reading and processing what was actually said (Corbin & Strauss, 1990). Guided by the extant theoretical work on insight and the mental itch, we individually identified and labeled relevant statements to a basic theme. We then discussed our themes and resolved our differences of opinion, settling on agreed upon terminology. The basic themes were organized in global themes (see Table 9.1). Since both authors coded all the data together, there was 100% agreement on how the statements should be categorized (Neuendorf, 2016).

Findings

We present our findings from representative evidence compiled through data reduction following the interviews (Cacciotti, Hayton, Mitchell, & Giazitzoglu, 2016). Of the six possible categories previously mentioned, two were defined as not having utilized insight. However, despite previously indicating that they had not experienced an insight moment while they developed their business, both students from those categories discussed an insight moment in their interview. In support of our findings we include some actual quotes in Table 9.2.

TABLE 9.1 Study 1 Themes	
Basic Themes	**Organizing Themes**
1. It was like I was seeing through new eyes	Insight
2. It was like seeing this for the first time	
3. It was more than just solving one problem—this would change everything	
5. I had an uneasy feeling in my head	Mental Itch
6. I had an urgency	
7. It was more then something I had to do, I felt I needed to have a good solution	
8. It was hard controlling my urge to think about it	
9. Thinking about it was exciting to me	Affective Response
10. Frustration	
11. It got pretty competitive with my friends	

TABLE 9.2 Study 1 Representative Evidence	
Representative quotations	**Organizing Theme**
"I might've been studying for tests and like I was just thinking about stuff. Um, my thoughts never are one thing. They're never one thing. So it, it was definitely while I was thinking about something else."	Insight
"Um, actually it was like an Aha moment in the shower because I have my best thoughts in the shower."	
"Cause I had two events that caused me to think of, okay, this is my idea, this is how I'm going to do it."	
"I was sitting up here at the athletic academic center and I was trying to think of ideas. I was like, well, I need to find something I'm passionate about so it's not going to be boring or I'm going to actually, you know, maybe someday go through with it. It was really the Aha moment."	
"All through like I guess trying to think of something that I was missing."	Mental Itch
"And that was kind of hard for me because we had to have entrepreneurial solutions. I knew I had to come up with something and I could just stop thinking about it."	
"Honestly, I just started thinking like, I, I just like, like I have no idea what I'm going to do. I don't feel like I have any good ideas."	
"I'm worried about trying to figure out where's the money coming from and where is the knowledge coming from."	Affective Response
"Um, and then like going through the whole process of like, I don't know... brainstorming was kind of frustrating a little bit. It's like trial and error. Like does this work?"	
"I did not expect to come up with something so cool."	

A key finding common among the students was the mention of time spent thinking of an entrepreneurial business before their insight experience. One of the six students mentioned that she had thought of the business developed for class before the semester began, but again, her experience involved a lengthy time period before she actually experienced the insight moment. Time was a factor because students did not immediately know how to accomplish the task, which is similar to impasse, commonly associated with the experience of insight. The other factor common for all the students was that they were doing or thinking about something else when at least one of their insight moments occurred. Four of the students interviewed said they wanted to solve a meaningful problem with their business. They had several ideas but were looking for something they considered entrepreneurial.

Study Two

The objective of study two was to extend the use and role of insight in the entrepreneurial process with those who had actually created ventures, rather than students who were pitching ideas. Twelve entrepreneurs participated in interviews from seven states who were LinkedIn contacts of the first author, which represents a response rate of 10% from the 117 invitations that were sent out. The average age of the respondents was 49.9 years and the majority have owned their own businesses for more than 15 years. After some demographic information was gathered, participants were asked two questions. Six of the participants were asked to recall the best thing that has ever happened in their business and five were asked to recall the worst thing that has ever happened in their business. The second question was, "Because you own a business, you must have believed it was an opportunity worth pursuing. Since you started running your business what new opportunities have you pursued?" The objective of the questions was to help participants remember and relive some of what has occurred in their entrepreneurial process.

To capture the insight experience, participants were given the following prompt and question: "Sometimes things suddenly click into place in your mind when you think of something new, similar to an 'ah-hah' moment. Have you experienced anything like that since you have owned your business?" Follow up questions asked about their problem-solving routine, the frequency of insight for them and the amount of trust they place in an insight once it has occurred. Interview sessions lasted between 16 and 42 minutes and were conducted and recorded using the Zoom platform.

Analysis

The analysis of the data was conducted in the same manner as study one. After completing the interviews, the audio was transcribed using Temi, an online speech to text transcription service. As in study one, both authors began the coding process by reading and taking time to reflect and process the data (Corbin & Strauss, 1990). We incorporated the same strategy to label key statements as basic themes. We spent time discussing and coming to an agreement about where the statement should be placed and if they needed to be placed in multiple categories. We then constructed broader, global themes that would reflect the intent of the data (see Table 9.3). Both authors coded all the data so ultimately, we arrived at complete agreement.

Findings

The findings of study two are grounded in the representative evidence compiled in Table 9.4. The sample of experienced entrepreneurs described their experience with insight in the entrepreneurial process of an actual

TABLE 9.3 Study 2 Themes	
Basic Themes	**Organizing Themes**
1. Everything looked different all of a sudden	Insight
2. I would never see things the same	
3. I had a new understanding, it really sunk in	
5. It was like seeing this for the first time	
6. It was almost magical	
7. It seemed to come out of nowhere	
8. I had an uneasy feeling in my head	Mental Itch
9. It was almost like a nagging itch	
10. It was hard controlling my urge to think about it	
11. Thinking about it was exciting to me	Affective Response
12. It was irritation for me but sad for others	
13. It can be painful sometimes	
14. Frustration	

business, significantly shifting the focus of previous insight research from laboratory experimental problem solving (Karwowski, Reiter-Palmon, & Tinio, 2014; Weisberg, 2013, 2015).

A primary focus of entrepreneurs following a significant event is to take inventory of what occurred and determine a suitable course of action to follow. Of the entrepreneurs interviewed, all said insight played some role in their entrepreneurial journey. One entrepreneur mentioned the reason she became an entrepreneur was because of an insight that occurred while working at her previous job. Following the insight moment, she said, "It's been 10 years and I'm like, I just can't do this . . . I can't do this thing anymore, you know, having my job dangled over my head like a Damocles sword every day." She referred to the moment as seeing herself under the sword and something inside her changed. She would never go back to the way she was. Another entrepreneur recounted a battle with Amazon because they claimed her company was selling "knock off" products. The ordeal was understandably quite a setback. She described the mental anguish she went through trying to solve the problem in much the same way the mental itch literature suggests (Jarman, 2016). The primary difference between the students in Study 1 and the entrepreneurs in Study 2 was the lived experiences of the entrepreneurs. Personally significant positive and negative life experience played a significant role in the way the entrepreneurs approached their business decision making. One entrepreneur stated "I spend little time thinking in the context of my feelings. If I experience a 'worst thing' then most of my energy will go towards (a) reflecting

TABLE 9.4 Study 2 Representative Evidence	
Representative quotations	**Organizing Theme**
"I started putting the pieces together, thinking of a way to go forward."	Insight
"My insight ideas usually come when I'm trying to go to sleep at night."	
"Mainly the little insights I get are you know, when I'm working with a client. Once I find something specific, you know, there's a bit of a trend and the ideas just expand from there."	
"For me insight is like going down a rabbit hole. How deep am I going into this thing?"	
"Always have to be observant, times change. If you pay attention you gain insight on what to do next."	
"Insight for me comes when comes from having true mastery of understanding. The more I know, the more I connect with other ideas."	
"A lot of my insights come to me when my partner and I spitball ideas back and forth."	
"Because I had been kind of freaking out because I wasn't having any luck. I was stuck, but then it came out of the blue."	Mental Itch
"Amazon suspended our account saying we were selling products that were 'knock-offs'. It killed our sales. We were stuck for weeks before a solution came to me."	
"When the housing market crashed I didn't know what to do. Do I even have a business?"	
"I started my business to help kids who are like I was. For no other reason than I want them to know that someone actually gives a rats ass."	Affective Response
"That all happened because we were having a baby."	
"Overnight I lost 80% of my business due to one individual. Felt betrayed and fearful. Had poured my heart and soul into the endeavor. Anyone with inside knowledge of the situation expressed dismay and disgust. Couldn't pout for long. I had 5 employees who had made life changing decisions in following me and who depended on me for their livelihood. Picked myself up and began the long road back."	
"Legislative changes eliminated 80% of business in one year. Felt dispirited and hopeless but made alterations and persevered."	
"I was nervous, anxious, and excited all at the same time."	
"Regulatory changes in my industry have made my revenue model more difficult and leaves me feeling a mixture of ticked, frustrated and discouraged at times."	

on what went wrong, (b) determining what I can do immediately in the short-term, and (c) a long-term response." In this case, the entrepreneur tried to remove the emotion of the experience, but was still affected by it. He went on to say "I have had one business failure in my 35-year career. The questions that I asked related to how I could have acted differently in the years leading up to the failure. The failure helped me to recognize how essential cash is to any operation, how judicious I must be with spending (whether in good times or bad) and how much stronger my analytics must be on a weekly basis to know where exactly the company is financially." He saw his insight moments as both a learning tool and a rudder to direct his next steps. What was common of the insight experience for the entrepreneurs was the apparent correctness of the answer (DeYoung et al., 2008) even without verification.

CONCEPTUAL DEVELOPMENT

Our analysis suggests there are a number of aspects of insight that factor significantly in the entrepreneurial process. In their depiction of the entrepreneurial experience, Morris et al. (2012) highlight the importance of experience, affective and learning outcomes, and improvisational behavior en route to the emergence of both the entrepreneur and entrepreneurial venture. In building on that model, we suggest incorporating insight into an entrepreneurial experience model better explains the reality of the phenomenon and extends past emergence to include the day-to-day responses of entrepreneurs who experience affective events and utilize insight moments to influence the direction of their subjective entrepreneurial process (Packard, 2017).

In the proposed model (see Figure 9.1), insight and impasse play an important role in confident action. It is important to note that confident action does not necessarily occur in a linear path from the proceeding variables, but rather is part of a dynamic ongoing process. The dynamic model is intended to represent the possibility of multiple variables occurring simultaneously and in no particular order until the ultimate judgment is made to proceed with or abort the business. The results seem to indicate entrepreneurs place greater confidence in entrepreneurial action following the insight occurrence. In a number of cases, entrepreneurs choose to take action immediately following an experienced event and reported mixed results. Additionally, when entrepreneurs reported not knowing what to do, but choosing not to "just do something," but instead allowed for time to pass, they ultimately experienced an insight moment. We suspect it is possible for impasse to remain unresolved and ultimately result in the decision to abort or proceed as usual with the business, but that was not the case for any of our study participants. In light of this we suggest:

Proposition 1: *Within the dynamic entrepreneurial process, the experience of a personally significant affective event requires an insight moment in order to take confident action.*

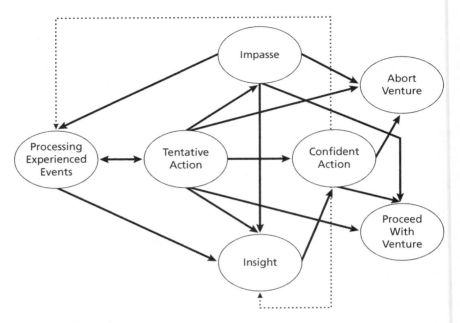

Figure 9.1 Proposed insight model. *Notes:* The solid arrows between processing experienced events and tentative action highlight their interaction. Important to note, confident action does not necessarily flow from a linear path, but is part of a dynamic process, simultaneously occurring with the other variables until the ultimate judgment is made to proceed or abort.

> **Proposition 2:** *Entrepreneurs who allow impasse to occur prior to taking action experience an insight moment that results in confident action.*

In this regard, insight is incorporated into the dynamic entrepreneurial process following the experience of a personally significant affective event. In consideration of a philosophy of entrepreneurship and asking what are the objectives, we contend that entrepreneurship is a purposeful activity where entrepreneurs respond to life's problems and seek the most effective ways to solve them (Dewey, 1929). Experience supplies the problems that need solving and real-life problem solving occurs through entrepreneurship, often with the aid of insight moments.

DISCUSSION

The primary theoretical question of the study is how does the experience of a personally experienced affective event relate to the use of insight in real world problem solving. In particular, the goal was to refine the core tenets of problem solving within the entrepreneurial process. The data extends findings regarding the cognitive and emotional processes responsible for problem solving in the entrepreneurial process, and are activated by the experienced triggering event (Barringer & Ireland, 2008). Impasse or the mental itch serves to heighten cognitive activation (Jarman, 2016) that ultimately produces a perceived correct but unverified answer to the experienced problem (Weisberg, 2015). Second, this work advances the methods in the entrepreneurship and psychology literatures by being one of the first to explore insight during real world problem solving. The qualitative design provides important clues into the factors associated with the entrepreneurial process, following the experience of a significant experienced triggering event (Suddaby et al., 2015).

Affective events theory was extended in the entrepreneurship literature with the current research by describing a link between an affective experienced event and an insight moment. As a subjective conceptualization, the entrepreneurial process inexorably links the entrepreneur with their environment and simultaneously the environment to the entrepreneur (Weiss & Cropanzano, 1996). Consequently, it is impossible to separate experienced events from how the subjective entrepreneurial process is constructed and evolves for the entrepreneur. If, as discussed, insight is a key factor in the path toward confident action, it should also be incorporated into the entrepreneurial process discussion.

Future Research

We suggest future research should expand in two ways. First, the entrepreneurial process is under-theorized and limited in application without an expanded view of entrepreneurial judgment (Foss & Klein, 2012; McMullen, 2015) that includes the role of insight for entrepreneurial problem solving. Second, empirical work should include the development and validation of an insight scale that captures its use in the entrepreneurial process. Specifically, our proposed model would require a scale that incorporates the insight moment with the experience of impasse to capture the proposed link to confident action.

Practical Implications

The present research has a number of practical implications for entrepreneurs. Despite many entrepreneur's tendency to be confident in their ability to act, our research seems to confirm the assertion of Baron,

Hmieleski, and Henry (2012) where they suggested possible downsides to being overly positive. Our results suggest entrepreneurs as a group would be well-suited to allow impasse to serve its course. It would be wise in many cases to allow time to process before taking action. Entrepreneurs might benefit from seeking the perspective of others before acting, and to "set with" what has happened long enough to allow the cognitive activation provided by impasse to produce an insight moment.

Limitations

Although this study extends our understanding of the insight moment in the entrepreneurial process, our research design does have limitations. Albeit we attempted to limit the impact of recall bias (Podsakoff & Organ, 1986) by having participants detail a previous experience and the emotion elicited, we cannot overcome completely the fact that this is retrospective research and the data was self-reported. Second, our sample was limited in scope to the United States, it may not accurately reflect or generalize to the entire population of entrepreneurs. Third, we acknowledge selection bias as all of participants were actively engaged in the entrepreneurial process, which does include those who may have engaged at some point in the process but have since chosen to abort.

CONCLUSION

With our conceptual model we attempted to elucidate the role of insight in the entrepreneurial process. Building on extant theoretical knowledge, we sought to extend the perspective of the entrepreneurial process by developing a framework that more accurately reflects entrepreneurs' lived experiences. We offer propositions based on our findings and encourage subsequent empirical and theoretical consideration.

REFERENCES

Audretsch, D., Keilbach, M., & Lehmann, E. (2006). *Entrepreneurship and economic growth.* New York, NY: Oxford University Press.
Baron, R. A. (2006). Opportunity recognition as pattern recognition: How entrepreneurs "connect the dots" to identify new business opportunities. *Academy of Management Perspectives, 20*(1), 104–119.
Baron, R. A., & Ensley, M. D. (2006). Opportunity recognition as the detection of meaningful patterns: Evidence from comparisons of novice and experienced entrepreneurs. *Management Science, 52*(9), 1331–1344.

Baron, R. A., Hmieleski, K. M., & Henry, R. A. (2012). Entrepreneurs' dispositional positive affect: The potential benefits—and potential costs—of being "up." *Journal of Business Venturing, 27*(3), 310–324.

Barringer, B. R., & Ireland, R. D. (2008). *What's stopping you?: Shatter the 9 most common myths keeping you from starting your own business.* Upper Saddle River, NJ: FT Press.

Baumol, W. (1986). Productivity growth, convergence, and welfare: What the long-run data show. *American Economic Review, 76*(5), 1072–1085.

Blanchette, I., & Dunbar, K. (2001). Analogy use in naturalistic settings: The influence of audience, emotion and goals. *Memory and Cognition, 29,* 730–735.

Bluedorn, A. C., & Martin, G. (2008). The time frames of entrepreneurs. *Journal of Business Venturing, 23*(1), 1–20.

Brown, L. M. (2016). The family effect in establishing a family business. *NCFR Report: Family focus: Entrepreneurship and family business.* National Council on Family Relations. Retrieved from https://www.ncfr.org/ncfr-report/focus/family-focus-entrepreneurship-and-family-business

Brown, L., Packard, M., & Bylund, P. (2018). Judgment, fast and slow: Toward a judgment view of entrepreneurs' impulsivity. *Journal of Business Venturing Insights, 10,* e00095.

Bruner, E. (1986). Experience and its expressions. In V. Turner & E. Bruner (Eds.), *The anthropology of experience* (pp. 3–32). Urbana: University of Illinois Press.

Bylund, P. L., & McCaffrey, M. (2017). A theory of entrepreneurship and institutional uncertainty. *Journal of Business Venturing, 32*(5), 461–475.

Cacciotti, G., Hayton, J. C., Mitchell, J. R., & Giazitzoglu, A. (2016). A reconceptualization of fear of failure in entrepreneurship. *Journal of Business Venturing, 31*(3), 302–325.

Casson, M., & Wadeson, N. (2007). The discovery of opportunities: Extending the economic theory of the entrepreneur. *Small Business Economics, 28*(4), 285–300.

Choi, Y. R., & Shepherd, D. A. (2004). Entrepreneurs' decisions to exploit opportunities. *Journal of Management, 30*(3), 377–395.

Companys, Y., & McMullen, E. (2007). Strategic entrepreneurs at work: The nature, discovery, and exploitation of entrepreneurial opportunities. *Small Business Economics, 28*(4), 301–322.

Corbett, A. C. (2005). Experiential learning within the process of opportunity identification and exploitation. *Entrepreneurship Theory and Practice, 29*(4), 473–491.

Corbin, J., & Strauss, M. (1990). Grounded theory research: Procedures, canons, and evaluative criteria. *Qualitative Sociology, 13*(1), 3–21.

Creswell, J., & Plano Clark, V. (2011). *Designing and conducting mixed methods research* (2nd ed.). Los Angeles, CA: SAGE.

Csikszentmihalyi, M. (1990). *The psychology of optimal experience.* New York, NY: Harper & Row.

Csikszentmihalyi, M. (1996). *Creativity: Flow and the psychology of discovery and invention.* New York, NY: Harper Perennial.

Desjarlais, R. (1997). *Shelter blues.* Philadelphia: University of Pennsylvania Press.

Dewey, J. (1929). *Experience and nature* (Paul Carus lectures). New York, NY: Norton.

DeYoung, C. G., Flanders, J. L., & Peterson, J. B. (2008). Cognitive abilities involved in insight problem solving: An individual differences model. *Creativity Research Journal, 20*(3), 278–290.

Dimov, D. (2007). From opportunity insight to opportunity intention: The importance of person-situation learning match. *Entrepreneurship Theory and Practice, 31*(4), 561–583.

Durso, F. T., Rea, C. B., & Dayton, T. (1994). Graph-theoretic confirmation of restructuring during insight. *Psychological Science, 5*(2), 94–98.

Epstein, S., Pacini, R., Denes-Raj, V., & Heier, H. (1996). Individual differences in intuitive-experiential an analytical-rational thinking styles. *Journal of Personality and Social Psychology, 71*(3), 390–415.

Fiet, J. O. (1996). The informational basis of entrepreneurial discovery. *Small Business Economics, 8*(6), 419–430.

Fleck, J. I., & Weisberg, R. W. (2004). The use of verbal protocols as data: An analysis of insight in the candle problem. *Memory & Cognition, 32*(6), 990–1006.

Foss, N., & Klein, P. (2012). *Organizing entrepreneurial judgment: A new approach to the firm.* New York, NY: Cambridge University Press.

Gielnik, M., Zacher, H., Wang, M., & Chen, G. (2018). Age in the entrepreneurial process: The role of future time perspective and prior entrepreneurial experience. *Journal of Applied Psychology, 103*(10), 1067–1085.

Grégoire, D. A., Barr, P. S., & Shepherd, D. A. (2010a). Cognitive processes of opportunity recognition: The role of structural alignment. *Organization Science, 21*(2), 413–431.

Grégoire, D. A., Shepherd, D. A., & Lambert, L. S. (2010b). Measuring opportunity-recognition beliefs: Illustrating and validating an experimental approach. *Organizational Research Methods, 13*(1), 114–145.

Gruber, H. E. (1995). Insight and affect in the history of science. In R. J. Sternberg & J. E. Davidson (Eds.), *The nature of insight* (pp. 397–431). Cambridge, MA: MIT Press.

Hennessey, B. A., & Amabile, T. M. (2010). Creativity. *Annual Review of Psychology, 61*, 569–598.

Hill, G., & Kemp, S. M. (2018). Uh-oh! What have we missed? A qualitative investigation into everyday insight experience. *Journal of Creative Behavior, 52*(3), 201–211.

Holyoak, K. J., & Thagard, P. (1995). *Mental leaps: Analogy in creative thought.* Cambridge, MA: Bradford.

Jarman, M. S. (2014). Quantifying the qualitative: Measuring the insight experience. *Creativity Research Journal, 26*(3), 276–288.

Jarman, M. S. (2016). Scratching mental itches with extreme insights: Empirical evidence for a new theory. *Psychology of Aesthetics, Creativity, and the Arts, 10*(1), 21–31.

Karwowski, M., Reiter-Palmon, R., & Tinio, P. (2014). Creative mindsets: Measurement, correlates, consequences. *Psychology of Aesthetics, Creativity, and the Arts, 8*, 62–70.

Koestler, A. (1964). *The act of creation.* New York, NY: Macmillan.

Kounios, J., & Beeman, M. (2009). The aha! moment: The cognitive neuroscience of insight. *Current Directions in Psychological Science, 18*(4), 210–216.

Ludwig, A. M. (1995). *The price of greatness: Resolving the creativity and madness controversy.* New York, NY: The Guilford Press.

McMullen, J. (2015). Entrepreneurial judgment as empathic accuracy: A sequential decision-making approach to entrepreneurial action. *Journal of Institutional Economics, 11*(3), 651–681.

McMullen, J., & Dimov, D. (2013). Time and the entrepreneurial journey: The problems and promise of studying entrepreneurship as a process. *Journal of Management Studies, 50*(8), 1481–1512.

Morris, M. H., Kuratko, D. F., Schindehutte, M., & Spivack, A. J. (2012). Framing the entrepreneurial experience. *Entrepreneurship Theory and Practice, 36*(1), 11–40.

Neuendorf, K. A. (2016). *The content analysis guidebook.* Thousand Oaks, CA: SAGE.

Ohlsson, S. (2011). *Deep learning: How the mind overrides experience.* Cambridge, England: Cambridge University Press.

Ortony, A., Norman, D., & Revelle, W. (2005). Add-affect and proto-affect in effective functioning. In M. Arbib (Ed.), *Who needs emotions?* (pp. 173–202). New York, NY: Oxford University Press.

Packard, M. (2017). Where did interpretivism go in the theory of entrepreneurship? *Journal of Business Venturing, 32*(5), 536–549.

Packard, M. D., Clark, B. B., & Klein, P. G. (2017). Uncertainty types and transitions in the entrepreneurial process. *Organization Science, 28*(5), 840–856.

Patton, M. (2002). *Qualitative research and evaluation methods* (3rd ed.). Thousand Oaks, CA: SAGE.

Perkins, D. N. (2000). *The Eureka effect. The art and logic of breakthrough thinking.* New York, NY: Norton.

Podsakoff, P., & Organ, D. (1986). Self-reports in organizational research: Problems and prospects. *Journal of Management, 12*(4), 531–544.

Proulx, T., & Inzlicht, M. (2012). The five "A"s of meaning maintenance: Finding meaning in the theories of sense-making. *Psychological Inquiry, 23*(4), 317–335.

Sawyer, R. K. (2012). Explaining creativity: The science of human innovation (2nd ed.). New York, NY: Oxford University Press.

Schumpeter, J. (1934). *The theory of economic development; An inquiry into profits, capital, credit, interest, and the business cycle.* Cambridge, MA: Harvard University Press.

Shane, S. (2000). Prior knowledge and the discovery of entrepreneurial opportunities. *Organization Science, 11*(4), 448–469.

Shepherd, D. A., & DeTienne, D. R. (2005). Prior knowledge, potential financial reward, and opportunity identification. *Entrepreneurship Theory and Practice, 29*(1), 91–112.

Suddaby, R., Bruton, G. D., & Si, S. X. (2015). Entrepreneurship through a qualitative lens: Insights on the construction and/or discovery of entrepreneurial opportunity. *Journal of Business Venturing, 30*(1), 1–10.

Throop, C. J. (2003). Articulating experience. *Anthropological Theory, 3*(2), 219–241.

Vallerand, R. J., Salvy, S. J., Mageau, G. A., Elliot, A. J., Denis, P. L., Grouzet, F. M. E., & Blanchard, C. (2007). On the role of passion in performance. *Journal of Personality, 75*(3), 505–534.

Weisberg, R. W. (1995). Prolegomena to theories of insight in problem solving: A taxonomy of problems. In R. J. Steinberg & J. E. Davidson (Eds.), *The nature of insight* (pp. 157–196). Cambridge, MA: MIT Press.

Weisberg, R. W. (2006a). *Creativity: Understanding innovation in problem solving, science, invention, and the arts.* Hoboken, NJ: Wiley.

Weisberg, R. W. (2006b). Modes of expertise in creative thinking: Evidence from case studies. In K. A. Ericsson, N. Charness, P. Feltovich, & R. R. Hoffman (Eds.), *Cambridge handbook of expertise and expert performance* (pp. 761–787). Cambridge, MA: Cambridge University Press.

Weisberg, R. W. (2013). On the "demystification" of insight: A critique of neuroimaging studies of insight. *Creativity Research Journal, 25*(1), 1–14.

Weisberg, R. W. (2015). Toward an integrated theory of insight in problem solving. *Thinking & Reasoning, 21*(1), 5–39.

Weiss, H. M., & Beal, D. (2005). Reflections on affective events theory. In N. M. Askanasy, W. Zerbe, & C. E. J. Hartel (Eds.), *Research on emotion in organizations: The effect of affect in organizational settings* (Vol. 1, pp. 1–21). Oxford, England: Elsevier.

Weiss, H. M., & Cropanzano, R. (1996). Affective events theory: A theoretical discussion of the structure, causes and consequences of affective experiences at work. In B. Shaw & L. L. Cummings (Eds.), *Research in organizational behavior* (pp. 1–74). Greenwich, CT: JAI Press.

CHAPTER 10

EXPLORING THE RELATIONSHIP BETWEEN FOREIGN COMPETITION AND ENTREPRENEURSHIP IN A HOST COUNTRY

Ana Venâncio
Farzana Chowdhury

ABSTRACT

Globalization has increased trading activity among countries. We examine how China foreign competition and human capital influence entrepreneurial activity in a host country. We propose that foreign competition fosters knowledge spillovers and consequently leads to firm entry. We build on the competence based argument to suggest that these spillovers are strengthened by the availability of human capital. Based on a comprehensive panel dataset of employees and new firms between 1994 and 2008, we find that the impact of China foreign competition on domestic entrepreneurial activity is not always positive rather the availability of human capital moderates this relationship. We also find strong support for the positive effect of foreign competition on quality of the initial team.

Entrepreneurship and Behavioral Strategy, pages 263–294

INTRODUCTION

Globalization has increased trade relations between nations over the years. However, the question regarding the gains from foreign competition remains open. Previous literature has argued that foreign competition increases productivity in the host country through positive spillovers (Bloom, Draca, & Van Reenen, 2016; Buckley, Clegg, & Wang, 2007; Feinberg & Majumdar, 2001; Spencer, 2008; Zhang, Li, Li, & Zhou, 2010). Also, foreign competition increases competition for resources and market share in the host countries (Bandelj, 2008; Graham & Krugman, 1995). The consequences of foreign competition are important because it affects not only economic growth and productivity (Cartiglia, 1997; Eaton & Kortum, 2001, 2002; Frankel & Romer, 1999; Grossman & Helpman, 1990; Manning, 1982; Rodrik, 1997; Yanikkaya, 2003) but also the political and cultural activity in a country (Coyne & Williamson, 2012; Rodrik, 1998; Varsakelis, 2001; Wacziarg, 2001). At the firm-level, foreign competition is responsible for reshuffling resources and output from less to more efficient firms (Bernard, Jensen, & Schott, 2006a, 2006b; Melitz, 2003; Pavcnik, Blom, Goldberg, & Schady, 2004), for technology upgrading (Bloom et al., 2016; Freeman & Kleiner, 2005), and for increasing offshore activities (Feenstra & Hansen, 1996). These trends reflect the need for increased attention to foreign competition's influence on the economic outcomes of the host country, particularly on entrepreneurship.

In this study, we examine the role of foreign competition on entrepreneurship and examine the moderating role of human capital on this relationship. We seek to provide insights into the importance of human capital in identifying opportunities as foreign competition increases. Additionally, we analyze the composition of the founding teams to investigate how the initial team is affected when a new venture faces foreign competition.

To illustrate these issues, we examine Portugal's manufacturing sector before and after China's accession to the World Trade Organization. We analyze trade with China because, over the last two decades, the country's exports have increased by more than 15% per year (Bloom et al., 2016). There are three reasons why our examination of the Portuguese manufacturing sector holds particular promise. First, the relative importance of the Portuguese manufacturing sector has declined significantly over the last 2 decades. Second, Portugal is likely to bear the brunt of China's competitive advantages because a substantial part of its production and exports is concentrated in either labor-intensive goods or on labor-intensive stages of the production cycle. Consequently, Portugal competes in the same industries as China. Third, we have access to extraordinary panel data on new firms and their initial workforce. Our analysis draws on a matched employer-employee dataset combined with international trade data from Eurostat over the period, from 1994 to 2008. The data cover detailed information about all manufacturing workers and entrepreneurs and their background history. Also, our data make it possible to match founders and their initial team with new ventures characteristics.

The topics raised in our study are theoretically appealing because they emphasize foreign competition as a source of knowledge as well as a business opportunity for the host country. Additionally, it is reasonable to assume that increased foreign competition will put downward pressure on wages (Auer, Degen, & Fischer, 2013) and consequently trigger individuals to search for alternative occupations, possibly become an entrepreneur. The quality of the entrepreneurial activity either productive or unproductive will depend on the motivation of the entrepreneur (Baumol, 1996). Thus, understanding how increased trade competition affects entrepreneurial activity is important to welfare analysis and to enable policy makers to develop sound policies toward the high-quality firm entry.

Our findings demonstrate that the impact of foreign competition on domestic entrepreneurial activity is not always positive rather the availability of human capital moderates the relationship between foreign competition and entry. We propose that foreign competition fosters knowledge spillovers and consequently leads to new firm entry. This study demonstrates that the entrepreneurship literature needs to develop new theories with regards to access to resources in different contexts. Also, we find strong support for the positive effect of foreign competition on quality of the initial team. Entrepreneurial firms are in need of various resources and rarely possess all the required resources for exploring/exploiting opportunities and for being successful. Thus, the initial team serves as a buffer against liabilities of newness as it allows the start-up to establish credibility with customers, and to create an institutional identity (Stinchcombe, 1965). This research brings new light to the role of teams on entrepreneurial activity when facing foreign competition.

CONCEPTUAL FRAMEWORK AND HYPOTHESES

Foreign Competition and Entry

Foreign competition can be a "double-edged sword," it can have positive as well as negative impacts on the economy. On one hand, foreign competition fosters the adoption of new technology and uncovers business opportunities. On the other hand, it can force firms to go out of business, reducing the demand for unskilled workers.

Models of international trade with heterogeneous firms predict that, in the short run, foreign competition increases the minimum productivity level that is required to stay in business, and consequently reduces the number of firm entries (Bernard et al., 2006a; Melitz, 2003).

Foreign firms compete for the same customers and crowd out domestic firms that have fewer resources (De Backer & Sleuwaegen, 2003),[1] increasing the barriers to entry for new firms.

Although increasing imports imply higher competitive pressure for firms, it also creates more business opportunities and promotes innovation. Individuals with entrepreneurial characteristics and opportunity recognition ability will be able to take advantage of this newly created opportunity or fill in the void created. In general, entrepreneurs in a society act as "gap fillers" by discovering and exploiting opportunities (Schumpeter, 1942; Shane & Venkataraman, 2000). An entrepreneur with appropriate resources such as institutional support, human capital and financial resources can explore and exploit opportunities to create new products, new processes, or new markets (Bowen & De Clercq, 2008; Evans & Jovanovic, 1989; Fairlie & Krashinsky, 2012; Gentry & Hubbard, 2004; Hurst & Lusardi, 2004; Quadrini, 1999; Stenholm, Acs, & Wuebker, 2013).

Foreign competition helps host country entrepreneurs to uncover entrepreneurial opportunities in several ways. A series of Eaton & Kortum's studies (2001, 2002) found that foreign competition influences growth in the local area through technology spillovers. Existing studies define spillover as transfer or diffusion of knowledge in the host country due to the presence of the foreign competition (Kim & Li, 2014; Meyer, 2004). Acharya and Keller (2009) found that imports play an important role in the technology transfer process. Also, Bloom et al. (2016) found that increased import competition with China caused a significant technological upgrading in European firms through both faster diffusion and innovation. They use several measures of technical change and innovation namely patenting, IT intensity and R&D expenditure. Thus, foreign competition pushes new and existing firms to develop new products. To escape competition, high productive firms compete on quality, using their productivity advantage to upgrading their mix of products (Bernard et al., 2006a; Melitz, 2003). Additionally, new products, services, or processes introduced by foreign competitors increase the demand in the host country (O'Malley & O'Gorman, 2001). On the other hand, entrepreneurs in the host country can take advantage of this increased demand by imitating foreign products (Javorcik, 2004). Since the host country entrepreneur has local knowledge, which a foreign competitor lacks, he/she can improve on the existing product. Moreover, local entrepreneurs can uncover new markets that foreign competitors are not aware of or overlooked (O'Malley & O'Gorman, 2001). Both foreign competitors and local entrepreneurs can benefit each other by combining their competitive advantage, also known as "forward linkage" (Ayyagari & Kosová, 2010). Foreign competitors lack local connections or relationships with appropriate local business and professional organizations (Ayyagari & Kosová, 2010; Blalock & Simon, 2009; Javorcik, 2004). In contrast, local entrepreneurs can take advantage of these networks to reach new markets. Another venue through which foreign competition can spur entrepreneurial activity in a country is by partnering with local entrepreneurs. By partnering with local entrepreneurs, they can produce new products that are more suitable for the local market (Pitelis & Teece, 2010). Thus, foreign competition increases local demand for new or improved products and creates new markets.

Another mechanism through which foreign competition triggers entrepreneurial activity is through job displacements. The common view is that foreign competition reduces employment (Revenga, 1997), particularly among low-skilled workers (Autor, Dorn, & Hanson, 2013). To respond to foreign competition, firms adopt technologies and activities that favor high skilled workers (Yeaple, 2005) or switch to high-quality products and hence labor quality (Verhoogen, 2008). Neoclassical economists argued that this "skill-based technical change" forces a group of individuals out of the labor market.[2] Individuals who lack the needed skill move to entrepreneurship because of the shortage of alternative job opportunities (Storey, 1994) but also due to changes on their risk frame. In loss frame events, individuals become more receptive to bear the risk.[3] On these grounds, high rates of or increases in, unemployment would lead to higher rates of new firm formation.

To sum up, we argue that foreign competition may reduce or trigger entrepreneurial activity. Nevertheless, as both push and pull effects positively affect entrepreneurial activity,[4] we expect:

Hypothesis 1: *Foreign competition is positively associated with firm entry.*

Moderating Role of Founder's Human Capital on Foreign Competition and Entry

Foreign competition affects individuals in different ways depending on labor market configuration and their level of human capital. Human capital includes both formal knowledge acquired through formal education and training as well as tacit knowledge acquired through work experience and non-formal education (Davidsson & Honig, 2003). It also pertains to generic and specific human capital (Becker, 1975; Colombo & Grilli, 2005). Specific human capital is industry or firm specific (Dakhli & De Clercq, 2004; Sandberg & Hofer, 1987; Siegel, Siegel, & MacMillan, 1993). Individuals with higher human capital are generally more likely to become founders, and founders' human capital largely determines the initial conditions of the start-up such as their initial size (Colombo, Delmastro, & Grilli, 2004; Mata & Machado, 1996), their chances of surviving (Brüderl, Preisend-örfer, & Ziegler, 1992) and their growing prospects (Bosma, Van Praag, Thurik & De Wit, 2004; Colombo & Grilli 2005; Koeller & Lechler, 2006). An entrepreneur with high human capital will have the inspiration to grow and to build a successful venture (Ardichvili, Cardozo & Ray, 2003; Mitchell et al., 2002; Shepherd & DeTienne, 2005). Also, founders with higher human capital are more efficient in organizing and managing operations, in attracting customers, negotiating better contracts with suppliers and raising more capital from investors (Brüderl et al., 1992).

Human capital that is transferable across firms and industries is important for running a business (Becker, 1975) but also for perceiving and interpreting unconnected information (Schultz, 1975). Thus, individuals with high human capital are more likely to recognize and pursue an opportunity (Arenius & De Clercq, 2005; Arenius & Minnitti, 2005; Busenitz et al., 2003; Davidsson & Honig, 2003; Shepherd & DeTienne, 2005). Levie and Autio (2008) presented that higher level of education is positively related to identifying entrepreneurial opportunity. Shane and Venkataraman posited that "two broad categories of factors that influence the probability that particular people will discover particular opportunities: (a) the possession of the prior information necessary to identify an opportunity, and (b) the cognitive properties necessary to value it" (2000, p. 222). Entrepreneurs with industry specific knowledge are better able to recognize an opportunity than someone who does not possess that information. Ucbasaran, Westhead and Wright, presented that "specific human capital may represent a better 'guide' for entrepreneurs to identify opportunities than general human capital alone" (2008, p. 158). Foreign competition creates entrepreneurial opportunity in the local market and individuals with high human capital are better prepared and able to recognize an opportunity and take advantage of that.

Entrepreneurs do not always pursue all the opportunities they identify (Shane & Venkataraman, 2000; Witt, 1998), rather the cost of pursuing the opportunity can be an important component of an entrepreneur's decision. If the opportunity cost of exploiting an opportunity (e.g., independence, time, effort, money) is lower for an individual than staying in the regular wage job then he/she will transition to entrepreneurship. Individuals with higher human capital have higher expectations than their counterparts. Bowen and De Clercq (2008) found a positive relationship between higher education and starting high-growth oriented businesses. Therefore, entrepreneurs with high human capital can use their knowledge to pursue the attractive opportunity.

To sum up, the spillover effect of foreign competition on entrepreneurship can be influenced by the availability of human capital. Based on the arguments above, we expect:

Hypothesis 2: *The positive relationship between foreign competition and entry is strengthened by the availability of highly qualified individuals.*

Linking Foreign Competition and Initial Team

Existing literature suggests that foreign competition increases the productivity of domestic firms as well as the quality of domestic products (Aitken & Harrison, 1999; Blomström & Kokko, 1998; Buckley et al., 2007; Feinberg & Majumdar, 2001; Zhang et al., 2010). For an entrepreneur to imitate or to create a new product and create a new organization/venture, the characteristics of the founding team are an important resource (Chandler & Hank, 1998).

The competence-based studies argue that the combination of unique capabilities are the main sources of the firm's competitive advantage (Grant, 1996). For instance, a production process involves teamwork and in order for the process to be successful, members of the team need to have complementary skills and share these skills to complete the tasks (Alchian & Demsetz, 1972; Kremer, 1993). Therefore, coordinating a team of people who can complement each other can create a productive organization. Existing literature has established that people can be an important resource as it helps to create a sustainable competitive advantage (Pfeffer, 1994; Prahalad, 1983; Wright, McMahan, & McWilliams, 1994). High-quality initial workforce creates a competitive advantage for a new venture. For example, Mata and Portugal (2002) argue that the education of a firm's workforce can be regarded as a measure of ownership advantages. Dahl and Klepper (2015) find that employees hired in the earliest stages of the start-up are a key element of future firm success. Members of the initial team can divide tasks among members in an efficient manner to be productive. Also, the initial team helps new ventures to overcome resource constraints. At the initial stage of its life cycle, venture needs several crucial resources. In order to acquire these resources, they need to establish legitimacy and overcome the liability of the newness (Aldrich & Auster, 1986; Carroll & Delacroix, 1982; Stinchcombe, 1965), also known as "soft power" (Santos & Eisenhardt, 2009). Soft power is defined as "subtle influence mechanisms that cause others to willingly behave in ways that benefit the focal agent" (Santos & Eisenhardt, 2009, p. 663). The initial team can use their previous networks, experience to establish legitimacy.

Founders and initial team rely on each other to learn new tasks (Stinchcombe, 1965) and to establish new roles for individuals involved and routines (Choi & Shepherd, 2005; Nelson & Winter, 1982). By establishing routines, these new ventures gradually reduce inefficiency. The initial team members help ventures to gain legitimacy. The high-quality initial team can also help new ventures to acquire the necessary resources to either compete with or form an alliance with foreign competition. Studies have shown that venture capitalists often use the availability of human capital as selection criteria for investing in the firm; in this case, human capital is considered in terms of the founders' management skills and experience (Zacharakis & Meyer, 2000). Therefore, the initial workforce can give the venture capitalist the confidence to make an investment in the firm.

At the initial stage, general and industry-specific human capital, leadership style, and mental models are helpful for creating a successful new venture (Coad, Daunfeldt, Johansson, & Wennberg, 2014; Kazanjian & Drazin, 1989; Miller & Friesen, 1984). The effective management of this human capital may ultimately determine the success of the new venture (Adler, 1988; Reich, 1991). Therefore, we expect the initial team members to be hired based on their technical skills to complete tasks and to fit the organizational culture (Aldrich & Ruef, 2006). Initial teams with a high level of human capital create organizational memory, culture and norms that are conducive to entrepreneurial activity.

Availability of human capital can also help in the knowledge transfer process in an organization.[5] Cyert and March (1963) argued that in an organization individuals learn from each other through interactions by sharing the information and knowledge they already have from previous experience and new knowledge acquired through different sources such as customers, suppliers, and other stakeholders in the new venture. A venture with high human capital is better able to absorb and apply this knowledge to create competitive advantage (Argote & Ingram, 2000). Based on this logic, we hypothesize that:

Hypothesis 3: *Foreign competition is positively associated with the quality of the initial team.*

METHODOLOGY

Sample

The hypotheses are tested using Portuguese data. We combine a longitudinal matched employer-employee database, *Quadros de Pessoal* (QP) with the EUROSTAT database on international trade.

QP database originates from a mandatory survey submitted annually to the Portuguese Ministry of Employment and Social Security by Portuguese private firms with at least one paid employee. The database has detailed information at the individual and firm level. As individuals and firms are cross-referenced by a unique identifier, the database makes it possible to identify the founders and their initial workforce. With these data, we construct two databases: individuals and entrepreneurs. For the first database, we select all individuals with age between 19 and 59[6] who worked in manufacturing firms in mainland Portugal between the period of 1993 and 2007.[7] To reduce the number of multiple observations per individual, we ensure that an individual only appears once in the data. Next, we identify their background history and analyze their employment status in the following year (1994 and 2008). Individuals can either continue working as paid employees, move to entrepreneurship or become non-employed.[8] In total, we have a sample of 1,214,502 individuals, of whom 34,378 are entrepreneurs. These data allow us to evaluate the impact of foreign competition on firm entry and compare the characteristics of founders and non-founders in specific years.

Table 10.1 provides general characteristics of the individuals' sample separately for entrepreneurs and workers. Workers are mostly male (54%), medium educated (13%), highly educated (5%), foreign nationality (3%), and are 32 years old, on average. Their hourly income is 3.90€ and they worked for five years on average and 2% of them previously set up a new venture. Entrepreneurs are older (39 years old), more educated, medium educated (14%), highly educated (7%), and earn larger earnings (4€ per hour). The great majority of them (83%) have entrepreneurial experience.

The second database, entrepreneurs' database, allows us to evaluate the characteristics of the initial team. From QP, we select all manufacturing start-ups established in mainland Portugal between 1994 and 2008. In a second step, we identify the founders and their background history.[9] As in the previous database, we restrict data to founders between 20 and 60 years of age. Finally, for each start-up, we identify the initial workforce hired in the entry year. We exclude start-ups where the only employees are the founders. We ended up with 10,037 founders and 36,683 employees of 7,068 new firms.

Table 10.2 presents the descriptive statistics for the entrepreneurs' database. On average, start-ups are established by one founder and after the first 3 years, approximately 1,845 firms fail to correspond to a mortality rate of 26%. Start-ups are small and employ on average six workers. The initial workforce earns on average 522 Euros and only 9% and 2% of them have medium and high education, respectively. Founders in our sample are mostly male (71%), low educated (80%) and with 37 years of age. On average, 23% of the founders establish their venture in the same industry where they previously worked.

TABLE 10.1 Descriptive Statistics For the Individuals

Characteristics	Total			Workers			Entrepreneurs		
	Obs.	Mean	SD	Obs.	Mean	SD	Obs.	Mean	SD
Entry	1,214,502	0.03	0.17						
Gender (Male)	1,214,502	0.55	0.50	1,180,124	0.54	0.50	34,378	0.72	0.45
Age	1,214,502	31.81	10.77	1,180,124	31.59	10.71	34,378	39.31	10.08
Medium Education	1,214,502	0.13	0.33	1,180,124	0.13	0.33	34,378	0.14	0.35
High Education	1,214,502	0.05	0.23	1,180,124	0.05	0.22	34,378	0.07	0.25
Nationality (Foreign)	1,214,502	0.03	0.16	1,180,124	0.03	0.16	34,378	0.01	0.11
Non Employed	1,214,502	0.31	0.46	1,180,124	0.31	0.46	34,378	0.25	0.43
Tenure	1,214,502	4.91	3.81	1,180,124	4.89	3.80	34,378	5.70	3.97
Entrepreneurial Experience	1,214,502	0.05	0.21	1,180,124	0.02	0.15	34,378	0.83	0.37
Hourly Income	1,103,847	3.90	3.76	1,098,220	3.89	3.76	5,627	4.63	4.59

Notes: Obs. = Observations; *SD* = Standard Deviation

TABLE 10.2   Descriptive Statistics For the Start-Ups, Entrepreneurs, and Their Initial Teams

Characteristics	Obs.	Mean	SD
Firm Characteristics			
N Founders	7,068	1.47	0.69
Size	7,068	5.61	8.88
Survival	7,068	0.74	0.44
Initial Team Members Characteristics			
Share of Medium Education	10,037	0.09	0.23
Share of High Education	10,037	0.02	0.10
Average Income	9,889	522.43	191.50
Founder Characteristics			
Gender (Male)	10,037	0.71	0.45
Age	10,037	36.99	9.29
Medium Education	10,037	0.15	0.36
High Education	10,037	0.04	0.21
Nationality (Foreign)	10,037	0.01	0.08
Industry Experience	10,037	0.23	0.42

Notes: Obs = Observations; S.D. = Standard Deviation

Next, we use trade information from the EUROSTAT international database to construct our measure of foreign competition. This database captures all bilateral international transactions by product level between European countries and any country in the world. We select imports from China to Portugal and aggregate them from eight-digit product level to four-digit ISIC (rev 3.1) industry level using the Pierce and Schott (2009) concordance. Our measure of foreign competition evaluates the exposure of a region to Chinese imports[10] and it is derived from the Eaton and Kortum (2002) model of trade[11] and adapted by Autor et al. (2013) to account for regional economies. We use:

$$FC_{cy} = \sum_j \frac{E_{jcy}}{E_{jy}} \times IMPS_{PTjy} \qquad (10.1)$$

where c denotes county, y denotes year, and j denote industry.

We apportion the value of imports originating from China (M_{jy}^{China}) as a share of total world imports to Portugal (M_{jy}^{World}) by four-digit industry and year

$$IMPS_{PTjy} = \frac{M_{jy}^{China}}{M_{jy}^{World}}$$

to a region according with their initial share of industry employment. The fraction

$$\frac{E_{jcy}}{E_{jy}}$$

represents the county's start of the year share of total employment in industry j. A region is more exposed to foreign competition when it accounts for a larger share of industries experiencing an increase of imports from China. There are 278 counties in mainland Portugal, each of them with substantial geographic variation in terms of industry specialization. Most of the industries are agglomerated in specific counties. For instance, the footwear industry is concentrated on Felgueiras, Santa Maria da Feira, and Oliveira de Azemeis, and the glass industry is located in Marinha Grande and Alcobaça.

Table 10.3 reports the regional average of our foreign competition measure for the years 1994, 2000, and 2008 considering different countries: China, Central Eastern European Countries (CEEC), low-income countries and high-income countries. CEEC includes Bulgaria, Croatia, Czech Republic, Hungary, Poland, Romania, Slovakia, and Slovenia. High-income countries include Australia, Denmark, Finland, Germany, Japan, New Zealand, Spain, and Switzerland. The selection of low-income countries follows the World Bank definition in 1993, excluding China. On average, a region faced foreign competition from China of 0.5% and 1.1% in 1994 and 2008, respectively. These numbers reflect the rise of Chinese imports share. Águeda and Lisbon are the counties more affected by Chinese competition. From 1994 to 2008, China competition increased by 0.59%. For comparison, the next columns provide our foreign competition measure using the

TABLE 10.3	Regional Average of Foreign Competition			
	Foreign Competition			
	(1) China	(2) CEEC	(3) Other Low-Inc	(4) High-Inc
Portugal				
1994	0.52%	0.15%	0.13%	2.72%
2000	0.71%	0.34%	0.11%	3.10%
2008	1.11%	0.61%	0.30%	2.35%
United States				
1994	2.92%			
2000	4.54%			
2008	8.68%			

Source: Computed by the authors.

import share from CEEC, low-income countries (excluding China) and a group of high-income countries. Except for high-income foreign competition, foreign competition from CEEC and low-income countries grew over time. For example, the CEEC and low-income foreign competition grew by 0.46% and 0.17%, respectively. Nevertheless, this expansion was smaller than in the case of Chinese foreign competition.

Further details of our data construction and measures are provided in the Appendix.

Econometric Approach and Variables

Entry and Founders Profile

To evaluate if foreign competition increases firm entry, we estimate the following model using the individuals sample:

$$Entry_{iy} = \theta_y + \alpha_j + \omega_c + \beta FC_{cy} + X_i'\lambda + \varepsilon_{ijcy} \qquad (10.2)$$

where i denotes an individual, c denotes county, y denotes year and j industry.

$Entry_i$ is an indicator variable that equals 1 if individual i founds a start-up, and 0 if that individual does not open a firm.

Our variable of interest is foreign competition, FC_{cy}, measured as the weighted average of China import share in county c and year y. Our empirical strategy relates the probability that any individual found a start-up to foreign competition measured at the county level.[12] Our first hypothesis predicts an increase on firm entry due to an increase on foreign competition, thus we expect the coefficient to be positive and statistic significant.

Our estimation strategy intends to capture the supply side effect of China import increase. However, if Chinese imports are related to demand side effects, then our estimates may underestimate the true impact as both firm entry and Chinese imports may be correlated with unobserved shocks to demand. To account for the potential endogeneity of our foreign competition variable, we employ the instrumental variable strategy. We argue that the growth in Chinese imports stems from the rise in manufacturers competitiveness, lower trade barriers, dismantle of central planning and accession to the WTO. Similarly to Autor et al. (2013), we use as instrument:

$$FCI_{cy} = \sum_j \frac{E_{jc(y-5)}}{E_{j(y-5)}} \times IMPS_{USiy} \qquad (10.3)$$

The instrument differs from the foreign competition measure in two respects. First, in place of Chinese import share to Portugal ($IMPS_{PTiy}$), it uses

Chinese import share to the United States ($IMPS_{USiy}$). Second, in place of the start-of-year employment levels by industry and region, this expression uses employment levels from the prior 5 years. The employment levels on a region might be affected by anticipated China imports, thus we use lagged employment to mitigate this simultaneity bias. Nonetheless, if the demand shocks are correlated between Portugal and the United States both our estimates understate the true effect of foreign competition on firm entry.

Equation 10.2 also includes a vector of individual characteristics, X_i: gender, which equals 1 for men, 0 for women; two variables for founder's age (age and age squared); foreign nationality, which equals 1 for foreign individuals, 0 for Portuguese individuals; two indicator variables for education: "medium education" for individuals with a high school diploma or equivalent, and "high education" for those reporting bachelor's degree or more advanced degree; tenure, measured as the logarithm of the number of years of work experience in the last job; non-employment, which equals 1 for individuals absent of the database in the prior year, 0 otherwise.[13] In reporting the estimated coefficients, our omitted categories are female individuals who did not finish high school.

This specification also includes year dummies, θ_y to control for the macroeconomic setting; regional dummies, ω_c, to control for regional differences in start-up dynamics and region-specific economic development; and industry dummies, α_j, to account for heterogeneous entrepreneurial opportunities across industries. Standard errors for this specification are clustered at the start-up level.

Initial Team Profile

Next, we evaluate if foreign competition affects the quality of the initial workforce by estimating the following model using the entrepreneurs' database:

$$Team_{iy} = \theta_y + \alpha_j + \omega_c + \beta FC_{cy} + X_i'\lambda + \varepsilon_{ijcy} \qquad (10.4)$$

where i denotes founder, c denotes county, y denotes entry year, and j industry.

Our dependent variable evaluates the educational level of the initial workforce using two variables: the share of workers with high school diploma (share of medium educated workers) and the share of workers reporting bachelor's degree or more advanced degree (share of high educated workers).

Again, we are interested in the coefficient associated with foreign competition, FC_{cy}. We expect this coefficient to be positive and statistically significant.

Also, we control for founder demographic and educational characteristics because existing literature suggest that founders with high human capital are more likely to hire highly qualified workers (Dahl & Klepper, 2015). We include founders' gender, age, and age squared, foreign nationality, high and medium education and industry experience. The latter variable is measured by a dummy variable equaling 1 for founders that previously worked on the same four-digit industry code, 0 otherwise. Additionally, we control for the initial size of the venture because ventures with larger labor workforce have more human capital and more resources (Klepper, 2001). In reporting the estimated coefficients, our omitted categories are female founders who did not finish high school.

RESULTS

Table 10.4 reports the results of the regression estimations of foreign competition on new firm entry. Models 1, 2, and 3 show the estimates for the probit model while Models 4 and 5 the IV-probit estimates. Model 1 features our main variable of interest, foreign competition, and year, industry and region fixed effects. The coefficient of foreign competition is negative, suggesting that an increase in foreign competition reduces the predictive probability of entry. This negative relationship is consistent with all the models included in Table 10.4. Thus, we do not find support for our Hypothesis 1.

In Model 2, we add a set of demographic and education controls. Consistent with previous literature, we find a U-shaped relationship between age and firm entry (Ucbasaran et al., 2008). The likelihood of entry increases until a certain age and then it declines. As for the other demographic and education variables, we can infer that male and well-educated individuals are relatively more likely to transition into entrepreneurship than are other individuals. In terms of experience, we find that individuals with longer careers in paid employment and non-employed individuals are less likely to transition to entrepreneurship. In contrast, individuals with previous entrepreneurial experience are more likely to become entrepreneurs.

To verify that foreign competition leads to an increase in the entry of high qualified entrepreneurs (Hypothesis 2), we interact the two educational variables (medium and high education) with our foreign competition measure and add these interactions to Equation 10.2. The coefficient estimates are reported in Models 3 of Table 10.4. The interaction effect of foreign competition and medium education is positive and significant. This positive relationship also holds when we include the interaction of higher education and foreign competition. These results suggest that individuals with more education are more likely to enter the market as foreign competition increases. Hypothesis 2 is thus supported.

Models 4 and 5 of Table 10.4 report the IV-probit estimates. These estimates are quite similar to probit estimates but larger in magnitude. The

TABLE 10.4   Results of Foreign Competition and Entry

Model Specification	(1) Coeff.	(1) s.e.	(2) Coeff.	(2) s.e.	(3) Coeff.	(3) s.e.	(4) Coeff.	(4) s.e.	(5) Coeff.	(5) s.e.
Foreign competition (FC)	-0.477	(0.251)†	-0.414	(0.359)	-0.804	(0.369)*	-1.174	(0.168)***	-1.592	(0.189)***
FC*Medium education					1.493	(0.328)***			1.618	(0.337)***
FC*High education					0.851	(0.456)†			1.135	(0.461)*
Control Variables										
Gender (Male)			0.113	(0.008)***	0.113	(0.008)***	0.112	(0.008)***	0.112	(0.008)***
Age			0.065	(0.002)***	0.065	(0.002)***	0.065	(0.002)***	0.065	(0.002)***
Age square			-0.077	(0.003)***	-0.077	(0.003)***	-0.077	(0.003)***	-0.077	(0.003)***
Nationality (Foreign)			-0.197	(0.025)***	-0.195	(0.025)***	-0.195	(0.024)***	-0.193	(0.024)***
Medium education			0.182	(0.011)***	0.135	(0.015)***	0.169	(0.011)***	0.119	(0.015)***
High education			0.211	(0.016)***	0.183	(0.023)***	0.188	(0.016)***	0.151	(0.023)***
Non-employment			-0.109	(0.011)***	-0.109	(0.011)***	-0.114	(0.011)***	-0.113	(0.011)***
Tenure			-0.116	(0.006)***	-0.116	(0.006)***	-0.120	(0.006)***	-0.119	(0.006)***
Entrepreneurial experience			2.496	(0.008)***	2.496	(0.008)***	2.503	(0.008)***	2.503	(0.008)***
Constant	-1.862	(0.074)***	-3.647	(0.108)***	-3.640	(0.108)***	-3.605	(0.052)***	-3.597	(0.052)***
Method	Probit		Probit		Probit		IV Probit		IV Probit	

Notes: All estimations have White's heteroskedasticity–consistent standard errors and covariance matrices. $N = 1,213,210$. Industry, year and region fixed effects included but not reported. Two–tailed t-test with $***p < 0.001$, $**p < 0.01$, $*p < 0.05$, $†p < 0.1$. Coeff. = regression coefficient; s.e. = standard error.

coefficient associated with our foreign competition measure becomes more negative and the significance level changes from 5% to 1%. Also, the interaction of foreign competition and higher education becomes larger and the significance level changes from 10% to 5%. Note that we use a weighted average of China import share to the United States as an instrument for foreign competition, and we find support for a positive correlation between those variables. For both specifications, the coefficients associated with the instrument in the reduced equation are positive and significant ($\beta = 0.102$, $p < 0.01$) and the results are available upon request.

Table 10.5 presents the results for the quality of the initial workforce. Models 1 and 2 show the results for the share of high educated workers and Models 3 and 4 presents the estimates for the share of medium educated workers. We present both the OLS and IV model side by side; the results of both specifications are similar. The coefficient associated with foreign competition is positive and significant and the IV estimate is also significant but larger in magnitude. These results suggest that ventures established in regions facing higher foreign competition are more likely to hire highly educated workers. We also find a positive and significant effect of foreign competition on the share of medium educated workers, nevertheless, the coefficient loses statistical significance in the IV regression (Model 4 of Table 10.5). These results are consistent with the predictions of Hypotheses 3 which suggest that foreign competition increases the quality of the initial team. As suggested by the previous literature, we find that well-educated founders are more likely to hire similarly educated workers. The coefficients associated with the high and medium education of the founder are positive and significant for both the share of high and medium educated workers. However, founders' demographic characteristics do not statistically affect the share of high and medium educated workers. The only exception is founder's age for the share of medium educated workers. In this case, we find a U-shape relationship. Size has a negative association with the share of high and medium educated workers, suggesting that larger ventures will hire less educated workers.

We have one additional analysis intended to inform us about the relative quality of the initial workforce. We repeat the analysis reported for education, but now we use as the dependent variable the logarithm of employees' monthly average income (in 2008 Euros). Unfortunately, for some of the workers, their salaries are not disclosed and consequently the sample size is smaller. Model 5 and 6 of Table 10.5 present the results for OLS and IV specification. The coefficient associated with foreign competition is positive and significant, suggesting that ventures established in regions facing higher foreign competition pay higher salaries to their workers than other ventures. As noted previously, the IV coefficient is larger in magnitude. These results are consistent with the predictions of Hypotheses 3, using

TABLE 10.5 Results of Foreign Competition and Initial Workforce

Model Specification	Share of High Educated Workers				Share of Medium Educated Workers				Income			
	(1)		(2)		(3)		(4)		(5)		(6)	
	Coeff.	s.e.	Coeff	s.e.	Coeff	s.e.	Coeff	s.e.	Coeff	s.e.	Coeff	s.e.
Foreign Competition (FC)	0.241	(0.068)***	0.438	(0.110)***	0.197	(0.106)†	0.208	(0.153)	0.980	(0.183)***	1.188	(0.211)***
Control Variables												
Gender (Male)	0.003	(0.002)	0.003	(0.002)	0.003	(0.005)	0.003	(0.005)	0.006	(0.008)	0.006	(0.008)
Age	–0.000	(0.001)	–0.000	(0.001)	0.005	(0.002)**	0.005	(0.002)**	0.000	(0.003)	0.000	(0.003)
Age square/100	0.001	(0.001)	0.001	(0.001)	–0.005	(0.002)*	–0.005	(0.002)*	0.002	(0.004)	0.002	(0.004)
Nationality (Foreign)	0.004	(0.021)	0.004	(0.021)	0.021	(0.033)	0.021	(0.033)	–0.075	(0.098)	–0.076	(0.097)
Medium education	0.007	(0.003)*	0.006	(0.003)†	0.155	(0.011)***	0.155	(0.011)***	0.065	(0.011)***	0.063	(0.011)***
High education	0.106	(0.015)***	0.105	(0.015)***	0.083	(0.016)***	0.083	(0.016)***	0.136	(0.022)***	0.135	(0.022)***
Industry experience	–0.002	(0.002)	–0.002	(0.002)	0.001	(0.006)	0.001	(0.006)	0.016	(0.008)†	0.016	(0.008)†
Size	–0.004	(0.002)**	–0.004	(0.002)*	–0.013	(0.003)***	–0.013	(0.003)***	0.039	(0.005)***	0.039	(0.005)***
Constant	0.255	(0.121)*	0.020	(0.034)	0.020	(0.105)	–0.312	(0.049)***	6.384	(0.099)***	6.361	(0.101)***
N	10,037		10,037		10,037		10,037		9,889		9,889	
Adjusted R²	0.127		0.125		0.142		0.142		0.161		0.161	

Notes: All estimations have clustered standard errors at the firm level. Industry, year and region fixed effects included but not reported. Two–tailed *t*-test with ***$p < 0.001$, **$p < 0.01$, *$p < 0.05$, †$p < 0.1$. Coeff. = regression coefficient; s.e. = standard error.

wages as a proxy for the quality of the workforce. Founder's education and industry experience have a positive association with the average income of the workforce indicating that founder with higher human capital pay larger salaries. The size of the venture positively affects the salary of the workforce, suggesting that larger ventures pay larger salaries.

Again, we use an instrument for foreign competition the weighted average of China import share to the United States. All the coefficients associated with the instrument in the reduced equations are positive and significant ($\beta = 0.102$, $p < 0.01$) and the results are available upon request.

Below we provide results related to additional robustness checks we conducted. The results are available upon request. We have conducted several analysis checks. First, we computed alternative measures for foreign competition. In the earlier analysis, we use a weighted average of China import share as our foreign competition measure. This is by no means the only way to measure foreign competition. We computed alternative measures by changing the weights and the import share. First, we apportion imports according to counties share of total industry sales instead of apportioning according to share of employment. As another measure, we replace the China imports share, with the China net imports (imports–exports) share. These alternative measures yield similar estimates to the ones presented in the section above.

Second, our results are consistent in restricted samples. As noted before our instrumental variables strategy seeks to isolate the supply shocks of China imports increase. Nevertheless, our IV estimates might understate the true effects if the demand shocks are correlated between Portugal and the United States. To address this concern, in untabulated results, we dropped industries where the rise of Chinese imports might be due to an increase in domestic demand. We exclude the consumer electronics industry and we find that the foreign competition negatively affects firm entry. The interactions of the medium and high education with the foreign competition are both positive and significant. In terms of the quality of the initial team, we find a positive and significant effect of foreign competition on the share of high educated workers.

Third, we allow a dynamic response for our foreign competition measure by including lag lengths (1-, 2-, and 3-year lags) on our foreign competition measure. In the analyses reported above, we used the current level. In this case, the coefficients of foreign competition on entry continue to be negative and statistically significant and the interactions between medium education and foreign competition continue to be positive and significant. The interactions between high education and foreign competition are positive but only statistically significant for 1-year lag. In terms of the quality of the initial team, we find a positive and significant effect of foreign competition on the share of high educated workers.

Finally, we evaluate the impact of foreign competition on the size of the initial team. We measure size as the logarithm of a total number of initial employees. We find a negative and significant effect of foreign competition in size. The IV estimate is larger in magnitude and also significant. These results suggest that ventures established in regions facing high foreign competition are likely to be smaller than other ventures.

DISCUSSION AND CONCLUSIONS

Increased globalization has increased relationships among countries. However, the debate regarding the impact of foreign competition on the economic activity of the host countries continues. To the best of our knowledge, this is the first empirical study that explicitly examines how foreign competition affects entrepreneurial activity.

We use a comprehensive dataset from Portugal for the period from 1994 to 2008 to analyze how China foreign competition affects new firm entry. Our results show that foreign competition reduces new firm entry, but with the availability of human capital has an opposite effect, fosters firm entry. Our findings suggest that foreign competition may not always be a bad thing rather it can be a motivating factor for individuals with high human capital. We found that the interaction of foreign competition and human capital have a positive relationship with firm entry. Our findings have important implications for policy makers and domestic firms. For policy makers, our findings help them better understand how they need to be flexible in a changing environment and adopt policies that help to foster entrepreneurial activity.

We further argue that foreign competition influences the profiles of the initial workforce and our findings suggest that foreign competition spillovers help to create high-quality founding teams. In addition to the cognitive abilities, the individual entrepreneur also acts as "a champion" to mobilize and combine resources to accomplish his/her goal. Therefore, as foreign competition creates opportunities for them to exploit, they would also push themselves to make the venture successful by creating a high-quality team. This high-quality founding team will employ strategies to acquire and channel resources to make the venture successful.

Theory suggests that trade yields aggregate gains. Our study highlights the dynamics of foreign competition spillovers. Foreign competition either forces to create or improves entrepreneurial ecosystems. In general, established firms tend to control or have overwhelming access to critical resources such as markets, high-quality human capital, and financial capital than nascent firms. Foreign competition can act as an "external force" to break the existing structure and create opportunities for entrepreneurs who were either reluctant to enter the entrepreneurial activity or did not see an opportunity that they were willing to pursue. Foreign competition can also force policymakers to adopt policies that are more conducive to entrepreneurial activity.

We examined the role of foreign competition in generating entrepreneurial activity and influencing the founding teams in Portugal. Whether our findings are generalizable to other countries remain to be seen because regulations, development level (Schwab & Sala-i-Martin, 2011), labor management and intellectual property are different (Hitt, Li, & Worthington, 2005). Future studies may also explore how strategic alliances form due to foreign competition. Foreign firms may want to remain in the host country and be interested in increasing their market share in the host country. One possible way of increasing market share is by forming alliances with local firms. Another area of future exploration is international entrepreneurship/export related ventures.

NOTES

1. Faced with increased import competition, low-tech firms shrink or fail while high-tech firms are sheltered out (Bloom et al., 2016).
2. Another view argues that import competition might not lead to an increase in the demand for skill. In fact, the new technologies might be used to replace skilled workers or even expand tasks performed by the unskilled workers (Acemoglu & Autor, 2011; Goos, Manning, & Salomons, 2014).
3. The prospect theory suggests that individuals are more willing to bear risk in loss frame events (Tversky & Kahneman, 1991). Being unemployed is likely to make individuals more receptive to risk.
4. If an individual takes on entrepreneurial activity in order to meet the basic need then he/she is pushed into entrepreneurship. On the flip side, if an individual enters into entrepreneurial activity at his/her own will and ability by recognizing an opportunity, then it would reflect "pull" effect.
5. Singley and Anderson (1989, p. 1) defined transfer at the individual level as "how knowledge acquired in one situation applies (or fails to apply) to another."
6. We select this age range to exclude individuals with limited career histories and close to retirement.
7. We focus our analysis in the period between 1994 and 2008 to exclude the effects of the economic and sovereign debt crises. The economic crisis is considered to have started in 2009, the first year with negative GDP growth in every quarter (with a contraction of around 2%). Due to the high levels of public deficit and public debt, the country requested a bailout package from the International Monetary Fund and European Union in April 2011.
8. Non-employed individuals include unemployed, self-employed, and civil servant individuals. The database does not allow us to accurately distinguish between these cases.

9. We exclude start-ups for which we could not identify at least one founder or their background history. For each individual, QP includes some cases in which the record changes in gender and year of birth. We consider observations with multiple changes in the gender or year of birth to be errors, corresponding to individuals whose identification number was not recorded, or wrongly identified by the respondent. We drop individuals whose gender and year birth change in more than 75% of the total number of observations.

10. We use China import surge because the country experienced productivity gains, transitioned to a market oriented economy, and had its quotas and trade barriers eliminated due to its accession to the WTO in 2001.

11. Eaton and Kortum (2002) develop a Ricardian trade model that incorporates differences in technology, input costs and geographic barriers. Their model bears semblance to the standard gravity model.

12. Our empirical approach is closely related to a large body of literature studying the impact of trade on the labor market and using regional economies as unit of analysis (see e.g., Autor et al. [2013], Topalova & Khandelwal [2011]). Alternative estimation strategies treat industry or occupation as the unit of analysis (Bernard et al., 2006b; Bloom et al., 2016).

13. In this case, non-employed individuals are new entrants to the labor market, unemployed, self-employed or public servant individuals.

ACKNOWLEDGMENTS

The authors are grateful to the Portuguese Ministry of Employment and Social Security and Gabinete de Estratégia e Planeamento (GEP) for access to the matched employer-employee data. This work was supported by the Fundação para a Ciência e a Tecnologia (Portuguese Foundation for Science and Technology) [Project UID/SOC/04521/2019]. Views expressed herein are those of the authors and do not necessarily reflect those of any branch or agency of the Government of Portugal.

APPENDIX: DATA AND VARIABLES

Matched Employer–Employee Database

The longitudinal employer-employee dataset, *Quadros de Pessoal* (QP) originates from a mandatory survey submitted annually in October by all firms with at least one employee. This database collects information on an average of 227,000 firms and two million individuals per year, covering virtually all employees and firms in the Portuguese private sector. The data do not include information on self-employed, unemployed and public servant individuals. This database is available annually from 1985 onward, however, we restrict our analysis to the period between 1993 and 2008.

The database contains three related sets of records: one at the firm level, other at the establishment level and another at the employee level. Employees, firms, and establishments are cross-referenced by a unique identifier. Each year, firms report their year of incorporation, location (county), main industry, the number of employees, the number of establishments, initial capital, ownership structure and sales. At the establishment level, firms report the number of employees, location, and main industry. At the individual level, the database contains information on gender, age, date of hire, education (number of years of education and field of education), occupation, labor status, working hours, and October's earnings. However, the employee records are unavailable for the year 2001 and include redundant data or data with frequent changes in gender and/or year of birth. We consider these observations to be errors, corresponding to individuals whose identification number was not inserted or wrongly identified by the respondent. We drop individuals whose gender and year birth change in more than 75% of the total number of observations.

With these data, we construct two databases: individuals and entrepreneurs databases. For the first database, we select all individuals with age between 19 and 59 who worked in manufacturing firms in mainland Portugal between the period of 1993 and 2007. To reduce the number of multiple observations per individual, we ensure that an individual only appears once in the data. Next, we identify their background history and analyze their employment status in the following year (1994 and 2008). Individuals can either continue working as paid employees, move to entrepreneurship or become non-employed. In total, we have a sample of 1,214,502 individuals, of whom 34,378 are entrepreneurs.

For the second database, we select all manufacturing start-ups established in mainland Portugal between 1994 and 2008 from QP. In a second step, we identify the founders and their background history. As in the previous database, we restrict data to founders between 20 and 60 years of age. Finally, for each start-up, we identify the initial workforce hired in the entry year. We exclude start-ups were the only employees are the founders. We ended up with 10,037 founders and 36,683 employees of 7,068 new firms. We have adopted the following definitions:

Entrepreneurs are business owners with legally independent firms with at least one employee. We exclude from the analysis self-employed individuals because they do not appear in the matched employer-employee dataset. Individuals are identified as business owners through a labor status variable that distinguishes business owners from paid employees.

Entry is computed as the minimum of the year of foundation reported in the database, the year that the firm first appeared in the database and the year of hire of the first employee. Using this procedure, we eliminate possible merger/acquisitions or changes of denomination or legal structure.

Start-ups are entrepreneurial ventures founded by entrepreneurs.

Initial Team includes all individuals, excluding the founders, who are employed in the first year of activity of the start-up.

Size is the initial number of employees of a start-up. This measure is computed as the total number of individuals in the employee records in the entry year. We exclude the founding team.

Gender (Male) is a dummy variable equaling one for men and zero for women.

Age is coded in years in the database.

Education is coded in years in the database. We measure education with two categorical variables: *High Education* is a dummy variable equalling one for founders with bachelors, masters or doctoral degrees; *Medium Education* is a dummy variable equalling one for individuals reporting a high school diploma or vocational school degree.

Nationality (Foreign) is dummy variable equaling 1 for foreign and 0 for Portuguese individuals. This variable is only available in the data after the year 2000. We complete any missing information in the years before 2000 by tracking the individual's nationality is the following years.

Tenure is the number of years an individual has worked in the last employer.

Industry Experience is coded one for entrepreneurs that previously worked in the same industry (four digit level) as that of their new ventures. Industry classification changed in 1994 and 2007, and there is no unequivocal relation between the old and new codes. To mitigate errors, we use all unique relations to translate old to new codes and, vice versa. Then, we compute the variable industry experience for the new and old codes and aggregate both results.

For 2007, this problem is mitigated because the database provides information on the new and old industry classification.

Income is the monthly regular earnings, which include the base salary, regular bonus, and other regular wage components. Regular earnings are expressed in 2008 Euros using the CPI index.

The definitions of the main variables are presented in Table 10.A.1.

TABLE 10A.1 Definition of the Variables	
Variable	**Definition**
Start–Up Characteristics	
N founders	Number of business owners in the founding year.
Size	Start–up's initial number of employees.
Survival	Dummy variable equaling 1 for start-ups that survive their first three years and 0 otherwise.
Initial Team Member Characteristics	
Share of Medium Education	Percentage of workers with a high school diploma or vocational school degree in the total number of employees.
Share of High Education	Percentage of workers with bachelor's, master's, or doctoral degrees in the total number of employees.
Average income	Average monthly regular earnings (in 2008 Euros) of the initial workforce.
Individual and Founder Characteristics	
Gender (Male)	Dummy variable equaling 1 for male and 0 for female entrepreneurs.
Age	Age of the founder in the entry year.
Age Squared/100	Age squared divided by 100.
Medium Education	Dummy variable equaling one for individuals reporting a high school diploma or vocational school degree, and 0 otherwise.
High Education	Dummy variable equaling 1 for individuals with bachelor's, master's, or doctoral degrees, and 0 otherwise.
Nationality (Foreign)	Dummy variable equaling 1 for foreign and 0 for Portuguese individuals.
Industry Experience	Dummy variable equaling 1 for founders that establish a venture in the same four digit industry, 0 otherwise.
Entrepreneurial Experience	Dummy variable equaling 1 for individuals that previously founded a venture, 0 otherwise.
Tenure	Number of years an individual has worked in the last employer.

EUROSTAT Database on International Trade

EUROSTAT database includes product level information on all bilateral imports and exports between European countries and any country in the World available back to 1994. The trade statistics are broken down by eight-digit Combined Nomenclature (CN) product level. The following indicators are available: gross trade value (in million euros), unit value and gross volume. In this study, we select trade data between Portugal and other countries.

In order to ensure consistency between the EUROSTAT database and the matched employer-employee database, we use the crosswalk in Pierce & Schott (2009) and Autor et al. (2013), which assigns 10-digit HS product code to four-digit US Standard Industrial Classification (1987 SIC). Next, we match the four-digit SIC to the four-digit International Standard Industrial Classification of All Economic Activities (ISIC Rev. 3), using the international concordance table (available in http://unstats.un.org/unsd/cr/registry/regdnld.asp?Lg=1). Details on our industry classification are available on request.

We apply our conversation table between six-digit HS product code and four-digit ISIC industries to all imports. Next, we aggregate imports across four export country groups: China; low-income countries; Central Eastern European Countries (CEEC); and high-income countries. CEEC include Bulgaria, Croatia, Czech Republic, Hungary, Poland, Romania, Slovakia, and Slovenia. High-income countries include Australia, Austria, Belgium, Luxembourg, Finland, Japan, New Zealand and Switzerland. The selection of low-income countries follows the World Bank definition in 1993. We consider the following countries: Afghanistan, Albania, Angola, Armenia, Azerbaijan, Bangladesh, Benin, Bhutan, Burkina Faso, Burundi, Cambodia, Central African Republic, Chad, China, Comoros, Republic of the Congo, Equatorial Guinea, Eritrea, Ethiopia, The Gambia, Georgia, Ghana, Guinea, Guinea-Bissau, Guyana, Haiti, India, Kenya, Lao, Lesotho, Madagascar, Malawi, Maldives, Mali, Mauritania, Moldova, Mozambique, Nepal, Niger, Pakistan, Rwanda, Saint Vincent and the Grenadines, Samoa, Sao Tome and Principe, Sierra Leone, Somalia, Sri Lanka, Sudan, Togo, Uganda, Vietnam, and Yemen. We did not include Burma because data on EUROSTAT was not available.

COMTRADE Database on International Trade

To construct our instrumental variable, we use data from UN Comtrade Database. This database includes product level information on all bilateral imports and exports between any pair of countries in the World available back to 1994. The trade statistics are broken down by six-digit Harmonized Standard (HS) product level.

We select the import data from China to the United States of America and from other countries to the United States for the period between 1994 and 2008.

In order to ensure consistency between the Comtrade database and the matched employer-employee database, we use the crosswalk in Pierce & Schott (2009) and Autor et al. (2013), which assigns 6-digit HS product code to four-digit US Standard Industrial Classification (1987 SIC). Next, we match the four-digit SIC to the four-digit International Standard Industrial Classification of All Economic Activities (ISIC Rev. 3), using the international concordance table (available in http://unstats.un.org/unsd/cr/registry/regdnld.asp?Lg=1). Details on our industry classification are available on request.

REFERENCES

Acemoglu, D., & Autor, D. (2011). Skills, tasks and technologies: Implications for employment and earnings. In D. Card & O. Ashenfelter (Eds.), *Handbook of labor economics* (Vol. 4, pp. 1043–1171). Amsterdam, The Netherlands: Elsevier.

Acharya, R. C., & Keller, W. (2009). Technology transfer through imports. *Revue Canadienne d'Économique, 42*(4), 1411–1448.

Adler, P. S. (1988). Managing flexible automation. *California Management Review, 30*(3), 34–56.

Aitken, B. J., & Harrison, A. E. (1999). Do domestic firms benefit from direct foreign investment? Evidence from Venezuela. *American Economic Review, 89*(3), 605–618.

Alchian, A. A., & Demsetz, H. (1972). Production, information costs, and economic organization. *American Economic Review, 62*(5), 777–795.

Aldrich, H., & Auster, E. R. (1986). Even dwarfs started small: Liabilities of age and size and their strategic implications. *Research in Organizational Behavior, 8*, 165–186.

Aldrich, H. E., & Ruef, M. (2006). *Organizations evolving.* London, England: SAGE.

Ardichvili, A., Cardozo, R., & Ray, S. (2003). A theory of entrepreneurial opportunity identification and development. *Journal of Business Venturing, 18*(1), 105–123.

Arenius, P., & De Clercq, D. (2005). A network-based approach on opportunity recognition. *Small Business Economics, 24*(3), 249–265.

Arenius, P., & Minniti, M. (2005). Perceptual variables and nascent entrepreneurship. *Small Business Economics, 24*(3), 233–247.

Argote, L., & Ingram, P. (2000). Knowledge transfer: A basis for competitive advantage in firms. *Organizational Behavior and Human Decision Processes, 82*(1), 150–169.

Auer, R. A., Degen, K., & Fischer, A. M. (2013). Low-wage import competition, inflationary pressure, and industry dynamics in Europe. *European Economic Review, 59*, 141–166.

Autor, D. H., Dorn, D., & Hanson, G. H. (2013). The China syndrome: Local labor market effects of import competition in the United States. *American Economic Review, 103*(6), 2121–2168.

Ayyagari, M., & Kosová, R. (2010). Does FDI facilitate domestic entry? Evidence from the Czech Republic. *Review of International Economics, 18*(1), 14–29.

Bandelj, N. (2008). *From communists to foreign capitalists: The social foundations of foreign direct investment in postsocialist Europe.* Princeton, NJ: Princeton University Press.

Baumol, W. J. (1996). Entrepreneurship: Productive, unproductive, and destructive. *Journal of Business Venturing, 11*(1), 3–22.

Becker, G. S. (1975). Investment in human capital: Effects on earnings. In G. S. Becker (Ed.), *Human capital: A theoretical and empirical analysis, with special reference to education* (pp. 13–44). Boston, MA: National Bureau of Economic Research.

Bernard, A. B., Jensen, J. B., & Schott, P. K. (2006a). Survival of the best fit: Exposure to low-wage countries and the (uneven) growth of US manufacturing plants. *Journal of International Economics, 68*(1), 219–237.

Bernard, A. B., Jensen, J. B., & Schott, P. K. (2006b). Trade costs, firms and productivity. *Journal of Monetary Economics, 53*(5), 917–937.

Blalock, G., & Simon, D. H. (2009). Do all firms benefit equally from downstream FDI? The moderating effect of local suppliers' capabilities on productivity gains. *Journal of International Business Studies, 40*(7), 1095–1112.

Blomström, M., & Kokko, A. (1998). Multinational corporations and spillovers. *Journal of Economic Surveys, 12*(3), 247–277.

Bloom, N., Draca, M., & Van Reenen, J. (2016). Trade induced technical change? The impact of Chinese imports on innovation, IT and productivity. *Review of Economic Studies, 83*(1), 87–117.

Bosma, N., Van Praag, M., Thurik, R., & De Wit, G. (2004). The value of human and social capital investments for the business performance of startups. *Small Business Economics, 23*(3), 227–236.

Bowen, H. P., & De Clercq, D. (2008). Institutional context and the allocation of entrepreneurial effort. *Journal of International Business Studies, 39*, 747–768.

Brüderl, J., Preisendörfer, P., & Ziegler, R. (1992). Survival chances of newly founded business organizations. *American Sociological Review, 57*(2), 227–242.

Buckley, P. J., Clegg, J., & Wang, C. (2007). Is the relationship between inward FDI and spillover effects linear? An empirical examination of the case of China. *Journal of International Business Studies, 38*(3), 447–459.

Busenitz, L. W., West, G. P., Shepherd, D., Nelson, T., Chandler, G. N., & Zacharakis, A. (2003). Entrepreneurship research in emergence: Past trends and future directions. *Journal of Management, 29*(3), 285–308.

Carroll, G. R., & Delacroix, J. (1982). Organizational mortality in the newspaper industries of Argentina and Ireland: An ecological approach. *Administrative Science Quarterly, 27*(2), 169–198.

Cartiglia, F. (1997). Credit constraints and human capital accumulation in the open economy. *Journal of International Economics, 43*(1–2), 221–236.

Chandler, G. N., & Hanks, S. H. (1998). An examination of the substitutability of founders human and financial capital in emerging business ventures. *Journal of Business Venturing, 13*(5), 353–369.

Choi, Y. R., & Shepherd, D. A. (2005). Stakeholder perceptions of age and other dimensions of newness. *Journal of Management, 31*(4), 573–596.

Coad, A., Daunfeldt, S. O., Johansson, D., & Wennberg, K. (2014). Whom do high-growth firms hire? *Industrial and Corporate Change, 23*(1), 293–327.

Colombo, M. G., & Grilli, L. (2005). Founders' human capital and the growth of new technology-based firms: A competence-based view. *Research Policy, 34*(6), 795–816.

Colombo, M. G., Delmastro, M., & Grilli, L. (2004). Entrepreneurs' human capital and the start-up size of new technology-based firms. *International Journal of Industrial Organization, 22*(8), 1183–1211.

Coyne, C. J., & Williamson, C. R. (2012). Trade openness and cultural creative destruction. *Journal of Entrepreneurship and Public Policy, 1*(1), 22–49.

Cyert, R. M., & March, J. G. (1963). *A behavioral theory of the firm.* Englewood Cliffs, NJ: Prentice-Hall.

Dahl, M. S., & Klepper, S. (2015). Whom do new firms hire? *Industrial and Corporate Change, 24*(4), 819–836.

Dakhli, M., & De Clercq, D. (2004). Human capital, social capital, and innovation: A multi-country study. *Entrepreneurship & Regional Development, 16*(2), 107–128.

Davidsson, P., & Honig, B. (2003). The role of social and human capital among nascent entrepreneurs. *Journal of Business Venturing, 18*(3), 301–331.

De Backer, K., & Sleuwaegen, L. (2003). Does foreign direct investment crowd out domestic entrepreneurship? *Review of Industrial Organization, 22*(1), 67–84.

Eaton, J., & Kortum, S. (2001). Trade in capital goods. *European Economic Review, 45*(7), 1195–1235.

Eaton, J., & Kortum, S. (2002). Technology, geography and trade. *Econometrica, 70*(5), 1741–1779.

Evans, D. S., & Jovanovic, B. (1989). An estimated model of entrepreneurial choice under liquidity constraints. *Journal of Political Economy, 97*(August), 808–827.

Fairlie, R. W., & Krashinsky, H. A. (2012). Liquidity constraints, household wealth, and entrepreneurship revisited. *Review of Income and Wealth, 58*(2), 279–306.

Feenstra, R. C., & Hanson, G. H. (1996). *Globalization, outsourcing, and wage inequality* (Working paper No. w5424). National Bureau of Economic Research, Boston, MA.

Feinberg, S. E., & Majumdar, S. K. (2001). Technology spillovers from foreign direct investment in the Indian pharmaceutical industry. *Journal of International Business Studies, 32*(3), 421–437.

Frankel, J., & Romer, D. (1999). Does trade cause growth? *American Economic Review, 89*(3), 379–399.

Freeman, R. B., & Kleiner, M. M. (2005). The last American shoe manufacturers: Decreasing productivity and increasing profits in the shift from piece rates to continuous flow production. *Industrial Relations: A Journal of Economy and Society, 44*(2), 307–330.

Gentry, W. M., & Hubbard, R. G. (2004). Entrepreneurship and household saving. *Advances in Economic Analysis & Policy, 4*(1), 1–55.

Goos, M., Manning, A., & Salomons, A. (2014). Explaining job polarization: Routine-biased technological change and offshoring. *American Economic Review, 104*(8), 2509–2526.

Graham, E. M., & Krugman, P. (1995). *Foreign direct investment in the United States.* Washington, DC: Institute for International Economics.

Grant, R. M. (1996). Toward a knowledge-based theory of the firm. *Strategic Management Journal, 17*(Winter Special Issue), 108–122.

Grossman, G. M., & Helpman, E. (1990). Trade, innovation, and growth. *American Economic Review, 80*(2), 86–91.

Hitt, M. A., Li, H., & Worthington, W. J. (2005). Emerging markets as learning laboratories: Learning behaviors of local firms and foreign entrants in different institutional contexts. *Management and Organization Review, 1*(3), 353–380.

Hurst, E., & Lusardi, A. (2004). Liquidity constraints, household wealth, and entrepreneurship. *Journal of Political Economy, 112*(2), 319–347.

Javorcik, B. S. (2004). Does foreign direct investment increase the productivity of domestic firms? In search of spillovers through backward linkages. *American Economic Review, 94*(3), 605–627.

Kazanjian, R. K., & Drazin, R. (1989). An empirical test of a stage of growth progression model. *Management Science, 35*(12), 1489–1503.

Kim, P. H., & Li, M. (2014). Injecting demand through spillovers: Foreign direct investment, domestic socio-political conditions, and host-country entrepreneurial activity. *Journal of Business Venturing, 29*(2), 210–231.

Klepper, S. (2001). Employee startups in high-tech industries. *Industrial and Corporate Change, 10*(3), 639–674.

Koeller, C. T., & Lechler, T. G. (2006). Economic and managerial perspectives on new venture growth: An integrated analysis. *Small Business Economics, 26*(5), 427–437.

Kremer, M. (1993). The O-ring theory of economic development. *Quarterly Journal of Economics, 108*(3), 551–575.

Levie, J., & Autio, E. (2008). A theoretical grounding and test of the GEM model. *Small Business Economics, 31*(3), 235–263.

Manning, R. (1982). Trade, education and growth: The small-country case. *International Economic Review, 23*(1), 83–106.

Mata, J., & Machado, J. A. (1996). Firm start-up size: A conditional quantile approach. *European Economic Review, 40*(6), 1305–1323.

Mata, J., & Portugal, P. (2002). The survival of new domestic and foreign-owned firms. *Strategic Management Journal, 23*(4), 323–343.

Melitz, M. J. (2003). The impact of trade on intra-industry reallocations and aggregate industry productivity. *Econometrica, 71*(6), 1695–1725.

Meyer, K. E. (2004). Perspectives on multinational enterprises in emerging economies. *Journal of International Business Studies, 35*(4), 59–276.

Miller, D., & Friesen, P. H. (1984). A longitudinal study of the corporate life cycle. *Management Science, 30*(10), 1161–1183.

Mitchell, R. K., Busenitz, L., Lant, T., McDougall, P. P., Morse, E. A., & Smith, J. B. (2002). Toward a theory of entrepreneurial cognition: Rethinking the people side of entrepreneurship research. *Entrepreneurship Theory and Practice, 27*(2), 93–104.

Nelson, R., & Winter, S. (1982). *An evolutionary theory of economic change*. Cambridge, MA: Belknap Press.

O'Malley, E., & O'Gorman, C. (2001). Competitive advantage in the Irish indigenous software industry and the role of inward foreign direct investment. *European Planning Studies, 9*(3), 303–321.

Pavcnik, N., Blom, A., Goldberg, P., & Schady, N. (2004). Trade liberalization and industry wage structure: Evidence from Brazil. *World Bank Economic Review, 18*(3), 319–344.

Pfeffer, J. (1994). *Competitive advantage through people*. Boston, MA: Harvard Business School Press.

Pierce, J. R., & Schott, P. K. (2009). *Concording US harmonized system categories over time*. Working paper No. w14837, National Bureau of Economic Research, Boston, MA.

Pitelis, C. N., & Teece, D. J. (2010). Cross-border market co-creation, dynamic capabilities and the entrepreneurial theory of the multinational enterprise. *Industrial and Corporate Change, 19*(4), 1247–1270.

Prahalad, C. K. (1983). Developing strategic capability: An agenda for top management. *Human Resource Management, 22*(3), 237–254.

Quadrini, V. (1999). The importance of entrepreneurship for wealth concentration and mobility. *Review of Income and Wealth, 45*(1), 1–19.

Reich, R. B. (1991). *The work of nations: Preparing ourselves for 21st-century capitalism*. New York, NY: Knopf.

Revenga, A. (1997). Employment and wage effects of trade liberalization: The case of Mexican manufacturing. *Journal of Labor Economics, 15*(S3), S20–S43.

Rodrik, D. (1997). *Has globalization gone too far?* Washington, DC: Institute for International Economics.

Rodrik, D. (1998). Why do more open economies have bigger governments? *Journal of Political Economy, 106*(5), 979–1032.

Sandberg, W. R., & Hofer, C. W. (1987). Improving new venture performance: The role of strategy, industry structure, and the entrepreneur. *Journal of Business Venturing, 2*(1), 5–28.

Santos, F. M., & Eisenhardt, K. M. (2009). Constructing markets and shaping boundaries: entrepreneurial power in nascent fields. *Academy of Management Journal, 52*(4), 643–671.

Schultz, T. W. (1975). The value of the ability to deal with disequilibria. *Journal of Economic Literature, 13*(3), 827–846.

Schumpeter, J. (1942). Creative destruction. In J. Schumpeter (Ed.), *Capitalism, socialism and democracy* (pp. 82–85). New York, NY: Harper.

Schwab, K., & Sala-i-Martin, X. (Eds.). (2011). *The global competitiveness report 2011–2012*. Geneva, Switzerland: World Economic Forum.

Shane, S., & Venkataraman, S. (2000). The promise of entrepreneurship as a field of research. *Academy of Management Review, 25*(1), 217–226.

Shepherd, D. A., & DeTienne, D. R. (2005). Prior knowledge, potential financial reward, and opportunity identification. *Entrepreneurship Theory and Practice, 29*(1), 91–112.

Siegel, R., Siegel, E., & MacMillan, I. C. (1993). Characteristics distinguishing high-growth ventures. *Journal of Business Venturing, 8*(2), 169–180.

Singley, M. K., & Anderson, J. R. (1989). *The transfer of cognitive skill (No. 9).* Cambridge, MA: Harvard University Press.

Spencer, J. W. (2008). The impact of multinational enterprise strategy on indigenous enterprises: Horizontal spillovers and crowding out in developing countries. *Academy of Management Review, 33*(2), 341–361.

Stenholm, P., Acs, Z. J., & Wuebker, R. (2013). Exploring country-level institutional arrangements on the rate and type of entrepreneurial activity. *Journal of Business Venturing, 28*(1), 176–193.

Stinchcombe, A. L. (1965). Social structure and organizations. In J. G. March (Ed.), *Handbook of organizations* (pp. 142–193). Chicago, IL: Rand-McNally.

Storey, D. J. (1994). *Understanding the small business sector.* Working paper, University of Illinois at Urbana-Champaign's Academy for Entrepreneurial Leadership Historical Research Reference in Entrepreneurship, Champaign, IL.

Topalova, P., & Khandelwal, A. (2011). Trade liberalization and firm productivity: The case of India. *Review of Economics and Statistics, 93*(3), 995–1009.

Tversky, A., & Kahneman, D. (1991). Loss aversion in riskless choice: A reference-dependent model. *Quarterly Journal of Economics, 106*(4), 1039–1061.

Ucbasaran, D., Westhead, P., & Wright, M. (2008). Opportunity identification and pursuit: Does an entrepreneur's human capital matter? *Small Business Economics, 30*(2), 153–173.

Varsakelis, N. C. (2001). The impact of patent protection, economy openness and national culture on R&D investment: A cross-country empirical investigation. *Research Policy, 30*(7), 1059–1068.

Verhoogen, E. (2008). Trade, quality upgrading and wage inequality in the Mexican manufacturing sector. *Quarterly Journal of Economics, 123*(2), 489–530.

Wacziarg, R. (2001). Measuring the dynamic gains from trade. *World Bank Economic Review, 15*(3), 393–429.

Witt, U. (1998). Imagination and leadership—The neglected dimension of an evolutionary theory of the firm, *Journal of Economic Behaviour and Organization, 35*(2), 161–177.

Wright, P. M., McMahan, G. C., & McWilliams, A. (1994). Human resources and sustained competitive advantage: A resource-based perspective. *International Journal of Human Resources Management, 5*(2), 301–326.

Yanikkaya, H. (2003). Trade openness and economic growth: A cross country empirical investigation. *Journal of Development Economics, 72*, 57–89.

Yeaple, S. R. (2005). A simple model of firm heterogeneity, international trade, and wages. *Journal of International Economics, 65*(1), 1–20.

Zacharakis, A. L., & Meyer, D. G. (2000). The potential of actuarial decision models: Can they improve the venture capital investment decision? *Journal of Business Venturing, 15*(4), 323–346.

Zhang, Y., Li, H., Li, Y., & Zhou, L. (2010). FDI spillovers in an emerging market: The role of foreign firms' country origin diversity and domestic firms' absorptive capacity. *Strategic Management Journal, 31*(9), 969–989.

ABOUT THE CONTRIBUTORS

Joan L. Brown is a doctoral candidate in social foundations of education at Oklahoma State University, Stillwater, OK, after earning from there a master's degree in human development and family science. Her research interests include education policy, school and neighborhood inequities, school and place renaming, racial awareness, the democratic method, and civic engagement. Email: joan.brown@okstate.edu

Lincoln Brown is an assistant professor at Southwestern Oklahoma State University, Weatherford, OK. He received his PhD in entrepreneurship from Oklahoma State University, Stillwater, OK. Earlier, he had an extended career as a programming engineer in the aircraft industry, and had founded and operated seven ventures. His research is focused on the entrepreneurial process and how affective experiences impact decision making and the subsequent opportunities available to the entrepreneur. Email: lincoln.m.brown@okstate.edu

Farzana Chowdhury is an assistant professor at Durham University Business School, Durham, UK. She has a PhD from Indiana University, Bloomington, IN. She has published in *Entrepreneurship Theory and Practice* and *Small Businesses Economics*. Email: farza.chowdhury@gmail.com

Alice Comi is a postdoctoral researcher at the Design Innovation Research Centre of the University of Reading, UK, where she has recently completed a research project on interorganizational relationships, funded by the Swiss National Science Foundation. She received her PhD in communication

Entrepreneurship and Behavioral Strategy, pages 295–300

sciences from the University of Lugano, Switzerland. During her doctoral studies, she was a visiting researcher at the University of Cambridge, UK, and the University of St. Gallen, Switzerland, where she studied organizational theory and research methods. Her professional background includes a teaching assistantship at the Institute of Marketing and Communication Management, University of Lugano, Switzerland, a PR internship at the Swiss Broadcasting Corporation, and consulting projects for pharmaceutical companies such as Pharmaton, Switzerland, and Merck Serono, Italy. Email: a.comi@reading.ac.uk

T. K. Das is professor of strategic management at the Zicklin School of Business, Baruch College, City University of New York, New York. He is concurrently a member of the university's doctoral faculty. Professor Das received his PhD in organization and strategic studies from the Anderson Graduate School of Management, University of California at Los Angeles (UCLA). He also has degrees in physics, mathematics, and management, and a professional certification in banking. Prior to entering the academic life, Professor Das had extensive experience as a senior business executive. He has research interests in strategic alliances, strategy making, organizational studies, temporal studies, and executive development. Professor Das is the author or editor of 26 academic research books on strategy and strategic alliances and also author of six booklets on bank management for practicing executives. His research articles have appeared in over 45 journals, of which some of the later ones include *Academy of Management Executive, Academy of Management Review, British Journal of Management, Journal of International Management, Journal of Management, Journal of Management Studies, Organization Science, Organization Studies*, and *Strategic Management Journal*. Professor Das currently serves on the editorial boards of several academic journals, and is a former senior editor of *Organization Studies* and editorial board member of a number of other journals. He is the founding (and current) series editor of three book series published by Information Age Publishing—*Research in Behavioral Strategy, Research in Strategic Alliances*, and *Research in Strategy Science*. Email: TK.Das@baruch.cuny.edu

Gjalt de Jong is professor of sustainable entrepreneurship in a circular economy, University of Groningen, Faculty Campus Fryslân, Groningen, Netherlands. He received a Master of Science in economics and a PhD in business administration from the same university. Professor de Jong supervises research, education, and business solutions for successful sustainable entrepreneurship and the circular economy, including strategy, leadership, organizational structure, business context, strategic alliances, public policy, and multi-value performance. He supervises multiple PhD students, and is the director of the university's Centre for Sustainable Entrepreneurship and of the university's master program in sustainable entrepreneurship. He is a member of the faculty board and of various regional entrepreneurship and research institutes. Email: g.de.jong@rug.nl

Martin J. Eppler is a full professor at the University of St. Gallen, Switzerland, where he is also the managing director of the institute for media and communication management. He has been a guest professor at various universities in Asia and Europe, and an advisor to organizations such as Daimler, Ernst & Young, the United Nations, and the Swiss Military. He studied communications, business administration, and social sciences at Boston University, MA, the Paris Graduate School of Management, France, and the universities of Geneva and St. Gallen, Switzerland. He has published more than 100 academic papers and ten books, mostly on knowledge communication, management, and visualization. Email: martin.eppler@unisg.ch

Frances Fabian is an associate professor of strategic management and entrepreneurship in the Department of Management, Fogelman College of Business and Economics, University of Memphis, Memphis, TN. She received her BA from Smith College, Northampton, MA, MPP from Harvard Kennedy School, Cambridge, MA, and her PhD from the University of Texas at Austin, Austin, TX. Her research interests include information environments and their implications for decision making, with theories drawing from both cognition and perspectives on the conceptualization of environments. She has published in journals such as *Academy of Management Review, Strategic Management Journal, Journal of Management Studies, Management International Review, Journal of World Business, Journal of International Management, Communications for the Association of Information Sciences, IEEE in Engineering Management,* and *Human Resource Management Review.* Email: ffabian@memphis.edu

Jiasi Fan is an assistant professor of international business at the University of International Business and Economics, Beijing, China. She received a PhD degree in business administration from the University of Groningen, Groningen, Netherlands. Her research interests center around the internationalization of small companies, foreign direct investment in emerging markets, and concepts and measurements of managerial attention in an international perspective. She is an active member in the Academy of International Business and the Academy of Management. Email: j.fan@uibe.edu.cn

David Jorgensen is a doctoral candidate in the Department of Management, Fogelman College of Business and Economics, University of Memphis, Memphis, TN, studying strategic management and entrepreneurship. He earned both a Bachelor of Science and a Master of Business Administration from Utah Valley University, Orem, UT. His research interests include competition, alternative approaches to the entrepreneurial process, personality, impression management, and pedagogy. He has published in the *Journal of Vocational Behavior.* Email: dfjrgnsn@memphis.edu

Burak Cem Konduk is an assistant professor of management at Juniata College, Huntingdon, PA, where he teaches analytics, management, entrepreneurship, and strategy at both undergraduate and graduate level. He earned his PhD from Georgia State University, Atlanta, GA, and holds a BA from Bilkent University, Ankara, Turkey, an MS from EDHEC Business School, Nice, France, and an MBA from Sabanci University, Istanbul, Turkey. He has held permanent or visiting positions at NYU Stern School of Business, New York, NY, Georgia State University, Atlanta, GA, and the University of North Georgia, Dahlonega, GA. His research focuses on competition, behavioral strategy, and data mining. He has published in journals such as the *Journal of Strategy and Management* and the *Journal of General Management.* In addition to various teaching awards, he has received research fellowships, scholarships, and grants from both national and international organizations. Email: konduk@juniata.edu

Guido Möllering is the director of the Reinhard Mohn Institute of Management at Witten/Herdecke University, Germany, where he also holds the Reinhard Mohn Endowed Chair of Management. He earned his PhD in management studies at the University of Cambridge, UK, and his habilitation (postdoctoral degree, venia legendi) in business administration at Freie Universität Berlin, Germany. His main areas of research are interorganizational relationships, organizational fields, and trust. He has published several books, notably *Trust: Reason, Routine, Reflexivity* (2006, Emerald), and articles in leading journals such as *Organization Science* and *Journal of International Business Studies.* He is a senior editor of *Organization Studies* and editor-in-chief of *Journal of Trust Research.* Email: guido.moellering@uni-wh.de

Oleksiy Osiyevskyy is an assistant professor of entrepreneurship and innovation at the Haskayne School of Business, University of Calgary, Calgary, Canada. In his scholarship, Oleksiy concentrates on the problem of achieving and sustaining firm growth through successfully engaging in entrepreneurial strategies. Particular areas of expertise include analyzing and designing innovative business models, improving corporate innovation practices, and evidence-based strategies for developing high-growth new ventures. He received the prestigious Canadian Izaak Killam Memorial Scholarship during his PhD studies, and numerous awards from the United States Association for Small Business and Entrepreneurship. Email: oosiyevs@ucalgary.ca

Corina Paraschiv is a professor in decision sciences at Paris Descartes University in Paris, France. Her areas of expertise include behavioral decision making and experimental economics. She received her PhD in management science in 2002 and her MSc in decision sciences in 1998 from Ecole Normale Superieure de Cachan, France. Her main research interests are decision making under risk and under ambiguity, intertemporal choice, and experience-based decisions. She developed applications in a variety of fields, from e-commerce and consumer behavior to housing markets, transportation research, and entrepreneurship. Her work has been published in leading journals, including *Management Science*. She was awarded the INFORMS' Decision Analysis Publication Award in 2009. Since 2013, she is a member of the prestigious French institution, Institut Universitaire de France. Email: corina.paraschiv@parisdescartes.fr

Amir Bahman Radnejad is an assistant professor of strategy and entrepreneurship at the State University of New York, Brockport, NY. He received his PhD in strategy and global management from the University of Calgary, Calgary, Canada. He also holds an MSc in innovation management and entrepreneurship from the University of Manchester, UK, and a bachelor's degree in chemical engineering from the University of Tehran, Iran. His research interests include innovation strategies, technology alliances, open innovation, and sustainable development. His work on sustainable energy development has garnered numerous awards, including the Enbridge Corporate Sustainability award in 2012 and 2015. Email: aradnejad@brockport.edu

Anisa Shyti is an assistant professor in the Accounting Department at IE Business School in Madrid, Spain. She is also a visiting assistant professor of economics in the Social Science Division of New York University in Abu Dhabi, United Arab Emirates. Earlier, she was a lecturer in Bocconi University in Italy, ESCP Europe, and IESEG School of Management in Paris, France. She received her PhD in management sciences in 2014 from HEC Paris, France, and her MSc in business administration from Bocconi University in Italy in 2005. Her research focuses on decision making under uncertainty in business related topics. Specifically, she investigates how overconfidence impacts individual attitudes towards exogenous and endogenous ambiguity. Through lab and field experiments, she also examines ambiguity attitudes of entrepreneurs and non-entrepreneurs. Email: anisa.shyti@ie.edu

Kanhaiya Kumar Sinha is an assistant professor of entrepreneurship at the Labovitz School of Business and Economics, University of Minnesota, Duluth, MN. His research interests include human capital and its impact on entrepreneurial outcomes, innovation in SMEs, learning and entrepreneurship orientation, governance strategies in an entrepreneurial environment, and human capital indicators of new venture performance variability. He has received best paper awards in the Academy of Management annual conferences. He has extensive work experience in steel and mines, oil and gas, telecom, and business process outsourcing industries in multiple countries and cultures. Email: sinhak@d.umn.edu

Bing-Sheng Teng is an associate professor of strategic management and associate dean for MBA at Cheung Kong Graduate School of Business in Beijing, China. He was previously an associate professor of strategic management with tenure at George Washington University, Washingtom, DC. His research has been published in such top journals as *Academy of Management Review* and *Organization Science*. His expertise on Chinese management led to frequent interviews by the popular media such as *Wall Street Journal* and *Business Week*. Email: bsteng@ckgsb.edu.cn

Hans van Ees is professor of governance and institutions at the Faculty of Economics and Business of the University of Groningen, Groningen, Netherlands. He is dean of the University College Groningen. His research deals with corporate governance, theory of business groups (in emerging markets), board of directors, sustainable corporate performance, and building trust within and between organizations. He is regularly involved in executive teaching, training, consultancy, and contract research for private companies and the Dutch government on issues related to good governance, executive compensation, and industrial democracy. He is director of undergraduate programs in economics and international economics and business. Email: h.van.ees@rug.nl

Ana Venâncio is an assistant professor of finance and entrepreneurship at ISEG—Lisbon School of Economics and Management, Universidade de Lisboa, Lisbon, Portugal, and a researcher at ADVANCE, Lisbon, Portugal. She has a PhD in technological change and entrepreneurship from Carnegie Mellon University, Pittsburgh, PA. She has published in the *Economic Journal* and *Applied Economics*. Her research focuses on identifying the barriers and constraints to entrepreneurial activity and understanding the crafting of public policies to foster high-growth entrepreneurial firms. Email: avenancio@iseg.ulisboa.pt

Chenjian Zhang is an assistant professor in strategy and entrepreneurship in the School of Management, University of Bath, UK. He earned his PhD in sociology at Bremen International Graduate School of Social Sciences, University of Bremen, Germany. His main research interests are in social networks, entrepreneurship, and institutional theory. He has published articles in leading journals such as *Strategic Management Journal* and *Management and Organizational Review*. Email: c.zhang2@bath.ac.uk

INDEX

Made in the USA
Monee, IL
22 May 2023

34259244R00181